Hermeneutics and Method

IVO COELHO

Hermeneutics and Method: The 'Universal Viewpoint' in Bernard Lonergan

UNIVERSITY OF TORONTO PRESS
Toronto Buffalo London

© University of Toronto Press 2012
Toronto   Buffalo   London
www.utppublishing.com
Printed in Canada

ISBN 978-0-8020-4840-0 (cloth)
ISBN 978-1-4426-1491-8 (paper)

Lonergan Studies series

Canadian Cataloguing in Publication Data

Coelho, Ivo.
Hermeneutics and method : the 'universal viewpoint' in Bernard Lonergan

(Lonergan studies series)
Includes bibliographical references and index.
ISBN 978-0-8020-4840-0 (bound).   ISBN 978-1-4426-1491-8 (pbk.)

1. Lonergan, Bernard, J.F. (Bernard Joseph Francis), 1907–1984 – Contributions in hermeneutics   2. Theology – Methodology.
3. Hermeneutics – History – 20th century.   I. Title
II. Series: Lonergan studies

BL118.C63   2001   230'.2'01   C00-932036-9

University of Toronto Press acknowledges the financial assistance to its publishing program of the Canada Council for the Arts and the Ontario Arts Council.

This book has been published with the help of a grant from the Bombay Province of the Salesians of Don Bosco.

University of Toronto Press acknowledges the financial support for its publishing activities of the Government of Canada through the Book Publishing Industry Development Program (BPIDP).

To Paul and Luiza Coelho

Contents

Preface / xiii

Abbreviations / xvii

Introduction / 3

PART ONE: *INSIGHT*

1 **Early Anticipations of the Universal Viewpoint** / 17
    1 The Pure Form of Speculative Development / 17
    2 Psychological Introspection and Wisdom / 19
        2.1 Psychological Introspection / 19
        2.2 Wisdom / 21
        2.3 The Method of Interpretation / 28

2 **The Universal Viewpoint: Background Notions** / 31
    1 Heuristic Structures / 31
        1.1 The A Priori / 31
        1.2 Heuristic structures / 33
    2 Dialectical Heuristic Structure / 36
    3 The Method of Metaphysics / 40
    4 Metaphysics as Dialectic / 44
    5 Concluding Summary / 48

viii Contents

3 The Universal Viewpoint in Chapter 17 of *Insight* / 49
  1 Meaning and Truth / 49
    1.1 The Structure of Meaning / 49
    1.2 The Development of Meaning / 53
    1.3 Truth / 53
  2 Hermeneutical Method / 54
    2.1 The Problem of Interpretation / 54
      2.1.1 Appropriation / 54
      2.1.2 Communication / 56
      2.1.3 The Problem of Interpretation / 58
    2.2 Hermeneutical Method / 58
  3 The Notion of the Universal Viewpoint / 60
    3.1 A Heuristic Structure / 60
    3.2 A Heuristic Structure for Meaning / 63
    3.3 Levels and Sequences of Expression / 65
    3.4 Hermeneutical Method / 66
    3.5 The Ascent to the Universal Viewpoint / 68
    3.6 The Universal Viewpoint, Metaphysics, and Wisdom / 71
  4 Concluding Summary / 74

4 Expansion and Transformation of the Universal Viewpoint / 78
  1 The Expansion of the Universal Viewpoint / 78
    1.1 Expansion / 78
    1.2 Transformation / 81
    1.3 Limits / 84
  2 The Theologically Transformed Universal Viewpoint / 88
    2.1 Fundamental Theology / 88
    2.2 Theological Hermeneutics / 90
    2.3 Interdisciplinarity / 94
  3 Conclusion / 95

PART TWO: FROM *INSIGHT* TO *METHOD IN THEOLOGY*

5 Upper Blade for Hermeneutics or History / 101
  1 1954: 'Theology and Understanding' / 101
  2 1957: *Divinarum personarum ...* / 103
  3 1959: *De intellectu et methodo* / 105
  4 1959: Lectures on the Philosophy of Education / 108
  5 1959–60: *De systemate et historia* and 'The Philosophy of History' / 109
  6 1961: *De Deo trino: Pars analytica* / 110
  7 Conclusion / 111

6 Basic Context / 113
1. 1962: General Method / 114
2. 1962: Basic Context / 118
3. Stages of Meaning / 123
4. Conclusion / 124

7 Methodical Horizon / 125
1. 1963: Total and Basic Horizon / 125
2. Spring 1963: Methodical Horizon / 128
3. Conclusion / 131

8 New Theological Foundations / 133
1. 1964: Focus on Theological Foundations / 133
   - 1.1 Antecedents / 133
     - 1.1.1 Emerging New Theological Foundations / 133
     - 1.1.2 The Distinction between Positive and Dogmatic Theology / 134
   - 1.2 Method as Foundational / 136
2. 1965: Breakthrough / 139
3. 1967–68: Achievement of New Theological Foundations / 141
   - 3.1 The New 'Largely Empirical' Theology / 141
   - 3.2 New Theological Foundations in Religious Conversion / 142
   - 3.3 The Primacy of the Existential / 142
   - 3.4 The New Notion of Faith / 144
4. Conclusion / 145

PART THREE: *METHOD IN THEOLOGY*

9 Transcendental Method / 151
1. The Need for a New Horizon for Theology / 151
   - 1.1 The Method of Theology (1964) / 151
   - 1.2 'MiT 1965' (Batch V.10) / 152
   - 1.3 'MiT 1965' (Batch V.7) / 153
   - 1.4 The Material of 1966–67 / 154
2. Transcendental Method as Horizon / 155
   - 2.1 'Ch. I: Method' (1968) / 155
   - 2.2 'Ch. III: Horizons and Categories' (1968) / 156

10 Research, Interpretation, History / 159
1. 1969: 'Ch. VI: Research' / 159
2. 1969: 'Ch. VII: Interpretation' / 161

    2.1 Interpretation as Functional Specialty / 161
    2.2 Understanding the Text / 162
    2.3 Judging the Correctness of the Understanding of the Text / 162
    2.4 Statement of Interpretation / 164
        2.4.1 A Supplementary Mode of Expression / 166
  3 1969: 'Ch. VIII: History' / 168
  4 1969: 'Ch. IX: History and Historians' / 170
  5 Conclusion / 172

11 Dialectic and Foundations / 174
  1 1966–68: The Comprehensive Viewpoint as Goal of Dialectic / 174
  2 1969: Dialectic and Foundations / 176
    2.1 Dialectic / 176
    2.2 Foundations / 179
    2.3 Horizons and Categories / 180
  3 1970: Dialectic and Foundations / 180
    3.1 Dialectic / 181
    3.2 Foundations / 183
  4 1971: The Collaborative Dimension of Dialectic / 184
  5 Conclusion / 187

12 The Universal Viewpoint in *Method in Theology* / 189
  1 The Universal Viewpoint and Transcendental Method / 189
    1.1 Method as Horizon / 189
    1.2 Method as 'General Dynamics': The Shift from Faculty Psychology / 192
    1.3 Method as Contemporary Stage of the Ascent to the Universal Viewpoint / 195
  2 The Universal Viewpoint and Theological Method / 197
  3 The Universal Viewpoint and the Functional Specialty Dialectic / 200
  4 Wisdom and Theological Method / 203

Conclusion / 206
  The Interpretation / 206
  The Development / 207
  Relevance / 213

Appendix A: Archival Material: Chronology / 217

Appendix B: A Note on the Emergence of Chapters 7–11 of
Method in Theology / 221

Notes / 223

Bibliography / 293
1 Primary Sources / 293
2 Secondary Sources / 316

Index / 323

Preface

The present book originated in a doctoral thesis submitted to the Gregorian University in Rome. I wanted my doctoral topic to have something to do with being a Christian in India today; I wanted it to be 'on the border' of philosophy and theology; I wanted something seminal as well as holistic. I spent the better part of a year searching, and it was through a set of coincidences that I settled upon Lonergan's notion of the universal viewpoint. I had come determined to set aside Lonergan, both because I thought I knew enough of him and because he seemed somehow inadequate. I settled subsequently for Lonergan and Ricoeur, then dropped Lonergan in favor of Ricoeur after a seminar with P. Henrici revealed the folly of attempting to study two authors. Terry Tekippe, however, who happened to be in Rome for a teaching stint at the Greg, encouraged me to take up Lonergan and spoke about the possibility of studying further a topic he himself had explored, the universal viewpoint. This coincided perfectly with my interest in hermeneutics, but I had no idea at that time that it had to do also with theological foundations and therefore with inculturation; and the crowning joy was to discover that the universal viewpoint flowered into dialogue. This might be called coincidence, but I prefer to use a name that is among the many things retrieved by Lonergan from the treasure of tradition: providence.

The thesis was defended in 1994. Somewhat dissatisfied, however, I decided to put in more work in the snatches of time left me by new responsibilities. The result has been an almost complete re-elaboration of parts two and three, with the benefit of the discovery of a more organic connection between the universal viewpoint and generalized method, the key being the notion of horizon that replaces the notion of 'viewpoint' in 1963.

The universal viewpoint is an important but somewhat obscure notion in Lonergan's *Insight*. One problem is the name itself, which sounds pretentious to postmodern ears. But the main problem is that this allegedly important notion quite disappears in later works, to surface only in a very marginal way in *Method in Theology*. The question that frames the present work might therefore be put in terms of the detective metaphor familiar to Lonergan readers: whatever happened to the universal viewpoint?

The question of theologizing in context is by no means a new one, but the Balasuriya affair and the recent Asian Synod of the Catholic church have thrown it into focus once again. It is being expressed in a variety of ways in the current literature: how are we to guard the deposit of faith as well as proclaim the gospel to all nations? How are we to achieve a genuine inculturation of the faith? How are we to rearticulate the faith in a way comprehensible to cultures that are not so dependent on the Western tradition? How are we to combine fidelity to tradition with the need for innovation? How are we to combine creativity with continuity? How are we to handle the historicity of Christian doctrine? Or even more radically, it is being asked: is orthodoxy needed? Is not orthopraxy enough?

These questions raise crucial and difficult issues: the link between reality and expression, or between experience and expression; the question of meaning, and its relation to experience on the one hand and to expression on the other; the relevance of doctrines to religious and to Christian experience; the question of historicity, or the question of tradition; the question of truth, and the very meaning of truth itself; the question of authority and criteria: who is to decide on the authenticity of new formulations, and how?

Clearly, these are issues that are by no means relevant only to Christians in India or in Asia. These issues confront anyone who is concerned with cross-cultural transitions, whether temporal or spatial. They are questions therefore that are being asked the world over. They are hermeneutical issues.

The universal viewpoint is relevant to all this, simply because it is a hermeneutical tool. It is a key tool in the appropriation of the meaning of another. It is an important part of Lonergan's life-long concern with the historicity of Christian doctrines.

I have been trying to show the relevance of the present study, but I must hasten to add that this is a work of 'research' and 'interpretation' in Lonergan's specialized sense. This means that the work of application, no doubt of greater interest, will have to await some other occasion. The present offering restricts itself to determining what Lonergan meant by the universal viewpoint, and to the development of that notion up to the completion of *Method in Theology* in 1971. While the post-*Method* works have not been completely neglected, there is no attempt to study them systematically. A more complete work would have to take this into account. A study of Lonergan's sources – Aristotle mediated by Newman and Aquinas; Hegel; the big names in the development of the *Geisteswissenschaften* – would also certainly be very useful.

Finally, a word of thanks. I would like to thank the Salesian Province of Bombay, and in a special way the provincials in the years 1990–2000, Fr Loddy Pires, Fr Joaquim D'Souza, and Fr Tony D'Souza. I am grateful to my guide, Fr Carlo Huber, not only for his unfailing encouragement during the years of my work in Rome, but also for introducing me to the Italian Catholic Scouting Movement (AGESCI); Fred Crowe, for what I have learnt from his writings, but also for the embodiment of 'concern' that he has been; Terry J. Tekippe, for the initial inspiration and for having gone out of his way in countless ways since; Giovanni B. Sala, Michael Shields, Robert Doran, and Philip McShane, for the time spent and inspiration provided; Joaquim D'Souza, Jose D. Maliekal, and the late Richard V. De Smet, friends and partners in dialogue; Don Giacomo Tagliabue, parish priest of the lovely little village of Suello in the country of Manzoni, for his friendship and support; the Salesian community of Testaccio, for four pleasant years in Rome; friends both in India and elsewhere who make life worth living; my dad and mum, my brother and sister and their families, for their love and understanding; and finally my community of the last six years, for having made it possible to somehow finish this work.

Ivo Coelho, SDB
Feast of Don Bosco
Nashik, 31 January 2000

Abbreviations

Note: The following are all works of Lonergan. 'LRI Archives' refers to the archives of the Lonergan Research Institute of Regis College, 10 St Mary Street, Suite 500, Toronto, Ontario M4Y 1P9 Canada. Where necessary, I have indicated the year under which a particular item is listed in the chronological bibliography of primary sources.

1C *Collection*. 2nd ed. Collected Works of Bernard Lonergan 4. 1988.
2C *A Second Collection: Papers by Bernard Lonergan, S.J.* Philadelphia: Westminster, 1974.
3C *A Third Collection. Papers by Bernard J.F. Lonergan, S.J.* New York/Mahwah: Paulist Press; London: Geoffrey Chapman, 1985.
AF *Analysis fidei. The Early Latin Works of Bernard J.F. Lonergan.* Ed. F.E. Crowe, assisted by C. O'Donovan and G. Sala. Regis College, Toronto, 1973. Unpublished. [Cf. bibliography, under *1952*.]
DCC *De constitutione Christi ontologica et psychologica supplementum confecit Bernardus Lonergan, S.I.* 4th edition. Rome: Gregorian University Press, 1964. [Cf. bibliography, under *1956*.]
DDT-I *De Deo trino: I. Pars dogmatica.* 2nd ed. Rome: Gregorian University Press, 1964. [Cf. bibliography, under *1963*.]
DDT-II *De Deo trino: II. Pars systematica seu divinarum personarum conceptio analogica.* 3rd ed. Rome: Gregorian University Press, 1964. [Cf. bibliography, under *1963*.]
DDTPA *De Deo trino: Pars analytica.* Rome: Gregorian University Press, 1961.

xviii Abbreviations

DMT 1962   *De methodo theologiae.* Course given at the Gregorian University, Spring 1962. Autograph typescript, LRI Archives Batch v.1, item c. Unpublished.

DMT 1962 Batch v.4   LRI Archives Batch v.4. Folder containing mostly handwritten pages probably related to *De methodo theologiae* of 1962 and to the Summer Institute on The Method of Theology, Regis College, Toronto, 1962. Unpublished.

DMT 1962 Batch v.5   LRI Archives Batch v.5. Folder containing mostly handwritten pages probably related to *De methodo theologiae* of 1962. Unpublished.

DMT 1962 Student Notes   De methodo theologiae. Notes taken by students (60 pp.), but almost certainly copied from Lonergan's own notes, from the course given at the Gregorian University, Spring 1962. Unpublished.

DMT Spring 1963   Folder entitled 'De methodo theologiae 1963.' LRI Archives Batch v.11, 1963. Handwritten notes for the course given at the Gregorian University, Spring 1963. Unpublished.

DMT Fall 1963   Folder entitled 'De methodo theol. 1963.' LRI Archives Batch v.9. Handwritten notes pertaining to the course *De methodo theologiae* at the Gregorian University, Fall 1963. Unpublished.

DMT Fall 1963 Daly   *De methodo theologiae.* Notes made by Tom Daly and typed by John Begley, of the course given at the Gregorian University, Fall 1963. Unpublished.

DP   *Divinarum personarum conceptionem analogicam evolvit Bernardus Lonergan, S.I.* Rome: Gregorian University Press, 1957.

DSH   *De systemate et historia.* LRI Archives Batch v.8, item i. Autograph typescript of notes (18 pp.) for the course given at the Gregorian University, Rome, Fall 1959. Unpublished.

GF   *Grace and Freedom: Operative Grace in the Thought of St.Thomas Aquinas.* London: Darton, Longman & Todd; New York: Herder and Herder, 1971. [Cf. bibliography, under *1941, 1942, 1971.*]

GOI   'The *Gratia Operans* Dissertation: Preface and Introduction.' *Method: Journal of Lonergan Studies* 3:2 (1985) 9–46. [Cf. bibliography, under *1940.*]

Hermeneutics 1962 MS   Hermeneutics. Autograph typescript of the lecture during the Institute on The Method of Theology, Regis College, Toronto, 1962. LRI Archives, file entitled 'Various Papers.' Unpublished.

Hermeneutics 1962   Hermeneutics. Notes for lecture during the Institute on the Method of Theology, Regis College, Toronto, 20 July 1962. Mimeographed edition, Thomas More Institute, Montreal, 1963. Unpublished.

History 1962   History. LRI Archives Batch IX.7, item f. Notes for lectures on history at the Institute on The Method of Theology, Regis College, Toronto, 1962.
IM 1959   *De intellectu et methodo.* LRI Archives Batch V.2, item a. Autograph typescript of chapter I of the course given at the Gregorian University, Rome, Spring 1959. Unpublished.
IM 1959 Student Notes   *De intellectu et methodo.* Notes taken by F. Rossi de Gasperis and P. Joseph Cahill from the course given at the Gregorian University, Rome, Spring 1959. Unpublished.
IN   *Insight: A Study of Human Understanding.* San Francisco: Harper & Row, 1978. [Cf. bibliography, under *1953*.]
INCW   *Insight: A Study of Human Understanding.* Collected Works of Bernard Lonergan 3. 1992. [Cf. bibliography, under *1953*, *1992*.]
KL   Knowledge and Learning. Notes for lectures in the Institute in the Graduate School of Gonzaga University, Spokane, Washington, 15–26 July 1963. LRI Library file 357-1. Unpublished.
KL Laporte   Knowledge and Learning, 1963. Notes made during lectures by J.M. Laporte. LRI Library file 357-2. Unpublished.
KL Tyrrell   Knowledge and Learning, 1963. *Reportatio* by B. Tyrrell. LRI Library file 357-3. Unpublished.
MiT 1965 Batch V.7   Folder entitled 'MiT 1965.' LRI Archives Batch V.7. Handwritten and typed pages, 1965. Unpublished.
MiT 1965 Batch V.10   Folder entitled 'Method in Theology 1965.' LRI Archives Batch V.10. Handwritten and typed pages, 1965. Unpublished.
MiT 1969   Method in Theology. Institute at Regis College, Toronto, 7–18 July 1969. Transcript by N. Graham. Unpublished.
MiT 1970   Method in Theology. Institute at Boston College, Boston, 15–26 June 1970. Transcript by N. Graham, Toronto, 1984. Unpublished.
MiT 1971   Method in Theology. Institute at Milltown Park, Dublin, 2–14 August 1971. Transcript by N. Graham, Lonergan Center, Regis College, Toronto. Unpublished.
'MiT VII'   'MiT VII: The Tasks of Theology.' LRI Archives Batch VI.2. Probable date 1968 (cf. appendix A). Unpublished.
MoT 1962   The Method of Theology. Summer Institute at Regis College, Toronto, 9–20 July 1962. Transcript by N. Graham, Lonergan Center, Regis College, Toronto, 1984. Unpublished.
MoT 1964   The Method of Theology. Summer Institute at Georgetown University, Washington, 13–17 July 1964.
MoT 1964 Wilker   The Method of Theology. Summer Institute at George-

xx   Abbreviations

town University, Washington, 13–17 July 1964. Notes (16 pp.) taken by Sr Rose Wilker. Unpublished.

MT   *Method in Theology.* Toronto: University of Toronto Press, 1990. [Cf. bibliography, under *1971.*]

The Nottingham lecture   'Method in Catholic Theology.' *Method: Journal of Lonergan Studies* 10:1 (1992) 1–26. [Cf. bibliography, under *1959, 1992.*]

PGT   *Philosophy of God, and Theology: The Relationship between Philosophy of God and the Functional Specialty, Systematics.* Philadelphia: The Westminster Press, 1973. [Cf. bibliography, under *1972.*]

PTP   *Philosophical and Theological Papers 1958–1964.* Collected Works of Bernard Lonergan 6. 1996.

'Questionnaire'   'Questionnaire on Philosophy.' *Method: Journal of Lonergan Studies* 2:2 (1984) 1–35. [Cf. bibliography, under *1976.*]

SH   Folder entitled 'System and History.' LRI Archives Batch v.8, 1959. The folder contains sheaves of handwritten and typed notes probably prepared for sessions of the course *De systemate et historia* given at the Gregorian University, Rome, Fall 1959. Unpublished.

TE   *Topics in Education. The Cincinnati Lectures of 1959 on the Philosophy of Education.* Collected Works of Bernard Lonergan 10. 1993. [Cf. bibliography, under *1959, 1993.*]

TPSR Graham   Transcendental Philosophy and the Study of Religion. Institute at Boston College, Boston, 3–12 July 1968. Transcript by N.W. Graham from tapes of lectures, 1984. Unpublished.

UB   *Understanding and Being: The Halifax Lectures on* Insight. Collected Works of Bernard Lonergan 5. 1990. [Cf. bibliography, under *1958, 1990.*]

VB   *Verbum: Word and Idea in Aquinas.* Notre Dame: University of Notre Dame Press, 1967. [Cf. bibliography, under *1946, 1947, 1949, 1967.*]

WN   *The Way to Nicea: The Dialectical Development of Trinitarian Theology.* London: Darton, Longman & Todd, 1982. [Cf. bibliography, under *1963, 1976.*]

Hermeneutics and Method

Introduction

Our aim is to study the development of Bernard Lonergan's notion of the universal viewpoint, and we may begin by trying to indicate just what is meant by the term universal viewpoint. When it first appears in chapter 17 of *Insight*,[1] the notion of the universal viewpoint is a heuristic structure or an a priori for interpretation. Very simply, a heuristic structure is a cognitional tool enabling discovery of an unknown. The famous x used in algebra as a name for the unknown quantity that is sought is an elementary example of a heuristic notion. The point to be grasped is that human knowledge is a question, not merely of data, but also of heuristic anticipation. This is most clear in physics, where the procedures of measuring and curve-fitting are complemented by other procedures derived from mathematics, such as differential equations. Human knowledge is marked therefore by a double-pronged approach, a pincer movement, a scissors-action, with a lower blade arising from data and an upper blade descending from general anticipations. When therefore the notion of the universal viewpoint is described as a heuristic structure, what is meant is that it forms part of the upper blade of hermeneutical method.

But why is an upper-blade procedure necessary in interpretation? According to Lonergan, interpretation is beset by a twofold problem: the first is the need to avoid projecting one's own viewpoint onto the text, and the second is the need to communicate successfully to a variety of audiences. The first is the problem of relativism born of the bias of the interpreter. The second is the problem of the relativity of interpretation to the audience to which it is addressed. The creation of a hermeneutical upper blade is an attempt to solve these problems, and the notion of the universal viewpoint is a part of this hermeneutical upper blade.

We have been saying that the upper blade begins from rather general considerations. Lonergan proposes that the areas to be considered in hermeneutics are meaning and expression. The heuristic structure relevant to meaning is the notion of the universal viewpoint, while the heuristic structure relevant to expression is the notion of 'levels and sequences of expression.' Further, Lonergan conceives the universe of meanings, not merely as the totality of meanings, but as an ordered totality of viewpoints, where viewpoints themselves are ordered accumulations of insights and meanings. Thus, the notion of the universal viewpoint is described as 'a potential totality of genetically and dialectically ordered viewpoints.'[2] But how is one to grasp such a potential totality of ordered viewpoints? This is a question of taking advantage of the invariant elements of human consciousness, for if human meaning is a product of human consciousness, then grasp of that consciousness is a key to the universe of human meaning and the totality of viewpoints.

We have been trying to indicate in a preliminary way the meaning of the term universal viewpoint, and we may go on now to a further specification of our topic. This may be done by fixing the broad outlines of the development and the *status quaestionis*. In *Insight*, the term 'universal viewpoint' receives a brief mention in the introduction: it is the goal or term of the moving viewpoint from which the book is written.[3] In the body of the book, as we have noted already, the universal viewpoint makes its first appearance in the third and final section of chapter 17. In the subsequent chapters of *Insight*, it occurs only sporadically, while the epilogue speaks of a theologically transformed universal viewpoint.[4] The term disappears almost completely in the post-*Insight* period, though there is the similar notion of 'basic context' in a lecture of 1962 on hermeneutics.[5] However, in the article 'Functional Specialties in Theology,' published in 1969, Lonergan speaks of dialectic as aiming at the 'high and distant goal' of a comprehensive viewpoint.[6]

This state of affairs continues in *Method in Theology*:[7] the term universal viewpoint appears just twice, once in a footnote, and the second time in a reference to *Insight*.[8] The footnote tells us that what was in *Insight* termed a universal viewpoint is now realized by advocating a distinct functional specialty named dialectic.[9] Again, the term comprehensive viewpoint is mentioned in the chapter on 'Functional Specialties,'[10] but is never mentioned again in the book, not even in the chapter called 'Dialectic.'

Such a state of affairs could not have gone unnoticed for long. In fact, even before the publication of *Method*, the question about the relationship between the universal and the comprehensive viewpoint is the subject of an exchange between Terry J. Tekippe and Lonergan. The discussion is reported in the appendix of Tekippe's dissertation, 'The Universal Viewpoint and the Relationship of Philosophy and Theology in the Works of Bernard Lonergan.'[11] Before coming to that discussion however, a word is in order about Tekippe's dissertation itself. The central question here is the relationship between what Tekippe calls the generalized universal viewpoint and the theological viewpoint:[12] both seem to be universal, and yet the theological viewpoint cannot simply be identified with the universal viewpoint.[13] The solution hinges on the distinction between heuristic and actual horizon; such a distinction, we are told, is one that Lonergan himself does not make, 'at least not very explicitly.'[14] Both the generalized universal viewpoint and the theological viewpoint are universal, because both are merely heuristic and not fully actual horizons. However, the theological viewpoint is both more actual and more concrete than the generalized universal viewpoint.[15] The reason is that it adds to the latter a further range of meanings that, however, are merely further specifications of being. Now the real world is the concrete world in which God's grace is operative; and so a viewpoint that attains this real world is to be regarded as more concrete, while a viewpoint that does not deal with this fact of grace operates in fact under a certain degree of abstraction.[16]

The relationship between the universal viewpoint and the comprehensive viewpoint is touched upon in an appendix. Basing himself on the 1969 article 'Functional Specialties in Theology,'[17] Tekippe notes that there is a clear discrepancy between the universal viewpoint of *Insight* and the comprehensive viewpoint of the functional specialty dialectic, for the former is an actual heuristic structure, 'proximate achievement,' while the latter is a high and distant goal, 'even an ideal.'[18] Yet when questioned on this point at the 1971 Dublin course, 'Lonergan responded that the two viewpoints were one and the same, that the universal viewpoint was no less potential than the comprehensive viewpoint.'[19] Pressed further,[20] Lonergan held to his position and made the following response:

> I've read through the contrasting passages here, but I'm not convinced – like I never thought that I had attained the high and distant goal of the comprehensive viewpoint when I was writing *Insight*. I said, there is this possibility, and this could guide the movement towards attaining a universal viewpoint, and I said what sort of a thing this universal viewpoint would be, but to state it and put it [? tape unclear] would be to write an Hegelian treatise, and I never aimed to write like Hegel. And I'm still on that position that it's up to – that it's a matter of experience, understanding and judgment to arrive at an understanding of – and dialectic – to arrive at an account of all the different positions that different [? tape unclear] people held.[21]

The debate is rendered 'even more complicated' by a subsequent discussion in which Lonergan 'accepted without question the technical precision' proposed by Tekippe, that the universal viewpoint was *an actual viewpoint* from which could be grasped a potential totality of genetically and dialectically related viewpoints.²² For, granted such a precision, Tekippe feels that the discrepancy between the universal viewpoint and the comprehensive viewpoint becomes even more clear: the former is an actual viewpoint, while the latter is a high and distant aim. Yet Lonergan's public statements 'have not been retracted, and the forthcoming *Method in Theology*, unless changed since the galley proofs, will document the same confusion.'²³ Still, Tekippe feels that the substantial proposal of the universal viewpoint is carried over into *Method*, any discrepancy being accounted for quite adequately by the change of context between *Insight* and *Method*.²⁴ He would not however exclude the possibility of some shift, for 'Lonergan's answer ... would suggest that, while he would be unlikely to disown the universal viewpoint, he might be less sanguine about the ease of attaining it or the usefulness it would have, once attained.'²⁵

Are we then to assume an oversight on the part of Lonergan on the question of the relationship between the universal and the comprehensive viewpoints? It would seem that such an assumption cannot easily be made. For first, we are dealing with a second response to the question, and besides, Tekippe had forwarded a written presentation containing parallel passages on the universal viewpoint and the comprehensive viewpoint. Second, there is the acceptance of the technical precision. In the third place, there is the reference made by Lonergan himself to Tekippe's dissertation in a paper of 1973:

> In this connection I might mention a doctoral dissertation presented at Fordham by Terry J. Tekippe on *The Universal Viewpoint and the Relationship of Philosophy and Theology in the Works of Bernard Lonergan*. It illustrates very well an intermediate position between what I had worked out in *Insight* and, on the other hand, the views presented in *Method in Theology*.²⁶

The context of this observation is the relationship between *Insight* and Lonergan's later thinking. Noting that he has not been moved to change his mind 'about the first three chapters [of *Insight*] on metaphysics,' Lonergan indicates that the third section of chapter 17 has been given 'a more concrete expression in chapters seven to eleven of *Method*' and that a 'systematic account of the problems of interpretation' in *Insight* 'yield place in the later work to an orderly set of directions on what is to be done towards moving to the attainment of universal viewpoint.'²⁷

At least in Lonergan's mind then, (1) chapters 7 to 11 of *Method* represent not an abandonment but a development of the position of the third section of chapter 17 of *Insight*, (2) this change is the difference between a systematic account of problems and a practical account of method, and (3) the universal viewpoint is understood here as a 'high and distant' goal. As in the response to Tekippe in 1971, we have here an affirmation of basic continuity, and yet the universal viewpoint is affirmed to be an ideal goal. We are faced here with the problem of evaluating an author's self-interpretation. Is the basic continuity to be granted, while asserting a difference between the universal viewpoint in *Insight* and the universal or comprehensive viewpoint in *Method*? Or is the latter difference so great as to eliminate even the basic continuity? Or is there perhaps another answer?

The question of the relationship between the universal viewpoint and the comprehensive viewpoint comes up once again for consideration in the doctoral dissertation of Charles Hefling, entitled 'Lonergan on Development: *The Way to Nicea* in Light of His More Recent Methodology.'[28] It is precisely in the context of a reference to Tekippe's dissertation that Hefling summarizes his own position: 'considered with regard to how it *functions*, the universal viewpoint (which in *Method* Lonergan prefers to call the 'comprehensive viewpoint') remains the keystone of his proposal. How such a viewpoint is *reached*, on the other hand, is something that does change considerably between *Insight* and *Method*.'[29] Both the universal viewpoint and the comprehensive viewpoint are viewpoints 'from which it would be possible to understand the many diverging viewpoints that give rise to conflict.'[30] Still, the universal viewpoint of *Insight* has to be expanded and transformed in order to function within theology; and since this is a process patterned on classical fundamental theology,[31] the upper blade of the theological hermeneutics of *Insight* includes not only metaphysical categories but also revealed truths and dogmatic decisions.[32] *Method*, by contrast, recognizes the existential priority of the horizon of deliberation;[33] accordingly, in a sense 'theological transformation of a comprehensive viewpoint is something that is already taking place.'[34] Further, the special theological categories that form part of the upper blade of theological method are derived from religious interiority through self-appropriation. But such self-appropriation itself occurs in ongoing interaction with data, and so there results a process in which the categories of the upper blade themselves become increasingly more determinate.[35] The comprehensive viewpoint then is not something that is already constructed. It is in process; it is a high and distant goal of theological method. Not only is the Christian church a *Selbstvollzug*, but 'the comprehensive viewpoint is part of that *Selbstvollzug*. For what is "seminal" in *Dialectic* and increasingly explicit in *Foundations* is very much "a high and distant" goal.'[36]

If I understand Hefling well, he is saying that, in contrast to the upper blade of theological hermeneutics in *Insight*, which 'includes the theologically transformed universal viewpoint,' the upper blade of theological method in *Method* is something that is not simply 'attained' but is rather in process of being constructed; and since that process coincides with the process of self-constitution of the church, the comprehensive viewpoint of *Method* is to be considered a high and distant aim. This interpretation agrees with and expands upon Lonergan's own remark that in *Method*, the universal viewpoint is realized by advocating a distinct functional specialty, dialectic.[37] If Hefling is right here, then we have an explanation of how the comprehensive viewpoint but not the theologically transformed universal viewpoint of *Insight* is a high and distant aim.[38] But what of the universal viewpoint of chapter 17 of *Insight*? Was that a high and distant aim? It would seem so, if we go by what Lonergan says to Tekippe at the 1971 Dublin Institute:

> There is no discrepancy. The universal viewpoint in *Insight* is potential in so far as I am talking about it. It not [*sic*] having everything lined up here and now. Its actuation, even in *Insight*, is a high and distant goal.[39]

In the light of this, it would seem that there is work to be done. For Hefling, while offering an explanation of the shift from *Insight* to *Method*, and while showing how the comprehensive viewpoint is a high and distant aim in *Method*, does not enter into the question of whether and how the universal viewpoint is an equally high and distant goal in *Insight*. Careful reading of Lonergan's response reported above will already yield a clue: the universal viewpoint is potential; it is its *actuation* that is a high and distant goal, already in *Insight*. But clues must be pushed, and that is what the present study intends doing.

Robert Doran holds for a basic continuity between the hermeneutical positions of *Insight* and of *Method*:

> [H]owever new may be the position of *Method in Theology* regarding critical history, the ultimate condition of possibility of approximating a correct interpretation of another's meaning and a responsible historical opinion regarding what was going forward in another time and place remains one's understanding of oneself. And the basic statement regarding the pertinence of this condition of interpretation is given in chapter 17 of *Insight*.[40]

The term universal viewpoint is not used in this statement, but elsewhere

Doran remarks that the universal viewpoint of *Insight* receives its proper context and development in the chapter on dialectic in *Method*, and that this chapter is itself made possible by the prior discussion of history.[41] The difference is that in *Method*, the universal viewpoint is constituted by the self-appropriation of consciousness not only as cognitional but also as moral and religious. 'The universal viewpoint is now rooted in the objectification of religious, moral, intellectual, and psychic conversion that constitutes theological foundations.'[42]

Again, Doran speaks of a historical ascent to the universal viewpoint and interprets chapter 17 of *Insight* as an extension of emergent probability into the world of meaning.[43] In this he is supported by Philip McShane.[44] It would seem that an ascent to the universal viewpoint has something to do with the universal viewpoint as high and distant aim, and so we have here a suggestion worth exploring.

Finally, the writings of Frederick Crowe contain illuminating remarks about the universal viewpoint and precious suggestions for research. Thus, an article of 1964 notes that one of the things Lonergan learned from Aquinas was the habit of the universal viewpoint.[45] Again, an article of 1984 links up Thomist wisdom with the universal viewpoint and with transcendental method. For many years, observes Crowe, Thomist wisdom was a dominant category for Lonergan; but in *Method* it has all but disappeared, if not in the functions it served, at least in the terminology and in the perspective from which problems were approached:

> Even in *Insight* its functions were being taken over by the 'universal viewpoint', and that too has yielded in *Method* to a transcendental method reaching its full human potential in dialectic, transformed then by conversions that are mainly the work of God, in order to take possession of new foundations for another formulation of the truths we live by, the whole being complemented now by an explicit principle of feedback.[46]

Since further Crowe links up wisdom with Lonergan's early search for foundations,[47] and places the beginning of that search in the 'Introduction' to Lonergan's doctoral dissertation,[48] we have here, as far as the universal viewpoint is concerned, a line of research reaching backwards to the Thomist notion of wisdom of the *Verbum* articles[49] and to the *Gratia Operans* introduction, and forward to the transcendental method of *Method*, culminating in the functional specialties dialectic and foundations.

From this survey of the state of research on the development of Lonergan's notion of the universal viewpoint, we might note the following points. First, while basic continuity between *Insight* and *Method* is admitted by all, Tekippe finds a discrepancy between the universal viewpoint of *Insight* and the comprehensive viewpoint of *Method*. In this he is opposed by Lonergan himself, and by Hefling. Second, there would seem to be required a new investigation into the notion of the universal viewpoint, given that Tekippe's dissertation was completed before the publication of *Method*, and that Hefling's work itself does not take up the question of whether and how the universal viewpoint was a high and distant aim already in *Insight*. Third, Crowe, Doran, and McShane provide hints for this investigation: Crowe suggests a research into the pure form of speculative development of 1940 and into the Thomist wisdom of the *Verbum* articles; Doran and McShane suggest that chapter 17 of *Insight* be read in terms of emergent probability. Accordingly, we set ourselves the task of clarifying the notion of the universal viewpoint in *Insight* and of following its development up to *Method in Theology*. As for post-*Method* developments, they will not be completely ignored, but there will be no attempt to follow them systematically.

The thesis upheld is that, because of a complex shift that Lonergan makes from 'faculty psychology' to 'intentionality analysis' and from the primacy of metaphysics to the primacy of method, the functions of the universal viewpoint are taken over by transcendental method. However, the universal viewpoint does survive in some way in *Method in Theology*: it remains a part of the upper blade of transcendental method, and it is also the goal to which that method heads through the functional specialty dialectic. I have tried to capture the dynamics of this relationship between the universal viewpoint and method in the title of my study, 'Hermeneutics and Method: The "Universal Viewpoint" in Bernard Lonergan.'[50]

The relevance of the present work might be indicated in three points. A first point is the centrality of the notion of the universal viewpoint in the hermeneutics of *Insight*: without it, we are told quite clearly, no objective interpretation is possible.[51] Determining the development of the universal viewpoint is therefore quite crucial to an understanding of Lonergan's hermeneutics.

Second, if Crowe is right in saying that the universal viewpoint yields place to transcendental method, then our study is not about some peripheral point but about the very core of Lonergan's life work.

Third, our age is increasingly aware of disparate universes of discourse, of the profusion of language-games, of incommensurable paradigms and of cultural parameters. Involved here are questions of cross-cultural communication and of dialogue. The notion of the universal viewpoint is intimately related to such questions; but just how it is related is something that had best be reserved for the conclusion of this study.

There remains the question of methodology, and since I am engaged in interpreting an author who has written on hermeneutics and on method, it would seem fitting to relate my own attempt to his theory. Accordingly, the present study would be an instance of the functional specialties, research and interpretation, for it assembles the data regarding the universal viewpoint, and attempts to determine the meaning of that data.

The limits of the research have been mentioned already: the period extending from *Insight* to *Method*. The primary materials examined have included most of Lonergan's published works, a major part of the 'semi-published' and unpublished material (class notes prepared by Lonergan, students' notes on Lonergan's courses, transcripts of institutes and lectures), as well as pertinent material from the Archives at the Lonergan Research Institute in Toronto. An attempt to date some of the undated archival material may be found in appendix A.

As far as interpretation is concerned, my effort to understand Lonergan on the universal viewpoint has been largely a matter of 'spiraling into his meaning through the self-correcting process of learning.' In other words, it is an instance of the functional specialty interpretation, rather than of the hermeneutics of chapter 17 of *Insight*. Still, something more is involved. For understanding the text presupposes an understanding of *die Sache* of the text, an understanding of what the text is speaking about; when that is not enough, one must move on to an understanding of the context (which is what Lonergan means by his 'Understanding the Author'), and eventually to understanding oneself.[52] But when one is studying the universal viewpoint, the object of study has to do with the 'concrete subject that is oneself,' and so understanding the object coincides with understanding oneself. If then one is to understand Lonergan on the universal viewpoint, the pre-understanding required is familiarity with the workings of one's mind and eventually of one's heart. More briefly, understanding Lonergan on the universal viewpoint presupposes that understanding of the object which is understanding oneself. This, it will be seen, amounts to saying that a work that attempts to express a universal viewpoint cannot be understood apart from the universal viewpoint. Accordingly, there is a sense in which the present work approaches the hermeneutics of *Insight*; but it might be more exact to say that this is merely a reflection of the continuity between *Insight* and *Method*. Still, this study does not attempt to engage formally in the functional specialty dialectic, and much less in the functional specialty foundations. This does not mean that positions have not been taken; it only means that determining the meaning of a text is merely one element on the way to these specialties, and that such a contribution is often all that is possible or can be demanded of any single individual.[53]

It might be added that, if the difference between the functional specialties interpretation and history is that between the 'hermeneutic' context of a single author and the 'historical' context of a series of authors,[54] then the present study is not an instance of the functional specialty history, for it does not attempt to situate Lonergan in a historical context but limits itself to the determination 'of the meaning of a single author on a particular point.'

Since, however, what is being studied is a development, the method has been to identify points of transition and to concentrate on the question of identity in difference. Ideally, such a study presupposes a range of particular studies, and should have been undertaken only upon the completion of such studies. Still, at least as far as a single author is concerned, it is probably only within the ongoing context of his thought that the meaning of any single text or group of texts can be determined. The point I would make is that while the present work leaves place for a range of further studies on particular points regarding the universal viewpoint or on the universal viewpoint in more limited contexts, still, there is an interaction between such particular studies and more general ones, and in this consists the apology for the present study.

A task that has not been attempted is the examination of Lonergan's own sources. Thus, for example, there are clear indications that, while the proximate source of Lonergan's notion of wisdom is Aquinas's mediation of Aristotle, the remote source is probably Newman's mediation of Aristotle.[55] In the same vein, there is probably much to be gained for an understanding of Lonergan's notion of dialectic, which is so closely related to his notion of the universal viewpoint, by an examination of his early reading of Hegel. A third if more remotely relevant area to be examined would be the *Sitz-im-Leben* of Lonergan's thinking on hermeneutics as constituted especially by the debate on biblical interpretation raging in Catholic circles at around the time *Insight* was being written. Yet another valuable source would be Lonergan's reading of the *Geisteswissenschaften.*

Since what is being studied is a development, the criterion used in distribution of material and in division of parts is chronological. The study divides into three parts, the points of division being the completion of *Insight* in 1953, and the achievement of new theological foundations in around 1968. Accordingly, the first part might be said to deal with the context of *Insight*, the second with the period between *Insight* and *Method*, and the third with the context of *Method.* Each part consists of four chapters. The first part deals with the antecedents of the universal viewpoint, situates it in the context first of *Insight* and then of chapter 17 of *Insight*, and examines its expansion and transformation in the final part of the book. The second part tries to determine the metamorphosis of the universal viewpoint in the post-*Insight* period: from 1954 to 1961 it appears under the guise of the upper blade for hermeneutics or history; in 1962 it becomes 'basic context'; and in 1963 it is replaced by methodical horizon. The final chapter of this part takes up the question of the search for new theological foundations. This provides a transition to the third part, which begins by discussing whether transcendental method itself is methodical horizon, goes on to study the first five functional specialties (research, interpretation, and history in chapter 10 and dialectic and foundations in chapter 11), and finally concludes with a chapter on the universal viewpoint in *Method in Theology*.

PART ONE

Insight

1

Early Anticipations of the Universal Viewpoint

We begin by examining three notions from Lonergan's early writings that seem to be early anticipations of the universal viewpoint: the 'pure form of speculative development' found in the introductory pages of his doctoral dissertation (1940),[1] the technique of psychological introspection found in the *Verbum* articles (1946–49),[2] and the notion of wisdom, also to be found in the *Verbum* articles. As has been indicated in the Introduction, this is a line of research suggested by Crowe; whether or not it pays off should become evident as we go along.

1   The Pure Form of Speculative Development

The *Gratia Operans* introduction presents the problem of interpretation as one of avoiding two extremes: that of imposing current categories on to the text, and that of a pure positivism. The first extreme is represented by Bañezian and Molinist attempts to read Aquinas from the viewpoint of current theology; such interpretation results in a distortion of the texts.[3] The second extreme instead is the modern temptation; the problem here is not only the risk of ending up with mere compilations of texts, but also the impossibility of approaching a text with a blank mind, for 'even historians have intelligence and perform acts of understanding; performing them, they necessarily approach questions from a given point of view; and with equal necessity the limitations of that point of view predetermine the conclusions they reach.'[4]

The key to the solution lies in the discovery of some neutral set of categories. What is needed is 'a point of vantage outside the temporal dialectic, a matrix or system of thought that at once is as pertinent and as indifferent to historical events as is the science of mathematics to quantitative phenomena.'[5] Such a vantage point Lonergan finds in the human mind, and this vantage point is neutral 'because the human mind is always the human mind.'[6] Thus, he proposes to construct 'an *a priori* scheme that is capable of synthesizing any possible set of historical data irrespective of their place and time, just as the science of mathematics constructs a generic scheme capable of synthesizing any possible set of quantitative phenomena.'[7] Such a scheme is attained 'by an analysis of the idea of a development in speculative theology.'[8] Speculative thinking develops in a predictable way, and the form of this development provides the required set of neutral categories. Crowe has summarized this scheme thus:

> [T]he general form of any speculative development ... oscillates between general and particular in the following way. We have an insight on a specific point; we generalize it and make it the whole explanation; we learn it is insufficient for a complete explanation, so we go behind it to a more general factor; we make this in its turn the whole explanation, only to discover that it too is insufficient by itself; we go back to our first insight, the specific one, but now we make a synthesis of the general and specific, and have a better approximation to a complete explanation.[9]

Given the pure form of speculative development, interpretation is the result of a 'pincer' movement[10] from the general to the particular, and from the particular to the general.[11] The first movement consists in discovering the general form of speculative development in the data. The second movement consists in assembling the explicit statements on one's specific topic in a given set of authors.[12] Such a movement, Lonergan points out, 'is essentially the same as when a mathematician works out an equation from general considerations and then a physicist evaluates the unknown coefficients by objective measurements.'[13] The advantage is that we are able to find a correlation among statements made by different people at different times 'merely in virtue of the assumption that the people in question were all men, all thinking, and historically interdependent in their thought.'[14]

Lonergan notes that this procedure does not consist in proposing and verifying hypotheses; thus all guesswork is excluded. 'Instead of hypotheses there is used the *a priori* scheme of speculative development, which is not a hypothesis but a demonstrable conclusion.'[15] The point here is that, since the scheme does not arise from the data under consideration, the possibility of prejudging the issue is avoided. Still, it must not be thought that the use of such a scheme makes interpretation a deductive process. Interpretation remains an inductive procedure, for though the scheme is a priori, the filling in of the scheme is not a priori. There is thus no question of a demonstration of what Aquinas meant. Inductive conclusions can be certain when negative, but are no more than probable when positive; for 'the only possible way to demonstrate an interpretation is to enumerate the entire list of speculative possibilities, demonstrate that the enumeration is complete (that is the difficult point), and then exclude all views except one.'[16] This is an interesting remark in view of the description of the universal viewpoint as envisaging the range of possible meanings,[17] though of course the universal viewpoint is not an enumeration but rather a grasp of a virtual totality of viewpoints,[18] just as grasp of the rule for integers is a grasp of a virtual totality of concepts.[19]

The use of such a procedure avoids the twin dangers affecting interpretation. Positivism is avoided by taking into account 'the exigence of the human mind for some scheme or matrix within which data are assembled and given their initial correlation.'[20] The danger of distorting data to uphold one's hypothesis is avoided, for the scheme is taken not from the data but solely 'from a consideration of the nature of human speculation on a given subject.'[21] Moreover, such a procedure allows the inquiry to be historical, and this is necessary, given the fact that Aquinas's thought on grace underwent development.[22]

2 Psychological Introspection and Wisdom

Like the *Gratia Operans* dissertation, the *Verbum* articles (1946-49) are an exercise in interpretation. There is no mention, however, of the pure form of speculative development. The reason would seem to be that the object of study here is not a speculative development in a series of authors but rather the meaning of a notion or concept in a single author. Still, as will be seen, there are echoes of the pincer movement, and this not only in the method used but also in the very content of the study itself.

2.1 Psychological Introspection

The aim of the *Verbum* articles is to establish what Aquinas meant by *intelligere*[23] or by intelligible procession of an inner word.[24] The thesis is that by *intelligere* Aquinas meant understanding.[25] As in the case of *gratia operans*, we have here a problem of conflicting interpretations.[26] Part of the problem is that Aquinas expressed his grasp of psychological facts in metaphysical categories and theorems.[27] Lonergan's solution is to approach the texts by means of familiarity with psychological fact: 'to follow Aquinas here one must practice introspective rational psychology.'[28]

Grasp of the nature of one's acts of understanding is 'the key to the whole of Thomist psychology.'[29] Preliminary concern with psychological fact

> will lend a sureness, otherwise unattainable, to the interpretation of the metaphysical categories; for the Thomist application of metaphysics to the tasks of psychological analysis cannot be studied in some preliminary vacuum. That application exists only in psychological contexts; and it is easier to interpret metaphysics as applied to psychology when one is aware of the psychological facts involved. Without such awareness interpretation has to limp along on more less remote and certainly non-psychological analogies.[30]

Such a method becomes in effect a bridge between the centuries, and the bridge, as in the *Gratia Operans* introduction, lies in the fact that the human mind is always the same: '[T]he principal aim has been to build a bridge from the mind of the twentieth-century reader to the mind of the thirteenth-century writer. Both possess psychological experience; in both that experience is essentially the same; both can by introspection observe and analyze such experience.'[31]

Psychological introspection then is the key to the interpretation of Thomist psychology. But Lonergan has a further point to make: that Aquinas both knew about psychological introspection and practiced it. Thus he remarks:

> At once the assumption of the method employed and the contention derived from the data assembled in these two chapters [i.e., chapters 1 and 2] have been that Aquinas did practice psychological introspection and through that experimental knowledge of his own soul arrived at his highly nuanced, deeply penetrating, firmly outlined theory of the nature of human intellect.[32]

In fact, the possibility of such introspection is central to Aquinas's analysis of human knowing, given that for him the procession of the inner word is neither unconscious nor automatic but rather intelligent and rational.[33] If Aquinas is right, then psychological introspection regarding the inner word is possible: one can know about the inner word not only through deduction and not only through the study of Aquinas's texts, but also through familiarity with the workings of one's own mind.

To enter a little more deeply into the issue, it is necessary to explore the links between introspection and wisdom. For while indirect evidence that Aquinas practiced introspection is spread throughout the first two of Lonergan's articles, direct evidence is invoked in connection with epistemological wisdom. Just why this is so should become clear in the next section, but we might say right away that the link is self-knowledge. For psychological introspection is a question of becoming familiar with the workings of one's own mind; but epistemological wisdom in Aquinas has itself to do with self-knowledge. Accordingly, Lonergan can observe that his presentation of the data in Aquinas on the soul's knowledge of itself serves a double purpose: not only does it answer the question about the precise extent to which Aquinas subscribed to the critical program, but also it serves as 'a justification of the procedure followed in these articles, a presentation of the evidence for our belief that the Thomist theory of intellect had an empirical and introspective basis.'[34]

2.2 Wisdom

The topic of wisdom comes up in *Verbum* in connection with judgment, and more precisely, in connection with the critical question. This critical question is to be distinguished from the criteriological question. The criteriological question is concerned with the mechanism of judgment: it asks how one arrives at the point where one feels compelled to make a judgment.[35] The critical issue instead may be put thus: '[G]ranted the subjective necessity of some judgments as knowable and known, how does the mind proceed from such immanent coercion to objective truth and, through truth, to knowledge of reality?'[36] Aquinas's answer to the former question is the *resolutio in principia*, a return from the intellectual syntheses reached by developing insights to their sources in sense and in the naturally known first principles.[37] His answer to the critical question instead is to be found in his discussions of the virtue of right judgment which is wisdom.

What does wisdom have to do with the critical question? The critical question regards judgment, and wisdom is the virtue of right judgment. Wisdom has to do with the real as real, and it is in judgment that we know the real.[38] Wisdom in fact has a dual role. Principally it is first philosophy, or ontology, or natural theology; it is concerned with universal order, and so it is the 'highest, architectonic science, a science of sciences.'[39] But 'it also has some of the characteristics of an epistemology,'[40] for it is also concerned 'with the transition from the order of thought to the order of reality.'[41] But how exactly does wisdom handle this transition from thought to reality? Well, we test the truth of statements by reducing them to their sources in sense and in the first principles; but it is wisdom that validates the first principles of the intellect themselves by validating their component terms.[42]

Now such a point would seem to have been made already by Aristotle. Still, remarks Lonergan, Aristotle cannot be said to have raised the critical problem; he never discusses how our immanent activities contain a transcendence; his thinking on judgment amounts merely to a generalization of the criteriological question.[43] Further, it would seem that Aquinas himself was acutely aware of the incompleteness of Aristotelian gnoseology.[44] For Aristotle's basic gnoseological theorem is that knowing is by identity; but this theorem, while it avoids serious problems with respect to knowledge in the absolute Being, also raises the problem of knowledge of the other as far as human intellect is concerned.[45] For 'the act of the thing as intelligible is the act of understanding, but the act of the thing as real is the *esse naturale* of the thing and, except in divine self-knowledge, that *esse* is not identical with knowing it.'[46] As far as human knowledge is concerned, the theorem of knowing by identity needs to be completed by another theorem, that of knowing by intentionality. In us, understanding needs to be complemented by reflection. It is only by reflection on the identity of act that one arrives at the difference of potency.[47]

In his effort to elaborate the moment of rational reflection, Aquinas turned to Augustine's vision of eternal truth.[48] In the process he brought the second operation of the intellect, the act of rational reflection, into its own: this act had to bear the weight of the transition from knowledge as perfection to knowledge of the other.[49] However, there was a problem here, for Augustine's vision of eternal truth is ultimately Platonic in its presuppositions: it holds that we all know the same truth because we all gaze upon the one eternal Truth. Such a view went against Aquinas's fundamental and systematic option for the Aristotelian view that we know, not by confrontation, but by what we are.[50] Aquinas's way out was to posit that we know, not by gazing upon Eternal Light, but by means of our own intellectual light, which is a created participation of the Eternal Light. It is through this intellectual light that we pass from knowledge by identity to knowledge of the other.[51]

However, this is merely an ontology of knowledge. As an epistemology it is 'null and void,' for it presupposes that we know validly both ourselves and God. The question therefore arises: does Aquinas have an epistemology? If he has, it will have to be along the following lines: since we know by what we are (and not by what we see), it follows that we know we know by knowing what we are.[52] Whether or not Aquinas has an epistemology reduces then to discovering whether he affirmed the latter type of self-knowledge. Did he? Here Lonergan appeals to a text 'in which Aquinas did maintain that our knowledge of truth is derived from our knowledge of ourselves': 'secundum hoc cognoscit veritatem intellectus quod supra se ipsum reflectitur.'[53] For sense knowledge is both true and conscious, but is not conscious of its own truth.[54] Intellectual knowledge instead is not merely true but also aware of its own truth. It is not merely aware empirically of its acts, but also reflects upon their nature and in this way knows its own proportion to knowledge of reality.[55] Lonergan believes that, in the passage quoted above, 'Aquinas subscribed, not obscurely, to the program of critical thought: to know truth we have to know ourselves and the nature of our knowledge, and the method to be employed is reflection.'[56]

This brings us to the section 'Self-knowledge of the Soul,' and to our question about the link between psychological introspection and epistemological wisdom. From Aristotle, Aquinas learned that, since the human soul is *in genere intelligibilium* merely a potency, it knows itself not by direct grasp of its essence, but rather by grasp of understanding in act.[57] On his own, Aquinas distinguished between an empirical awareness of our acts and a scientific grasp of their nature. The latter is reached only by study; and it is reached precisely by appealing to the former.[58] Introspective method for Aquinas is therefore a question of establishing scientific self-knowledge by appealing to our prior empirical awareness of our inner acts, and explicit statements to that effect are not lacking. Thus Lonergan can remark:

> [T]he introspective method employed in this and the preceding article may be said to rest upon an explicit statement: 'anima humana intelligit se ipsum per suum intelligere, quod est actus proprius eius, perfecte demonstrans virtutem eius et naturam'; grasp the nature of your acts of understanding and you have the key to the whole of Thomist psychology. Indeed you also have what Aquinas considered the key to Aristotelian psychology: 'unde et supra Philosophus per ipsum intelligere et per illud quod intelligitur, scrutatus est naturam intellectus possibilis.'[59]

The point therefore is to ask how the human soul understands itself by its act of understanding. Here Lonergan goes on to examine the question of intellectual light. This leads back to the critical problem and so to the link between psychological introspection and epistemological wisdom.

The human soul does not grasp itself by its own essence; nonetheless it is true that 'in some fashion it does know its own intellectual light by its own intellectual light.'[60] The note of caution here stems from the fact that normally intellectual light 'is seen, not as an object, but "in ratione medii cognoscendi."'[61] The mere fact that one is understanding something 'does not make it inevitable that one reflexly directs one's attention to the intellectual light involved in the act.'[62] Clearly then, while intellectual light in a certain way always knows itself *per se ipsum*,[63] introspective grasp of intellectual light by means of intellectual light calls for a further effort. Such is the 'appeal to experience' by which Aquinas established his psychological theory.

Now Aquinas pushed the notion of intellectual light beyond the Aristotelian theory of agent intellect, not only by identifying agent intellect with the ground of intellectual light[64] but also by relating intellectual light not merely to the first but also to the second operation of intellect.[65] This is of course connected with his overcoming of the limitations of Aristotelian gnoseology by appealing to Augustine, and it is here that hints about Aquinas's epistemology must be sought, for it is by this light that we get beyond relativity to immutable truth, and that we discern appearance from reality.[66] It is here that we must search for the way intellect is aware of itself not merely empirically but rather by penetrating to its own essence and thus knowing its own proportion to reality.[67] But, warns Lonergan, 'it is somewhat hazardous to attempt to specify the exact course of such reflection,' for Aquinas himself 'did not offer an account of the procedure he would follow; so it is only by piecing together scattered materials that one can arrive at an epistemological position that may be termed Thomistic but hardly Thomist.'[68] Still, Lonergan considers that two points may be granted because sufficiently clear in Aquinas: (1) that the epistemological reflection in question involves 'a sort of reasoning' that is not however a deduction[69] but rather 'a development of understanding by which we come to grasp just how it is that our minds are proportionate to knowledge of reality,'[70] and (2) that the content of the reasoning consists in a grasp of the native infinity of intellect.[71] We may note that Lonergan regards this Thomistic epistemological position as a *reflection*: it is by reflection on the nature of intellectual light that we know the proportion of our intellects to reality; it is by such reflection that we resolve the critical problem. Epistemological reflection is therefore a question of *scientific* self-knowledge rather than empirical self-knowledge.

The reflection or reasoning goes as follows. That Aquinas asserted the native infinity of intellect is clear;[72] further, such infinity is also a datum of rational consciousness, for it appears both in the restless spirit of inquiry as well as in the absolute exigence of reflective thought 'which will assent only if the possibility of the contradictory proposition is excluded.'[73] Thus the intellect naturally knows being, and gives its assent only when the absolute of being is reached. When we grasp this clearly, we grasp the proportion of our intellects to reality. For we know by what we are; so we know that we know by reflecting on what we are; by reflecting, that is, on the nature of our intellect, on its native capacity to grasp being and to be satisfied with nothing less than being. Lonergan concludes:

> Just as Thomist thought is an ontology of knowledge inasmuch as intellectual light is referred to its origin in uncreated Light, so too it is more than an embryonic epistemology inasmuch as intellectual

light reflectively grasps its own nature and the commensuration of that nature to the universe of reality.[74]

The difficult point in the above is of course to understand just how a grasp of the native infinity of intellect implies a grasp of the proportion of intellect to reality. At this point Lonergan offers two remarks, which we will try to elucidate. First of all, to know the real involves knowledge of the universe in some way.[75] We might add: to grasp the commensuration of intellectual light to reality means grasping its commensuration to the whole of the universe. But this means that knowing the real involves wisdom. For when one is an expert in a particular field, one judges with ease, and one's judgments are secure; when instead one finds oneself in a strange field, one hesitates to judge. Now when the issue is judgment of reality, the relevant field is really unlimited, for reality is not some aspect of things, but the whole of each thing, and it is not just some one particular thing, but the whole universe of things.[76] Hence, judgments of reality call for an expertise or a wisdom that is unlimited, that regards the universe.

But do we have such wisdom that regards the universal scheme of things? No, for such wisdom belongs only to God. How then do we pass judgments and attain the truth about things? The fact is that, though we do not possess the perfect wisdom that belongs to God, still we do possess some participation in it, and that is our intellectual light. Intellectual light within us is marked by a native infinity; it is therefore a rudimentary view of the whole, and so an inchoate wisdom.[77] On the basis of this elementary knowledge of the universe we grow in wisdom. It follows that our knowledge of the real is a development. We move only slowly towards the ability to make competent and proper judgments. Thus the child has to learn to distinguish fact and fiction; the young person has to acquire a certain maturity before he or she can profit from the study of ethics; and each of us is expert only within the domain of the familiar, but outside that domain we turn to the experts.[78]

But how do we grow in wisdom? By a process of internal differentiation of the rudimentary view of the whole given in intellectual light.[79] This differentiation is by a process of dichotomy: divide being into material and nonmaterial, subdivide the material into the living and the non-living, and so on. This process leaves out nothing, and at the same time we are moving towards ever more detailed knowledge of the whole. So we always have a view of the whole; what we do is to block off areas by means of dichotomies, and operate in the context of this view of the whole.[80] Growth in wisdom can be also by learning from others.[81] In the light of the degree of wisdom we have attained, we make judgments; we also know the limits of our wisdom, and refrain from making judgments in those areas that are unfamiliar to us.[82]

But if we reach being by means of intellectual light, do we know that we so reach being? Yes, because though the human soul does not know itself by its own essence, we know our intellectual light by means of intellectual light itself. It follows that we not only reach being but also know that we reach being.

Lonergan's second comment is that we and our knowing are instances of being; we are therefore within being and not outside of it.[83] The critical problem therefore is reformulated: it is not a question of moving from the subject to an object outside the subject; rather, we know being and beings, and within this knowledge we grasp also the difference between subjects and objects.[84] The radical clarification of this comes of course in the *Insight* chapters on self-affirmation, being, and objectivity.

Clearly such a 'Thomistic' epistemological reflection is a question of psychological introspection, for it consists in intellectual light grasping itself as critical wonder. Clearly also it does not occur every time we pass a judgment, for 'the mere fact that one is understanding something does not make it inevitable that one reflexly directs one's attention to the intellectual light involved in the act,'[85] and again, '[n]ot in every judgment do we reflect to the point of knowing our own essence and from that conclude our capacity to know truth.'[86] Further, such epistemological reflection may be said to be the highest point in psychological introspection.[87] But epistemological reflection is merely wisdom in its epistemological role, and so the highest point in psychological introspection seems to coincide with epistemological wisdom.

But perhaps epistemological wisdom is to be identified not merely with a part of psychological introspection but with the whole of it. Such an interpretation finds support in the distinction between empirical, scientific, and normative self-knowledge.[88] Normative self-knowledge is described as lying 'in the act of judgment which passes from the conception of essence to the affirmation of reality.'[89] Such normative self-knowledge

> is concerned not with this or that soul, but with what any soul ought to be according to the eternal reasons; and so the reality of soul that is envisaged is not sorry achievement but dynamic norm. Now knowledge of the norm, of the ought-to-be, cannot be had from what merely happens to be and, too often, falls far short of the norm. Normative knowledge has to rest upon the eternal reasons. But this resting, Aquinas explained, is not a vision of God but a participation and similitude of Him by which we grasp first principles and judge all things by examining them in the light of principles.[90]

There follows the statement that 'wisdom through self-knowledge' is 'a progress from empirical through scientific to normative knowledge.'[91] Not only then would the highest point in introspection coincide with epistemological reflection, but growth in self-knowledge through introspection would itself seem to coincide with the genesis of wisdom and with epistemological wisdom.

We have been noting the duality of wisdom between epistemology and metaphysics, but Lonergan also insists on the unity of wisdom.[92] The current practice, he says, of separating manuals and courses of epistemology and metaphysics reinforces the impression of a violent and irreducible contrast between the two, as if being were one thing and knowing another. The truth instead is that there is the most intimate relationship between knowing and being, for we know by what we are, and we know that we know by knowing what we are.[93] The very distinction between subject and object is a distinction within being, for the critical problem, as we have seen, is not a question of moving 'from within outwards, of moving from a subject to an object outside the subject' but is rather a problem of moving 'from above downwards, of moving from an infinite potentiality commensurate with the universe towards a rational apprehension that seizes the difference of subject and object in essentially the same way that it seizes any other real distinction.'[94] Therefore if ontology is first *quoad se*, epistemology is first *quoad nos*. Wisdom is stretched out between two poles, between our immanent intellectual light and the uncreated Light that is the object of its striving, between the inchoate wisdom given in the former and the infinite Wisdom that is the latter. Between these two poles wisdom moves to knowledge of itself and of its Source in a dialectical oscillation.[95]

Further, wisdom seems to provide a term of comparison between the pure form of speculative development and psychological introspection. Like the pure form of speculative development that is a hermeneutical upper blade, epistemological wisdom is also a hermeneutical upper blade. Unlike the pure form of speculative development that anticipates development and so is diachronic, introspection is concerned with grasp of the structure of human knowing and so is synchronic. But what we would draw attention to is the pincer movement involved not only in the pure form but also in the technique of introspection. For as we have noted above, the critical problem is a question of moving 'from above downwards,' 'from an infinite potentiality commensurate with the universe towards a rational apprehension that seizes the difference of subject and object in essentially the same way that it seizes any other real distinction.'[96] This is more than merely a tenuous link based on the use of the metaphor of the movement from above downwards. For the metaphor in question is an expression of the fact that the inchoate wisdom given in intellectual light constitutes a permanent feature of human knowing, and that it is a rudimentary view of the whole and so a universal anticipation:

> As our intellects are potential, so our knowledge of the real is a development ... Still, in all this progress we are but discriminating, differentiating, categorizing the details of a scheme that somehow we possessed from the start. To say that any X is real is just to assign it a place in that scheme; to deny the reality of any Y is to deny it a place in the universal scheme.[97]

Thus wisdom itself is an upper blade, and this is clearly confirmed by post-*Insight* references to it. The *Verbum* articles themselves note that intellectual light contains virtually the whole of science,[98] but the Latin course of 1959 entitled *De systemate et historia* notes further that it is this light of agent intellect giving rise to questions that is the upper blade at the very beginning of a science. It goes on to add that as the science progresses, the systematic knowledge that has been achieved itself functions as the upper dynamic.[99] This is of course in keeping with the fact that progress in knowledge is a question of 'discriminating, differentiating, categorizing the details' of the universal scheme already possessed at the start,[100] and further confirmation may be had from the example of doctor and patient given in the *De methodo theologiae* course of 1962: from his or her prior knowledge of medicine the doctor diagnoses the illness; but such diagnosis in turn may lead to an enrichment of medical knowledge.[101] And we have seen that *Verbum* itself describes human wisdom, because merely accidental, as having to move towards knowledge of itself and of its source in a dialectical oscillation between our immanent intellectual light and the uncreated Light that is the object of its striving.[102]

In sum: wisdom has an epistemological and a metaphysical aspect, where epistemology must be seen as revealing the intrinsic link between knowing and being rather than as moving from knowing to being. The method of psychological introspection coincides with wisdom in its epistemological aspect. Finally, wisdom itself constitutes the original upper blade of human knowing. From this it follows not only that all human knowing is marked by a pincer movement, but also that various upper blades such as mathematics, the pure form of speculative development, and self-knowledge are merely particular instances of the original upper blade that is wisdom.

2.3 The Method of Interpretation

We may end this chapter by turning to the discussion of the method of interpretation in the epilogue to the *Verbum* articles. As in the *Gratia Oper-*

ans introduction, the problem in interpretation is the need to avoid both imposition of categories and positivism, but now Lonergan notes that both these extremes are rooted in neglect of the role of understanding in interpretation. Contemporary historical study is beset by the temptation to positivism, the temptation to so rely on method as to exclude the goal of understanding; but method is mere superstition when the aim of understanding is excluded.[103] The temptation of the manual writer, by contrast, is the 'conceptualist illusion.' He tends to think that interpreting Aquinas is a matter of quoting and arguing. Ignoring the fact that inner words are products of understanding, he tends to overlook the enormous initial task of having to develop one's understanding. But the fact is that without such a development, one usually ends up repeating the words of Aquinas without being able to mean what Aquinas meant.[104]

Such a position follows from what has been established about *verbum*. The inner word proceeds from the act of understanding, and this procession is neither unconscious nor merely sensitively conscious but rather is intelligently or rationally conscious. The inner word itself is an act of meaning, and acts of meaning give rise further to the outer word or expression, which may be spoken, written, or else merely imagined.[105] It follows that interpretation is a question of mounting backwards from the outer word to the inner word or act of meaning, and to the act of understanding itself. Thus we begin from the data, which are illuminated by intellectual light; there follows thinking in order to understand, at the end of which emerge the act of direct understanding and the inner word proportionate to it; this is followed by critical inquiry and rational reflection, the act of reflective understanding, and the rational procession of the inner word of judgment. Is then interpreting Aquinas a simple matter of reading and understanding? Well, the analysis has spoken of thinking in order to understand, and of the process of rational reflection, and it is here that the difficulty lies. For the role of habits has not been mentioned: given a habitual understanding of a particular field, the moment of thinking is reduced to a minimum; one has only to read in order for understanding to follow. Lacking such a habit, one has first to undertake the labor of acquiring it before one can understand with ease. The problem of interpretation then is the problem of acquiring a habitual understanding like that of the author; given that, there is not much difficulty in mounting up from Aquinas's texts to understanding what he meant and understanding as he understood.[106]

A little reflection should make clear that we are confronted here with a vicious circle: we cannot understand unless we already possess a habit of understanding; but such a habit of understanding is itself the result of many acts of understanding. The solution consists in appealing to the dynamism of the process: one mounts up to the mind of Aquinas by a 'slow, repetitious, circular labor':

> Only by the slow, repetitious, circular labor of going over and over the data, by catching here a little insight and there another, by following through false leads and profiting from many mistakes, by continuous adjustments and cumulative changes of one's initial suppositions and perspectives and concepts, can one hope to attain such a development of one's own understanding as to hope to understand what Aquinas understood and meant.[107]

Such then is the comment on interpretation in the epilogue to the *Verbum* articles. Curiously, there is no mention here of the technique of psychological introspection, of the fact that 'it is only by introspection that one can discover what an introspective psychologist is talking about.'[108] The reason for such an omission may perhaps be the fact that psychological introspection is not yet a generalized method of interpretation: it is applicable only in the case of texts dealing with the workings of the human mind. Still, it is not difficult to relate introspection to what has been said. For clearly, introspection is itself a way of mounting up to the self-knowledge or habitual understanding similar to that of Aquinas.[109] It must be added here that such introspection takes place not apart from but in interaction with the Thomist texts: this would seem to be borne out by the first two *Verbum* articles that we have been examining. This is merely a particular instance of the general rule that introspection does not take place in a vacuum, for '[w]e can know what understanding is by understanding anything and reflecting on the nature of our understanding; for the *species* of the object understood is also the *species* of the understanding intellect.'[110] The point is that some *species* is needed, some object is required. The 'dialectical oscillation' in which we move towards wisdom[111] does not take place in the concrete without 'a dialectical interplay of sense, memory, imagination, insight, definition, critical reflection, judgment.'[112]

We have been noting that introspection is not as yet a generalized technique of interpretation, and we must add that the pure form of speculative development was not sufficiently general either. This pure form was the form of speculative development, and not, for example, of dogmatic development.[113] Still, we have also noted that the pure form was diachronic while psychological introspection is synchronic. The point is that, between the pure form and the technique of psychological introspection, we have in fact the basic elements of the universal viewpoint. In the chapters to follow we hope to show that the universal viewpoint is a generalized tool of interpretation that is both synchronic as well as diachronic.

2

The Universal Viewpoint: Background Notions

The universal viewpoint is a heuristic structure that is introduced and discussed in a chapter of *Insight* entitled 'Metaphysics as Dialectic.' Accordingly, an examination of the notion of heuristic structures in general and of dialectical heuristic structure in particular, of the method of metaphysics and of metaphysics as dialectic, will serve to establish the general context of the universal viewpoint. It will be seen further that all four topics have to do in some way with wisdom, and so the present chapter serves also as a link between the pure form of speculative development, the technique of psychological introspection, and the universal viewpoint.

1 Heuristic Structures

1.1 The A Priori

Both because Lonergan's notion of heuristic structures is itself related to the notion of the a priori,[1] and because the notion of the universal viewpoint is contrasted to a Kantian type of a priori,[2] we preface our account of heuristic structures with this brief note on the a priori in Lonergan.

In *Insight* the term a priori does not occur very frequently, and when it does, its use seems to be marginal.[3] Thus insights are said to be a priori and synthetic, but in a sense quite different from Kant's. For one thing, Lonergan does not hold for some fixed set of a priori syntheses; instead, every insight is an a priori synthesis. Further, such an a priori synthesis is only possibly relevant to data; and so insight is followed by verification or judgment.[4] Since then there is this ongoing interaction between insight and data, between the a priori and the a posteriori, it follows that insights are a priori only in a relative sense. Besides insights, heuristic structures and canons of method also constitute an a priori, in the sense that they settle in advance the general determinations, not only of the knowing, but also of the known.[5] However, the notion of being is never referred to as an a priori.

In the Halifax lectures of 1958 Lonergan makes a further effort to relate his own ideas to Kant's notion of the a priori. Taking as his starting point Kant's definition of the a priori as complete independence from experience, Lonergan points out that the issue is first of all a question of fact: how much of knowing is from the subject, and how much from the object? But besides this question of fact, there is also the question of significance: what value is to be attached to this notion of the a priori? The answer to this question depends on one's notion of what knowing ought to be. On the confrontationist model, knowing is a matter of taking a look; accordingly anything that comes from the subject is not knowing at all. But when knowing is conceived as an ontological perfection of the subject, in some cases it may include knowing something else, but that is incidental. On this model, 'the question of the a priori, of what comes from the subject and what comes from the object, is of minor moment.'[6]

In the light of this clarification, Lonergan asks about the sense in which the notion of being is a priori. He notes that the notion of being, our capacity to ask questions, is from nature; but actual wondering has at least an occasion supplied from experience. In other words, the potency is from nature, but the exercise involves experience.[7]

> Briefly, then, the intention of being functions as a finality. It is radically from nature, and it functions in knowledge as a finality, a guide, a criterion, a requirement. It is absolutely transparent; it is not an a priori that determines what you will know, but it demands, it initiates, the process of knowing, guides the process, and sets criteria by which one carries out the process correctly or incorrectly.[8]

Lonergan concludes that a posteriori and a priori, experiencing and not experiencing, are not the fundamental categories in which a satisfactory answer to the question is obtained. The fundamental categories are rather what we know by nature and what we know by acquisition.[9]

If in *Insight* then the a priori is at best marginal, in the Halifax Lectures its importance is relativized in favor of other categories. However, Lonergan continues to use the term a priori in the broad sense[10] up to 1974, when he explicitly restricts its meaning: 'The operators [of intentional dynamism] are a priori, and they alone are a priori. Their content is ever an anticipation of the next level of operations and thereby is not to be found in the contents of the previous level.'[11] In 1975 there occurs the description of heuristic structures as 'a conjunction both of data on the side of the object and of an operative criterion on the side of the subject.'[12] Once the a priori has been given a strict sense, a heuristic structure is not just the a priori question, but the question determined by a set of data; it is not just intellectual light, but intellectual light as applied.[13]

1.2 Heuristic Structures

The notion of heuristic structure is central to *Insight*. It is in fact an effort to elaborate the pincer movement mentioned in the *Gratia Operans* introduction, and in the light of the reference there to mathematics as an example of this movement,[14] it is interesting to note that *Insight* first identifies and appropriates this movement in the field of mathematics and the natural sciences, and then generalizes it to the whole of human knowing.

The first approach then is through a consideration of scientific inquiry. Scientific inquiry is methodical, and method consists in ordering means to achieve an end. But how can means be ordered to an end, when the end is knowledge, and the knowledge is not yet acquired? The answer is heuristic structure: name the unknown; work out its properties; use the properties to direct, order, guide the inquiry.[15] In algebra the unknowns to be known are named simply 'x'; in prescientific thought, what is to be known by understanding data is named 'the nature of ...': the nature of light, the nature of heat, etc. Scientific thought anticipates that the unknowns are not merely 'natures of ...' but rather correlations between measurable aspects of data. A further sophistication comes through the techniques of the infinitesimal calculus: now the empirical inquirer 'can move towards the determination of his indeterminate function by writing down differential equations which it must satisfy.'[16] There may be added further a principle of invariance and of equivalence.[17]

Now these sophistications of heuristic structures are the result of the labors of mathematicians. Empirical science begins in data to end in systems of laws. Its ideal goal is complete explanation of all data, excepting the empirical residue. Mathematics instead begins from the empirical residue and explores the totality of ways in which enriching abstraction can confer intelligibility on any materials that resemble the empirical residue. These movements then are complementary, for the mathematician begins where the empirical scientist would end; and if the mathematician does his/her work thoroughly, his/her enumeration of intelligible systems is bound to contain systems that empirical science will verify.[18] There is therefore set up a scissors movement (and this, we might note, is another way of speaking about the pincer movement). 'Not only is there a lower blade that rises from data through measurements and curve fitting to formulae, but also there is an upper blade that moves downward from differential and operator equations and from postulates of invariance and equivalence.'[19]

Inbuilt into our knowing, then, there is an anticipation of what is to be known. By inquiring, intelligence anticipates the act of understanding for which it strives. 'The content of that anticipated act can be designated heuristically. The properties of the anticipated and designated content constitute the clues intelligence employs to guide itself towards discovery.'[20] But such guided inquiry is methodical inquiry, and so explicitating heuristic structures provides a basis for method.[21] Canons of method are in fact rules for inquiry, formulated on the basis of the explicitated heuristic structures[22] with the intention of governing the fruitful unfolding of the immanent heuristic structures.[23]

Heuristic structures therefore anticipate a form to be filled, whereas method regards the process of filling the anticipated form. Heuristic structures are anticipated contents, whereas method is a set of directives regarding the process of reaching those contents.[24]

Again, we have noted that heuristic structures and canons of method constitute an a priori. By this is meant that they 'settle in advance the general determinations, not merely of the activities of knowing, but also of the content to be known.'[25] It is this characteristic of heuristic structures and of the a priori that is important to Lonergan; the question of whether heuristic structures are from the subject or from the object is, as we have seen, quite secondary.

Now scientific inquiry is concerned with understanding, and so its heuristic structures are anticipations of understanding.[26] But besides direct understanding there is also reflective understanding, and so human knowing anticipates not only the content of understanding but also the content of judgments. The Halifax lectures of 1958 put it thus: 'Just as there is heuristic structure with regard to acts of understanding, so there is a total heuristic structure; there is the total goal of intelligent and rational consciousness as such. We have named that goal "being."'[27] Since the notion of being anticipates all cognitional contents whatsoever, it is the *supreme heuristic notion*. Prior to every content, it is the notion of the to-be-known through the content.[28] But heuristic structures are operative even before being known,[29] and this is true also of the notion of being: before it can be known, it is already immanent and operative. The immanent and operative notion of being is the pure, detached, unrestricted desire to know. The pure desire to know, points out Lonergan, is a spontaneous notion of being; and if it seems strange to refer to a desire as a notion, it must be noted that the desire in question is neither an unconscious tendency like the orientation of a fetal eye to sight, nor a merely empirically conscious desire like hunger, but a unique type of tendency and desire that is not merely empirically but also intelligently and rationally conscious.[30]

This spontaneous notion of being that is our pure desire to know is what *Verbum* referred to as intellectual light. Like intellectual light that was both spontaneous wonder and the spirit of critical inquiry,[31] the notion of being is our intelligent and rational consciousness.[32] The notion of being as the supreme heuristic notion is therefore a transposition into contemporary terms of the inchoate wisdom or rudimentary view of the whole that is given in intellectual light.

Consideration of the notion of being makes it clear that even the most elementary anticipations are a sort of upper blade and already constitute a scissors movement.[33] The fact is that all human knowing is characterized by an upper blade. The anticipations of mathematics are merely a further sophistication of the original upper blade that is the spontaneous notion of being. But this is a point we have noted already: the inchoate wisdom given in intellectual light sets up the original pincer movement.[34]

Chapter 2 of *Insight* had spoken of the unspecified heuristic concept, which is a name given to the content of the anticipated act of direct understanding.[35] Chapter 12 generalizes this to obtain the fundamental heuristic notion of being that anticipates the content not only of direct but also of reflective understanding. Chapter 14 carries this generalization further by speaking of heuristic notions rather than heuristic concepts. As in empirical science, so also in general, heuristic notions are a question of naming the unknown, determining its properties, and using these properties to guide inquiry; but here the properties of the unknown are obtained by studying the general characteristics of the act by which the unknown will become known.[36] Thus a heuristic notion is now described as 'the notion of an unknown content' that is determined 'by anticipating the type of act through which the unknown would become known,'[37] whereas a heuristic structure is described as an ordered set of heuristic notions.[38]

A further point to be noted is that heuristic structures are the key to both development and continuity in knowledge. Heuristic structures are basically the questions that are structurally inbuilt into our knowing. But such basic questions do not change; what changes are answers. Thus, various answers have been given down the ages to the question, What is fire, but that question itself has remained the same. On the other hand, there is a sense in which heuristic structures themselves undergo development. For it must not be thought that heuristic structures are completely indeterminate. Besides the content that fills the heuristic structure, there is the content that is the heuristic structure itself. That the heuristic structure is itself 'something very definite' is clear from the fact that it is something that can be grasped and affirmed.[39] Now as determinate contents, heuristic structures themselves undergo development. Thus, the discovery of the significance of measurement led to a shift from the vague 'nature of' to the precise 'indeterminate function to be determined.' Classical method has been complemented by statistical, and both may be complemented by genetic and dialectical methods.[40] All such development is however a question of differentiation, further specification, and sophistication of the fundamental heuristic notion of being. This point is not new: already in *Verbum* Lonergan had pointed out that growth in wisdom is a question of 'discriminating, differentiating, categorizing the details of a scheme that somehow we possessed from the start.'[41] The original scheme here is, of course, the inchoate wisdom that is given us in the notion of being that is our intellectual light.

Thus, *Insight* replaces the intellectual light of the *Verbum* articles with the pure desire to know, and the inchoate wisdom given in intellectual light with the spontaneous notion of being. Further, the notion of being is the supreme and fundamental heuristic notion, while all other heuristic notions and structures are merely further differentiations of this fundamental notion. It is obvious then that Thomist wisdom in its genetic aspect is the inspiration for the heuristic notions and structures of *Insight*.

2 Dialectical Heuristic Structure

The previous section has followed Lonergan's identification of heuristic structures in the field of mathematics and of natural science, and the generalization of this notion, first in chapter 12 of *Insight* and then in chapter 14. Already in chapter 7 however, the notion is extended to the field of the human sciences. This is done by noting that the human situation is not a pure intelligibility, but rather a mixture of the rational and the irrational, of intelligibility and lack of intelligibility. This means that a method for the human sciences cannot be merely empirical:

> [A]n excellent method for the study of electrons is bound to prove naive and inept in the study of man. For the data on man are largely the product of man's own thinking; and the subordination of human science to the data on man is the subordination of human science to the biased intelligence of those that produce the data.[42]

Still, just as the lack of intelligibility in the spatio-temporal continuum gives rise to the infinitesimal calculus, and just as the lack of intelligibility in random deviations from ideal frequencies gives rise to statistical method, so the lack of intelligibility in human opinions, choices, and decisions gives rise to the dialectical theorem.[43] This theorem is defined as

a concrete unfolding of linked but opposed principles of change.
Thus there will be a dialectic if (1) there is an aggregate of events of a determinate character, (2) the events may be traced to either or both of two principles, (3) the principles are opposed yet bound together, and (4) they are modified by the changes that successively result from them.[44]

Such a dialectical theorem, by its distinction between insight and bias, progress and decline, 'contains in a general form the combination of the empirical and the critical attitudes essential to human science.'[45] Thus, dialectic serves as the upper blade of a generalized empirical method: 'it stands to generalized method as the differential equation to classical physics, or the operator equation to the more recent physics.'[46]

Dialectic provides no more than the general form of a critical attitude. Each department of human science will therefore have to work out its own criteria, 'but it will be able to do so by distinguishing between the purely intellectual element in its field and, on the other hand, the inertial effects and the interference of human sensibility and human nerves.'[47] Accordingly, fuller study of the human mind should provide us with further general elements relevant to determining a far more nuanced yet *general critical viewpoint*.[48] Such fuller study is precisely what chapters 8 to 13 of *Insight* are engaged in. Thus, if dialectic is a question of opposed principles in interaction, chapter 8 draws attention to the duality in human knowing. There is to be found in us an animal knowing, constituted completely on the level of experience and dominated by the biological pattern of consciousness, and also a properly human knowing, constituted by the three levels of experiencing, understanding, and judging, and dominated by the purely intellectual pattern of experience. The problem set by these two types of knowing is not one of elimination but of *critical distinction*; for, unless distinguished sharply by a critical theory of knowledge, these two types of knowing become confused and generate aberrations that affect scientific and philosophic thought.[49] Attainment of a critical position means distinguishing between different patterns of one's own experience and refusing to commit oneself intellectually unless one is functioning within the intellectual pattern. Failure to reach the *full critical position* results in the babel of philosophies; 'and it is by dialectical analysis, based on the full critical position, that one can hope to set up a philosophy of philosophies in the fully reflective manner that at least imperfectly was initiated by Hegel and still is demanded by modern needs.'[50]

Now it is important to note that the full critical position is attained, not in chapter 11 on self-affirmation, but in chapter 14, for the text cited above goes on to note that 'these points can be developed only after we have answered questions on the nature of rational consciousness, of critical reflection, of judgment, of the notions of being and objectivity.'[51] Grasp of this point is dependent on advertence to the fact that already in *Verbum*, and more clearly in *Insight*, Lonergan has effected a transformation of the critical problem. The critical problem for Lonergan is not the question of how a knower gets beyond himself to a known: that is merely a misleading question, which *Insight* refers to, not as the critical problem, but as the problem of transcendence.[52] The critical problem is rooted in the polymorphism of our consciousness. This polymorphism gives rise to divergent meanings of the basic terms knowing, being, objectivity. Resolving the critical problem is therefore a question of determining the true meaning of knowing, of being, and of objectivity;[53] and this problem arises, not in chapter 11 on self-affirmation of the knower, nor even in chapter 13 on the notion of objectivity, but only in chapter 14 on the method of metaphysics.[54] Chapter 11 does indeed affirm that the deepest foundation of our knowing is our rational consciousness,[55] and shows that the judgment of self-affirmation is incontrovertible.[56] Again, chapter 13 dispatches in a single paragraph the pseudo-problem of transcendence.[57] Still the notions of being and of objectivity remain strangely open to being determined in a variety of ways. For the spontaneous notion of being may be thematized in a variety of ways: being may be identified with matter, or the sensible, or the ideal, or whatever.[58] The notion of being is in fact named protean,[59] for it 'does not decide between empiricism and rationalism, positivism and idealism, existentialism and realism, but leaves that decision to the content of correct judgments that are made.'[60] Further, like the notion of being the notion of objectivity itself remains open:

> If judgments occur in the appropriate pattern, then it involves a plurality of knowing subjects and known objects. If in effect there is only one true judgment, say, the affirmation of the Hegelian Absolute Idea, our notion of objectivity undergoes no formal modification. If true judgments are never reached, there arises the relativist position that acknowledges only experiential and normative objectivity.[61]

If further evidence is needed, it may be had from the military metaphor of breakthrough, encirclement, and confinement invoked as an image for the way in which evidence for metaphysics is to be presented. This metaphor reveals that self-affirmation is merely the breakthrough, that acknowledgment of the protean notion of being is merely encirclement, but that confinement comes only through dialectic:

> The confinement is effected through the dialectical opposition of

twofold notions of the real, of knowing, and of objectivity, so that every attempt to escape is blocked by the awareness that one would be merely substituting some counterposition for a known position, merely deserting the being that can be intelligently grasped and reasonably affirmed, merely distorting the consciousness that is not only empirical but also intelligent and not only intelligent but also reasonable.[62]

Such dialectic is carried out, of course, not in chapters 11 to 13, but basically in chapter 14.

The critical problem begins to be raised therefore only in chapter 14 of *Insight*, and the question here is not only the determination of the meanings of knowing, being, and objectivity, but also, as promised in chapter 8, the achievement of a philosophy of philosophies;[63] and both are achieved by means of the dialectical theorem. Chapter 14 begins by noting that antitheses can easily be set up against the positions on knowing, being, and objectivity outlined in the previous three chapters;[64] this is once again a confirmation of the 'openness' of the notions presented in these chapters. Still, these chapters are not useless, for they make possible a sharp formulation of the antitheses. They also make it possible to say that the variety of antithetical positions regarding the fundamental notions of knowing, being, and objectivity, and so the variety of philosophies, are a result of the polymorphism of human consciousness. For the task of philosophy is not the observation of some simple entity by some simple mind.[65] Already there is the complexity that human knowing unfolds on several levels; to this is to be added the further complexity that human consciousness is not pure intelligence but rather a shifting variety of patterns and blends of patterns.[66] Now complexity in the mathematical, empirical, and other fields is mastered through the use of inverse insights. Further, since in the present case we are dealing with the human field, the obvious tool would be the dialectical theorem, for this theorem anticipates both intelligibility and lack of intelligibility. Through the use of this theorem, the 'mind and grasp' of the philosopher 'become the single goal in which contradictory contributions attain their complex unity.'[67] The heuristic structure of that unity is the principle that positions invite development and counterpositions invite reversal.[68] Thus, the application of dialectical heuristic structure to the history of philosophy yields a philosophy of philosophies: 'In the light of the dialectic, then, the historical series of philosophies would be regarded as a sequence of contributions to a single but complex goal.'[69]

But what is the relevance to us of Lonergan's transformation of the critical problem? A more adequate answer should emerge at the end of the next section on the method of metaphysics, but already we might point out that selection of the meaning of basic terms such as being was the work of wisdom, and that it was wisdom that handled the critical problem in *Verbum*. If then it is generalized empirical method that handles the critical problem in *Insight*, it is this method that takes over the epistemological function of wisdom. Generalized empirical method, in other words, would be a new form of wisdom.

Before moving on to the next section, we might draw attention to the fact that basic counterpositions are by no means erroneous cognitional theories; rather, they are erroneous *formulations* of cognitional theory.[70] Thus, Lonergan insists that cognitional theory alone does not suffice to establish the meanings of knowing, being, and objectivity, and that 'the formulation of cognitional theory cannot be complete unless some stand is taken on basic issues in philosophy.'[71] But how is it, we might ask, that genuine discoveries can be formulated wrongly? The reason is that any single judgment is but a single increment in knowing.[72] Accordingly, the making of even a single correct judgment calls for a context of other correct judgments,[73] and this context is the result of past insights and judgments that remain with us and form a habitual orientation, thus governing the direction of attention, evaluating insights, guiding formulations, influencing new judgments.[74] Context therefore influences formulation. Now adequate formulation of cognitional theory must be done within the purely intellectual pattern of experience; but since human consciousness is polymorphic, formulation of cognitional theory is often inadequate. We might add that the issue is linked to wisdom. For the universal context or the universal principle of correct judgment is wisdom.[75] Given such a universal context or adequate wisdom, formulations of cognitional theory would be exact. But human wisdom is not perfect, and so discoveries are made but are not always properly formulated. What then is the way out? Once again it is wisdom; or else it is the new form of wisdom that is generalized empirical method. But more of this in the section that follows.

3 The Method of Metaphysics

Metaphysics exists in three forms or stages: latent, problematic, and explicit. On the level of proportionate being, explicit metaphysics is defined as the conception, affirmation, and implementation of the integral heuristic structure of proportionate being.[76] Now the method of metaphysics is basically a process from latent through problematic to explicit metaphysics. It is a question of making explicit the latent heuristic structures, integrating them, and implementing them. It is therefore primarily a process to self-knowledge.[77] But a method is a set of directives that guide a process to a result.[78] What then are the directives that make up metaphysical method? The first directive is to begin from interest and to lead the 'pupil' on to adequate self-knowledge. This means that the method of metaphysics is primarily pedagogical.[79] This preliminary stage ends when the subject reaches an intelligent and reasonable self-affirmation.[80] Such self-affirmation is the required self-knowledge. Does this mean that self-knowledge is attained in chapter 11? While this appears to be the case, we must note that 'the formulation of cognitional theory cannot be complete unless some stand is taken on basic issues in philosophy.'[81] Accordingly, adequate self-knowledge is attained, not with the self-affirmation of chapter 11 but through the dialectic of chapter 14 that fixes the meanings of the basic terms. Once this stage has been reached, the method becomes self-directive. For self-knowledge

> makes explicit the pursuit of the goal that has been implicit in the pure desire to know. From that explicit pursuit there follow the directives, first of reorientating one's scientific knowledge and one's common sense, and secondly, of integrating what one knows and can know of proportionate being through the known structures of one's cognitional activities.[82]

The *preliminary pedagogical stage* therefore coincides with generalized empirical method moving towards the full critical position. In the epilogue and in the introduction of *Insight* this is also referred to as a process of self-appropriation[83] or as 'a personal appropriation of one's own rational self-consciousness.'[84] Self-appropriation is not a question of setting forth a list of abstract properties of human knowledge, but rather a matter of attaining personal familiarity with the concrete dynamic structure immanent and recurrently operative in one's own cognitional activities.[85] Self-appropriation is therefore a 'private crucial experiment,' which consists 'in one's own rational self-consciousness clearly and distinctly taking possession of itself as rational self-consciousness.'[86] But rational consciousness taking possession of itself is another way of speaking about intellectual light grasping itself by itself, for intellectual light is the inquiring and critical spirit in human beings.[87] Accordingly self-appropriation would seem to be another name for psychological introspection. But psychological introspection has been shown to coincide with wisdom in its epistemological aspect; and so self-appropriation through generalized method, or the preliminary phase of metaphysical method, would seem to coincide with epistemological wisdom.

A first confirmation of this hypothesis, that self-apropriation through generalized method coincides with epistemological wisdom, is to be had from the fact that generalized empirical method echoes key features of epistemological wisdom. Thus, *Verbum* had described 'wisdom through self-knowledge' as a movement from empirical through scientific to normative self-knowledge,[88] but the upper blade of generalized method is the dialectical theorem that is a combination of the empirical and critical or normative attitudes.[89] Again, in *Verbum* it was epistemological wisdom that had handled the critical problem, but now it is through generalized method that the critical question is resolved. But more detailed confirmation may be had from a consideration of the explicit references to wisdom in *Insight*.

A first occurrence of the term wisdom is to be found in the context of the distinction between analytic propositions, which can be produced indefinitely and at will, and analytic principles, whose terms have been found to be existent by some independent judgments.[90] There is explicit notice that the source of the distinction is Aquinas's notion of wisdom. 'Aquinas advanced that conclusions depend upon principles and that principles depend upon terms; but he was not ready to accept any terms whatever; he added that proper terms are selected by wisdom, and by wisdom he meant an accumulation of insights that stands to the universe as common sense stands to the domain of the particular, incidental, relative, and imaginable.'[91]

The next occurrence of wisdom is in the context of the dialectic of metaphysical methods, and it applies the distinction drawn earlier between analytic propositions and principles. If one supposes that the method of metaphysics is fundamentally deductive, one has to ask about the origin of its first principles. These first principles cannot be analytic propositions, or else metaphysics will be empty. They must then be analytic principles; but in that case there occurs Aquinas's requirement that the proper terms of these principles be selected by wisdom. But where are we to obtain the necessary wisdom? Aquinas had recognized two types of wisdom: the wisdom that is a gift of the Holy Spirit, and the wisdom that is Aristotle's first philosophy. However, when we ask about the method of metaphysics, there can be presupposed neither a religion nor a philosophy, and so there arises the need for a third type of wisdom.[92] The condition of possibility of the method of concrete deduction is therefore 'the genesis of a wisdom that is prior to metaphysics.'[93] Here Lonergan points out that Aquinas did not concern himself explicitly with such a wisdom. Still (in an obvious reference to his own 'Thomistic' epistemological reflection in *Verbum*), he believes that there can be found in Aquinas's writings 'a sufficient number of indications and suggestions to form an adequate account of wisdom in cognitional terms.'[94] The problem, however, is that this is a 'delicate operation,' because the influence of the polymorphism of human consciousness is so great that there is little consensus to be found among the various attempts that have been made to construct Thomist epistemologies.[95]

The third reference occurs in the section on Hegelian dialectic, in the same discussion of the dialectic of metaphysical methods. Since deductive methods call for a wisdom that is prior to metaphysics, and since directive methods are not satisfactory either, one is forced to the conclusion that philosophic method should concern itself 'with the structure and the aberrations of human cognitional process.'[96] Thus, Hegelian dialectic proposes that the method of philosophy consist in the process that turns positions into their opposites only to bring forth new positions, with the repetition of this process until the totality of positions and their opposites form a dialectical whole.[97] Lonergan agrees with the idea that philosophic method should concern itself with the structure and aberrations of human cognitional process, but his own dialectic is quite different from that of Hegel. Such a dialectic results in a metaphysics 'that brings to contemporary thought the *wisdom* of the Greeks and of the medieval schoolmen as reached by Aristotle and Aquinas.'[98] Wisdom here refers to metaphysics; but dialectic has to do with the method of metaphysics and so would seem to be the third type of wisdom called for earlier.

The suggestion that arises from these texts is that the wisdom required to select the terms of the analytic principles relevant to metaphysics is a cognitional and dialectical wisdom. But it is through generalized method, through an appropriation of one's intelligent and rational consciousness, that *Insight* moves towards a breakthrough to, encirclement, and confinement of the meaning of the basic terms of philosophy. Accordingly generalized method, with its upper blade in the dialectical theorem, would seem to coincide with the required cognitional and dialectical wisdom. This is in fact confirmed in the lectures on the philosophy of education (1959), which ask why Aquinas chose Aristotle's first philosophy and not something else, and how he knew that he had to develop and correct it. The answer is that there is no recipe for producing men of good judgment; one has to grow into wisdom.[99] A little later the question is taken up again, this time in terms of the selection of the notion of being. Since wisdom is not a foundation from which we begin, but rather a foundation towards which we tend,[100] it is only 'by studying different philosophic systems, comparing them, and seeing the different consequences of the different systems that one arrives at the wisdom of one's own that entitles one to prefer one notion of being to another.'[101]

In its preliminary phase, then, the method of metaphysics is dialectical. It is a genetic wisdom in cognitional terms that determines the meanings of knowing, being, and objectivity and so takes over the epistemological functions of Thomist wisdom.[102] Like wisdom, this method is a process of self-appropriation that begins from empirical self-knowledge and mounts through scientific self-knowledge to a normative self-knowledge. Accordingly, generalized method replaces the technique of psychological introspection.

We turn now to the second, *self-directive phase* of metaphysical method. This is described as a question of reorientation and integration. Reorientation is of common sense and of science; it amounts to applying dialectic to correct the biases and the counterpositions present in these fields.[103] But it is in the moment of integration that there takes place the transition from latent to explicit metaphysics. Lonergan describes this transition as a deduction, in which the major premise is 'the isomorphism that obtains between the structure of knowing and the structure of the known,' the set of primary minor premises 'consists of a series of affirmations of concrete and recurring structures in the knowing of the self-affirming subject,' and the set of secondary minor premises consists of reorientated science and common sense.[104] In an important article, Crowe has noted that the major premise is really an analytic proposition, and that it becomes an analytic principle only with the introduction of existence in the primary minor premises.[105] He notes further that the question of the ontological status of the metaphysical elements is handled, not through the deductive transition, but through the dynamic process described in terms of the military metaphor of breakthrough, encirclement, and confinement.[106] Breakthrough, encirclement, and confinement is of course a way of speaking about generalized method or the wisdom that is prior to metaphysics, and so we might add that it handles not only the question of the ontological status of the metaphysical elements but also the formulation of cognitional theory itself. Thus, just as wisdom validated the naturally known first principles by validating the apprehension of their component terms, so generalized method governs the transformation of isomorphism into an analytic principle and thus presides over the transition to explicit metaphysics.

4 Metaphysics as Dialectic

We have been speaking about the transition to explicit metaphysics outlined in chapter 14 of *Insight*, but we must note that this is just an outline, a program, a method. An exploratory execution of this program is essayed in chapters 15 to 17.[107] This is a question of applying the upper blade of the integral heuristic structure to the data provided by reorientated common sense and science.[108] Such application yields explicit metaphysics or an integrated view of the universe of proportionate being. Thus, in chapter 15 genetic method is applied to data to yield the world-view of emergent probability. On the human level, however, given the presence of aberration as well as development, genetic method is inadequate and has to give way to dialectical method.[109] This is done in chapter 17 on metaphysics as dialectic, by applying dialectical heuristic structure to historical data.[110]

The earlier chapters of *Insight* had used dialectic as a tool for criticism. Chapter 17 instead uses it as a tool for integration. Lonergan observes here that the appeal to polymorphism in the earlier chapters has been rather fragmentary, and that there is available in addition 'a general theorem to the effect that any philosophy, whether actual or possible, will rest upon the dynamic structure of cognitional activity either as correctly conceived or as distorted by oversights and by mistaken orientations.'[111] Still, this general theorem is abstract. Deductions from it yield merely general philosophical tendencies, which, though they might serve as hermeneutical tools, cannot really be considered as interpretations.[112] The creation of a hermeneutical method based on this theorem instead assures the movement into the field of concrete historical process.[113] Since, further, such hermeneutical method is created on the basis of the same set of primary minor premises that yielded a scientific metaphysics,[114] chapter 17 achieves an integration of the universe of meanings into the single unified view that is explicit metaphysics.

It might be noted that such explicit metaphysics remains a heuristic integration. For metaphysics 'is the whole in knowledge but not the whole of knowledge.'[115] The application of the integral heuristic structure to data envisages but does not immediately achieve universal knowledge. Thus, chapter 17 applies dialectical heuristic structure to the field of historical data, but such application yields not universal history but a hermeneutical method.[116] Explicit metaphysics as integral heuristic structure is an integration of human knowledge through the integration of all possible methods.

We have been saying that dialectical metaphysics forms part of explicit metaphysics, but we might press further and ask just what is this integral or unified view. Chapter 15 of *Insight* tells us that methods admit of 'structural unifications,' and gives the example of the combination of classical and statistical methods that yields the world-view of generalized emergent probability,[117] but does not say anything about the structural unification of genetic and dialectical methods. Still, the term used here is 'generalized emergent probability,' and the reason is that chapter 7 has already made it quite clear that emergent probability extends to the human realm as well: '[T]he advent of man does not abrogate the rule of emergent probability.'[118] Emergent probability on the human level is not merely intelligible but also intelligent process, for now there is the role played by insight and decision.[119] Further, human beings can discover emergent probability and attain a certain control over it.[120] Most interestingly, this discussion of emergent probability on the human level is intimately connected with dialectic, for human process is dialectical in its development, and accordingly it can be mastered only by a method that is not merely empirical but also normative.[121] The heuristic structure relevant to human process, in other words, is dialectical,[122] and the integral or comprehensive view is an emergent probability extended to the human level and so named a generalized emergent probability.[123]

In the light of the possibility of discovering emergent probability and attaining control over it, the relevance of Lonergan's formulation of dialectical method and of a dialectical metaphysics should begin to become clear. In this connection, the parallel between the terms 'generalized emergent probability' and 'generalized empirical method' seems suggestive. For emergent probability on the human level is a dialectical process, and so the method relevant to it is generalized empirical method with an upper blade in the dialectical theorem.[124] But this means that generalized empirical method is the required human control over generalized emergent probability. Since further generalized empirical method issues into a methodical metaphysics, *Insight* itself can be seen as a proposal for a new control over meaning. This in fact is the opinion of Philip McShane, who asks about 'the self-energy of *notio incarnata* that is an origin of species' and goes on to observe that 'Lonergan's life work represents a push towards a collaborative control of that origin ..., a control hinted at by the metaphysics sketched in *Insight*.'[125]

There is in fact more than a hint of this new control over meaning in the discussion of metaphysics, mystery, and myth in chapter 17 of *Insight*.[126] This discussion intends to be 'a genetic account' of mystery and myth.[127] Mystery and myth are manifestations of finality on the level of sensitive living, corresponding to 'the openness of inquiry and reflection and the paradoxical "known unknown" of unanswered questions.'[128] Further, the fact of such finality 'is interwoven with the very genesis of metaphysics, with the process in which the mind of man moves from a latent through a problematic to an explicit metaphysical view.'[129] Now the point is that that genesis is dialectical. Myth and metaphysics are opposites. They are related dialectically. It is only by that mistaken unfolding of the pure desire to know which is myth that we learn to avoid the pitfalls to which the unfolding is prone.[130]

Further, the structure of chapter 17 itself seems to reflect the general pattern of human development. The discussion of mystery and myth deals with the development of meaning (level of intelligence, distinction of sense from understanding). This discussion leads to the recognition of the need for an adequate control of meaning, and so there arises the discussion of truth in the second section (level of judgment, distinction of understanding from judgment).[131] Since further the third section is entitled 'The Truth of Interpretation,'[132] the methodical hermeneutics proposed there would seem to be part of the methodical control over meaning sought in the first section.

We have been saying that metaphysics as dialectic achieves the extension of emergent probability to the human level, and also the integration of the universe of meanings into single unified view that is explicit metaphysics. It is this explicitly dialectical metaphysics that is the highest viewpoint and the most comprehensive integration. Chapter 16 of *Insight* indicates this rather clearly:

> For man is the being in whom the highest level of integration is, not a static system, nor some dynamic system, but a variable manifold of dynamic systems. For the successive systems that express the development of human understanding are systems that regard the universe of being in all its departments ... Only the broadest possible set of concepts can provide the initial basis and the field of differences that will be adequate to dealing with a variable set of moving systems that regard the universe of being. Only a critical metaphysics that envisages at once positions and counterpositions can hope to present successfully the complex alternatives that arise in the pursuit of the human sciences, in which both the men under inquiry and the men that are inquiring may or may not be involved in the ever possible and ever varied aberrations of polymorphic consciousness.[133]

This 'variable manifold of dynamic systems,' which as chapter 17 indicates is related not merely genetically but also dialectically, is brought into the universe of being as an aspect or part of that being which is the human being. Thus, a metaphysics that is explicitly dialectical is the unified view that is the goal of the method of metaphysics.

We might conclude by relating metaphysics to wisdom. We have noted that dialectical method or generalized empirical method is equivalent to the epistemological wisdom or the 'Thomistic' epistemological reflection of the *Verbum* articles.[134] We can now add that such a dialectical method issues into a metaphysics that is not merely 'scientific' but also dialectical, and that this metaphysics takes the place of the metaphysical wisdom of the *Verbum* articles. The differences between such a metaphysics and Thomist wisdom should not of course be ignored. While the former is the fruit of method, the latter may be said to be only implicitly methodical; for though Aquinas not only used psychological introspection but also occasionally adverted to such use, such introspection is far from having become a reflectively enucleated method in his works.[135] Again, while the former is explicitly critical and dialectical, the latter does select the proper notion of being, but once again it neither adverts to nor thematizes that process, nor does it move on to a philosophy of philosophies and to an integration into metaphysics of the universe of meanings. We might say that the difference is Hegel, for not only does chapter 14 feel the need to add a note on Hegelian dialectic, but also chapter 17 is 'bounded by references' to Hegel's demand that philosophers account not only for their own views but also for the existence of contrary opinions.[136]

5   Concluding Summary

A first point to be noted is that *Insight* seems to be a transposition of key positions appropriated in *Verbum*. Thus, intellectual light becomes the pure desire to know, and intellectual light as inchoate wisdom becomes the fundamental heuristic notion of being. Further, just as all progress in wisdom is a question of differentiating and specifying the rudimentary grasp of the whole given in intellectual light, so all particular heuristic structures arise from differentiation of the fundamental heuristic notion. Again, just as metaphysical wisdom was universal order or a science of sciences or an architectonic science, so metaphysics consists in an integration of all the various particular heuristic structures that have arisen through differentiation of the notion of being. Further, just as wisdom performed its critical function through self-knowledge, which was a question of intellectual light grasping itself, so generalized empirical method moves towards self-knowledge through a process of self-appropriation, which is a question of rational self-consciousness grasping itself. Finally, just as wisdom validated the first principles themselves by selecting the proper notion of being, so generalized empirical method determines the meaning of the basic philosophical terms, transforms isomorphism into an analytic principle, and thus governs the transition from appropriated cognitional structure to explicit metaphysics.

Second, dialectical metaphysics is a part of explicit metaphysics, and this dialectical metaphysics achieves the integration of the universe of meanings into explicit metaphysics. Explicit metaphysics, of which dialectical metaphysics forms a part, is therefore, the highest and most comprehensive integration.

Third, it follows that metaphysics in its scientific and dialectical aspects takes the place of wisdom as grasp of universal order, the difference being that, unlike Thomist wisdom, it is explicitly and deliberately methodical as well as dialectical. Thus, for example, where Thomist wisdom was a science of sciences, dialectical metaphysics is a philosophy of philosophies.

3

The Universal Viewpoint in Chapter 17 of *Insight*

The immediate context of the universal viewpoint is hermeneutical method, while its larger context is dialectical metaphysics. But dialectical metaphysics has already been examined in the previous chapter, and so the present chapter need only situate the universal viewpoint within the context of hermeneutical method. However, this hermeneutical method itself follows from theories of objectivity and meaning.[1] Accordingly, the present chapter begins with the theories of meaning and objectivity presupposed by hermeneutical method, goes on to discuss hermeneutical method itself, and finally takes up the notion of the universal viewpoint.

1 Meaning and Truth

1.1 The Structure of Meaning

The psychological introspection of the *Verbum* articles, besides being a technique of interpretation, also yields a theory of meaning, for it indicates that from a grasp of the nature of the act of understanding 'we shall come to a grasp of the nature of inner words, their relation to language, and their role in our knowledge of reality.'[2] We note here just one point: that as far as Aquinas is concerned, there is a 'clear reduction of meaning to knowledge.'[3] This is because outer words refer, not directly to reality, but rather to inner words;[4] and inner words result, not from unconscious abstraction, but rather from the self-possession of an act of understanding. If, then, names refer to things through concepts in our intellects, it follows that the measure of the use of names is the knowledge in our intellects. If our knowledge is adequate, our use of names is adequate; but where our knowledge is not adequate, our use of names is not adequate.[5]

Such a reduction of meaning to knowledge is operative in *Insight* as well. This is indicated already in the preface, which notes that insight into insight can be expected to yield an apprehension of the meaning of meaning, and that insight into flight from understanding can be expected to explain aberrant views on the meaning of meaning. The reason given is that insight is an apprehension of relations, and meaning seems to be a relation between sign and signified; accordingly, insight will include an apprehension of meaning, and insight into insight will include an apprehension of the meaning of meaning.[6]

There would seem to be two aspects to such an apprehension of the meaning of meaning, and these would seem to correspond respectively to the criteriological problem and the critical problem, to cognitional theory and epistemology. The determination of cognitional theory can be expected to yield also the structure of meaning. But cognitional theory cannot be formulated without taking some stand on the basic issues of philosophy, and taking such a stand, we have seen, is really a question of settling the meaning of the basic terms knowledge, reality, and objectivity.[7] For the terms knowledge, reality, and objectivity take on different meanings as consciousness shifts from one pattern or blend of patterns of experience to another. 'But the meaning of every other term changes with changes in the meaning of the terms, knowledge, reality, objectivity, for the function of all language is to express presumptive knowledge of presumptive reality and affirm or deny the objectivity of the knowledge.'[8] But the determination of the meaning of the basic terms is a sapiential and critical task, and, further, explicit metaphysics is itself described as a generalized semantics or a new control of meaning;[9] so the apprehension of the meaning of meaning tends to coincide with the program of *Insight*.

Since our previous chapters have already spoken about the critical problem, we can restrict ourselves here to the structure of meaning. *Insight* speaks of principal and instrumental acts and terms of meaning, sources of meaning, and the core of meaning.

Principal acts and terms of meaning divide into formal and full. Formal acts of meaning are acts of conceiving, defining, thinking, supposing, considering, formulating.[10] Full acts of meaning are instead acts of assenting or dissenting.[11] Formal terms of meaning are often referred to as formulations, but include also concepts,[12] definitions, hypotheses, as well as mere thoughts, suppositions, and considerations.[13] Full terms of meaning are what is affirmed or denied.[14]

It must be noted that acts of direct and reflective understanding are neither formal nor full but merely potential acts of meaning.[15] The reason is that, while in the principal acts of meaning the distinction between meaning and meant has emerged, in acts of understanding such distinction has not yet emerged. Potential and principal acts of meaning are related as *intelligere* and *dicere*,[16] or as apprehensive and formative abstraction: while apprehensive abstraction is insight into phantasm, and grasps the universal in the particular, formative abstraction grasps the universal as common to several instances, sets up the object apart from its material conditions, and does this by meaning it or defining it; for while one cannot grasp the necessary and sufficient condition of circularity except in a diagram, one can mean 'circle' without meaning any particular instance of it.[17]

In addition to principal acts and terms of meaning, there are also instrumental acts of meaning and partial terms of meaning together with the rules governing their coalescence into the complete units of meaning that are sentences.[18] An instrumental act of meaning 'is the implementation of a formal or of a full act by the use of words or symbols in a spoken, written, or merely imagined utterance.'[19] Thus expressing need not be limited to speaking or writing; it may well be merely imagined, and such imagining need not always be visual, but may be also auditory or motor.[20] It is to be noted also that expression may be the implementation of either a formal or a full act of meaning,[21] and so may be merely a hypothesis, or else a judgment. Further, in addition to the principal insight that is the potential act of meaning, there is a practical insight governing the verbal flow and directing it towards its end of communication.[22]

Insight also speaks about sources of meaning and the core of meaning. Any element of knowledge may serve as a source of meaning: '[S]ources of meaning include data and images, ideas and concepts, the grasp of the unconditioned and judgment and, no less, the detached and unrestricted desire to know.'[23] As for the core of meaning, it is the desire to know. For being is the all-inclusive term of meaning; but the desire to know is the notion of being, and the notion of being not only intends but also underlies and penetrates all terms of meaning. Since the desire to know or the notion of being intends, underlies, and penetrates all terms of meaning, it is regarded as the core of all acts of meaning.[24]

We began this section with an observation about the reduction of meaning to knowledge. But if the meaning of meaning is to be grasped in the relations between the core of meaning, sources of meaning, and potential, principal, as well as instrumental acts and terms of meaning, then the reduction of meaning to knowledge includes the reduction of expression to knowledge, where 'reduction' means an explanation of expression in terms of knowing. *Insight* notes that there is to be found an isomorphism between knowledge and expression. Corresponding to the three levels on which knowledge arises, there are three components in expression:

For as affirmative or negative utterance, the expression corresponds to reflection and judgment. As a significant combination of words, the expression corresponds to insight and conception. As an instrumental multiplicity, the expression corresponds to the material multiplicity of experience and imagination.[25]

This isomorphism is not to be mistaken for an identity. Between judgment and assertion, there intervenes an act of willing to speak truthfully or deceitfully. Between understanding experience, and hitting upon the happy combination of phrases and sentences, there intervenes the further practical insight that governs the verbal flow towards its end of communication. Finally, while data consists of the manifold of sensitive presentations and imaginative representations, the manifold relevant to expression is a set of conventional signs.[26]

Knowledge and expression are therefore isomorphic but distinct; still, there must be recognized an interpenetration between the two. For coming to know is a process; at each stage it is helpful 'to fix what has been reached, and to formulate in some fashion what remains to be sought.'[27] Thus expression 'enters into the very process of learning'; and, on the other hand, 'the attainment of knowledge tends to coincide with the attainment of the ability to express it.'[28] Thus, development of knowledge results eventually in development of adequate modes of expression.[29]

If development of knowledge results eventually in development of adequate modes of expression, the development of modes of expression also has an effect on knowledge.[30] For though the principal insight and formulation are said to emerge simultaneously,[31] lack of adequate means of expression has an effect on one's grasp of one's own insight: one is not able to possess one's own discovery adequately if there are not available adequate means of expression, if there is not the adequate cultural development. Thus, Lonergan can say that the differentiation and specialization of modes of expression 'conditions not only the exact communication of insights but also the discoverer's own grasp of his discovery.'[32] So discoveries may well be made, but their implications may escape the discoverer himself. For grasping implications means grasping how the discovery is related to the contemporary state of knowledge, but lack of adequate means of expression may result in inadequate and even mistaken formulation, and such formulation either distorts or makes it difficult to grasp implications. That is why Lonergan adds that 'such grasp and its exact communication intimately are connected with the advance of positions and the reversal of counter-positions.'[33]

Such interpenetration of knowledge and expression 'implies a solidarity, almost a fusion, of the development of knowledge and the development of language.'[34] This brings us to the topic of the development of meaning and of expression.

1.2 The Development of Meaning

The genesis of metaphysics discussed in the first section of chapter 17 is really a discussion of the development of meaning.[35] For meaning includes insights as well as judgments, and, further, metaphysics is a generalized semantics or control of meaning.[36] By the 'hypothetical introduction of blind spots' into the integral heuristic structure of metaphysics Lonergan arrives at the categories of inadequate philosophies as well as of mythic consciousness.[37] If adequate self-knowledge and explicit metaphysics are a question of (1) clear distinctions between positions and counterpositions, (2) a shift from the descriptive to the explanatory viewpoint, and (3) a clear and firm grasp of the heuristic and progressive character of human understanding,[38] mythic consciousness is a lack of these compounded by the absence of 'the techniques of mastery and control that the study of grammar imparts to the use of words, the study of rhetoric to the use of metaphor, the study of logic to the communication of thought.'[39] Further, the discussion of myth and metaphysics reveals that the development of meaning is dialectical.[40]

Again, there is discussed also the development of expression.[41] In the process from ignorance to knowledge, there arises inevitably a problem of expression.[42] For new viewpoints must be communicated if they are to become generally accepted and established.[43] But communication involves an adaptation to the cultural level of the audience, for though there may be a new viewpoint, still the means of communication available are the old ones. There has to be carried out, therefore, a transformation of the meanings 'that change the reference of words from the sensible to the intelligible and the rational.'[44]

1.3 Truth

The development of meaning and the dialectic between myth and metaphysics raises the question of truth, and hence the second section of chapter 17 may be seen as a continuation of the discussion of the genesis of metaphysics, concerned with the 'effective criteria for passing judgments on anticipations and acts of understanding.'[45] Still, our immediate concern is with this section as relevant to the discussion of hermeneutical method and the universal viewpoint in the third and final section of chapter 17. This relevance, as we have noted already, consists in the fact that it brings together the 'theory of objectivity' obtained in earlier parts of *Insight*.[46]

54   Part One: *Insight*

A distinction is drawn between the definition of truth and the criterion of truth.[47] While truth may be defined in general as a relation of knowing to being,[48] the criterion of truth divides into proximate and remote. The proximate criterion is reflective grasp of the virtually unconditioned.[49] The necessity of adding a remote criterion to this proximate criterion arises from the fact that reflective understanding is itself conditioned by a context of other cognitional acts and contents.[50] The discussion of truth and expression notes the isomorphism, the distinction, and the genetic interpenetration of knowledge and expression, and goes on to make some observations about the process of the communication or the expression of truth.[51] The discussion of the appropriation of truth instead speaks about the various aspects and the problems involved in grasping truth and making it one's own.[52] These discussions of expression and of appropriation are both relevant to the question of the truth of interpretation, for interpretation is described as 'a second expression addressed to a different audience,'[53] which means that it is a question of appropriating the truth of another and communicating it anew. Since, further, one of the problems in the appropriation of truth is that of maintaining a proper orientation towards truth,[54] and since the remote criterion is a question of the proper unfolding of the pure desire to know and the absence of interference from other desires,[55] the discussion of the criterion of truth is itself integrated into the discussion of the truth of interpretation.

2   Hermeneutical Method

From 'the theories of objectivity and of meaning' of *Insight* flow both the statement of the problem of interpretation as well as the hermeneutical method that is the solution to that problem.

2.1   *The Problem of Interpretation*

Lonergan describes interpretation as a second expression addressed to a different audience,[56] or an expression of the meaning of another expression.[57] It follows that the starting point of the process of interpretation is some expression, the goal is a second expression addressed to a different audience, while the process itself involves appropriation as well as successful communication.

2.1.1   Appropriation

From the section 'The Appropriation of Truth' we may gather that grasping the truth of another, like the appropriation of truth in general, involves a problem of learning. Gradually one must acquire the set of habitual insights that accumulate into a viewpoint, and eventually move from lower to higher viewpoints.[58] This is a point made already in *Verbum*: one can read and understand an author only if one has first undergone the labor of reaching up to the level of the author.[59] The attainment of a habitual understanding or viewpoint matching that of the author's is therefore a condition of possibility of successful interpretation.

The appropriation of truth involves also the problem of identification. Insights grasp unities and correlations; but besides unities and correlations, there are the elements unified or correlated. Before insight is reached, one does not know just which might be the elements relevant to the insight; but once insight has been reached, one is able to distinguish in one's own experience what is relevant to the insight and what is not. 'However, ability is one thing, and performance is another. Identification is performance. Its effect is to make one possess the insight as one's own, to be assured in one's use of it, to be familiar with the range of its relevance.'[60] It is, we might say, the difference between apprehensive and formative abstraction, between insight into phantasm and the formulation of that insight. Such identification is essential if one is to teach, or, we might add, to communicate successfully:

> [T]he understanding that enables one to teach adds identification to insight. By that addition one is able to select and arrange and indicate to others the combination of sensible elements that will give rise to the same insight in them. One is able to vary the elements at the demand of circumstances. One is able to put the questions that elicit from the pupil indications of his blind spots, and then to proceed afresh to the task of bringing him to the prior insights he must reach before he can master the present lesson.[61]

Appropriating the truth of another is, however, peculiar, for the data of interpretation are for the most part 'spatially ordered marks on paper or parchment, papyrus or stone.'[62] This implies that all meaning must be reconstructed from the proximate sources of interpretation immanent in the interpreter. 'If the interpreter assigns any meaning to the marks, then the experiential component in that meaning will be derived from his experience, the intellectual component will be derived from his intelligence, the rational component will be derived from his critical reflection on the critical reflection of another.'[63] The point is that when it comes to interpretation, identification involves data not of sense but of consciousness. Clearly, reconstruction of meaning in the manner set out above calls for a mastery of one's own consciousness.

Appropriation of truth also involves a problem of orientation. Human consciousness is capable of various orientations,[64] but the appropriation of truth demands the possession of a habitual orientation towards truth.[65] Failure to maintain such an orientation results both in a distortion of what we know and the restriction of what we might know, for it involves the imposition of mistaken notions of reality, of objectivity, of knowledge upon what we already know.[66]

Because there exists a problem of orientation, interpretation cannot be a merely commonsense affair. For simple interpretation is based on a scholarly extension of common sense that may be named the historical sense, and, like common sense, this historical sense can neither analyze itself nor formulate its central nucleus, is open to individual, group, and general bias, and varies with every difference of place and time. Like common sense, therefore, the historical sense cannot handle the problem of orientation, and so is prone to the danger of subjective projection: it tends to interpret the words and deeds of other persons by reconstructing their experience and uncritically adding to it intellectual viewpoints that they do not share.[67] It is such subjective projection that is behind the phenomenon of the rewriting of history by each different culture and by each stage of progress and decline within a culture.[68]

It must be noted that, like common sense, the historical sense can and often does attain the virtually unconditioned.[69] Still, the problem of orientation cannot be avoided, for reflective grasp of the virtually unconditioned is itself conditioned by a context of other acts and contents,[70] both of which are prone to error, to bias, to the polymorphism of consciousness.[71] Accordingly, the reflective grasp must be questioned: has the proper orientation to truth been maintained all along? Has one been habitually and actually disinterested and detached? Has there been interference from other desires? Has one's inquiry and reflection been truly genuine? Further, is one's habitual context free from error and bias? To absolute objectivity, then, there has to be added normative objectivity,[72] and to the proximate criterion, a remote criterion of truth.[73] Only with such an addition can the problem of orientation be handled. It follows that there is no escape from historical relativism 'as long as men cling to the descriptive viewpoint' of common sense.[74] Appropriation of the truth of another involves, therefore, not merely learning and identification but also a shift from the descriptive to a properly explanatory viewpoint.

2.1.2 Communication

Communication is described as involving a re-expression of the appropriated meaning, and as being guided by a practical insight that depends not only on the principal insight (the meaning appropriated) but also on a grasp of the viewpoint of the new audience.[75]

These remarks may be illuminated by hints about the process of communication from the first two sections of chapter 17. Thus, the discussion of myth and allegory notes that words 'are effective tools only in the measure that the speaker or writer correctly estimates the cultural development of listeners or readers and chooses just the words that have a meaning for them.'[76] Again, the discussion of truth and expression observes that, since truth and falsity reside in judgment, expression cannot properly be said to be true or false, but rather adequate or inadequate.[77] Adequacy of expression is a question of correct estimation of the habitual accumulation of insights (or viewpoint) of the hearer or reader. For given the interpenetration between knowledge and expression, what is known, what is meant, and what is said can be distinguished, but are really just different aspects in what is the same thing, and efforts to explain what we mean sooner or later end with the assertion that what is meant is obvious. But this happens only as a matter of common coincidence, for commonly it happens that conversation occurs between people who share the same common sense, and writing is directed to readers who are already familiar with the subject under discussion. When instead there is significant difference between viewpoints, the gulf between knowledge and expression reappears. The practical insight governing the verbal flow towards its end of communication must then take into account not merely the principal insight to be communicated but also the viewpoint of the audience and the resources of language available to them.[78]

The problem here is the relativity of interpretations to audiences. Lonergan illustrates this by distinguishing between simple and reflective interpretation. Simple interpretation is the re-expression that results from grasping the truth of another and communicating it to some audience. Such simple interpretation, however, gives rise to a further question, Why must a faithful interpretation differ from the original expression? The attempt to answer this leads to reflective interpretation: one appeals to the fact that expression is relative to some audience, determines the differences between audiences, and incorporates such differences into the interpretation. Reflective interpretation then is a complex process in which the practical insight governing the verbal flow depends on a grasp not only (1) of the original insight and (2) of the identity of this insight with that communicated in the simple interpretation, but also on a grasp (3) of the viewpoints of the original and the new audiences, (4) of the new audience's grasp both of its own viewpoint and of its difference from that of the original audience, and (5) of the deficiencies in the new audience's grasp of its own viewpoint and of the way this viewpoint differs from that of the origi-

58   Part One: *Insight*

nal audience.[79] The problem is that such reflective interpretation is itself relative to a particular audience, and so the enormous labor involved would have to be repeated anew for every new audience. Second, there is the practical difficulty: is it really possible to conceive, determine, and communicate the habitual intellectual development of audiences, whether past or contemporary?[80]

2.1.3 The Problem of Interpretation

We may now state with Lonergan the basic problem of interpretation. Interpretation based on the historical sense suffers from three difficulties: (1) it is unable to assign grounds for interpretation;[81] (2) it is open to individual, group, and general bias; and (3) it is relative to a series of particular and incidental audiences. A scientific interpretation would therefore have to handle these three difficulties:

> But if interpretation is to be scientific, then the grounds for interpretation have to be assignable; if interpretation is to be scientific, then there will not be a range of different interpretations due to the individual, group, and general bias of the historical sense of different experts; if interpretation is to be scientific, then it has to discover some method of conceiving and determining the habitual development of all audiences, and it has to invent some technique by which its expression escapes relativity to particular and incidental audiences.[82]

The statement of the problem then matches the analysis of the process of interpretation: corresponding to the aspect of appropriation there is the problem of the range of conflicting interpretations rooted in bias; corresponding to the aspect of communication there is the problem of the relativity of interpretations to audiences.[83]

2.2 *Hermeneutical Method*

Since the problem of interpretation is rooted in its being based on a merely descriptive viewpoint, the solution is scientific interpretation or the shift to an explanatory viewpoint. As in the case of the pure form of speculative development, the basic inspiration here is from the procedures of empirical science.[84] However, since all knowledge is characterized by a scissors-structure, such inspiration does not amount to a reduction of interpretation to empirical science. The point is that some upper blade is always present in any effort to understand,[85] and that this upper blade is usually one's common sense or else a historical sense that is the fruit of scholarship. But common sense is successful only in the realm of the familiar, and we cannot travel into the past. It is necessary therefore to 'drop the descriptive viewpoint and adopt a viewpoint that unashamedly is explanatory.'[86] Mere collection of data is not enough; there have to be determined some approximation to the insights and judgments, decisions and feelings of the past.[87] But how is this to be done?

> Interpretation of the past is the recovery of the viewpoint of the past; and that recovery, as opposed to mere subjective projections, can be reached only by grasping exactly what a viewpoint is, how viewpoints develop, what dialectical laws govern their historical unfolding.[88]

But grasping the genetic and dialectical development of viewpoints amounts to grasping the historical progress towards adequate self-knowledge and explicit metaphysics. It means a recapitulation of that historical progress in oneself by appropriating the integral heuristic structure of proportionate being in interaction with contemporary mathematics, science, and common sense, and by making the transition to explicit metaphysics.[89] Making the shift to the explanatory viewpoint in interpretation presupposes therefore that self-scrutiny and self-knowledge that is prior to all interpretation and to the writing of history.[90]

All this is involved when the subsection 'Interpretation and Method' places the possibility of scientific interpretation in the creation of an appropriate upper blade for interpretation.[91] Such an upper blade consists of two elements, which regard meaning and expression respectively, and this corresponds well to the fact that the discussion of the genesis of metaphysics had spoken of the development of meaning as well as of expression, that the discussion of truth had spoken of the appropriation of truth as well as of the relationship of truth to expression, that the process of interpretation consists of appropriation as well as communication, and that the problem of interpretation is relativism as well as relativity to audiences.

It might be noted that the upper blade proposed here is a question of adding a higher-level control to the commonsense appropriation of meaning through the self-correcting process of learning.[92] Since this higher control consists in adequate self-knowledge and the consequent metaphysics, it is a question of adding self-appropriation to commonsense appropriation.[93] This is exactly the point made in the discussion of mythic consciousness: control over meaning is a question of growth in self-knowledge.[94] Thus, appropriation of the truth of another involves a self-appropriation. As we have noted earlier, the identification relevant to interpretation involves mastery of one's own consciousness. The need to maintain a habitual orientation towards truth merely specifies that such mastery should be a mastery of the polymorphism of our consciousness.

3 The Notion of the Universal Viewpoint

We come finally to the notion of the universal viewpoint. The notion of the universal viewpoint is defined as 'a potential totality of genetically and dialectically ordered viewpoints.'[95] The present section will explain just how it is a potential totality, in what sense it is a heuristic structure concerned with meaning, how it is related to the notion of levels and sequences of expression, and how it is relevant to scientific interpretation.

3.1 A Heuristic Structure

The universal viewpoint as dialectical heuristic structure recalls Hegelian dialectic, and the term 'universal viewpoint' itself recalls Hegel's universal history. Accordingly, among the first clarifications of the notion, Lonergan notes that the universal viewpoint is not universal history and not a Hegelian dialectic 'that is complete apart from matters of fact.'[96] But already in chapter 14 of *Insight* he had distinguished carefully his own use of the term 'dialectic' from that of Hegel:

> Hegelian dialectic is conceptualist, closed, necessitarian, and immanental. It deals with determinate conceptual contents; its successive triadic sets of concepts are complete; the relations of opposition and sublation between concepts are pronounced necessary; and the whole dialectic is contained within the field defined by the concepts and their necessary relations of opposition and sublation. In contrast, our position is intellectualist, open, factual, and normative. It deals not with determinate conceptual contents but with heuristically defined anticipations. So far from fixing the concepts that will meet the anticipations, it awaits from nature and from history a succession of tentative solutions ... Finally, the appeal to heuristic structures, to accumulating insights, to verdicts awaited from nature and history, goes outside the conceptual field to acts of understanding that rise upon experiences and are controlled by critical reflection; and so instead of an immanental dialectic that embraces all positions and their opposites, ours is a normative dialectic that discriminates between advance and aberration.[97]

If the universal viewpoint is not a Hegelian dialectic that is complete apart from matters of fact, it must not be thought that it is a Kantian type of a priori that is indeed to be applied to data, but is already in itself quite determinate.[98] Rather, the universal viewpoint

> is simply a heuristic structure that contains virtually the various ranges of possible alternatives of interpretations; it can list its own contents only through the stimulus of documents and historical inquiries; it can select between alternatives and differentiate its generalities only by appealing to the accepted norms of historical investigation.[99]

The operative word here is 'virtually.' Virtual grasp is illustrated in the grasp of the rule for the formation of integers, which is a grasp of the virtual totality that is the infinity of integers. Again, it is illustrated in the grasp of the set of primitive terms and propositions and rules of derivation, which is a grasp of the virtual totality of propositions that is a mathematical logical system.[100] These are of course examples of insights; but heuristic structures are anticipations of insights, and explicit heuristic structures are the result of insight into insight.[101] The point is that, if a single insight is expressed in many concepts, and if there are mathematical instances in which a single insight grounds an infinity of concepts,[102] it should not be a matter of surprise that insight into insight yields an understanding 'of the broad lines of all there is to be understood' and 'a fixed base, an invariant pattern, opening upon all further developments of understanding.'[103] But the universal viewpoint merely specifies that insight into insight includes insight into oversight, and thus arrives at the broad outlines not only of all there is to be understood, but also of the consequences of the flight from understanding.[104]

This may be illustrated by recalling the notion of being. We do not possess an idea of being: that would be the content of an act of understanding that grasps everything about everything, and such an act we do not have. All the same, we do possess a notion of being. From where do we obtain this? By thematizing our pure desire to know, which intelligently and rationally heads towards being, principally by acknowledging the questions, What is it? and Is it? In a similar fashion, we do not possess knowledge of universal history, or a unified view of all the data of interpretation. All the same, we can obtain a heuristic structure that anticipates such a unified view, and this we do simply by anticipating that human meaning develops genetically as well as dialectically.

But the notion of being is also the fundamental heuristic notion, and so we might inquire further into its relationship to the universal viewpoint. The answer is that the notion of the universal viewpoint is the structure of the notion of being as protean. For the integral structure of the pure notion of being gives rise to a scientific metaphysics, but the integral structure of the notion of being as protean gives rise to a dialectical metaphysics.[105] That is why the subsection 'Interpretation and Method' can say that the universal viewpoint or the upper blade for the totality of meanings 'is the assertion that the protean notion of being is differentiated by a series of genetically and dialectically related unknowns.'[106] For the unknown in question is the range of possible meanings. But the key to the universe of meanings is the protean notion of being,[107] and the protean notion of being unfolds through experience, understanding, and judgment as confused or as distinguished and related, and functioning under some particular pattern or blend of patterns of consciousness.[108] Grasp of the universal viewpoint is therefore grasp of the structure of the protean notion of being,[109] for 'once the structure is reached, the potential totality of viewpoints is reached,'[110] and any meaning can be reconstructed in oneself by some combination of the elements of experiencing, understanding, and judging under some dominant orientation of consciousness.[111]

We might turn for a moment to the discussion between Tekippe and Lonergan as to whether or not the universal viewpoint was a high and distant goal already in *Insight*.[112] To begin with, we note that the text of chapter 17 of *Insight* neither makes nor maintains a distinction between the terms 'universal viewpoint' and 'notion of the universal viewpoint,' but instead uses them quite freely and interchangeably. Thus, while section 3 is entitled 'The Notion of the Universal Viewpoint,' the very first sentence runs as follows: 'By a *universal viewpoint* will be meant a potential totality of genetically and dialectically ordered viewpoints.'[113] This indicates that both 'the notion of the universal viewpoint' and 'universal viewpoint' refer to the heuristic structure, to the potential totality of viewpoints. However, we must add that once the notion of heuristic structures is grasped, there should be no difficulty in drawing a distinction between the universal viewpoint as high and distant goal, and the notion of the universal viewpoint as actual heuristic structure. For a heuristic notion or structure is the notion of an unknown content to be known. It is a notion in the sense that it anticipates the as yet unknown goal, and this anticipation is built into the structure of knowing itself. Clearly then a heuristic notion, while being linked in the closest possible way to its goal, still remains distinct from it. The best example here is the distinction between being and the notion of being: clearly, the two are not identical, for being is the objective or goal of the pure desire to know, while the notion of being is the pure desire itself. In a similar way, the universal viewpoint is the 'high and distant goal' of the notion of being as protean, while the protean notion of being, differentiated both genetically and dialectically, is itself the notion of the universal viewpoint.

Further, both the universal viewpoint as goal and the notion of the universal viewpoint are viewpoints. However, the goal is a viewpoint that is yet to be attained, for we do not possess that habitual accumulation of insights that is an actual ordering of the actual totality of viewpoints. The notion or heuristic structure instead is a viewpoint that is quite within reach, for it arises upon that habitual accumulation of insights that is adequate self-knowledge and the consequent metaphysics.

Clearly then, it is not only possible but also essential to maintain both that the universal viewpoint is a high and distant goal already in *Insight*, and that the notion of the universal viewpoint is an actual heuristic tool or an actual viewpoint from which to move towards attainment of the ideal goal. Such a position, far from involving some sort of confusion, belongs to the very core of the notion of the universal viewpoint.

Following Lonergan, however, we ourselves will use the term 'universal viewpoint' to mean 'the notion of the universal viewpoint,' unless explicitly indicated otherwise.

3.2 A Heuristic Structure for Meaning

We have been trying to explain that the notion of the universal viewpoint is a grasp of a virtual totality. Now the totality that is grasped is a totality of viewpoints. It is concerned with meaning, and more precisely 'with the principal acts of meaning that lie in insights and judgments.'[114] Since, however, principal acts of meaning include insights as well as judgments, 'context' would be a more adequate term than 'viewpoint,' for while a viewpoint is defined as a coalescence of insights, a context is defined as a coalescence of insights as well as judgments.[115] This might be the reason why the subsection 'The Sketch' speaks of pure formulations, not of meanings and of viewpoints, but of contents and of contexts,[116] and also why the 1962 lecture 'Hermeneutics' uses the term 'basic context' where one might have expected 'universal viewpoint.'[117] At any rate, it is clear that the universal viewpoint as heuristic structure for meaning envisages both insights as well as judgments.

We have noted that appropriation of meaning is a question of reconstructing meaning from immanent sources of meaning. This provides the clue to the universal viewpoint: since all meaning is reconstructed from immanent sources of meaning, the universal viewpoint will consist in adequate self-knowledge, familiarity with one's immanent sources of meaning, and the ability to recombine them in various ways to approximate to various possible meanings.[118] It is a question of extrapolating from one's immanent sources of meaning to the meaning of a writer at a different stage of human development.[119]

In our discussion of *Verbum* we had noted that psychological introspection was a restricted tool of interpretation, since it was relevant only to authors practicing psychological introspection or at most to texts dealing with the human mind.[120] We might note now that both psychological introspection and the notion of the universal viewpoint are related to self-knowledge, though psychological introspection was a movement towards self-knowledge, while the universal viewpoint presupposes adequate self-knowledge.[121] In contrast to psychological introspection, however, the universal viewpoint is a generalized tool of interpretation, for it recognizes that self-knowledge, being a grasp of the immanent sources of meaning, is the key not only to authors practicing introspection but to the entire universe of meanings.[122] In this connection it might be noted that the Halifax lectures on *Insight* (1958) avoid the term universal viewpoint altogether. Its place is taken by the term self-appropriation,[123] and self-appropriation, as we have shown, is merely *Insight*'s way of speaking about psychological introspection.[124]

The universal viewpoint is an *ordered* totality of viewpoints, and the ordering is genetic and dialectical.[125] We might note first that genetic sequences and the emergence of higher viewpoints are rooted in the operators that are the exigences of intellectual development,[126] or in the pure desire to know unfolding through questions for intelligence and for reflection. The dialectical alternatives in which genuine discoveries are formulated are instead rooted in the polymorphism of human consciousness. Second, the ordering of the totality of viewpoints is itself potential,[127] for once it is anticipated that viewpoints will be ordered genetically as well as dialectically, the principle of the ordering is grasped. Third, the universal viewpoint is related to the pure form of speculative development as a more general to a less general tool of interpretation. For the pure form was relevant only to speculative development, and consisted in a genetic anticipation, but the universal viewpoint is relevant to the development of meaning in general and anticipates that such development will be not only genetic but also dialectical. There is of course the further difference that the universal viewpoint, unlike the pure form of speculative development, arises upon the imposing philosophic base of *Insight*.

If now we ask just how it is that the universal viewpoint functions, we will be led to the notion of levels and sequences of expression. For grasp of the universal viewpoint is grasp of a potential totality of ordered viewpoints. But such grasp alone is not enough, even when combined with the ability to work backwards through the fact that the totality is ordered. Some particular interpretation must be selected from among the range of possible ones, and this is where the notion of levels and sequences of expression comes in.

3.3 Levels and Sequences of Expression

The whole point of the notion of levels and sequences of expression is to provide a link between data and meaning. Now the data of interpretation are expressions. If there can be identified different modes of expression, and if these modes can be classified in terms of meaning, then from the type of expression represented in the text we could mount to the stage of meaning or viewpoint of the text.[128] The notion of levels and sequences of expression does precisely this: it exploits the fact that expression 'is an instrument of the principal acts of meaning that reside in conception and judgment,'[129] and that, further, the discovery of a new viewpoint can become generally established only through successful communication, which involves the transformation of old modes of expression and the creation and establishment of new ones.[130] This means that when a stage of meaning has become established, there will be a mode of expression to bear witness to its existence.[131] There exist, therefore, 'correlations between fields of meaning and modes of expression';[132] accordingly, expressions themselves provide an index to the level of meaning.[133]

Though *Insight* does not remark on this, the notion of levels and sequences of expression may perhaps be seen as a lower blade to the upper blade of the universal viewpoint: like the techniques of measurements and of curve-fitting, this notion helps in selection of the relevant viewpoint by setting boundary conditions.[134] Thus, the universal viewpoint moves from the potentially ordered universe of meanings downwards towards data, while the notion of levels and sequences of expression moves from data upwards.

Coming to the notion itself, first, levels of expression are distinguished by relating them to sources of meaning in both writer and reader.[135] Further, it is noted that expression can become specialized: advertisers and propaganda ministries aim at psychological conditioning; literary writing aims at stimulating intelligence and reflection through the medium of images and symbols; scientific writing is concerned with promoting understanding, while philosophic writing could be said to be concerned with the reader's judgments.[136]

In the second place, the genetic element is adverted to, for specialized modes of expression had to be invented and propagated.[137] The question of dialectical sequences of modes of expression, however, does not enter, for expression may be more or less adequate, but not properly true or false.[138]

The distinction of levels of expression grounds not an actual but a potential classification of expressions. Being merely potential, it does not impose rigid classifications upon the interpreter. Still, it is not useless: being based on the structure of human knowing and willing, it is sound; being systematic, it has all sorts of systematic implications. At the very least, it can help prevent the grosser blunders of those who assume that all expression lies on some single level with which they happen to be most familiar.[139] Again, the anticipation of sequences of expression is not a static classification. As in any genetic process, the really significant element here lies not in the classifications themselves but in the operators of the development. Thus, for example, in periods of transition there is to be expected the phenomenon of new thinking struggling to express itself as well as break free of old modes of expression.[140] In such situations the literary genre, far from revealing the meaning, only serves to mask or even betray it.[141]

Finally, if the notion of levels and sequences of expression is a classification of expressions in terms of the sources of meaning, and if the universal viewpoint itself consists in a grasp of the sources of meaning, then either the former may be regarded as an extension of the universal viewpoint to the field of expression, or at least both may be regarded as arising from the single common base that is Lonergan's cognitional theory.[142]

3.4 Hermeneutical Method

An examination of the way the universal viewpoint is expected to function cannot be omitted in a study of the universal viewpoint. Accordingly, we proceed to Lonergan's sketch of the functioning of hermeneutical method.[143]

The hermeneutical canon of relevance demands that interpretation begin from the universal viewpoint and proceed to pure formulations of contents and of contexts.[144] It should be stressed that such extrapolation occurs in interaction with data, and that further, as we have noted above, it involves not merely the universal viewpoint but also the notion of levels and sequences of expression. The formulations are named 'pure' in order to indicate that they arise from the universal viewpoint and are addressed to an audience that grasps the universal viewpoint,[145] and that accordingly they are free from the interference of the polymorphism of consciousness.[146] Such pure formulations will not normally correspond to the actual textual expression, for the simple reason that the author was working presumably not from the universal but from some particular viewpoint.[147] Further, since the notion of the universal viewpoint is the structure of the protean notion of being, the pure formulations that result from the application of the upper blade to data are described as 'determinate differentiations of the protean notion of being.'[148]

Now if it be granted that the pure formulations result from an interaction between the universal viewpoint, the notion of levels and sequences of expression, and data, then the rest of the procedure is concerned with control. The pure formulations are mere hypotheses, and so there is required a canon of parsimony.[149] From the pure formulations one proceeds to hypothetical expressions. The pure formulations of content will not coincide with the actual expression, but there are the pure formulations of the context, and so a hypothetical expression may be arrived at by transposing the pure formulations of content into the pure formulations of the context under the limitations of the resources of expression available to the author.[150] A first control is that the hypothetical expression must match the actual expression, and that there must be a one-to-one correspondence between the totality of hypothetical expressions and the totality of actual expressions. Conflicting interpretations of the same expression will instead call for re-examination of the procedure. A second control is that the totality of pure formulations of contexts must exhibit a genetic and dialectical order. A third control is that the totality of assumptions regarding available resources of expression must match the genetic sequence of modes of expression. Further controls arise from the fact that the method calls for distinctions between (1) the interpreter's accounts of contents and contexts, (2) his/her assumptions regarding available resources of expression, and (3) his/her account of how the author would express his/her message (content), given his/her context and resources of expression.[151] When pure formulations or explanatory differentiations of the protean notion of being are verified, there emerges the scientific interpretation that was the goal of hermeneutical method.

Through the envisaging of ordered totalities of documents, meanings, and expressions, interpretation becomes scientific. For envisaging ordered totalities amounts to relating the elements among themselves, and at the same time makes control possible. Thus, a canon of explanation demands that 'the interpreter's differentiation of the protean notion of being must be not descriptive but explanatory' and that it should aim at relating 'not to us, but to one another, the contents and contexts of the totality of documents and interpretations.'[152] The canon also points out that it is through such a move from description to explanation that there arises 'the possibility of scientific collaboration, scientific control, and scientific advance towards commonly accepted results.'[153]

The last point must be explained at once, and we may do so by pointing out that envisaging of the totality implies that the controls become increasingly more effective with approximation to the totality of interpretations. If then the canon of explanation demands scientific collaboration, the canon of successive approximations notes that the collaboration will extend over generations. Still, the existence of the possibility of multiple controls itself makes such collaboration possible, and so the canon of successive approximations concerns itself principally with laying down common critical principles.[154]

We might note here just how the method assures the handling of the remote criterion of truth. Individual and group bias will be handled by collaborative control, for such biases tend to vary with individuals and with groups.[155] General bias, on the other hand, cuts across individuals and groups, and is handled by operating from the universal viewpoint, for this amounts to taking one's stand on the invariant and normative structure of knowing.[156] Collaborative control will itself handle general bias in the measure that collaborators are operating from the universal viewpoint. Still, there is no automatic attainment of correct interpretations. Thus, the canon of parsimony notes carefully that radical surprises are excluded '*in the measure* that the universal viewpoint is reached.'[157] This note of caution is linked to the fact that there are degrees of certitude, whose ground lies in the 'obscure region' of the remote criterion. Only if this region were to be completely clarified would certitude reach the absolute of infallibility.[158] But can it do so? This question is taken up, not in chapter 17 but in the final part of *Insight*, which goes beyond knowing to consider human doing, discovers the problem of moral impotence and the need for liberation, and asks about the possibility of a solution. But we may note already that the attainment of truth is linked to the human person in his or her entirety. There is in fact no recipe for producing men and women of good judgment.

3.5 The Ascent to the Universal Viewpoint

We have been saying that hermeneutical method results in explanatory differentiations of the protean notion of being. But what exactly are these explanatory differentiations? And how are they related to viewpoints and to stages of meaning or of human development?

Explanatory differentiations of the protean notion of being are pure reconstructions of habitual orientations or particular viewpoints or contexts.[159] They are described as involving three elements:

> First, there is the genetic sequence in which insights gradually are accumulated by man. Secondly, there are the dialectical alternatives in which accumulated insights are formulated, with positions inviting further development and counterpositions shifting their ground to avoid the reversal they demand. Thirdly, with the advance of culture and of effective education, there arises the possibility of the differentiation and specialization of modes of expression; and since this development conditions not only the exact communication of

insights but also the discoverer's own grasp of his discovery, since such grasp and its exact communication intimately are connected with the advance of positions and the reversal of counterpositions, the three elements in the explanatory differentiation of the protean notion of being fuse into a single explanation.[160]

But to speak of genetic and dialectical sequences of contents and contexts, and of genetic sequences of modes of expression, is to relate these not to us but to one another. Accordingly, the differentiations of the protean notion of being are named explanatory.[161]

Chapter 17 also makes occasional mention of stages of meaning or of human development.[162] Thus, the second principle of criticism describes extrapolation of meaning as 'to the meaning of a man at a different stage of human development.'[163] Again: '[B]ecause all stages of development are linked genetically and dialectically, it should be possible to retrace through intervening documents the series of developments and reversals that bridge the gap from the past to the universal viewpoint.'[164] Further, the third principle of criticism notes that 'once any stage in the development of meaning has become propagated and established in a cultural milieu, there will result an appropriate mode of expression to bear witness to its existence.'[165] Most clearly, the fourth principle of criticism notes that evidence for interpretation 'supposes the coherence of the hypothesis with the universal viewpoint, with the genetic and dialectical relations between successive stages of meaning, with the genetic sequences of modes of expression and the recurrent gaps between meaning and expression'.[166]

How, we might ask, are stages of meaning related to explanatory differentiations? We may note that, just as explanatory differentiations involve the three elements of genetic sequences of viewpoints, dialectical formulations of these, and genetic sequences of modes of expression, so stages of meaning are described as being linked genetically and dialectically, and as becoming established through the attainment of an appropriate mode of expression. Accordingly, it would seem that stages of meaning are the *historical* differentiations of the protean notion of being, whereas explanatory differentiations are the interpreter's reconstructions of these historical differentiations.

In this connection it might be noted that the discussions of myth and mystery in the first section of chapter 17 are examples of extrapolations on the basis of the universal viewpoint.[167] Still, such extrapolations are not interpretations, and so cannot be adduced as instances of explanatory differentiations or pure formulations. They occupy rather an intermediate position between the universal viewpoint and pure formulations, and may be regarded as models, like the stages of meaning sketched out in *Method*.[168]

But there has been mentioned 'the series of developments and reversals *that bridge the gap from the past to the universal viewpoint.*'[169] The genesis of adequate self-knowledge and of explicit metaphysics may therefore be regarded also as an ascent to the universal viewpoint.[170] This should not be surprising, given that the universal viewpoint is a corollary of adequate self-knowledge and metaphysics.[171] For there is a historical differentiation of the notion of being, which is the progressive thematization of the various components of the notion of being. Further, as we have been saying, this process has genetic as well as dialectical characteristics. Thus,

> positions develop primarily inasmuch as sense is distinguished from understanding and both sense and understanding from judgment, and they develop secondarily inasmuch as the positions are distinguished sharply and effectively from the counterpositions. Pythagoras and Parmenides, Plato and Aristotle, Augustine and Aquinas are the great names in the primary process, while the breakdown of medieval scholasticism and the methodological efforts of modern philosophy set the problems of the secondary development, and the advance of mathematics and empirical science provides the precise information needed to effect it.[172]

The ascent to the universal viewpoint is the finality of the universe of being becoming increasingly more conscious of itself and taking control over itself.[173] It is a question of an emergent probability on the properly human level that is not merely intelligible but also intelligent.[174] Attainment of explicit metaphysics and the universal viewpoint is a new stage in the control of meaning; it is human discovery of emergent probability, and is part of the effort to attain control over this emergent probability.[175] Such control involves sharp distinctions between positions and counterpositions, a clear shift from description to explanation, and a firm grasp of the heuristic and progressive character of human intelligence through the discovery of effective criteria to distinguish between merely heuristic and explanatory understanding.[176]

We may speak therefore of a historical progress towards the notion of the universal viewpoint, a personal progress towards the notion of the universal viewpoint, and the further progress towards the high and distant goal of complete explanation that results from the ever greater specification of the heuristic structure in interaction with the lower blade of data. The book *Insight* is one person's attainment of the notion of the universal viewpoint, and this attainment is itself made possible by the historical stage of meaning at which we have arrived.[177]

3.6 The Universal Viewpoint, Metaphysics, and Wisdom

How is the notion of the universal viewpoint related to explicit metaphysics? Chapter 2 above has shown that dialectical metaphysics is a part of explicit metaphysics. Metaphysics as dialectic achieves the integration of the universe of meanings into explicit metaphysics; and such an explicitly dialectical metaphysics is the highest viewpoint and the most comprehensive integration. But if explicit metaphysics is the highest viewpoint, what then of the universal viewpoint? How, we might ask, is the notion of the universal viewpoint related to explicit metaphysics?

Chapter 17 of *Insight* tends to imply that the notion of the universal viewpoint and explicit metaphysics are distinct. Thus, the notion of the universal viewpoint is described as a corollary of 'our own philosophic analysis,'[178] as grounded in adequate self-knowledge and the consequent metaphysics,[179] or as grounded in a grasp of cognitional structure.[180]

Other evidence, however, seems to suggest that the universal viewpoint is more than merely a heuristic structure for interpretation.

The introduction, for example, describes *Insight* as having been written from a moving viewpoint: it begins from a minimal viewpoint and context, proceeds by raising questions that lead to an enlargement of that viewpoint and context, and repeats this device as often as is required 'to reach the universal viewpoint and the completely concrete context that embraces every aspect of reality.'[181] Again, the discussion of levels of expression points out that the highest type of writing is philosophic writing, for philosophic writing is concerned with judgments.[182] But documents are graded from the purely artistic to ever more conscious and deliberate efforts to communicate a particular or universal viewpoint exactly,[183] and so it would seem that philosophic writing is really an effort to communicate a particular or universal viewpoint exactly. This suggestion is strengthened by the mention of Hegelian dialectic as the initial essay in philosophic writing that envisaged the totality of viewpoints.[184] Further, the philosopher is described as repeating 'either on the grand scale of the totality of questions, or with respect to particular issues, the breakthrough that brings to light the empirically, intelligently, and rationally conscious unity of the knower, the encirclement effected by the protean notion of being, and the confinement that results from identifying being with the intelligently grasped and reasonably affirmed.'[185] The mention here of the military metaphor links the description of philosophic writing quite unmistakably to generalized empirical method, and so confirms that *Insight* is itself an effort to communicate the universal viewpoint.

Again, there is the mention of the term 'universal viewpoint' in the original preface of *Insight*.[186] The context here is the problem of the many and conflicting answers given to the question, What is man? There is no generally accepted principle of selection, and even within specialized fields there seems to be no method 'that can confront basic issues without succumbing to individual temperament and personal evaluations.'[187] This problem of human self-knowledge is no more a merely personal problem; it has taken on the dimensions of a social crisis. The answer, says Lonergan, lies in a collaboration; but *Insight* itself is concerned with the conditions preliminary to an effective collaboration.[188] These conditions are 'a common vision of a common goal,' and such a vision will be attained 'in the measure that potential collaborators move towards a personal appropriation of their rational self-consciousness,' in the measure they discover in themselves 'the structure of developing intelligence,' in the measure they reach 'the invariants of intellectual development.'[189] There follows the remark about the universal viewpoint:

> Prof. Cassirer has told us that, from the viewpoint of a phenomenology of human culture, the explanatory definition of man is *animal symbolicum* rather than *animal rationale*. But in the measure that men appropriate their rational self-consciousness, not only do they re-establish the *animal rationale* but also they break through the phenomenological veil. For, as will be argued, they can reach a universal viewpoint from which individual temperament can be discounted, personal evaluations can be criticized, and the many and disparate reports on man, emanating from experts in various fields, can be welded into a single view.[190]

It seems to be implied here that the universal viewpoint is the needed 'common vision of a common goal,' and that the way to it is through self-appropriation. The universal viewpoint would thus seem to be not merely a heuristic structure for interpretation, but rather the aim of *Insight* itself.

What then is the relationship between the notion of the universal viewpoint and metaphysics? Are they distinct? Or do they perhaps coincide, so that to speak of metaphysics or to speak of the universal viewpoint amounts to one and the same thing?

Let us note first of all that Lonergan describes metaphysics as free from the restrictions of particular viewpoints,[191] as the highest viewpoint in human knowledge,[192] as an integral viewpoint,[193] but never as a universal viewpoint. Again, he never speaks of the notion of the universal viewpoint as coinciding with metaphysics. The reason for this would seem to be that the notion of the universal viewpoint is an anticipation of the structure of the universe of meanings, whereas metaphysics is an anticipation of the structure of the universe of being. Now the universe of meanings clearly does not coincide with the universe of being. To affirm or suggest that it does would amount to a post-Hegelian type of idealism. Thus, it cannot be said that the notion of the universal viewpoint coincides with metaphysics.

Having said this, it must be admitted that the universal viewpoint and metaphysics are each in its own way unrestricted. There is in fact a complex relationship between the two.

Insofar as the universe of meanings is being, it is included within the universe of being. It follows that the heuristic structure of meaning is part of the heuristic structure of being. In other words, the notion of the universal viewpoint forms part of the integral heuristic structure that is metaphysics.

Insofar as the universe of being is a set of meanings, it is itself included in the universe of meanings.[194] It follows that metaphysics, insofar as it is a set of meanings, comes under the purview of the notion of the universal viewpoint. Thus, the notion of the universal viewpoint is able to hold together the correct metaphysics as well as the range of faulty and even anti-metaphysical systems.

Thus, from the viewpoint of being, metaphysics includes the notion of the universal viewpoint as one heuristic structure among others, but from the viewpoint of meaning, the notion of the universal viewpoint includes the 'correct metaphysics' as one viewpoint among others.

We could ask, however: in the ultimate analysis, what is basic – meaning or being? As far as *Insight* is concerned, the answer is clear: what is basic is being. Since the human being is a being whose being is partly constituted by meaning, meaning enters the universe of being as a constitutive element of that being which is human being. It follows that, in the ultimate analysis, the notion of the universal viewpoint is one heuristic structure among the many integrated by an explicit metaphysics.

But what about those statements that seem to indicate a different meaning for the universal viewpoint, statements that describe the universal viewpoint as the goal towards which *Insight* is moving, or that speak of 'the universal viewpoint of an intelligent and reasonable being,' or that imply that the universal viewpoint is a 'common vision of a common goal'? There is probably no need to assume a different meaning for the term in these contexts. For, as we have seen, the high point of world process is the human being, and the highest level of integration in the human being is a variable manifold of dynamic systems that regard not so much the individual in which the integration takes place, but rather the universe of being.[195] The set of concepts that is needed to handle this complex state of affairs can only be a metaphysics that is able to envisage both positions and counterpositions, a metaphysics that is explicitly dialectical, a metaphysics that includes a heuristic structure and a method for handling the universe of meanings. Since then the highest level of integration is a variable manifold of dynamic systems, or a genetically and dialectically ordered totality of viewpoints, Lonergan can speak of the universal viewpoint as the goal towards which *Insight* is moving, or of 'the universal viewpoint of an intelligent and reasonable being,' or of the universal viewpoint as a 'common vision of a common goal.'

We have been trying to relate the notion of the universal viewpoint to metaphysics, and now we may draw attention to its relationship with wisdom. We may recall that *Verbum* had spoken of wisdom as having two aspects, epistemological and metaphysical, and that *Insight* had carried out a transposition of these two aspects, so that epistemological wisdom becomes generalized empirical method, while metaphysical wisdom becomes a metaphysics that is not only critical and scientific but also explicitly dialectical.

We may now note that the notion of being is an inchoate wisdom or rudimentary view of the whole; metaphysics as integral heuristic structure is an unrestricted view that is a grasp of universal order, included in which is the universe of meanings; in particular, metaphysics in its dialectical aspect supplies a universal viewpoint that is the order grasped in the universe of meanings, included in which is the universe of being insofar as it is a set of meanings. Thus, the universal viewpoint may be regarded as a type of wisdom insofar as it is a grasp of order in the universe of meanings. But the place of the metaphysical aspect of wisdom is taken by an explicit metaphysics that is critical and scientific as well as dialectical, for it is this metaphysics that integrates the universe of meanings into the universe of being by integrating into itself a heuristic structure and a method for handling the universe of meanings.

We may end by returning to Tekippe's contention that the universal viewpoint is operative in other contexts in *Insight* besides that of hermeneutics.[196] This may be explained by the fact that in *Insight* dialectical method is operative, either implicitly or explicitly, whenever it is a question of the properly human level: for instance, the history of philosophy, the dialectic of metaphysical methods, the four types of biases, cosmopolis. This contention of Tekippe's is supported by Swartzentruber as well as by Hefling, and there would seem to be tacit approval on the part of Lonergan himself.[197]

4 Concluding Summary

From the theories of meaning and of objectivity there follow the analysis of the process of interpretation, the statement of the problem, and its solution. The process of interpretation consists in appropriating the truth of another and communicating it successfully. The problem arises from the fact that, when this process is carried out on the basis of common sense, there is neither adequate control over bias nor possibility of escape from relativity to a series of audiences. The solution consists in shifting to an explanatory viewpoint.

Basically, the solution consists in adding an upper blade to the lower blade that is the appropriation of the meaning of another through the self-correcting process of learning. This upper blade consists in self-appropriation or adequate self-knowledge. For such self-appropriation is a grasp of one's own intelligent and rational consciousness, or of the structure of the protean notion of being. But this is a grasp of a potential totality of viewpoints, for all viewpoints arise from some combination of experience, understanding, and judgment under some particular orientation or blend of orientations of consciousness. Further, since we are dealing with the human realm, the only adequate anticipation here is dialectical, and so it can be anticipated that the potential totality of viewpoints will be ordered not only genetically but also dialectically. Such in brief is the notion of the universal viewpoint.

Still, the notion of the universal viewpoint must be complemented by another notion, for while the former is able to envisage the range of viewpoints, it is not able to select from among these the one relevant to the text being interpreted. Here is the relevance of the link between meaning and expression, for modes of expression bear witness to the emergence and establishment of new stages of meaning. When this link is formulated heuristically, we get the notion of levels and sequences of expression, which anticipates not only that there will be a specialization of expression corresponding to the various levels of human consciousness, but also that there will be a genetic differentiation and emergence of such specialized modes of expression. Given such an anticipation, and keeping in mind the lag between meaning and expression, the mode of expression or the literary genre of a text becomes an indication of the stage of meaning represented by the text.

Consideration of the notion of levels and sequences of expression sheds light on the functioning of the genetic anticipation in the notion of the universal viewpoint. As far as the dialectical anticipation is concerned, however, chapter 17 is not quite as clear, perhaps because dialectical method has already been discussed earlier. However, hints might be gathered from chapter 14 as well as from the discussion of the remote criterion of truth in chapter 17. A first point is that adequate self-knowledge enables one to identify and distinguish positions from counterpositions; this is the way general bias is handled. A second point is that positions tend to develop, whereas counterpositions tend to their own reversal or else keep shifting grounds in order to escape such reversal; already here we have a way of distinguishing genetic from dialectical sequences. A third point is that individual and group bias, as well as general bias, will be handled through collaborative control.

Finally, a series of other conclusions may be indicated rapidly. First, once it has been grasped that wisdom constitutes the original pincer or scissors movement, and that we move towards wisdom on the basis of the inchoate wisdom that is intellectual light, it becomes possible to understand that all heuristic notions and structures are a question of making explicit the goal of knowing that is already latent and operative in the process of knowing itself. Thus, just as the heuristic notion of being is the notion of the unrestricted objective towards which our pure desire heads, so the notion of the universal viewpoint is the notion of the unrestricted objective towards which the protean notion of being heads. There is then the ideal goal that is the unified totality of viewpoints, and there is the heuristic structure that is our anticipation of that ideal.

Second, the universal viewpoint brings together the diachronic and synchronic dimensions represented in the pure form of speculative development and the technique of psychological introspection respectively; it is therefore a generalization of these hermeneutic tools.

Third, we may distinguish (1) orientations or patterns of consciousness, (2) habitual orientations, or viewpoints, or contexts, or differentiations of the protean notion of being, or stages of meaning, or stages of human development, (3) modes of expression, or differentiations of expression, that are indications of the establishment of stages of meaning, and (4) explanatory differentiations of the protean notion of being, or pure formulations, that are reconstructions from the universal viewpoint of sequences of habitual orientations or particular viewpoints or contexts.

Fourth, we have identified the notion of the universal viewpoint as the human discovery of emergent probability and therefore the attainment of a new stage in the control over meaning. Accordingly, we distinguished a historical progress towards the notion of the universal viewpoint, a personal progress towards the notion of the universal viewpoint, and the further progress towards the universal viewpoint as ideal goal.

Fifth, there is a complex relationship between the notion of the universal viewpoint and the unrestricted viewpoint that is metaphysics. From the viewpoint of meaning, the universal viewpoint includes metaphysics as one viewpoint among others. From the viewpoint of being, metaphysics includes the notion of the universal viewpoint as one heuristic structure among others. Since in the ultimate analysis it is being that is basic, meaning is included within the universe of being, and the notion of the universal viewpoint is one aspect but not the whole of that heuristic anticipation of the universe of being that is metaphysics.

Sixth, the epistemological wisdom of the *Verbum* articles becomes the generalized empirical method of *Insight*, and the metaphysical wisdom of *Verbum* becomes the explicit metaphysics of *Insight*. Wisdom as providing an upper blade for knowing gives rise to the notion of 'heuristic structures' in *Insight*. Explicit metaphysics as integral heuristic structure is therefore a contemporary form of wisdom that is methodical and dialectical, and one of the heuristic structures in this integration is the notion of the universal viewpoint.

4

Expansion and Transformation of the Universal Viewpoint

The universal viewpoint established in chapter 17 on the level of a metaphysics of proportionate being undergoes an expansion and a transformation in the final chapters of *Insight*. The *expansion* occurs when the metaphysics of proportionate being opens out in chapter 19 into a metaphysics of being in general. The *transformation* is prepared by chapters 19 and 20, but mention of the theologically transformed universal viewpoint is to be found only in the epilogue. Examination of this expansion and transformation will serve both to corroborate the conclusions of our previous chapter and to set the stage for successive chapters, for the post-*Insight* evolution of the universal viewpoint takes place almost exclusively in the realm of theology.

1   The Expansion of the Universal Viewpoint

1.1 Expansion

Consideration of human doing in chapter 18 leads to the discovery of the problem of moral impotence.[1] This leads to the question about human capacity for transcendent knowledge. For mere discovery of a correct philosophy is not an adequate solution. Polymorphism is a permanent feature of human consciousness, and such polymorphism gives rise to the fourfold bias of the dramatic and practical subject and to the counterpositions. General bias discounts all philosophy, since its principal feature is disregard of any and every issue that goes beyond the sphere of the immediately practical. The pressure and prevalence of the counterpositions makes it probable that even those who admit the relevance of philosophy will misunderstand or otherwise distort the correct philosophy. Thus, it is unlikely that the correct philosophy will ever be accepted or mastered by a significantly large number of people.² The solution to the problem of moral impotence can therefore only be a new higher integration of human living.³ Now since such a higher integration is not merely another philosophy, it will go beyond the types of knowledge examined so far. Accordingly, before asking about the existence of the needed higher integration, there is need to ask whether we can know anything that transcends the sphere of proportionate being.⁴ Hence chapter 19 takes up the question of human knowledge of God.

Now chapter 19 affects the universal viewpoint in two ways. First of all, the question of the ultimate condition of the possibility of the positions is raised and answered. Secondly, with the expansion of the metaphysics of proportionate being, the universal viewpoint itself undergoes an expansion.

To take up the first point, we must note that, while being has been identified with the real in chapter 14,⁵ this identification itself rests on the de facto coincidence of being and knowing in us.⁶ Despite this identification of the real with being, the question about just what being is has never been answered.⁷ Now raising the question What is being? leads to the grasp and conception of the notion of God. The extrapolation consists in distinguishing the pure notion of being, the heuristic notion of being formulated on the basis of the pure notion, the restricted acts of understanding, conceiving and affirming being, and the unrestricted act of understanding being. None of the first three considerations enables us to answer the question What is being, for answering that question implies understanding everything about everything; it implies, in other words, an unrestricted act of understanding. The content of such an act would be the idea of being; and the idea of being would be absolutely transcendent, for once everything about everything is understood, there are no further questions, no going beyond, no transcending.⁸ By extrapolating further from our knowledge of the subject and of the structure of proportionate being, more determinations can be added to this transcendent idea of being;⁹ this procedure reveals it to be identical to the notion of God.

Asking what being is thus leads to the conception of the idea of being and the notion of God. Asking further about the ultimate intelligibility of the de facto coincidence of being and knowing in us leads to the affirmation that God exists.¹⁰ For if the real is being, and being is the completely intelligible, and complete intelligibility is the unrestricted act of understanding that is God,¹¹ it follows that if there is some de facto coincidence between the real and being, God exists. But the basic affirmation of such a coincidence was made in the chapter on self-affirmation; it follows then that God exists.¹² Thus, general transcendent knowledge asks and answers the question of the ultimate intelligibility of the de facto coincidence between the real and being in our knowing, and so is concerned with the ultimate condition of the possibility of the positions.[13]

The second point concerns the expansion of the universal viewpoint. This may be approached by considering the infinite act of understanding. Clearly, to grasp everything about everything would be to grasp the universal viewpoint in the sense of the actual and not merely potential totality of ordered viewpoints. But such an act of understanding is God,[14] and so God would have a grasp of the universal viewpoint. But the point to be noted is that, though we do not possess an infinite act of understanding, nevertheless a heuristic conception of such an infinite act can and has been attained. The conception and affirmation of the notion of God is therefore itself a universal viewpoint,[15] though not an actual but still merely a potential totality of ordered viewpoints. Still, when such a notion is conceived and affirmed, the universal viewpoint is not only preserved but also expanded. It is expanded, because in chapter 17 the universal viewpoint was worked out on the level of a metaphysics of proportionate being; once, however, the notion of God has been conceived and the existence of God affirmed, such a metaphysics undergoes an expansion.[16] It is preserved, because the base of operations from which the notion of God has been conceived has remained the same.[17] For 'a viewpoint is universal in the measure that (1) it is one and coherent, (2) it raises issues too basic to be dodged, and (3) its analysis of the evidence is penetrating enough to explain the existence of every other view as well as to establish its own.'[18] But the notion and affirmation of God is one and coherent, because God is one and coherent. Again, the notion of God was reached by asking what being is, and the affirmation of God was reached by affirming that the real is being and that being is the completely intelligible. But such questions touch upon the basic positions about being, knowing, and objectivity, and these are fundamental issues, 'too basic to be dodged.' Finally, the existence of other views can be explained by assigning different values to the variables in our polymorphic consciousness.[19] For the affirmation of God pertains to the positions 'not in any incidental fashion, but as necessary answers to the inevitable questions about the idea of being and the identity of being with the real.'[20] If this is true, then any departure from the positions will generate mistaken notions of the divine on the mythical as well as on the philosophical level, and will tend to corrupt even correct notions and affirmations of God if these are unsupported by 'an effective criticism of the influences that rise from the unconscious ... and that invade the realm of truth.'[21] It is this concern to support correct notions and affirmations about God with effective critical procedures that is the reason for any complexity, says Lonergan, in his procedure of conceiving and affirming the reality of God.²² His concern has been 'so to advance from proportionate to transcendent being that the universal viewpoint, attained in the earlier stages of the argument, might be preserved as well as expanded.'²³

Lonergan has been explaining how it is that the universal viewpoint has been preserved as well as expanded. But how can a viewpoint that is already universal be expanded? This is not difficult, for we have already noted that the fundamental heuristic notion of being is both all-encompassing and subject to development, and that all such development is by internal differentiation.²⁴ Again, we have noted that particular heuristic structures themselves undergo development.²⁵ The universal viewpoint is clearly already universal on the level of proportionate being; the expansion that it undergoes on the level of general metaphysics consists in its receiving new determinations from the conception and affirmation of God. A new area within the whole that is the notion of being has been chalked out and specified. The difference between the universal viewpoint and the 'theological viewpoint' is the difference between lesser and greater determination of a heuristic structure.

We might stress once again that the notion of God is itself the expanded universal viewpoint. In fact, to the series of unrestricted viewpoints – from the spontaneous notion of being through the heuristic notion of being to explicit metaphysics as conception, affirmation, and implementation of the integral heuristic structure of proportionate being, included in which is the notion of the universal viewpoint – we must now add the notion of God, while God himself would be being as well as the grasp of the actual totality of viewpoints, and so the high and distant goal of all our striving.²⁶

1.2 Transformation

The problem of moral impotence had led to the question about human capacity for transcendent knowledge. This capacity having been established, for we can in fact affirm the existence of God, chapter 20 returns to the problem of moral impotence or the problem of human liberation. The fact of evil becomes a problem when God is taken into consideration, for then the question arises about the goodness of God. But, says Lonergan, if God is good then there is not only a problem of evil but also a solution. The question then is not whether there is a solution to the problem of evil, but rather what is God's solution to the problem of evil. Discovery of this solution really calls for an empirical inquiry, but already in advance one can say something about the nature of such inquiry,²⁷ and so chapter 20 engages in a determination of the heuristic structure of the solution.²⁸

Now like chapter 19, chapter 20 also affects the universal viewpoint in two ways. First, the divine solution to the problem of evil provides the de facto condition of possibility of our fidelity to the positions. Second, it can be anticipated that the universal viewpoint itself will have a role to play in the anticipated human collaboration with the divine solution.

To take up the first point, we note that the problem of evil is the priority of living over learning and being persuaded; it is the human incapacity for sustained development; it is the fact that we lack the habitual accumulation of correct insights and a habitual willingness that matches the detachment and unrestrictedness of the pure desire to know. The solution therefore must reverse this priority; and so we can foresee that it will include the introduction of new habits in our intellect, will, and sensitivity.[29] The introduction of such habits provides the de facto condition of possibility of our fidelity to the positions.[30] Faith, hope, and charity 'constitute a dialectical higher integration inasmuch as they make possible the sustained development of rational self-consciousness by reversing counterpositions through faith and by overcoming evil through the firmness of hope and through the generosity of charity.'[31]

Hope aids, supports, reinforces the detached and unrestricted desire to know, which, as desire, is merely spontaneous. The acts of will to which it gives rise will not be a mere repetition of the intellect's desire, but will take issue with conflicting tendencies and considerations.[32]

Though hope aids and supports the pure desire to know, hope itself is not knowledge but only expectation of knowledge. There is therefore need of some actual knowledge that will supply hope with its object and assurance, and charity with its motives. 'There is needed in the present a universally accessible and permanently effective manner of pulling men's minds out of the counterpositions, of fixing them in the positions, of securing for them certitude that God exists and that he has provided a solution which they are to acknowledge and to accept.'[33] Now there is little possibility of people generally moving away from the counterpositions by immanently generated knowledge. However, besides immanently generated knowledge there is also belief or appropriation of reliable knowledge generated by others, and it is through the way of belief that faith operates.[34]

Now the possibility and the reasonableness of believing is linked to human collaboration in the generation and diffusion of knowledge. If then faith operates through the way of belief, we are led to affirm that the divine solution will involve a new and higher collaboration in the pursuit of truth, and that this will be a collaboration not simply among human beings but principally with God.[35] Our entry into the higher collaboration and our participation in its fruits will be some species of faith. Faith is a species of belief, because only thus can the required knowledge be universally accessible.[36] The act of faith will be an assent of intellect to truths transmitted through the collaboration, motivated by reliance on the truthfulness of God.[37]

A person will be intelligent and reasonable in his or her *acknowledgment* of the solution inasmuch as (1) he or she grasps the existence of the problem of evil and human inability to solve it, (2) infers that divine wisdom must know many possible solutions, divine omnipotence can effect any of them, divine goodness must have effected one of them, and (3) recognizes that in fact there has been in human history an emergent trend and later full realization of the solution whose heuristic characteristics can be determined.[38] A person will be intelligent and reasonable in his or her *acceptance* of the solution inasmuch as the foregoing judgments enable him or her to grasp as unconditioned the value of deciding to assent to the truths of the higher collaboration.[39] The close parallel with *Analysis fidei* of 1952 should not be missed:[40] such acknowledgment and acceptance are related respectively to the principal acts of the remote process leading to faith, and to the proximate process terminating in the act of faith itself.[41]

Thus, the divine solution makes it de facto possible to attain and maintain the positions, and this in two ways: hope strengthens and reinforces the pure desire to know, while faith supplies hope with its object and assurance and charity with its motives.[42]

To come to our second point, not only does the divine solution to the problem of evil make fidelity to the universal viewpoint possible, but the universal viewpoint itself enters and becomes part of the human collaboration in the solution. For the solution is for all human beings and universally accessible, and so there will be the collaboration that consists in making it known to others. The solution is permanent, and so there will be the collaboration that consists in transmitting it to successive generations. Since, further, human expression is relative to its audience, transmission of the solution will involve recasting it into the equivalent expressions of different places, times, classes, and cultures; this, we might note, is related to the simple interpretation of chapter 17. But it is possible to arrive at a universal viewpoint, and this possibility is reinforced by the divine solution to the problem of evil; and so we can anticipate that human collaboration will involve not merely the reexpression of the solution to all peoples of all times, but also scientific interpretation, or conception and expression of the solution in terms of the universal viewpoint.[43]

Chapter 20 then involves further determination of the expanded universal viewpoint of chapter 19.[44] For there has been acknowledged a new higher integration that is the divine solution to the problem of evil,[45] and there has been worked out in extensive detail the heuristic structure of that solution. If, further, one acknowledges and accepts this divine solution, there occurs, as is seen in the epilogue of *Insight*, a transformation of the universal viewpoint into the terminal viewpoint of the believer.[46]

We might note also the significant extension undergone by dialectical method in chapter 20. The general heuristic structure of the divine solution to the problem of evil is specialized by adding the further alternative hypotheses of natural, relatively supernatural, and absolutely supernatural solutions.[47] Now, on the supposition of a supernatural solution to the problem of evil, dialectic undergoes radical transformation. Where before it was bipolar, now it becomes tripolar. For on the level of knowing, dialectic was a question of a bipolar conjunction and opposition between the attachment and interestedness of sensitivity and intersubjectivity on the one hand, and the detachment and disinterestedness of the pure desire to know on the other. On the hypothesis of a supernatural solution to the problem of evil, however, human perfection itself becomes a limit to be transcended.[48] For to the inner conflict between attachment and detachment is now added the necessity of our having to go beyond our humanity in order to save it.[49] Acceptance of the divine solution means having to transcend the humanist viewpoint. Such a heightened inner tension does not lack its objectification in the succession of human situations.[50]

1.3 Limits

We have been examining chapters 19 and 20 of *Insight*, but now we must ask about the universal viewpoint in chapter 18 of the book. The oddity of our procedure has something to do with a certain limitation in the notion of the universal viewpoint itself, for with chapter 18 the argument of *Insight* enters into the realm of human doing, but the relationship of the universal viewpoint to human doing is not quite clear.

Chapter 18 of *Insight* contains only a single mention of the universal viewpoint. The context is the significance of satire and humor for the problem of human liberation.[51] We are free, but our effective freedom is restricted; to expand this effective freedom, we must develop in willingness. But the less developed one is, the less one sees the need for such development, and the less willing one is to set aside time and effort for it. There is of course the pure desire to know, and so the tension of limitation and transcendence is a conscious one; but this desire tends to be 'shouldered out of the busy day.' Here comes the role of satire: since it does not require any logical presuppositions, and because it is apparently purposeless, satire is able to 'break in upon the busy day.' Thus, it becomes an ally of the pure desire to know, unveils counterpositions, and hastens their reversal. Its function is to 'help man swing out of the self-centeredness of an animal in a habitat to the universal viewpoint of an intelligent and reasonable being.'[52]

Now the mention of the self-centeredness of the animal in its habitat and the viewpoint of the intelligent and reasonable being recalls the discussion of human development in chapter 15, and this consideration lends support to the links we have found between metaphysics, the universal viewpoint, and wisdom. For the law of limitation and transcendence in the field of human development results in a tension between the world of sense and the universe of being, between a self-attached and self-interested center in the world of sense, and entry into a universe of being to which one can belong and in which one can function only through detachment and disinterestedness.[53] Again, the law of genuineness demands the admission of that tension into consciousness. But such genuineness is ideal, going far beyond the detachment and disinterestedness we possess in the pure desire to know, for it presupposes the accumulations of direct, introspective, and reflective insights needed to discriminate between issues. Yet such discrimination cannot be acquired without asking the right questions. Here is a vicious circle: '[W]e cannot become wise and discriminating without concentrating on the right questions, and we cannot select those questions unless we already are wise and discriminating.'[54] This circle is of course broken by the self-correcting process of learning, but in the ultimate analysis we are confronted with the problem of human liberation. The implication seems to be that the universal viewpoint of the intelligent and reasonable being is therefore wisdom – or at least the dialectical aspect of the wisdom that is metaphysics. It is in some sense the viewpoint of the 'wise man' who orders everything[55] and recognizes his proper place within the universe of being: not the center, but one element, quite insignificant, within this universe.

There is, then, only a single mention of the universal viewpoint in chapter 18. The question arises therefore about the relationship of the universal viewpoint to the realm of human doing. We examine here the addition of a 'universal willingness' to the universal viewpoint; the extension of dialectic not only to the realm of general metaphysics but also to the realm of doing; and the mention of an 'upper context' in the epilogue where one might have expected the universal viewpoint.

First, there is the mention of a universal willingness.[56] Moral obligation is the demand for self-consistency between one's knowing and one's doing. This means that one's willingness has to match the detachment and unrestrictedness of the pure desire to know. But the fact is that we are not born with such a willingness. We have to grow in willingness, and in point of fact the willingness one has actually attained tends to narrow down and restrict the range of possible courses of action that might be opened up by one's unrestricted desire to know. 'For unless one's antecedent willingness has the height and breadth and depth of the unrestricted desire to know, the emergence of rational self-consciousness involves the addition of a restriction upon one's effective freedom.'[57]

What is needed, therefore, is an expansion of effective freedom that would match the unrestrictedness of the pure desire to know. What is needed is a universal willingness. Such universal willingness consists not merely in recognition of an ideal norm but also in adoption of an effective (and not merely an affective) attitude towards the universe of being that would match high aspiration with performance.[58] Such a universal willingness alone would reflect and sustain the detachment and disinterestedness of the unrestricted desire to know.[59] But such universal willingness is high achievement.[60]

Now the function of willingness runs parallel to the function of the habitual accumulation of insights.[61] But a habitual accumulation of insights is a viewpoint, and this suggests a parallel between universal willingness and the universal viewpoint. Both are habits and both are universal, but one arises on the level of knowing, while the other arises on the level of doing. Thus, the notion of universal willingness seems to be on the level of rational self-consciousness what the notion of the universal viewpoint is on the level of rational consciousness. But this in turn seems to highlight the fact that the universal viewpoint is an intellectual habit.

Second, if the universal viewpoint is distinct from universal willingness, this does not mean that it has nothing to do with human doing. For the pure desire to know grasps not only facts of the universe of being but also its practical possibilities, and in this way it extends its influence into the sphere of deliberate human acts. Because one and the same intelligent and rational consciousness grounds both knowing and doing, there arises inevitably the exigence for self-consistency between knowing and doing.[62] It is this that makes possible the formulation of a method of ethics in a way parallel to that of metaphysics.[63]

Still, the method of ethics consists in an extension of dialectical method; no mention is made of the universal viewpoint. Thus, just as metaphysics is a set of positions opposed by sets of counterpositions that arise from the incomplete domination of the pure desire to know, so in ethics values are true or false, orders are troubled by disorders, and desires are unnecessarily frustrated, 'because the detachment and disinterestedness of the pure desire easily fails to develop into fully rational self-consciousness.'[64] In fact, ethical positions and counterpositions are prolongations of their metaphysical counterparts;[65] and just as metaphysical counterpositions invite their own reversal, so 'the basically similar counterpositions of the ethical order, through the shorter and longer cycles of the dialectic of progress and decline, either enforce their own reversal or destroy their carriers.'[66] Thus, hedonism or sentimentalism is an ethical counterposition, for intelligently and rationally it claims that the meaning of good and bad is to be settled, not on the level of intelligence and reasonableness, but on the unquestioning and unquestionable level of experience alone.⁶⁷ Thus dialectical analysis on the ethical level deals, not with alternative formulations of genuine discoveries, but with the different sets of consequences following respectively on reasonable and unreasonable human choices.⁶⁸ The point we would make however is that, as far as the realm of human action is concerned, dialectical method seems to manifest a far greater flexibility than the notion of the universal viewpoint. In fact, chapter 1 of *Insight* already tells us that dialectical method 'is necessitated by the lack of intelligibility in man's unintelligent opinions, choices and conduct,'⁶⁹ and chapter 7 defines the dialectical theorem in a way that is broad enough to embrace knowing as well as doing.⁷⁰

Third, the suspicion that the notion of the universal viewpoint is in some way restricted when it comes to the level of human action finds further support in the fact that, when the epilogue of *Insight* has to speak about knowing as well as doing, it uses the term 'upper context' rather than 'universal viewpoint.' *Insight*, we are told, was so planned that from a succession of lower contexts there was to emerge an invariant and unrevisable upper context.⁷¹ Such an upper context, Lonergan points out, has in fact emerged, and it is constituted

> (1) by the invariant structures of experiencing, inquiring, and reflecting, (2) by the consequent isomorphic structures of all there is to be known of the universe of proportionate being, (3) by the fuller invariant structure that adds reasonable choice and action to intelligent and reasonable knowing, (4) by the profounder structure of knowing and known to be reached by acknowledging the full significance of the detached, disinterested, unrestricted desire to know, and (5) by the structure of the process in which the existential situation sets human intelligence the problem of rising above its native resources and seeking the divine solution to man's incapacity for sustained development.⁷²

But why is the 'fuller invariant structure' not referred to as a universal viewpoint? One reason is surely that such a move would result in an expansion of the base of operations that constitutes the universal viewpoint. For while the universal viewpoint received further determinations in chapters 19 and 20, still the base of operations was explicitly affirmed to have remained the same as in chapter 17.⁷³ At any rate, it is clear that Lonergan is hesitant to expand the base of the universal viewpoint.⁷⁴

The only other occurrence in *Insight* of the term 'upper context' is in the introduction.⁷⁵ Here the terms 'viewpoint' and 'context' occur several times together,⁷⁶ and when the term 'upper context' occurs a little later, in the discussion about Gödel's theorem, the invariant structure mentioned there never includes doing.[77] This would caution against giving too much weight to the use of 'upper context' instead of 'universal viewpoint' in the epilogue. At any rate, we could draw the minimal conclusion that, while the universal viewpoint is relevant to the level of doing, that level is never asserted to form part of the integral heuristic structure that is the base of the universal viewpoint. In view also of the greater flexibility enjoyed by dialectical method, the question might be raised whether the seemingly lesser flexibility of the universal viewpoint is not due to its being somehow involved in faculty psychology. This is not to overlook the point that *Insight* is involved in a massive shift from faculty psychology to the analysis of consciousness. Still, the fact remains that, where the psychological introspection of *Verbum* wanted to provide *psychological* categories for the interpretation of metaphysical ones, the universal viewpoint is instead a set of *metaphysical* categories for interpretation. If that is not totally fair, given the critical and methodical nature of the metaphysics of *Insight*, at the very least it must be admitted that the universal viewpoint follows upon the very ontological analysis of development in chapter 15. At any rate, to speak of metaphysics is to raise old questions about the relationship between metaphysics and ethics, knowing and doing, wisdom and prudence. It is to raise questions about the distinctions and relations between sensitive, intellectual, and volitional habits, and indeed between speculative and practical intellectual habits.

2   The Theologically Transformed Universal Viewpoint

One of the heuristic anticipations of chapter 20 was that the universal viewpoint would itself enter and become part of the human collaboration with the divine solution to the problem of evil.[78] The epilogue returns to this point when it indicates a threefold theological contribution of *Insight* to the higher collaboration: apologetical, methodological, and interdisciplinary.

2.1 Fundamental Theology

Insight is apologetical, or better, it is a contribution to the introduction to theology,[79] for it begins from a humanist viewpoint but leads to the demand that this viewpoint be theologically transformed.[80] The whole of *Insight* is therefore involved in the theological transformation of the universal viewpoint:

> The self-appropriation of one's intellectual and rational self-consciousness begins as cognitional theory, expands into a metaphysics

and an ethics, mounts to a conception and an affirmation of God, only to be confronted with a problem of evil that demands the transformation of self-reliant intelligence into an *intellectus quaerens fidem*.[81]

Now the introduction to theology is known not only as apologetics, but also as fundamental theology. Just what Lonergan understands by fundamental theology at the time of writing *Insight* is revealed by *Analysis fidei* of 1952: fundamental theology, together with sound philosophy, belongs to the secondary part of the remote process leading to faith.[82] Their purpose is to lead to the principal acts of the remote process, which are the four judgments by which the four premises of the logical process are affirmed to be true.[83] Not only philosophy but also fundamental theology is done on the basis of the natural light of reason,[84] and fundamental theology consists in demonstrating the existence of God, deducing the divine attributes, showing the authenticity of the New Testament, demonstrating the possibility and proof of miracles, and pointing to the wonderful propagation of the church, its sanctity, its unity and stability.[85]

Now while *Insight* itself might be considered an example of the 'sound philosophy' mentioned above, the final chapters of *Insight* clearly reflect the structure of fundamental theology: the proof of the existence of God, deduction of the divine attributes of omnipotence and goodness (chapter 19), the problem of evil and the existence of a divine solution to this problem because God is both omnipotent and good, the delineation of the general characteristics of such a solution, the obligation to search for and accept the solution that exists (chapter 20). Again, like fundamental theology, this process is done by the natural light of reason, or, as *Insight* puts it, on the basis of a purely humanist viewpoint. Finally, like fundamental theology *Insight* stops short at the threshold of the proximate process leading to faith.[86] Both the principal acts pertaining to the remote process as well as the proximate process itself are the concern of the individual. Chapter 20 of *Insight* then does not achieve the theological transformation of the universal viewpoint; such transformation occurs through acknowledgment and acceptance of the divine solution, and so remains a personal act. Saying that the final chapters of *Insight* reflect the structure of classical fundamental theology does not of course amount to saying that the two are equivalent. One of the major differences is that *Insight* does not enter into an actual examination of the claims of the Christian religion and of the Catholic church, but restricts itself to an elaboration of the heuristic structure of the divine solution.

It is to be noted that, while both chapters 19 and 20 of *Insight* make use of heuristic anticipation, the key point in the process is the deduction of God's existence in chapter 19.[87] Once the existence of God has been affirmed, the anticipation of his qualities of goodness and omnipotence leads to an affirmation of the divine solution to the problem of evil. The obligation to search for and accept the solution seems to follow instead from the 'natural ethics' of chapter 18 and from the establishment of the value of believing in the course of chapter 20.[88]

The theological transformation of the universal viewpoint therefore involves a process that is clearly patterned on classical fundamental theology. An important consequence is that a universal viewpoint theologically transformed in this way includes an assent to truths[89] as well as submission to the institutional structure entrusted with preservation of the collaboration.[90] The theologically transformed universal viewpoint itself would seem to be a methodical version of 'reason illumined by faith.'[91]

There might be noted a further aspect of the fundamental theology of *Insight*. Chapter 14 had informed us that 'heuristic notions and structures are not discovered by some Platonic recall of a prior state of contemplative bliss,'[92] but rather from an analysis of human intelligence in operation in various fields such as mathematics, science, and common sense.[93] Chapter 17 had spoken of the 'conditioning of metaphysics by self-knowledge and of self-knowledge by human development.'[94] Again, we ourselves have noted that the formulation of the notion of the universal viewpoint is itself the contemporary stage of a long historical ascent.[95] What then of the heuristic notion of God worked out in chapter 19,[96] and the heuristic structure of the divine solution essayed in chapter 20 of *Insight*? Are we to suppose that these have been formulated by a pure process of deductive extrapolation from premises established in earlier parts of the book? Or should it not be admitted that they presuppose, though not in the form of premises, the historical and personal data of religious and Christian experience? Some such situation would seem to be the case, for Lonergan's theological work of this period is clearly echoed in the final part of *Insight*. We have already noted the parallels between chapter 20 and *Analysis fidei*; to that, there might be added the echoes of the *Gratia Operans* articles in chapter 19;[97] in fact, the text itself contains a reference to these articles.[98] The point here is that, as Lonergan himself later recognized, the final part of *Insight* is out of harmony with the earlier parts of the book insofar as it fails to make explicit the fact that heuristic structures are appropriated through a long and deliberate appeal to personal and historical experience.[99]

2.2 Theological Hermeneutics

The second contribution of *Insight* to the higher collaboration is methodological. Chapter 20 had already spoken of simple as well as scientific interpretation as forming part of human collaboration in the divine solution.[100]

The epilogue returns to this when it points to the parallel between the discussion of the truth of interpretation and 'the Catholic fact.'[101] The discussion of the truth of interpretation had envisaged

> (1) initial statements addressed to particular audiences, (2) their successive recasting for sequences of other particular audiences, (3) the ascent to a universal viewpoint to express the initial statements in a form accessible to any sufficiently cultured audience, and (4) the explanatory unification from the universal viewpoint of the initial statements and all their subsequent reexpressions.[102]

But isomorphic with the above process of interpretation there is the Catholic fact. To the first and second points correspond the initial divine revelation and the communication and application of this message to a succession of particular audiences. To the third point correspond dogmatic decisions as well as speculative theology, while to the fourth point corresponds historical theology.[103] This parallel may be illuminated by a series of remarks.

First, a distinction is drawn between 'authoritative pronouncements that call for dutiful submission 'and 'definitive pronouncements that the church itself cannot contradict.'[104] Further, the 'ordinary' magisterium is described as standing to the 'extraordinary' magisterium as simple interpretation to scientific interpretation.[105]

Second, both the teaching authority of the church and the theologian are described as operating on the basis of the theologically transformed universal viewpoint, but a clear difference in authority between them is implied in the remark that 'in a preeminent and unique manner the dogmatic decision is, and the technical thesis of the dogmatic theologian can be, the true interpretation of scriptural texts, patristic teaching, and traditional utterances.'[106] There is then a difference between dogmatic theses based on the theologian's own authority, and authoritative pronouncements made by the church. Given this, it is difficult to agree with Hefling's remark that it would be 'an oversight of *Insight*' to ask here 'whether the status of true interpretation accrues to dogmatic theses in virtue of their conformity with doctrines already defined, or in virtue of historical scholarship.'[107]

Third, such dogmatic theology would not seem to be different from the speculative theology that seeks universal formulations of the truths of faith.[108] We might add that seeking universal formulations would correspond to the *via analytica*, the process from the *priora quoad nos* to the *priora quoad se*.[109] What then about the *via synthetica*, the process from the *priora quoad se* to an intelligible organization of what has been revealed? An allu-

92   Part One: *Insight*

sion to this process is found elsewhere in the epilogue, when Lonergan speaks of the relevance to theology of the oppositions between positions and counterpositions: '[T]he clarification we have effected of the role of understanding in knowledge recalls to mind the impressive statements of the Vatican Council on the role of understanding in faith; and a firm grasp of what it is to understand can hardly fail to promote the limited but most fruitful understanding of the Christian mysteries.'[110]

Fourth, it is implied that theological interpretation is necessarily scientific, so that interpretation based on a historical sense cannot be theological. The reasons for such a position would seem to be complex. On the one hand, both dogmatic-speculative theology and the extraordinary magisterium aim at universal formulations. On the other hand, the ordinary magisterium, though not aiming at universal formulations, is nevertheless true interpretation. But historical interpretation based on a historical sense neither aims at universal formulations nor possesses a guarantee of truth, and so does not qualify as theological interpretation.

Fifth, there would seem to be a two-way interaction between the teaching authority of the church and theologians, for if the pronouncements of this authority demand acceptance, we are also told that the church 'takes advantage of the *philosophia perennis* and its expansion into a speculative theology.'[111] As 'Theology and Understanding' of 1954[112] remarks, 'On the one hand, the dogmatic pronouncements of the church draw upon the previous formulations of theologians ... On the other hand, with each new dogmatic pronouncement the basis of the *via inventionis* receives an increment in clarity and precision.'[113]

Sixth, this activity of the church taking advantage of the *philosophia perennis* and its expansion into a speculative theology is compared to true interpretation mounting to a universal viewpoint.[114] Earlier also, the work of speculative theology was paralleled to 'the ascent to a universal viewpoint to express the initial statements in a form accessible to any sufficiently cultured audience.'[115] It is thus the process from simple to scientific interpretation that parallels in some way the process in the church from the series of expressions to different audiences to the universal formulations of a speculative theology.

Seventh, 'explanatory unification from the universal viewpoint of the initial statements and all their subsequent reexpressions'[116] is paralleled to the work of the historical theologian 'revealing the doctrinal identity in verbal and conceptual differences' between initial divine revelation, subsequent expressions of this revelation to a variety of different audiences, and the universal formulations of speculative theology and of dogmatic decisions.[117] In the light of what we have just discussed, to speak of such historical theology as operating from the universal viewpoint, and to speak of it

Expansion and Transformation of the Universal Viewpoint 93

as using a dialectical analysis that proceeds to the universal viewpoint, amounts to the same thing. In fact, the whole of the immediately preceding discussion about changeless concepts is relevant to historical theology. Concepts, we are told, change inasmuch as things change, inasmuch as human understanding of things develops, and inasmuch as that development is formulated coherently or incoherently.[118] Now theological interpretation concerns an unchanging divine revelation that, however, is to be apprehended ever more fully;[119] accordingly, the first alternative is to be excluded. The problem then reduces to asking whether it is possible to affirm conceptual identity in difference, and whether there is a way to determine such conceptual identity in difference.

The possibility of conceptual identity in difference arises from the distinction between explanatory concepts and heuristic concepts. For on the one hand, while explanatory concepts change, heuristic concepts themselves remain constant;[120] heuristic concepts therefore provide a principle of continuity. But on the other hand, there can be developments in heuristic concepts and structures themselves,[121] and explicit metaphysics as integral heuristic structure itself undergoes development.[122]

As for the determination of conceptual identity in difference, the problem arises from the possibility of dialectical formulations of heuristic structures, but the solution comes from the existence of a dialectical metaphysics:

> [A] dialectical analysis based upon a sufficiently accurate cognitional theory can proceed to a universal viewpoint that embraces at once (1) the positions in the contemporary stage of their development, (2) the positions at each prior stage of their development, and (3) the successive counterpositions of the past and present with their essential incoherence with the claim that they are grasped intelligently and affirmed reasonably.[123]

The general position here is quite clear: there exists a method that enables a unitary grasp of both positions and counterpositions, and such a method is not equivalent to a universal history.

Now though what has been said does not constitute a complete explanation of how a historical theology might function, it at least explains the possibility of conceptual identity in difference and provides a method to help determine such identity. Thus,

> behind every change there is an underlying unity, and that unity may be formulated explicitly on the level of heuristic anticipation or of consciously adopted method or of a dialectical metaphysics. Hence it

follows that changes in conceptualization do not imply any ultimate multiplicity and that behind any conceptual variation there is a conceptual constant that can be formulated from a universal viewpoint.[124]

Thus conceptual constants are heuristic concepts, while conceptual variations are either developments of heuristic concepts or else the series of explanatory concepts that arise as answers to the heuristic concepts.[125] Dialectical method, on the other hand, helps distinguish positions from counterpositions and genetic from dialectical sequences of viewpoints.

Here an objection might be raised: if historical theology works from the theologically transformed universal viewpoint, then the historical theologian already believes what he is out to demonstrate: doctrinal permanence in development. Such a historical theology would therefore seem devoid of any scientific value. In answer, it must first be said that such an objection might not be wholly fair to Lonergan. Some six years after the completion of *Insight*, in *De intellectu et methodo* (1959), Lonergan noted that submission to the magisterium does not reduce the work of historical theology to a dogmatic reiteration of doctrinal continuity,[126] and this I think holds good for the historical theology of *Insight* as well. The universal viewpoint is not a tool that functions automatically, not even when it is theologically transformed. The work of showing doctrinal continuity is a question of grasping the immanent intelligibility of transitions and the critical principle here is dialectical: the identification of cognitional and ethical positions and counterpositions.[127] Still, the fact that Lonergan himself later changed his ideas about historical theology indicates that the position of *Insight* was in some way unsatisfactory. The root of the problem would seem to be the role played by classical fundamental theology in the theological transformation of the universal viewpoint.[128] We will have occasion to return to this point in the chapters that follow.

2.3 Interdisciplinarity

The third contribution to the higher collaboration is interdisciplinary. This is the question of the relation between theology and the empirical human sciences. Aquinas worked the Aristotelian synthesis of philosophy and science into a larger Christian view that includes theology. However, the contemporary emergence of the empirical human sciences creates a fundamentally new problem. For the empirical human sciences deal with human beings in their concrete performance; but human beings in their concrete performance are affected by sin and the problem of evil; they are recipients of grace, and they accept or reject grace. Given this, the empirical human sciences cannot reach adequate analysis of their data without the help of theology.[129] The only properly comprehensive view of the concrete universe is therefore the theological. But can such a view be reconciled with the proper autonomy of the human sciences?

Lonergan proposes that the solution is to be found in the inner dynamism of inquiry itself. Thus, the first eighteen chapters of *Insight* are written solely in the light of human intelligence and reasonableness; but the inner dynamism of inquiry itself leads inevitably to the affirmation of God and to the search of intellect for faith. Thus the sciences are autonomous, they operate from a 'humanist viewpoint,' and in principle they alone are competent to answer their proper questions. In fact, however, scientists do not triumph over bias; they can do so only if they raise and answer successfully the further questions that lead to other fields. Subjective bias can be overcome by setting it against the expansive dynamism of the object, by means of the self-appropriation that consists in the fruitful interaction of subject and object.[130] Here Lonergan goes on to make some concrete suggestions, but for our purposes it suffices to take note, first, of the fact that the human sciences include history of literatures, and that therefore they include literary history of the Bible, patristic study, conciliar study, and all the particular human studies that enter into theology;[131] and, second, of the sapiential role of theology as *regina scientiarum*. The integration of positive studies into theology will be an important theme in Lonergan's subsequent considerations on theological method, and this integration will be done by an extension and adaptation of the sapiential role of theology.

3 Conclusion

Our aim has been to study the notion of the universal viewpoint in the context of *Insight*. It should have by now become evident that the key notion in our interpretation has been wisdom. Wisdom not only provides the key to an interpretation of the notion of the universal viewpoint, but also enables grasp of the development from the *Gratia Operans* dissertation of 1940 to the completion of *Insight* in 1953.

Wisdom, we have seen, has an epistemological aspect and a metaphysical aspect; it has, we might say, a subject pole and an object pole. This polarity may be discerned in the entire development, from the pincer movement of 1940 with its upper blade in the pure form of speculative development, to the notion of the universal viewpoint in *Insight*. Thus, in the *Verbum* articles we have the technique of psychological introspection, and the self-knowledge that served as a hermeneutical upper blade. In *Insight* we have the methods of mathematics and of the empirical sciences, and their respective heuristic structures; generalized empirical method with its upper blade in the dialectical theorem; the method of metaphysics and metaphysics as integral heuristic structure; and, finally, hermeneutical method and the universal viewpoint. When the final part of *Insight* is taken into consideration, there have to be added also theological method and the theologically transformed universal viewpoint. The key to all these is wisdom, for all growth towards wisdom takes place on the basis of wisdom, and so all heuristic structures (and this includes the hermeneutical tools of the *Gratia Operans* dissertation and of the *Verbum* articles) are merely further specifications of the original or fundamental heuristic notion of being, which because unrestricted is a view of the whole and so a rudimentary wisdom. Metaphysics, on the other hand, is the integration of all particular heuristic structures, and so is a new way of specifying what used to be wisdom as grasp of universal order. Since, further, the only adequate integrated view is dialectical, such a metaphysics supplies a universal viewpoint from which the totality of meanings can be integrated.

We might say then that in *Insight* the place of the habit of wisdom is taken by generalized method and by a metaphysics that is explicitly dialectical. Generalized method takes the place of the genetic aspect of wisdom, whereas explicit metaphysics takes the place of wisdom as grasp of universal order.

Second, there is a historical ascent to the universal viewpoint. This ascent is a process of differentiation of the protean notion of being. Such an ascent is another way of speaking about the genesis of adequate self-knowledge or of explicit metaphysics or of the development of adequate control over meaning. The attainment of explicit metaphysics would itself be the ascent to the universal viewpoint becoming reflectively conscious of itself and taking adequate control over itself.

Third, as far as interpretation is concerned, the notion of the universal viewpoint is the key to the reconstruction of the content and context of any expression, and also an anticipation of the ordered totality of viewpoints. It has therefore both a synchronic and a diachronic dimension. In its synchronic dimension it recalls the technique of psychological introspection, while in its diachronic dimension it recalls the pure form of speculative development.

Fourth, the notion of the universal viewpoint, while not unrelated to the level of doing, does not include that level. Dialectical method instead appears to enjoy greater flexibility. It would seem that the universal viewpoint is hampered by limitations arising from an incomplete shift away from faculty psychology. True, *Insight* begins not with metaphysics but with cognitional theory; still, the universal viewpoint is a metaphysical upper blade for interpretation. The overcoming of these limitations will be an important theme in the post-*Insight* years.

Fifth, the process leading to the theological transformation of the universal viewpoint is patterned on classical fundamental theology. The key moment in this process is the deductive transition into the theological realm through the proof of God's existence. Again, faith is an assent to revealed truths, and involves submission to the authority of the body entrusted with the safeguarding of this revelation. It will be seen that the presence of such classical elements in the theologically transformed universal viewpoint constitutes a tension within theological hermeneutics, and that a large part of the way to *Method in Theology* will be dedicated to the resolution of this tension.

PART TWO

From *Insight* to *Method in Theology*

5

Upper Blade for Hermeneutics or History

Part One has studied the universal viewpoint in the context of *Insight*. Part Two asks about the universal viewpoint in the period from 1954 (the completion of *Insight*) to about 1968. While a more natural break-off point might have been the 'breakthrough' to the set of eight functional specialties in February 1965, I have thought it better to include in Part Two not only the 'breakthrough' but also the 'encirclement,' at least as far as the acquisition of new theological foundations is concerned.[1]

1   1954: 'Theology and Understanding'

The epilogue of *Insight* had mentioned a historical theology which operated from the firmer and broader base that included the theologically transformed universal viewpoint, and which had the task of revealing doctrinal identity in the verbal and conceptual differences between initial revelation and subsequent expressions.[2] The article of 1954 'Theology and Understanding' sheds light on the problem to which the above historical theology is the solution. The problem is the question of the relations between speculative and positive theology. Scholars using the methods of positive research generate a vast amount of material, but neither they nor anyone else seems to be able to produce a synthesis that is more than transitory; but this means that the most noble task (*munus nobilissimum*) of showing doctrinal identity in the manifold apprehensions of revealed truths becomes very difficult.[3]

What is required is a methodical solution. Lonergan's observations at this point are cryptic, but I construe them as follows. First, the existing methods of positive research are strong on lower-blade techniques, but weak on upper-blade techniques. Second, the type of questions handled by lower-blade techniques are not very relevant to theology. Moreover, such questions are subject to the vicissitudes of developing scientific opinion. Third, the questions that are extremely relevant to theology are settled not so much by lower-blade techniques as by the implicit or explicit philosophical viewpoints invoked by scholars in their interpretation of scientific method. This problem must be solved; and the solution as in *Insight* is to create an adequate upper blade. For if method in the physical sciences can make use of higher-level techniques, there is no reason to oppose the use of 'higher-level controls' in the historical sciences. Fourth, what could such an upper blade be? The problem lies in conflicting accounts of scientific method, and these in turn are rooted in conflicting philosophies. The solution would seem to be 'a study of scientific methods in their presuppositions and assumptions.'[4] This is a question of reason becoming explicitly conscious of the norms of its own procedures. It would seem that such explicit consciousness is equivalent to a general method. Fifth, what is needed is an upper blade for theology. This may be obtained by the illumination of reason by faith. For if method is simply reason's 'explicit consciousness of the norms of its own procedures,'[5] then the illumination of reason by faith will result in the illumination of method by faith.

Thus, despite the absence of the term historical theology, I think it is sufficiently clear that the solution being hinted at is not different from that of the epilogue of *Insight*.

A related issue that must be mentioned is 'the problem of patterns of human experience, of the *Denkformen*.'[6] The *Imitatio Christi* contrasts feeling compunction and defining it, pleasing the Trinity and discoursing learnedly upon it. But Lonergan wishes to note that both feeling compunction and defining it involve knowing, that there are two distinct types of knowing, and that the methodological problem 'is to define the precise nature of each, the advantages and limitations of each, and above all the principles and rules that govern transpositions from one to the other.'[7] Now transpositions from one type of knowing to the other are relevant both to a study of the Catholic tradition and to an understanding of the nature of speculative theology. They are relevant to the former because the larger part of the relevant documents springs from the commonsense type of knowing. They are relevant to the latter because speculative theology springs from the theoretical type of knowing.[8]

We have been noting two issues, the challenge posed to theology by the entry of the methods of historical research, and the need for a methodical differentiation between two types of knowing. Now these problems are not unconnected, and the connection is revealed by a book review of 1955, which observes that there is 'an elementary stage of historical investigation that has to be content with ill-defined, descriptive concepts. So New Testament scholars work out explanations in terms of Semitic mentality, eschatology, and the like.' It ends by hoping 'that a more developed methodology will eventually eliminate such makeshifts in favor of sharply defined concepts and of well formulated dialectical principles of development.'[9] We may recall that the hermeneutical method of chapter 17 of *Insight* had drawn a sharp contrast between explanatory differentiations and descriptive reconstructions:

> If one takes one's stand on the ambivalence of average common sense ... then one can obtain a base of operations for entering into the mentality of another age and interpreting its documents only by some putative reenactment in oneself of its ambivalent blend of the aesthetic, dramatic, and practical patterns and of its forays into the biological and intellectual patterns. So there arise problems of determining, not differentiations of the protean notion of being, but imaginative and emotive reconstructions of the Nature Religions, of the Greek mysteries, of Eschatology and Apocalyptic, of traditional and Hellenistic Judaism, of the Christian *Urgemeinde* and Paulinism.[10]

Within the protean notion of being, 'the transition from one differentiation to another is the quite determinate and determinable process of changing patterns of experience, accumulations of insights, and sets of judgments'; but if we restrict ourselves to mere common sense, 'the transition from one imaginative and emotive reconstruction to another is condemned by its very nature to be a mere transmogrification; people begin by perceiving and feeling in one manner; they end by perceiving and feeling in another; and there are no imaginable precepts or reproducible revulsions of feeling that could link verifiably their beginning to their end.'[11] The point should be clear: explanatory differentiation between the two types of knowing is the required upper blade for historical investigation, and thus the key to the integration of historical studies into theology.

2   1957: *Divinarum personarum ...*

A more substantial discussion of historical theology may be found in the first chapter of *Divinarum personarum ...* of 1957. Section 3 of this chapter draws a distinction between a systematic type of exegesis that omits accidentals, and a new, historical type of exegesis that would be more concrete and comprehensive, considering the economy of salvation in its historical evolution. This historical exegesis is prepared for by research but is as yet largely unachieved.[12]

This seems to be taken up again in the section on the historical process. In order to grasp the nature of the historical process, we must first form general notions regarding historical development, and then achieve some understanding of the development both of dogma and of theology.[13] The first or historical question tends to correspond to the universal or humanist viewpoint of *Insight*. The fundamental problem is to find a transcultural principle of transition from one culture to another. Appealing to depth psychology, scholarship, and other sciences solves merely the objective or material aspect of the problem; on the side of the subject, the problem remains, for there are as many interpretations as there are scholars and schools.[14] In an echo of the article of 1954, we are told that there is a tendency to divide all questions into two types: those that can be solved 'scientifically,' and others that are abandoned to a seemingly inevitable relativism. Thus, historians either avoid all philosophical questions, or else hold on to a relativistic philosophy.[15] How this relativism can be attacked at its root, and how true interpretation is possible, has been discussed in *Insight*.[16]

Echoing both the call for a transcultural principle and the mention of depth psychology and scholarship is a remark in the Halifax lectures of 1958: 'For Eliade, the image is a transcultural language.'[17] Significantly, this remark occurs in the lecture on chapter 17 of *Insight*. The lecture goes on to discuss mystery and myth, and observes that the 'imaginative side enables self-appropriation to project itself not only into the childhood of one's own past but also into the childhood of humanity.'[18] In terms of the measure of self-appropriation, it is possible to achieve not only a classification of philosophies but also a division of stages in culture. Sorokin's sensate, idealistic, and ideational stages of culture in fact correspond to self-appropriation qua experience, qua intelligent, and qua judging.[19] There follows a discussion of how categories derived from self-appropriation provide an upper blade for historical study.[20] We may note that the universal viewpoint is never mentioned; its place is taken by self-appropriation.

The Halifax lectures bring us to 1958. The indications are that the achievements of *Insight* are being applied in various ways, without significant modifications, in the works of the period 1954–58. We may note, however, that the concrete context of Lonergan's interests gradually comes to the fore in this period: the method of theology. The occasion for the problem seems to be the entry of the methods of positive research into theology, and the problem itself, if we are to go by the hint given in the article of 1954, is the conflicting notions of science inherent in (traditional) theology and the new historical methods.[21]

3   1959: *De intellectu et methodo*

Both the problem of method and the question of transitions are taken up in a systematic way in *De intellectu et methodo* of 1959, which is really an extended application of *Insight* to theology. The procedure is to outline a general method and then extend it into theology.

The course begins by outlining in an extensive manner the problem facing contemporary theology. Thus the first chapter, entitled 'The Notion of the Question,' notes that contemporary theology faces a triple problem: the problem of foundations, of historicity, and of the 'chasm.' These problems are three logically distinct aspects of one real problem, that of method,[22] and all three have to do with transitions. The problem of the foundations has to do with the *basis* of the transitions from one 'ordering of questions' to another. The problem of historicity is the problem of *continuity* between one ordering and another. The problem of the chasm is the problem of the increasing *gap* between the sources of revelation and the various orderings of questions.[23] It is not difficult to see in this an expansion of the 'contemporary methodological issues' mentioned in the article of 1954. To take up only the problem of historicity, we are told that the massive proliferation of material produced by positive theology poses serious problems for theology. For it has become clear that St Paul and St Thomas use the same words in different ways, and there is no logical process between one usage and the other but only a leap. 'But if among the various historical ways of conceiving dogmas there is simply a leap, then the foundation of systematic speculative theology is simply done away with, as well as all continuity among the various ways of understanding dogmas.'[24] Hence the necessity not only of finding an integration between positive and speculative theology, but also of finding and clarifying its foundation and theoretic justification.[25]

If the problem is one of foundations, historicity, and the chasm, the root of the problem is identified as the notion of science. Thus, we are told that the concrete form in which the methodological problem arises today is the gap between a historical and literary investigation of the Bible in accordance with a still-developing notion of science and the notion of science implicit in scholastic philosophy and theology.[26]

The only adequate solution is to have foundations based on wisdom. This solution is taken up at greater length in the fourth chapter on method.[27] Method is the contemporary form of wisdom that will provide foundations and will also solve the problem of historicity and of the chasm.

Method is a practical notion, hence it consists of precepts. The relevant precepts are five: Understand, Understand systematically, Reverse counterpositions, Develop positions, Accept responsibility for judging.[28] These emerge from the theory of knowledge laid out in *Insight*.[29] There follows an outline of metaphysics as the basic heuristic structure valid for all fields of knowledge.[30]

But the generalized empirical method of *Insight* was not only empirical but also critical; its upper blade was the dialectical theorem. What of the method of 1959? The answer is to be found in the third, fourth, and fifth rules, and this answer will also confirm the connection we have been making in Part One between wisdom and dialectic. The universal principle of good judgment is wisdom, but there is no method, technique, or recipe for producing men and women of good judgment;[31] accordingly, there arises the fifth rule, which demands that responsibility for judgment be accepted. Still, method does not entrust the advance of science 'to the vagaries of individual opinion':[32] it includes a technique for overcoming individual, group, and general aberration. This is in fact the function of the third and fourth rules: they are dialectical, and imply a further judgment on individual judgments.

> Developing positions and reversing counterpositions are equivalent to judging judgments; and the definitions of positions and counterpositions are based on ultimate philosophic alternatives, that is, on the diverse manners in which individual judgment can go wrong not merely incidentally but in the grand manner of a superficial or a mistaken philosophy.
>
> It is true, of course, that others may and will disagree with my account of the matter. But from the nature of the case, I think that disagreement in the main will be limited to naming positions what I name counterpositions and to naming counterpositions what I name positions. There would result a number of distinct schools, but their number could not be very large, their epistemological assumptions and implications would be in the open, and the individuals that chose between them could do so with an adequate awareness of the issues and of their own personal responsibility in judging.[33]

Thus, just as the hermeneutical canon of successive approximations had envisaged a collaboration made possible by common critical principles,[34] in the present text the individual habit of wisdom is complemented by the collaboration introduced by dialectical technique.

The course of 1959 also echoes the historical ascent to the universal viewpoint. The five rules of general method are immanent in history.[35] There is, therefore, a historical ascent to the explicit conception of general method: method is the contemporary stage of an ascent that begins with the symbolic mode of thought, progresses to the mixed mode (where the *logos* discovers itself in opposition to *mythos* but is not able to completely free itself from it), to arrive at methodical scientific intelligence. This historical ascent is confirmed by the Nottingham lecture: '[I]ntersubjectivity and common sense are propaedeutic to a third stage when the *Logos* immanent in man comes to awareness of its potentialities and asks for a method that will lead to complete understanding.'[36] This third stage can be itself, however, 'only by taking stock of its earlier history, noting the limitations of previous modes, acknowledging their opposition to the new demands of intelligence and reasonableness, and opting consciously, deliberately, coherently, and thoroughly for the new way.'[37]

The general method of 1959, therefore, follows *Insight* rather closely. The major novelty is that, while *Insight* had spoken of generalized empirical method and formulated the integral heuristic structure, and while it had proposed canons of hermeneutical method, it had not really come down to formulating canons or rules of method in general. In this sense, the general method of 1959 may be regarded as complementing the achievement of *Insight*.

Theology of course calls for a radical transformation of the rules that constitute general method. Once again, this transformation does not depart in its essentials from that of *Insight*. The notion of faith, for example, is still classical: it includes revealed truths.[38]

There is explicit mention of historical theology. The notion seems to be the same as in the epilogue of *Insight*, for we are told that biblical or patristic theology must not be understood as merely philology or history of literary genres in human thought; it belongs to another genus, theology.[39] The discussion, however, is more elaborate. We are told that theology must develop its own categories for investigating its prescientific stages, and that this is perhaps the biggest problem, the fundamental methodological problem, facing the science of theology today.[40] The solution consists in recognizing the existence of different modes of human thought. Before the systematic understanding of theology,[41] there was already an understanding, but this was an intersubjective, symbolic, commonsense understanding.[42] To write the history of Christian thought and theology, therefore, one must be a historian and a theologian.[43] But more is required: one must have personally undergone the transition from the commonsense to the systematic mode of thought,[44] and one must be able to make use of this personal experience when studying the history of Christian thought.[45] This is of course the problem of transitions.

Once a transition is identified, it must be understood. Such understanding is a question of seeking the intrinsic intelligibility of the text, rather than praising the truth of dogmatic definitions. Again, it is a question of avoiding the appeal to hidden causes such as Hebrew, biblical, medieval, or Palestinian mentalities. One must appeal instead to the overall development of the human mind.[46] All scientific investigation takes place in a twofold movement: an a posteriori movement from below, and an a priori movement from above.[47] Historical theology also requires an upper blade: without such an upper blade it is quite impossible to 'discover, select, emphasize, evaluate, order, judge' data.[48] The upper blade relevant to the study of the prescientific stage of theology consists of the stages of development.[49] More fundamentally, we are told that the five precepts of general method themselves encompass the entire aprioristic element in any science.[50]

Thus, the course of 1959 is significant on several counts. First, it continues the discussion of the historical theology mentioned in the epilogue of *Insight* and elaborated in *Divinarum personarum* ... (1957). Second, it brings together the two issues we noted in the article of 1954, that of the relations between speculative and positive theology, and that of the *Denkformen*, by making it clear that explanatory differentiations between the two types of knowing serve as an upper blade for historical investigation. When such an upper blade undergoes theological transformation, we have a 'firmer and broader base' for historical theology. Third, however, we note that Lonergan's notion of theology is still very classical: despite the concern with historical theology, theology still seems to be mainly or primarily systematic theology, and theological transformation of method involves the classical notion of faith as assent to revealed truths.

4   1959: Lectures on the Philosophy of Education

The concern with an upper blade for history is found once again in the philosophy of education lectures of the summer of 1959, in the discussion of the necessity of an a priori relevant to general history.[51] This course is extremely important as far as our study is concerned.

First, extensive reading in Piaget for the course of 1959 leads to a new functional analysis of human development, in contrast to the explicitly and deliberately metaphysical analysis of chapter 15 of *Insight*, which was cast in terms of conjugate potencies, forms, and acts.[52] The new analysis may be found spread over three chapters on the human good,[53] and this account of the human good is itself a significant contrast to the cosmic or ontological account of the good of chapter 18 of *Insight*.[54] These chapters identify four stages of human development: (1) undifferentiated common sense, (2) differentiated common sense, (3) differentiation of consciousness by the emergence of the intellectual pattern, and (4) applied science, applied philosophy, the emergence of historical consciousness.[55] Such differentiations may be regarded as explanatory, for they result from a combination of the invariant structure of the human good (the good as object of desire, the good of order, value) and the differentials (intellectual development, sin, redemption).[56]

Second, the a priori relevant to general history is provided by this differentiation of the human good rather than by the differentiation of the notion of being as in *Insight*. Correspondingly, the stages are now referred to as 'differentiations of consciousness' rather than 'differentiations of the notion of being,' or even 'modes of thought' as in 1959. This is a significant shift from the purely cognitional viewpoint represented in chapter 17 of *Insight* to a more concrete and existential viewpoint.

Third, the course makes explicit mention of the shift from faculty psychology to the flow of consciousness.[57] This is in fact the background to what we have been noting. The new analysis of human development, the concentration on the human good, and the new a priori for general history are all part of the shift of emphasis from metaphysics to the flow of consciousness.

5   1959–60: *De systemate et historia* and 'The Philosophy of History'

As far as philosophy and theology are concerned, there is the problem of the multiplicity of available upper blades stemming from the multiplicity of philosophies. Accordingly, the course *De systemate et historia* (Fall 1959) as well as the 1960 lecture 'The Philosophy of History' note that the upper blade in this case must be a philosophy of philosophies,[58] and the autograph of the lecture seems to imply that this philosophy of philosophies is the universal viewpoint of *Insight*.[59] *De systemate* even notes that such an upper blade must be related to all philosophies as mathematics is to all hypotheses and theories of physics. What is most interesting is the further remark that a system of this type can be constructed in several ways: (1) as Hegelian dialectic; (2) as something initially potential, to be perfected and determined through research; (3) as a *conceptual* potency; (4) as a potency of some other type, such as *operational*.[60]

Now this 'operational potency' is probably related to the notion of operational habit found in the archival text 'De circulo operationum.'[61] At any rate, the latter is to be distinguished from the 'operative habit' of the scholastics insofar as operative habits reside in some single and determinate potency, whereas operational habits can reside in several potencies at once: for instance, art involves the whole person, body and soul. Further, operational habits need not be restricted to a single mind, for science is an explicitly conscious operational habit,[62] and it is so extensive that it cannot be contained in a single mind.[63] Now if 'operational potency' is the same as 'operational habit,' then we can say that the universal viewpoint defined in this way transcends the restriction both to some single faculty and to a single mind. But perhaps we should be careful: if operational potency is related to the universal viewpoint, it does not follow that they are identical. For the universal viewpoint not only is formulated in a metaphysical context, but also is itself identical with the heuristic structure of dialectical metaphysics. A consistent shift, therefore, from faculty psychology to the flow of consciousness would require a shift from the universal viewpoint to something less ontological, such as the operational potency or habit we are discussing.

The third part of the lecture of 1960 concerns itself with the creation of an upper blade for fields resistant to conceptualization, and discusses the notion of dialectic as well as that of stages of development or differentiations of consciousness. Fundamentally, dialectic is within the individual: it is the contradiction between counterpositions and the dynamic structure of the subject qua intelligent and reasonable, and it is a principle of movement. The effect of such dialectic is change not merely in statements, but in the reality of the subject himself or herself.[64] Besides this fundamental dialectic, there is also dialectic between individuals. The dialogues of Plato are in fact an instance of concrete group-use of dialectic in the individual sense.[65] Further, there is dialectic stretched out over time or in history: Aristotle's dialectic as learning from various opinions of the past, Hegelian and Marxist dialectics, and the liberal notion of progress. The dialectic of history is itself an effect of dialectic in individuals.[66] As for the stages,[67] there recurs the observation that vague talk about Hebrew and Greek mentalities must be replaced by something more exact:

> In order to do the historical work of extending history back into the relatively primitive, or to understand the differences of the earlier and later civilizations, there is needed some exact knowledge of that differentiation, that movement from the undifferentiated consciousness, the primitive, to the later and fuller differentiations of consciousness.[68]

6   1961: *De Deo trino: Pars analytica*

In Part One of *De Deo trino: Pars analytica* of 1961, there may be found an extended application of the upper blade consisting of the stages of human thought to a concrete instance of transition in Christian theology. The instance in question is the emergence of the systematic mode of thought with the use of the term *homoousion* at the Council of Nicea.[69] The final section of the first part of the work contains in fact an analysis of the differences between the Hebrew and the Greek cultures.[70] Further, dogmatic development is described as dialectical, for it is marked by inexact formulations as well as by aberrations.[71] Thus, Lonergan distinguishes a material and a formal principle, the dialectical process itself, and the term or goal of the process. The material principle is an objective contradiction, either explicit or implicit. The formal principle is the rational subject under the aspect of his/her rationality, illumined either by the light of natural reason alone, or by the light of reason strengthened by the greater light of faith.[72] The dialectical process is the actual elimination of the contradiction:

> For it is a natural tendency of reason to get rid of contradictions. If the contradiction in question is only implicit, it is first made explicit; then one side of the contradiction can be clearly affirmed and the other denied. Where reason is somewhat tardy, or the matter itself rather difficult, the process is gradual: one by one, different elements of the contradiction are made explicit, until eventually the whole contradiction is eliminated.[73]

The term is either heresy or advance in theology.[74] Further, the dialectical process is grasped, not in any single author, considered apart, but in a whole series of authors, each in his/her own way trying to resolve the basic contradiction until at last it is in fact totally eliminated.[75] Finally, Lonergan's analysis is itself a result of the application of the genetico-dialectical upper blade to the dialectic of history.

7   Conclusion

The period 1954–61 exhibits radical continuity with *Insight*; there is even an explicit mention of the universal viewpoint in 1960. The article of 1954 seems content with the Aristotelian notion of science but acknowledges some contemporary methodological issues touching mostly upon historical investigation and its impact upon traditional theology; the course of 1959 instead tends to become somewhat more diffident about the Aristotelian notion of science, while working out a theological method that is largely an extension of the achievement of *Insight*.

The philosophy of education lectures of 1959 begin to speak about a shift from faculty psychology to the flow of consciousness. This is matched by a new, psychological analysis of development in contrast to the metaphysical analysis of chapter 15 of *Insight* and by a human account of the good in contrast to the cosmic or intellectual account of chapter 18 of *Insight*. The new analysis of development, formulated with help from Piaget, leads to a significant new notion of habit that, in contrast to the scholastic one, is confined neither to some single faculty nor to a single mind. As far as the universal viewpoint is concerned, this is an extremely significant development, signaling a step forward in the overcoming of the limitations of the notion that we noticed in Part One. More precisely, the shift from faculty psychology to the flow of consciousness leads to a new notion of habit, but also logically to the dropping of the term universal viewpoint, the reason being that the universal viewpoint is a metaphysical construct.

Simultaneously, the required a priori for general history is no longer merely the protean notion of being, but rather the more concrete notion of the human good, which includes a consideration of sin and redemption. The a priori for the history of philosophy remains the philosophy of philosophies; significantly, it is only in this context that we find a reference to the universal viewpoint, but that too only in an unpublished text.

6

Basic Context

In contrast to *De intellectu et methodo* (1959), which introduced the problem of method in various ways before going on to a consideration of method itself, *De methodo theologiae* (1962) dispenses with preliminaries and straightaway presents general notions concerning method.[1] Only after that does it go on to determine the questions or problems.[2] This is done in two steps. The first problematic[3] is rooted in 'basic antitheses,' and is concerned with the status of theology as a science.[4] This, it would seem, is a new way of stating the problem of the chasm and the question of the relevance of speculative theology. The antitheses are between the sacred and the secular, the outer and the inner, the visible and the intelligible. Science is concerned with the intelligible world; but the vast majority of humanity is content to remain within the visible or inner or sacred world. Now religion has to do with the sacred and the inner but also with the visible world; but theology is confined to the intelligible world.[5] Hence, doubts arise about the usefulness of traditional theology. Further, once it has been established that theology is a science, we must determine whether it must be a Greek type of science or a modern type.[6]

The second problematic instead is related to the question about the relationship between theology and positive studies. *De methodo theologiae* (1962) notes that this problematic arises from ideas about the social order, from history and hermeneutics, and that it has to do with theology as a science mediated by the Word of God and the order of the Body of Christ.[7] The *meaning* of the Word of God and the *order* of the Body of Christ belong to the same genus as other meaning and order. They therefore form part of the object of the *Geisteswissenschaften*. However, if this state of affairs involves a reduction of Catholicism to the level of merely human meaning and order, it cannot be accepted by Catholics. So there arises the question of methodology: to what extent do theology and the human sciences coincide, and where do they begin to diverge?[8]

We may note that a discussion of this second problematic is to be found in the Regis course of 1962, but not in the student notes pertaining to the course given at the Gregorian University. However, an archival folder pertaining to the Gregorian course contains an item headed 'Problematica altera': in all probability these are Lonergan's notes for a treatment of the second problematic within the course given at the Gregorian University.[9]

Against this background, let us go on to examine the general method of 1962, the differentiation of hermeneutics and history and the notion of basic context, and stages of meaning.

1   1962: General Method

The general method of 1959, we have seen,[10] follows *Insight* rather closely: it is a set of directives arising upon the appropriated structure of human knowing. The treatment of general method in 1962 instead seems to be different. The basis seems to be operations in general rather than cognitional operations alone, and method is described as a question of operating upon operations,[11] or as a question of a mediation of interiority.[12] Again, there is a consideration of the operating subject in general rather than of the knower. Further, three conversions are mentioned simultaneously: intellectual, moral, and religious. Moreover, we are told explicitly that method concerns the operations of intellect as well as will, and that it deals with being as well as the good.[13] Judgments of value are also discussed (judgments of credibility and credentity), and we are told that these, being judgments, are answers to the question, Is it so?[14]

The novelty is the direct result of the developments of the preceding years. Already in the 1956 text *De constitutione Christi* ..., and more especially in the 1957 lectures on existentialism, there is a focus on the notions of the subject, of authenticity, and of conversion. Still, these notions are not really new: *Insight* has much to say on the subject and on genuineness,[15] and the theme of conversion goes back to the *Gratia Operans* dissertation. The more significant development is the enriched notion of operation and of habit derived through a reading of Piaget for the 1959 lectures on education.[16] Operations begin from what scholastic philosophers call natural habits or potencies. They are differentiated and perfected through repetition upon a variety of objects. There follow combinations of differentiated operations, groups of operations, and grouping of groups.[17] Now the group of operations is not a single habit but rather a set of habits; and where Aristotle's habits were broken up according to potencies, the group of operations is united by a single development. Accordingly, the new notion derived from Piaget accounts better for the unity of habits.[18] The point is one we have noted already before: the new notion of habit is confined neither to some single faculty nor to a single mind.[19]

The methodological viewpoint considers objects only through the operations. In the Aristotelian-scholastic tradition, objects defined acts, and acts in turn defined potencies. Now, instead, the formal object is defined as what is reached through some group of combination of operations; de iure it is what is reached through some ideal group of combinations of operations; de facto it is what is reached through some particular group of combinations of operations.[20] 'That concrete, *de facto* consideration of the formal object is the methodological way of viewing things.'[21] Such a methodological viewpoint has the advantage of overcoming the static character of the traditional approach. For the traditional definition of theology does not distinguish different stages in the development of theology,[22] nor does it distinguish directly between proper developments and aberrations. When instead the formal object is considered de facto, one can distinguish stages in the development of theology by means of differences in the relevant group of operations,[23] and one can raise questions of authenticity and of dialectic as well.[24] One stops speaking of 'the nature of theology' and speaks instead of the dogmatic-theological context, where 'context' is defined by the group of combinations of differentiated operations involved in making any of the statements of the context.[25] 'Consequently, the methodical consideration of the formal object as *de facto* it is reached by theologians makes room for a historical consideration.'[26]

The general method of 1962 seems to be equivalent to the generalized empirical method of *Insight*, with its upper blade in the dialectical theorem. Thus it is described as comparative, genetic, and dialectical.[27] Comparing texts of different authors reveals differences. Understanding the differences reveals them to be genetic or else dialectical. Dialectical analysis introduces the normative element.[28] The Regis lectures indicate two practical canons of dialectic, that positions are to be developed and counterpositions to be reversed.[29] By the fact that it is comparative, genetic, and dialectical, method is also synthetic: it puts things together and arrives at a genetico-dialectical understanding of the situation.[30]

In the course of the discussion of the 'first problematic,' the synthetic character of method is put in terms of 'worlds': method achieves an integration not merely of the intelligible world but of different worlds. (Worlds are a way of speaking about the objective component of differentiations of consciousness.) Method arises out of an appropriation of the inner world; we can say, therefore, that the visible world and the intelligible world are integrated by the mediation of the inner world.[31] More precisely, method integrates not the worlds themselves, but rather the corresponding groups of operations on the part of subjects.[32] Methodical analysis gives the key to radical integration:

> Now, just as the world of imagination and language is far larger than the world of immediate sensitive apprehension, as the world of science and theory is far larger than the world of imagination and language, so the world of interiority, including all possibilities of operation, puts together these different worlds and envisages them at the most radical point, i.e., how you go about it.[33]

This is not really new, for the dialectical integration achieved in *Insight* was precisely an integration through appropriation of the world of interiority.

Later in the course, the integration is described in terms of wisdom; we may recall that *De intellectu* of 1959 had placed foundations precisely in wisdom.[34] The theological problem is to integrate the inner, the visible, and the intelligible worlds.[35] The Thomist synthesis was worked out on the basis of Aristotelianism, but Aristotelianism, though integrated, is incomplete. It integrates the visible and intelligible worlds, and also in a way the inner and outer worlds, though there is some danger of the inner world being ignored. But its scientific ideal is incomplete, for it is concerned with the certain, the unchanging, the per se, the necessary, the universal. It needs to be completed by the modern scientific ideal, with its emphasis on the probable, the changing, the *per accidens*, the de facto, the particular.[36] In many ways the modern ideal fits better with the Catholic fact, for the central elements of the Catholic faith – the incarnation, the redemption, the events narrated in the scriptures – are neither universal nor necessary.[37] Still, the Greek ideal is not simply to be eliminated; it must be enriched and corrected.[38] This Lonergan does by reducing both ideals to the two basic questions, What is it? and Is it?[39] Such an integration is described as a new type of wisdom that takes over the functions earlier assigned to prudence, on the grounds that it handles not only the universal and the necessary but also the particular, the contingent, the changing.[40]

In 1962 method is also described for the first time as transcendental,[41] though the name 'transcendental method' itself is not frequently used.[42] The method is transcendental in the scholastic sense: the operations of intellect and will aim at everything that is and that is good.[43] But there is also another sense in which it can be said to be transcendental, and this is the peculiarly Lonerganian sense.[44] Method in this sense examines not so much individual operations as their combinations, and points out a similarity between this combination of operations and the combination among the objects of the operations. Thus, there will be a similarity between the combination of operations in building a house and, on the other hand, the structure of the completed house. Now there are operations that arise naturally or with hypothetical necessity, and it is these operations that are relevant to transcendental method:

> [B]y natural or hypothetical necessity such combinations of operations are performed that from them one can deduce similar combinations in the objects of those operations. For example, if human knowledge of a proportionate object proceeds through experience, understanding, and judgement, it follows that that proportionate object itself has a threefold composition.[45]

Lonergan points out that, while there is some similarity between the above method and that of Kant, still one cannot conclude to an identity in every respect. There is some similarity, for the method first considers not objects but operations, and it considers combinations of operations that, arising by natural or hypothetical necessity, are in a way a priori;[46] and according to Kant, 'that science or theory is transcendental which considers not the objects but the mode of cognition, and that mode itself not in any way at all but according to *a priori* possibility.'[47] However, there is no identity, for the method is opposed to cardinal points of Kantian doctrine.[48]

What conclusions can we draw? First, a note about the notion of science. In 1954, the Aristotelian notion of science was found quite adequate for formulating the nature of speculative theology, but certain contemporary methodological problems still remained. In 1959, the Aristotelian notion of science begins to be seen as a problem: it conflicts with the notion of science implicit in historical studies. The 1962 course considers it as an integrated but incomplete ideal; the modern ideal of science is in many ways more suited to the Catholic fact. The solution, however, is not elimination but integration. It becomes evident that *Insight* was an attempt at precisely such an integration: generalized method is a new type of wisdom that integrates the functions earlier assigned to prudence. It is able to handle the intelligibility not only of the universal and abstract but also of the particular and concrete; thus it is able to handle historical intelligibility.

Second, general method is defined in terms of operations and of the operating subject in general rather than in terms of cognitional operations alone; this move, it would seem, is made possible by the new notion of habit worked out with help from Piaget. Again, method is able to handle not only intellectual but also moral and religious dimensions of the subject. But we recall that the generalized method of *Insight* was able to provide not only a method of metaphysics but also a method of ethics. This was done by considering the fuller invariant structure that arises when

118 Part Two: From *Insight* to *Method in Theology*

doing is added to knowing. Thus already in *Insight* generalized empirical method was capable of handling operations of intellect as well as will, and of dealing not only with being but also with the good.

What then is new about the general or transcendental method of 1962? The novelty, I would say, lies in a more thoroughgoing shift from faculty psychology to the flow of consciousness, a more harmonious application of the 'priority' of cognitional theory over metaphysics. The developments of 1959 – the human account of the good and the new, non-metaphysical analysis of human development – lead to a more consistent shift to a properly methodological viewpoint, a viewpoint that considers objects only through operations and through the subject. We may insist that this is a shift and not an abandonment: faculty psychology is not invalid; but the methodological viewpoint has its advantages for a theology that is not static but ongoing.

2   1962: Basic Context

The lectures on the philosophy of education had called for a proper concept of history, and had attempted to work out such a concept. This attempt is continued in a more extensive way in the course *De systemate et historia* of the same year, and a good synthesis is reached in the 1960 lecture on the philosophy of history. Now the Regis course of 1962 is significant for the differentiation it achieves between hermeneutics and history: the hermeneutical-historical method of chapter 17 of *Insight* is differentiated into a hermeneutics based on common sense and a history based on common sense mediated by ongoing philosophy and by the human sciences. The cause of such a differentiation is the acknowledgment of historical consciousness, of the distinction between the natural and the human sciences, and of meaning as constitutive. The human sciences differ from the natural sciences insofar as their objects, unlike the objects of the natural sciences, are either wholly or at least partially constituted through intentional human acts, through meaning.[49] This means that, while in the natural sciences one attains a bit of understanding at the end of a process, in the human sciences instead understanding comes first.[50] Data for the human sciences is data with meaning. But this implies that the type of understanding relevant to the human sciences is commonsense understanding;[51] accordingly, particular texts and contexts can be studied only by commonsense understanding, and hermeneutics is an art rather than a science,[52] a question of enlarging one's horizon through a self-correcting process of learning.[53] Still, meaning itself undergoes development, and so there may be discerned a *Wendung zur Idee* both in commonsense understanding and in the objects of the *Geisteswissenschaften*.[54] There is, therefore, place for a comparative method that isolates points of change and heads into genetic and dialectical method. But such a procedure amounts to a history that is explanatory.[55]

In 1962, therefore, there emerges a hermeneutics that is not scientific, but rather a question of commonsense understanding, judging, and stating the meaning of the text.[56] In this new account of interpretation, however, there does seem to be some echo of the universal viewpoint.

A first echo may be found in the new account of understanding a text. The first requirement is that one understand the thing, *die Sache* of the text. How does one understand the thing? In general, by proceeding from the potential knowledge one already possesses. One has certain habits of understanding, knowledge, and wisdom; in reading an author, one simply actuates one's acquired habits. Those acquired habits regard things, objects, what people write about.[57] The point is that a blind person will not understand an account of pictorial art; similarly, a person who is quite unfamiliar with his/her own acts of understanding is not going to understand a discussion about understanding.[58] So the Principle of the Empty Head (widespread in positivist and Catholic circles) is to be firmly rejected.[59] A *Vorverständnis* is essential. Interpretation just cannot be a question of taking a good look at what is out there, for out there are merely black marks on paper. Anything the interpreter does beyond giving a new edition of the textual datum is the fruit of his/her own experience, understanding, judgment.[60] At this point Lonergan goes on to say that the more the interpreter's sensibility and affectivity is developed, the more fully his/her understanding is developed, the more profound and wise his/her judgment is, the better will be his/her position for understanding exactly what the author is talking about. The fully developed interpreter, he says, is in potency to selecting any of the possible meanings of the text and picking out the one that fits;[61] and people like Bultmann, Ebeling, and Gadamer are in agreement on this point.[62]

Is this an echo of the universal viewpoint? We must qualify. It certainly does not amount to the second canon of hermeneutics, the canon of explanation,[63] for there is here no demand for relating documents, texts, interpretations among themselves, no demand for discovering the genetic and dialectical sequences of viewpoints and the genetic sequences of modes of expression. Is it an echo of the first canon of hermeneutics, the canon of relevance, which demands that the interpreter begin from the universal viewpoint?[64] Perhaps, but we must note that no methodical self-appropriation is called for, much less the formulation of a dialectical and metaphysical set of categories.

To this we must add what is said under 'The Development of the Interpreter.'[65] The universal viewpoint of chapter 17 of *Insight* was based upon attainment of intellectual conversion; here instead Lonergan does not hesitate to say that the classics in letters, religion, or philosophy may demand not only an intellectual but even a moral and a religious conversion.[66] Further, he brings in the social and communitarian dimension here in a way that is perhaps more explicit than in *Insight*. The classics create the tradition or the milieu in which they will be understood. When this tradition is authentic, genuine interpretations are easily understood and accepted; when the tradition is unauthentic, genuine interpretations are met with ridicule.[67]

Still, despite some echoes of the universal viewpoint, both understanding a text and judging this understanding are commonsense affairs in 1962. But something of the scientific interpretation of *Insight* may be found in the account of the statement of one's understanding of the text. A merely commonsense statement is not enough, for very little communication is likely to be achieved, unless like the scholar the audience has itself gone through the vast labor of reaching the viewpoint of the text.[68] Besides, there is a shift towards system in the texts themselves, among interpreters and critics, as well as among audiences. Successful communication, therefore, calls for a set of categories common to both objects and subjects. These Lonergan would obtain from the human sciences and from philosophy and theology: the human sciences would provide basic anthropological categories, and philosophies and theologies would provide categories regarding conversion or its absence, for philosophies and theologies are scientific statements of the foundations of basic orientations.[69]

At this point there arises the problem of the foundations of scientific communication, and the question here is what philosophy or theology to choose. Bultmann's solution is to use Heidegger's existentials in his interpretation of St Paul; the Tübingen school used Hegelian thought as the spine of historical development; and the third section of chapter 17 of *Insight* had presented its own proposal regarding scientific communication, for it had asked about how interpretation might escape relativity to a variety of particular audiences.[70] This last proposal is taken up and reworked in terms of 'basic context.'

In what recalls the totality of materials for interpretation, the particular contexts, and the totality of contexts of the subsection 'The Sketch' of chapter 17 of *Insight*,[71] there are distinguished material context, hermeneutic formal context, and historical formal context. Hermeneutic formal context 'is the dynamic mental and psychic background from which the author spoke or wrote; it is the set of habits of sensibility and skill, of intellect and will, that come to second act in the text.'[72] Historical formal context 'is the genetico-dialectical unity of a series of hermeneutic formal contexts.'[73] Basic context instead is a context of contexts;[74] it is 'a heuristic notion, partly determined and partly to be determined. It is what becomes determined in the totality of successful efforts at exegesis.'[75] Further, it is described as the pure desire to know, and as the root of all expression. Basic context is a reality that undergoes development, proceeding 'from the undifferentiated through differentiation to an articulated integration,' and such development is both individual and historical.[76] Further, basic context undergoes triple conversion, and is also subject to aberration.[77]

Basic context is a genetic and dialectical upper blade for interpretation.[78] As the pure desire to know, it is present and operative not only in individuals, both authors and interpreters, but also in history.[79] Basic context not only echoes the dialectical analysis of *De Deo trino: Pars analytica* (1961) but also makes explicit reference to it, for the description of basic context as studying series of authors and going beyond their intentions is followed by references to Tertullian, Origen, and Athanasius.[80] Such a basic context, which operates on the level of the historical series of interrelated contexts,[81] is quite opposed to Romantic concentration on the aesthetic, intersubjective, and symbolic dimensions of meaning to the neglect of the process of transition from one context to another.[82]

Clearly, then, basic context takes the place of the universal viewpoint. But the change of name cannot be overlooked, for it is an indication of a certain discontinuity or novelty. Such discontinuity or novelty is not hard to find. For first, there is the differentiation of the scientific hermeneutics of *Insight* into a hermeneutics based on common sense and a history that is explanatory; and so where the universal viewpoint was a tool for understanding, judging, as well as stating the meaning of a text, basic context seems to be relevant only as far as stating the meaning of a text is concerned. Second, basic context reflects the general method outlined in 1962, for if method can handle not only intellectual but also moral and religious conversion, basic context is itself 'a reality that undergoes conversion, intellectual, moral, and religious.'[83] Finally, the name 'basic context' is itself significant in the light of the fact that the epilogue of *Insight* had used the term 'upper context' and not 'universal viewpoint' when it wished to refer to the fuller invariant structure that included the level of doing.[84] Interestingly, our text makes a series of references to *Insight*, and among these is the following: 'Epilogue, on the addition of the dimension of faith to human development and dialectic.'[85] This is an indication that basic context is to be placed on a par with the theologically transformed universal viewpoint rather than with the 'humanist' viewpoint of chapter 17 of *Insight*. At any rate, the basic difference, we could say, is the shift away from faculty psychology and metaphysics to an analysis of consciousness.

How, we might ask, is basic context related to method? In the same way as the universal viewpoint: it is a heuristic structure for interpretation, and so provides the upper blade of hermeneutical and historical method. This is made especially clear in the lectures on history in the 1962 Regis course.[86] Bultmann's perspectivism is described as subscribing to a merely phenomenological objectivity, 'the objectivity of the fact that the interpretation occurs, that it expresses a significance from an historically occurring point of view.'[87] Such objectivity 'escapes involvement in the basic context of a realist philosophy,' for it fails to realize that there is the further objectivity that asks whether the view that arises from history is part of a historical aberration or not.[88] Lonergan himself would hold for a history operating through the scissors action of an upper blade (developing philosophy, human sciences) and a lower blade of common and 'uncommon' historical research.[89] The Regis course notes that this upper blade is the basic context, or what *Insight* had referred to as the protean notion of being. The methodological possibility of this upper blade is a fundamental understanding of the human being, the self-knowledge that can be arrived at through self-appropriation. Such an upper blade is the contribution of a critical philosophy to historical method.[90] The echoes of *Insight* are unmistakable.

The autograph notes for the Regis lectures on history provide some more details about critical philosophy. Such a critical philosophy provides the foundations of historical method. It is at the basis of the methodological distinctions drawn between common and exceptional developments of common sense, between common sense and science, between common sense, science, and philosophy, and between philosophy, faith, and theology.[91] Again, critical philosophy provides an ultimate basis for a critique of the results of historical work, for it can discuss what the historian was doing and what he or she overlooked in each case, thus reducing oversights to their causes, both theoretical and existential.[92] But such was the task of basic context that went beyond the intentions of authors.[93] Basic context is the upper blade contributed by a critical philosophy to historical method.

Thus, in 1962 we have a differentiation between hermeneutics and history, and the universal viewpoint as heuristic structure for hermeneutics is replaced by basic context. Basic context is relevant to both hermeneutics and history, and it differs from the universal viewpoint in the direction of greater concreteness: unlike the universal viewpoint, which was formulated in a metaphysical context and on the basis of cognitional structure, basic context is described as undergoing triple conversion in history. Thus, basic context should be placed on a par with the theologically transformed universal viewpoint rather than with the universal viewpoint of chapter 17 of *Insight*. This is not to say that the two are equivalent; but we will be able to say more on this point only in the course of the discussion of new theological foundations in chapter 8 below.

3 Stages of Meaning

In the Graham transcript of the Regis course of 1962, the chapters 'Hermeneutics' and 'History' are preceded by the chapter 'Meaning.' The relevance of this chapter on meaning is the same, it would seem, as the relevance of the section 'Limitations of the Treatise' in chapter 17 of *Insight*. In fact, this is mentioned explicitly: in all texts except the strictly scientific treatise, the linguistic form of meaning blends with other forms; thus, it is important to be familiar with these other forms, if we are to understand any text apart from the strictly scientific treatise.[94] Besides linguistic meaning there is intersubjective, aesthetic, and symbolic meaning.[95] Human expression is not merely logical. It has a logical component in the strict sense, but there is also the logic proper to imagination and affectivity. Therefore, if one is to properly grasp linguistic meaning, one has to be aware of and take into account these other levels of meaning.[96]

At this point one would expect a discussion of sequences or stages of meaning, and the discussion of basic context does contain hints of this. Basic context, we are told, 'is a reality that develops, that proceeds from the undifferentiated through differentiation to an articulated integration. Such development is both individual ... and historical (from primitives to contemporary culture).'[97] It is related to scientific statements of the commonsense understanding of texts 'as the upper blade of a scientific method to the lower blade,' where scientific statement 'presupposes the commonsense understanding of the text and employs in stating that understanding (1) the categories constructed from the text and (2) the categories constructed by human science.'[98] Still, the matter is much clearer in a lecture of 1962 entitled 'Time and Meaning.'

'Time and Meaning' wants to offer 'a sketch of the way in which meaning develops.'[99] The purpose of such a sketch is to help bridge the 'islands' that result from the study of literatures, cultures, philosophy, religion, and to overcome irreducible entities such as the Semitic mentality, the Buddhist mentality, the Japanese mentality.[100] Such a procedure, which is really another way of speaking about the upper blade, is opposed both to the fragmentation of romanticism and to the universalism of classicism, for romanticism attends to the concrete, the singular, the individual, the personal, the historical at the expense of an overall view, while classicism so exalts the universal, the ideal, the normative, the exemplary, as to ignore and sideline things in their particularity.[101] It is a question of describing the types of meaning and then putting them together in different ways so as to approximate to the combinations that have existed at various times in the course of human development.[102] But such a procedure presupposes some analysis of human development, and for such an analysis Lonergan tells us that he wants to turn, not to the 'ontological analysis of development' of *Insight*, but rather to the more detailed account outlined, with help from Piaget, in *De methodo theologiae* and in the Regis course of 1962.[103] The combination of the types of meaning with this analysis of development results in 'a basic line from the undifferentiated to the differentiated consciousness and as well, various types of distortion resultant when certain elements are not sufficiently developed or others are overdeveloped.'[104] The connection between basic context and stages of meaning is not difficult to see: if basic context is related to the protean notion of being, then stages of meaning are (1) the differentiations undergone by basic context in the course of history, and (2) an upper blade for scientific statement of the understanding of a text, and for a history that is explanatory.

4   Conclusion

The developments of 1959 are integrated into a new account of general method in 1962. The novelty lies in a subtle shift of emphasis from metaphysics and the consequent faculty psychology to interiority and the methodological viewpoint. The total absence of the term universal viewpoint, and its replacement by the more concrete basic context, is to be seen as a function of this shift. The other significant development is the differentiation between hermeneutics and history achieved in 1962.

7

Methodical Horizon

1   1963: Total and Basic Horizon

The writings of 1962 revealed the replacement of 'universal viewpoint' by 'basic context.' The texts of 1963 instead contain clear indications of a shift from the language of 'viewpoint' to that of 'horizon.' The notion of horizon features in practically all the articles, lectures, and courses of 1963. This notion was first introduced in the 1957 lectures on existentialism.[1] In 1962 it was objective rather than subjective, for it was described as 'the world, the totality of objects with which one can promptly deal in virtue of one's acquired habits.'[2] In 1963 instead it is described as being fixed by two poles, objective and subjective. Each pole conditions the other: the objective pole is taken, not materially, but from the point of view of the subjective pole, and vice versa.[3] Thus, horizon is described as a concrete variation of the Aristotelian-Thomist notion of potency and formal object. The two notions differ inasmuch as the scholastic concept concentrates on the object and considers it abstractly. They also differ in terms of concreteness: in place of the single potency, the subject pole of horizon is the concrete subject; in place of the abstract *ratio*, the object pole of horizon is the totality of objects attained by the concrete subject. Finally, in horizon we have a term that denotes the whole constituted by both concrete subject and concrete totality of objects.[4] We may note that this notion of horizon incorporates and carries forward the new notion of habit constructed with help from Piaget in 1959, which was restricted neither to some single faculty nor to a single mind.[5] Again, we may note that the subject-object polarity of horizon echoes the description of method as transcendental, with its combinations of objects corresponding to combinations of operations arising from natural or hypothetical necessity.[6]

Such a notion of horizon is 'technically simpler' than the notion of viewpoint,[7] because, we might surmise, it lends itself more naturally to the subject-object polarity, and also because it expresses better the mutual conditioning between the poles. Accordingly, 'Metaphysics as Horizon' makes a shift to the language of horizon:

> [O]nce all restrictions are removed, there can be no ulterior and higher viewpoint from which new aspects come to light with a consequent revision and reordering of previous acquisition. So the unrestricted viewpoint is ultimate and basic: it is wisdom and its domain is being.
> Now it is technically simpler to express the foregoing in terms of 'horizon.' ... [I]n the horizon of the wise man, the philosopher of the Aristotelian tradition, the objective pole is an unrestricted domain, and the subjective pole is the philosopher practicing transcendental method, namely, the method that determines the ultimate and so basic whole.[8]

We note that neither metaphysics nor the universal viewpoint are named here. What is named is the 'unrestricted viewpoint,' which is 'ultimate and basic,' and this unrestricted viewpoint is identified with wisdom. When further there is mention of the 'horizon of the wise man,' we have here a shift from viewpoint to horizon, in the direction of greater concreteness. For further light on this 'horizon of the wise man' we must turn to the concluding section of the review.

The basic affirmation is that Lonergan is unwilling to identify the 'horizon of the wise man' with metaphysics: unlike Coreth, he would not 'equate metaphysics with the total and basic horizon, the *Gesamt- und Grundwissenschaft*.'[9] The reason given is that metaphysics coincides with the objective pole but not with the subjective pole of the total and basic horizon.[10] From an objective viewpoint, metaphysics would be the supreme science. From a methodological viewpoint, when objects are considered only through operations, metaphysics is just one science among many. For the subjective pole of the horizon of metaphysics is the pure inquirer; as such, it is still under a measure of abstraction. But the subjective pole of the total and basic horizon is the incarnate inquirer, 'liable to mythic consciousness, in need of a critique that reveals where the counterpositions come from,' developing 'in a development that is social and historical, that stamps the stages of scientific and philosophic progress with dates, that is open to a theology that Karl Rahner has described as an *Aufhebung der Philosophie*.'[11] From the critique of such a subject pole, taken in all its dimensions, 'from a total viewpoint,' there results 'a transcendental doctrine of methods.'[12]

The point is that critical procedure yields not merely a method of metaphysics, but a general or transcendental method. The method of metaphysics is merely one specification of such a general method. Other specifications would include not only the range of particular methods and the dialectical range of alternative philosophic methods but also the methods of ethics and of theology.[13]

Thus, as far as the subjective pole of total and basic horizon is concerned, the method of metaphysics is just one among many possible methods.[14] But the objective pole of metaphysics is being, and being coincides with the good;[15] and so though 'metaphysics, as science, does not equate with the subjective pole' of the total and basic horizon, '[m]etaphysics, as about being, equates with the object pole of that horizon.'[16]

The total and basic horizon is therefore a normative notion: its subjective pole is the philosopher practicing transcendental method, and its objective pole is being.

With Crowe we can note the continuity of this position with *Insight*: already in *Insight*, metaphysics was no longer the *Gesamt- und Grundwissenschaft*: it had fulfilled the *Gesamt*-function, but the *Grund*-function was already being taken over by cognitional theory. This would seem to be also Lonergan's own opinion, as may be seen from the following response to a question at the Dublin course of 1971:

> Where I differ from Coreth precisely you will find in the last paragraph of my article 'Metaphysics as Horizon,' ... Fundamentally, my point is that there is a dialectic, a range of opposing viewpoints, and that that is the fundamental problem in science and philosophy – especially in philosophy and theology.[17]

Even more explicitly, in a paper of 1973 Lonergan notes that already in *Insight*, though '[w]ithout the explicit formulations that later were possible, metaphysics had ceased for me to be what Fr. Coreth named the *Gesamt- und Grundwissenschaft*.'[18] The reasons given are that the empirical sciences were allowed to work out their own basic terms and relations, that the basic inquiry was cognitional theory and not metaphysics, and that the influence of faculty psychology had been broken in favor of intentionality analysis.[19]

Crowe, however, thinks that the later Lonergan would modify even this position. 'His final integral view seems better expressed in "Questionnaire on Philosophy"; now total philosophy has four parts: cognitional theory, epistemology, metaphysics, and existential ethics.'[20] Would this mean that in Lonergan's final thinking, metaphysics loses its claim even to the *Gesamt*-function? I would think not, for as far as the object pole of the total and basic horizon is concerned, being and the good coincide. What then could be said about Crowe's opinion? Perhaps only this: that while there is no fundamental novelty in Lonergan's final position, there is instead a clear grasp and a neat solution to the problem of the relationship between metaphysics and ethics. For when priority is given to the object, and metaphysics is considered as the total science, questions arise about the place of ethics in such a scheme of things. When instead priority is given to operations, and a general or transcendental method is derived from a critique of the concrete subject, this method can easily be extended to obtain not only a method of metaphysics but also a method of ethics and of theology. Unity is achieved by shifting consistently from a logical to a methodical viewpoint. That is why the 'Questionnaire' can say: the *Gesamt- und Grundwissenschaft* is not metaphysics, but a compound of cognitional theory, epistemology, metaphysics, and existential ethics.[21]

From the point of view of our study, the article of 1963 is very significant. If *Insight* gave the impression that metaphysics was the unrestricted viewpoint, the present article makes it very clear that it is not. The unrestricted viewpoint that is ultimate and basic is wisdom, and this wisdom is a total and basic horizon, the objective pole of which is being and the subjective pole is the philosopher practicing transcendental method. Metaphysics is merely one of the fruits of transcendental method.

As for the universal viewpoint, there is no mention of it in 'Metaphysics as Horizon,' but we should keep in mind the shift from the language of viewpoint to that of horizon.

2   Spring 1963: Methodical Horizon

In keeping with the declared shift from the language of viewpoint to that of horizon, the *De methodo* course of spring 1963 carries out a radical reworking of familiar notions in terms of horizon. In place of genetic sequences of viewpoints, the course speaks of relative horizons.[22] These are rooted in development, and result more from external factors than from inner conditions. Thus psychological development is the result of education, social development is the result of society, and cultural development is affected principally by the age in which one lives.[23] In place of dialectical sequences of viewpoints, the course speaks of transcendental horizons rooted in conversion. This conversion, though it has external conditions, is deliberate, free, responsible, existential choice, and so is principally in and by the individual.[24] Thus, relative horizons do not negate the existence of other horizons, but transcendental horizons introduce absolute oppositions: what lies beyond them does not exist for the individual concerned, has no value, cannot be known.[25]

Since there can be conversion as well as lack of conversion, there is need for further analysis of transcendental horizon. There are distinguished originary[26] and existential poles, and implicit and explicit fields. The originary pole is the structure of consciousness, and so is common to all. The existential pole is the subject constituting himself or herself; it is proper to the individual. The explicit or objectified field is a method, a philosophy, a theology. The implicit or exercised field is manifested in the way one operates, orders investigations de facto, etc.[27]

Now pole and field are correlative by definition. According to intention, originary pole and explicit field correspond. From the nature of things, the existential pole and the implicit field correspond, for *qualis quisque est, talis finis videtur ei*. Authenticity is the coincidence of the existential and the originary poles, and the consequent coincidence of implicit and explicit fields.[28] Unauthenticity may be radical or derived. It is radical when there is divergence between the existential and the originary poles. It is derivative and implicit when the implicit field corresponds to the unauthentic existential pole. When the explicit field is an objectification of the unauthentic existential pole and its corresponding implicit field, there obtains rationalization. When instead the explicit field objectively expresses the originary pole, but is distorted by the influence of the unauthentic existential pole, there obtains obnubilation.[29]

Now, given the possibility of a variety of existential poles rooted in the presence or absence of the three types of conversion, there exist a variety of transcendental horizons. Further, transcendental horizons may be objectified in various ways: symbolically, philosophically, theologically, or methodologically.[30] Accordingly there may be formed the notion of *methodical horizon*. Methodical horizon is one possible objectification of transcendental horizon. Materially it includes all transcendental poles and all transcendental fields. Formally it may be considered heuristically, and then it is such a totality as to be genetically and dialectically ordered; it may be considered historically, and then it is in some actual genetic and dialectical order.[31]

Methodical horizon is clearly another name for the total and basic horizon,[32] for it considers not only all possible transcendental fields but also all possible transcendental poles, and so it is unrestricted not only objectively but also subjectively. Again, the transcendental poles regard not merely intellectual but also moral and religious conversion.[33]

In the light of the distinction between relative and transcendental horizon, and of the analysis of transcendental horizon, Lonergan proceeds to outline a method in terms of horizon analysis. Method consists in determining the horizons of Christians, writers, historians, critics.[34] It is positive as well as critical. Positively, it is hermeneutics and history. Critically, it judges and discerns progress as well as aberration. It has an a priori element, for it anticipates that various elements of data will be either similar or dissimilar (comparative method), that the elements that are similar can be grouped together (organic method), that the elements that are dissimilar will be related either genetically or else dialectically (genetic and dialectical method).[35]

Such a method shows continuity in development, and thus handles the problem of continuity and of transposition from one context to another. For the originary pole experiences, inquires, doubts, deliberates, and it develops psychologically, socially, culturally. The existential pole undergoes or else fails to undergo intellectual, moral, and religious conversion. The implicit fields move to becoming explicit in philosophies, theologies, methodologies. In the absence of such distinctions, however, nothing remains except relative differences, psychological, social, cultural, and there emerge Hebrew, Greek, and other mentalities as irreducible and ultimate.[36]

In the preceding section we had noted that total and basic horizon is the new form of wisdom that does not coincide with but rather includes the horizon of metaphysics. In the present section it should have become evident that total and basic horizon, or methodical horizon, also tends to take over the functions of the notion of the universal viewpoint. It distinguishes itself from the universal viewpoint by its greater concreteness on the side of the subject. Since it is able to handle religious and moral as well as intellectual conversion, it is, like the basic context of 1962, closer to the 'completely concrete context' of the theologically transformed universal viewpoint of the epilogue of *Insight* rather than to the universal viewpoint of chapter 17 of *Insight*. This is not to say that the two are identical, however; the achievement of the new notion of faith allows the new horizon of theology to drop the classicist elements of the theologically transformed universal viewpoint of the epilogue of *Insight*. But more of this in chapter 8.

In conclusion we may note that the term 'methodical horizon' occurs only in the spring 1963 course, and that even here it is not a frequently used term. Again, the term 'transcendental method' is avoided on the whole,[37] possibly in order to avoid confusion with the term 'transcendental horizon.' Lonergan speaks more often simply of 'method,'[38] but makes it quite clear that this method is grounded on the transcendental element.[39] But the summer course of 1963, Knowledge and Learning, prefers to speak of absolute horizons instead of transcendental horizons, and the return to the term 'transcendental method' in the *De methodo theologiae* course of fall 1963 might perhaps be tied to this shift in terminology.

In the fall 1963 course, method is described as consisting of transcendentals on the side of the object as well as on the side of the subject. This course seems to be more 'conservative' than that of spring 1963, in the sense that methodical horizon is never mentioned, and transcendentals on the side of the subject include questions for intelligence and for reflection, experience, understanding, and judgment, but nothing pertaining to the level of doing. Still, the transcendentals on the side of the object include not only *ens, unum,* and *verum* but also *bonum*.[40] Objectifications of transcendentals on the side of the subject are named *communia* or common principles or notions; these are common precisely because they are the conditions of the possibility of any investigation whatsoever.[41] Such common principles are normally latent; they become explicit through the sciences and through philosophy, and this process can itself be perfected.[42] The process of objectification is of course dialectical.[43] Further, the common principles are described as constituting a transcendental heuristic structure for the investigation of the proper principles,[44] the latter being principles that do not possess philosophic generality but are instead proper to some particular field.[45]

The spring course of 1963 had spoken of major critics; the present course often describes transcendental method as 'critical,'[46] and *Insight* itself is referred to as 'fundamental critics.'[47]

The notion of horizon is added on together with the notion of meaning as a sort of appendix to the course. Both horizon and meaning are described as notions that are clearly fundamental,[48] and horizon is referred to as a fundamental heuristic notion for the investigation of meaning.[49] There follows the distinction between relative and absolute horizons, the mention of three types of conversion, and of four types of method (comparative, organistic, genetic, and dialectical). In an echo of method as horizon analysis, we are told that all study is a question of determining the relative and absolute horizons of authors.[50]

3 Conclusion

The developments of 1959 and 1962 pour into a new notion of horizon. This new notion of horizon is bipolar. Its subject pole incorporates the new and more concrete notion of habit developed with help from Piaget; its object pole is that set of objects corresponding to the group of operations forming the subject pole. This notion of horizon replaces the old Aristotelian-scholastic notions of potency and formal object, and is therefore one more step in the shift away from faculty psychology to interiority analysis. The clear identification of the 'horizon of the wise man' with a total and basic horizon that is not identical with metaphysics is to be placed in the light of this development.

We may draw, therefore, the following line of development: the *Verbum* articles speak of wisdom as having two aspects, epistemological and metaphysical. In *Insight*, these two aspects of wisdom may be identified with generalized empirical method and a metaphysics that is explicitly dialectical and so supplies a universal viewpoint. In the courses of 1962, the universal viewpoint becomes 'basic context,' the difference being that the latter is broader and more concrete than the former. In 1963, the functions of the universal viewpoint – or of basic context – are taken over by total and basic horizon or methodical horizon. Like basic context, the latter is broader and more concrete than the universal viewpoint.

A question that remains regards the relationship between transcendental method and methodical horizon. We have noted above that the subject-object polarity of horizon echoes the 1962 description of method as transcendental, as examining combinations of operations and concluding to similar combinations among the objects of the operations.[51] It is possible, therefore, that methodical horizon is another way of speaking about transcendental method itself. At the present stage, however, this has to remain at the level of a suggestion; but if this suggestion were substantiated, we would have a situation in which generalized method itself would take the place of the habit of wisdom.

8

New Theological Foundations

In our conclusions at the end of chapter 4 we had noted two sources of tension in the post-*Insight* period, the first being the involvement of the universal viewpoint in faculty psychology, and the second the elements of classical fundamental theology in the theological transformation of the universal viewpoint. Chapters 5, 6, and 7 have revealed the attempts to make a consistent shift from faculty psychology to interiority analysis and the effect of these on the universal viewpoint. The present chapter instead will focus on the attempt to overcome the classical notion of theology and its effect on theological transformation of the universal viewpoint. As will become evident, our two points are linked: new theological foundations arise through a consistent application within theology of the shift from faculty psychology to analysis of interiority.

1   1964: Focus on Theological Foundations

1.1 Antecedents

A series of developments form the background to the focus on foundations in the 1964 Georgetown course, of which we will note just two: the emergence of elements of new theological foundations in the years 1959–63, and the distinction between positive and dogmatic theology in 1963.

1.1.1 Emerging New Theological Foundations

Crowe has noted that *De intellectu et methodo* of 1959 represents 'the first documented thematizing of foundations as the problem occurs in theology.'[1] Foundations here are not yet the foundations of theology as such, but rather foundations of the transitions from one ordering of doctrines to another,[2] and the reason for this, says Crowe, is that theology is still conceived classically.[3] In fact, the Nottingham lecture of the same year affirms quite clearly that 'theology presupposes faith' and that faith, at least for the Catholic, includes judgment: it is 'an acceptance of truths revealed by God and taught by his church.'[4] The starting point of theology is, therefore, in the truths of revelation. Still, this position is not without its nuances, for it is also affirmed that '[t]here are, indeed, data that are just data as in the other sciences: most exegetical and historical questions are of that character.'[5]

The courses of 1962 make it very clear that method is able to handle all three conversions,[6] and this is significant for theological foundations. The classical notion of faith as including judgment continues to be affirmed up to 1965,[7] but significantly the deductive transition into the realm of theology through the proof of God's existence is never mentioned.[8] Linked to this failure to mention the deductive transition is the hint of a dissatisfaction with apologetics on the grounds that it is extrinsicist and that it tends to overlook the human mind.[9]

In such a context there must be situated the statement from *De methodo theologiae* (Spring 1963) that, though method of itself is a human science, it is automatically theology because it includes the transcendental horizon and hence the three conversions.[10] This statement is the immediate antecedent of the observation of 1964 that the turn of philosophy to the concrete subject is also its return to theology.[11]

1.1.2 The Distinction between Positive and Dogmatic Theology

The second development to be noted is the achievement of a clear distinction between positive and dogmatic theology. The important factor here is the challenge of the *Geisteswissenschaften*.[12] In chapter 6 we have seen how the struggle with the difference between the natural and the human sciences led in 1962 to the differentiation of the hermeneutics of *Insight* into a hermeneutics based on common sense and a history that is explanatory.[13] In the theological field this differentiation leads to a distinction between exegesis and positive dogmatic theology:[14] the former is concerned with particular contexts, while the latter is concerned with transpositions from one context to another.[15] Again, the former takes texts as data, but the latter begins from the word of God as true.[16] The works of 1963 systematize this distinction and stabilize it by means of a change in terminology. What was hitherto called exegesis, positive studies, positive investigations, positive research or specialized positive theologies is now called positive theology and what was referred to as positive theology, dogmatic theology, positive dogmatic theology, historical theology, or the *via historica* is now called simply dogmatic theology.[17] The point here is that positive research is now clearly accepted as an 'integral part' of theology.[18]

De Deo trino: I notes that dogmatic theology in the strict sense is concerned with the *munus nobilissimum* of exposing the dogmas and showing how they are contained in the sources.[19] It differs from positive theology in its proper object, its goal, its method. Positive theology is concerned with particular authors and contexts, but dogmatic theology is concerned with transitions over contexts.[20] The former does not seek to determine what must be taught by the church and believed by all; the latter is concerned with that which has been believed everywhere, always, and by all the faithful.[21] Positive investigation is *in oratione obliqua*: it does not itself propose doctrine about God, but instead narrates the theology of others of the past;[22] dogmatic theology instead is *in oratione recta*: it seeks to present doctrine about God.[23]

The positive and the dogmatic parts of theology differ not only in their proper objects and in their goals but also in their methods. Their questions are different: the former raises only those questions that arise immediately from the data, and does not seek a broad view except by the slow acquisition of details; such a broad view is instead the principal concern of dogmatic theology, for its whole problematic arises from the fact that the scriptures, the fathers, the theologians, and the councils seem to be saying different things.[24] Again, the positive theologian does not put aside the obscure, the rare, the doubtful, but the dogmatist who seeks the foundations of the dogmas cannot find the certain, the common, and the clear in the doubtful, the rare, and the obscure. Because of this, positive and dogmatic theology attend to different aspects of the data; and if they consider the same aspect, they proceed differently, the former wanting to someday determine the full meaning, the latter instead seeking that meaning which may be minimal, but must be certain and clear.[25]

With the establishment of the distinction between positive and dogmatic theology, Lonergan can speak of three clearly distinct parts of theology: the positive, the dogmatic, and the systematic. *De Deo trino: I* also names a fourth part, the instrumental, which produces critical editions, indices, bibliographies, and dictionaries.[26] But presiding over all these parts is the sapiential or methodical part, which distinguishes the other parts, assigns their functions and tasks, and directs their collaboration.[27] Method has, therefore, the sapiential function of integrating the various parts of theology by ordering them, and such integration would seem to be effected by relating the parts of theology to the structure of knowing.[28] We might note that the idea of functional specialization is beginning to emerge, for positive, systematic, and dogmatic theology are described as specializations of experience, understanding, and certitude respectively.[29]

1.2 Method as Foundational

If *De intellectu et methodo* of 1959 represents 'the first documented thematizing of foundations as the problem occurs in theology,'[30] the Georgetown Institute of 1964 represents a focus on the problem of theological foundations as such.[31] In keeping with the characterization in 1963 of method as sapiential, Lonergan declares: 'From my standpoint, method and [the] foundational [part of theology] more or less coincide.'[32] This means that theological foundations in 1964 are concerned not so much with the transition to faith as with theological method. It also means that the long introductory discussions about the problem of method in theology in the various editions of the trinitarian treatises are really discussions about foundations.

The emergence of a new notion of science, the shift from classicism to historical consciousness, and the emergence of new philosophies are the external factors in the problem of method in theology.[33] These factors have entered Catholic theology through positive studies.[34] Now such an addition of a new type of studies demands an organic adaptation of previous departments and so a transformation of the whole. Within such a whole,

> (a) the operative notion of science cannot be both Greek and modern, (b) the effective mode of consciousness cannot be both classicist and historical, (c) the philosophic ancilla in actual use cannot be both of the medieval and the modern type.[35]

This problem, points out Lonergan, is not of course grasped with such clarity; it surfaces rather in the form of the instability of both traditional 'dogmatic' theology and positive theology: the former is destroyed by the latter, and the latter is in turn destroyed by investigation into its epistemological and ontological presuppositions.[36]

Lonergan's solution is to place new theological foundations in the concrete subject, and here he brings forward the developments of 1962-63.

Insight had achieved a shift from faculty psychology to analysis of interiority, from logic to method, from a concentration on objects to a concentration on operations, but this shift was not always carried out in a consistent manner. The thematization of this shift in 1959 and the new notion of development and of the human good makes possible the account of general method presented in 1962, as well as the notion of total and basic horizon or methodical horizon of 1963. The institute on *Method in Theology* given at Georgetown University in 1964 in turn not only achieves an extremely clear thematization of the shift from logic to method,[37] but also pushes the method of 1962 further in the direction of the subject through its recognition of the ultimately existential character of any method. Thus, its discussion of the 'modern type of philosophy' notes that such a philosophy is concerned not with the per se, de iure subject, but rather with the concrete, self-constituting subject. But this means that a modern type of philosophy faces a critical problem:

> A modern type of philosophy acknowledges a basic critical problem: as it is concerned, not with reality insofar as, abstractly considered, it contains elements of necessity, but with the concrete universe, so it is concerned with the subject, not as per se or de iure he may be classically supposed to be, but as de facto he is, as de facto he makes himself what he is, as de facto he can be helped (though not dictated to) in making himself what he is to be.[38]

For the needed foundations, contemporary philosophy turns to the subject. These foundations are one's own experience of what it is to experience, understand, judge, be responsible. Such operations ground all philosophy, all science, all historical consciousness.

> The philosopher, scientist, historian ... that attends to [such operations], that understands their network, that discovers that such relationships are not just objects but the normative reality of his own intelligence, reasonableness, responsibility, has reached what is at once immediate and ultimate. Immediate, because that normative reality is his own being in its intellectual, rational, moral luminousness; ultimate, because that reality is already presupposed by any intelligent, reasonable, or responsible attempt to go beyond it.[39]

Further, the foundations provided are critical, for one *can* be intelligent, reasonable, responsible, but one does not *have to be* intelligent, reasonable, responsible.[40]

The repeated mention of responsibility in the above discussion should not be missed.[41] The solution to the critical problem cannot be imposed: one can merely help the de facto subject to make himself or herself what he/she is to be. Some will of course dodge responsibility, others will rationalize such escapism, still others will find no way out of relativism; but there exists 'the difficult way of *authenticity*, of discovering in oneself the exigences of one's own intelligence, rationality, responsibility, and of working out and accepting and living the consequences.'[42] Since such authenticity 'is not automatic, not to be assumed, presupposed, taken for granted,' but rather is something 'to be discovered, struggled for, conquered, won, achieved, maintained,' there is no automatic solution to the critical problem.[43] The existential aspects of method are coming to the fore. Lonergan does not in fact hesitate to say: 'Method is unpleasantly existential.'[44] The discussion ends with the remark that the turn of philosophy to the concrete subject is its return to theology:

> [A] philosophy that rejects extrinsecism, that begins from the self-appropriation of the subject = his self-mediation with respect to a tradition = mutual self-mediation within a tradition,
> begins with man as he concretely is, as a member of a community, as a receiver and transmitter of a tradition, as in need of conversion such a starting point is isomorphic with the starting-point of one that inquires into Christian claims
> while there are two formally distinct starting points, there is only one full solution: when one deals with man in the concrete, one is dealing with man under original sin, in need of grace, receiving it, and either accepting or rejecting it – one is in a theological context.[45]

Both the mention of the inquiry into Christian claims and the rejection of extrinsecism bring to mind the old fundamental theology or apologetics: where these concentrated on the preambles or presentation of the evidence for faith, the new theological foundations are concerned with the concrete subject.[46] Lonergan is aware of the difference: in fact, he distances himself explicitly from the old fundamental theology. The foundational part of theology is not fundamental theology but rather the presuppositions of all that theology does (in positive, dogmatic, or systematic theology).[47] It is concerned

> with the Catholic position as a whole, not in its entirety, but *in its roots*; *in conversion*; in the precise location of differences from other positions; in the precise formulation of Catholic presuppositions, the divisions of theology, their respective methods, the integration of the separate parts.[48]

But if theological foundations are distinct from fundamental theology, Lonergan still thinks of them in terms of the illumination of reason by faith. Since, further, 'reason' is human knowing as an operational structure,[49] illumination of reason by faith is the transformation of that structure by faith.⁵⁰ Again, if appropriation of the operational structure of human knowing is method, and provides critical philosophical foundations, then transformation of that structure by faith results in theological method and provides theological foundations. Further, while the other parts of theology are related to the levels of knowing, the foundational part is related to the intention of being itself;⁵¹ the latter relationship casts further light on the coincidence of the foundational part of theology with method.⁵²

Given that the starting point of both philosophy and theology is the concrete subject, the transformation here is to be understood not in terms of a shift from a philosophy *in statu naturae purae* to a supernatural theology, but rather in terms of the dynamism of a moving viewpoint. It could be added further that this would seem to be the case already in *Insight*. On this showing, the position of 1964 differs from that of *Insight* in emphasis rather than in substance. In like manner, the theological transformation itself yields results that are not different from the position of *Insight*: data is the word of God as true;⁵³ understanding is of mysteries;⁵⁴ judgment is within the church.⁵⁵ The major difference stems from the distinction between hermeneutics and history achieved in 1962 and the correlation of positive, systematic, and dogmatic theology to experience, understanding, and judgment respectively. Thus, where the epilogue of *Insight* had a historical theology operating on the 'broader basis' that included the theologically transformed universal viewpoint, now we have a positive theology *in oratione obliqua* and a dogmatic theology concerned with the *munus nobilissimum*; yet both form part of theological method, and both arise from theological transformation of the operational structure of human knowing.

Such a position hides a tension: positive theology is *in oratione obliqua*, and yet theological data is the word of God as true. The root of the tension would seem to be the classical notion of faith by means of which method is transformed. From the information available to us about the 1964 Institute, however, there is no indication that Lonergan is aware of this tension; but it would seem that this is one of the factors leading to the breakthrough of 1965.

2   1965: Breakthrough

The breakthrough of February 1965 to eight operational specializations⁵⁶ may be seen as a result of the logic of the correlation of theological parts to the structure of consciousness. For in 1964 there is regular mention of the level of responsibility,⁵⁷ and this level is even indicated in a diagram in the Wilker notes;⁵⁸ yet the operational structure continues to be referred to as the structure of human knowing, and there is no theological part corresponding to the level of responsibility.[59] In 1965, on the other hand, it is precisely this anomaly that is resolved. There is a clear affirmation of the four levels of consciousness[60] and of theological parts or operational specializations on each level. Further, theology is described as operating in two modes, for there is tradition to be assimilated, as well as assimilation of tradition; there is hearing as well as saying. The former is a question of determining what John and Paul and Isaiah said; it is *in oratione obliqua*; the latter is a question of deciding one's own personal stance; it is *in oratione recta*. There result accordingly eight operational specializations. The movement is from research through interpretation and history (*Historie* – the history that is written) to conversion, and then from foundations through doctrine and explanation to communication.[61]

The dogmatic theology of 1963 seems to have undergone differentiation into 'history,' which operates *in oratione obliqua*; 'conversion' and 'foundations,' which operate on the fourth level; and 'doctrines,' which operates *in oratione recta*. Dialectic continues to form part of history,[62] and within history it sets the fundamental alternatives of judgments,[63] while decisions are taken in the operational specialization, conversion. Conversion is one's encounter with history; it is an existential as well as an interpersonal decision.[64] Foundations, instead, deals with the objectification of conversions, that is, with positions and counterpositions,[65] or with basic categories, which amount to the same thing.[66] The echo of the basic context might be noted, for basic context was the foundation of categories required for scientific communication; and interestingly, the objectification of basic context occurs on the fourth level of consciousness.

Given that history is now *in oratione obliqua*, it might be said that the earlier positive theology has been replaced by the three operational specializations, research, interpretation, and history. But the starting point of theology in truths continues to be affirmed.[67] Still, it would seem that an effort to address the tension has begun in earnest. A first indication is the differentiation of the foundations of 1964: while method continues to underlie and ground the theological specializations, it is now referred to not as the foundational part of theology but as transcendental method; and in addition to this there is the operational specialization foundations. Second, 'foundations' as the fifth operational specialization is preceded by 'conversion' as the fourth specialization. It would seem therefore that, while general foundations underlie the whole of theology, the specifically theological principle has been shifted from the beginning of theology to the point of transition between the first and second phases of theology. Still, it remains that available evidence about the breakthrough does not reveal any qualification of the position that the starting point of theology is in revealed truths.

We could, therefore, agree with Crowe that the breakthrough of 1965 is precisely a breakthrough and not yet an encirclement,[68] and that classical elements persist, especially regarding the starting point of theology. There is, therefore, much work to be done before the position of *Method* is reached. The chief elements in the subsequent development are (1) the affirmation of a largely empirical theology, which removes any doubt about the starting point of theology; (2) the effort to specify the new foundations in religious conversion: the emergence of the notion of value, the affirmation of the primacy of praxis, the new description of religion, the new notion of faith, the inversion of the relationship between knowledge and love; and (3) the replacement of the functional specialty conversion by the functional specialty dialectic. The next section will take up the first two points, while the last point will be dealt with in Part Three.

3 1967–68: Achievement of New Theological Foundations

3.1 The New 'Largely Empirical' Theology

The title as well as the contents of the 1967 lecture 'Theology in Its New Context'[69] reveal its links to the 1964 discussions of the problem of theological method and of theological foundations. The emergence of a new context demands a new theology. The lecture draws a contrast between the old deductive theology with its starting point in truths, and the new largely empirical theology, which takes scripture and tradition not as premises but as data.[70] Acknowledgment of history, of evolution, and of development gives the lie to the classicist conception of theology, for no single theologian can master all the data of theology. Since, further, the results of particular research remain at best probable, a deductivist theology is quite out of the question.[71]

But acknowledgment of a largely empirical theology only makes more acute the question of theological foundations:

> One type of foundation suits a theology that aims at being deductive, static, abstract, universal, equally applicable to all places and to all times. A quite different foundation is needed when theology turns from deductivism to an empirical approach, from the static to the dynamic, from the abstract to the concrete, from the universal to the historical totality of particulars, from invariable rules to intelligent adjustment and adaptation.[72]

Again, the old fundamental theology consisted in objective statements; but these statements no less than the other treatises they claimed to found, themselves stand in need of foundations.[73] As a text of 1970 notes, the old fundamental theology wanted to be scientific and logical, but actual achievement tended to be merely rhetorical.[74] Even more clearly, a paper of 1973 notes that the arguments of the old fundamental theology do not prove: they merely deal with 'reasons which can justify the acceptance of faith as a moral option for a serious conscience.'[75] We might note that the fundamental theology mentioned in *Analysis fidei* and exemplified in the final part of *Insight* fits this description perfectly: it belonged to the remote process leading to the assent of faith, but the assent itself was a personal act.[76] Between traditional fundamental theology and the act of faith there was a hiatus, a leap.[77]

3.2 New Theological Foundations in Religious Conversion

The 1964 Institute, while noting that new theological foundations were to be placed in the concrete subject, and more specifically in conversion, had failed to specify such foundations adequately. 'Theology in Its New Context' instead begins to specify the new theological foundations, and it does so precisely through an analogy with the sciences. A first approximation notes that the foundation of a modern science is its method, where method is to be understood not so much as a set of rules but as the grounds governing such rules. Further, since this method is usually not formulated, the foundation may be described as the concrete reality of the subject as scientist.[78] A second approximation notes that conversion is fundamental to religion, and that conversion viewed as personal, communitarian, and historical coincides with living religion. Since, further, theology is reflection on religion, reflection on conversion can provide theology with its foundation. 'Just as reflection on the operations of the scientist brings to light the real foundation of the science, so too reflection on the ongoing process of conversion may bring to light the real foundation of a renewed theology.'[79]

Such theological foundations would bring the final part of *Insight* in line with the procedures followed in the earlier part. For *Insight* had established cognitional foundations by means of a long appeal to experience, by means of a generalized empirical method; but its last chapters had failed to appeal explicitly to religious experience.[80] But this is exactly what the proposal of 1967 attempts to do: it seeks theological foundations in a thematization of religious experience.

3.3 The Primacy of the Existential

While the broad outlines of the new type of theological foundations are laid down in 'Theology in Its New Context,' several key notions have to be developed before these outlines can be properly fleshed out. The first among these is the new notion of value and the concomitant affirmation of the primacy of the existential.

During a question session in 1976, Lonergan noted that in *Insight* the good was conceived metaphysically, as the intelligible in act. This, however, was the good from a divine viewpoint, from within the intellectualist tradition; it was not the human good, 'the human part of the story.'[81] The problem was that while *Insight* had distinguished the third and fourth levels from a psychological point of view, it had no corresponding psychological notion of the good.[82] Now if this is the case, the true emergence of the fourth level of consciousness is to be associated with the emergence of the psychological or human notion of the good; and such a notion emerges in the 1968 lecture 'The Subject.'[83] The psychological notion of the good is a transcendental notion and it regards value. Such an intention of the good or of value 'founds rational self-consciousness' and 'constitutes the emergence of the existential subject.'[84]

While the 1964 Institute had affirmed the 'unpleasantly existential' character of method, and while in 1965 method had been described as a pursuit of authenticity, the clear emergence of the fourth level of consciousness in 1968 leads further to an unambiguous affirmation of the primacy of the existential.[85] Each level of conscious intentionality takes precedence over the previous levels. Each preserves and perfects the previous level. It follows that the fourth is the most fundamental, decisive, highest level. It is the level on which we exist, become ourselves, become authentic or unauthentic persons.[86]

The affirmation of the primacy of the existential is yet another element in the overcoming of faculty psychology and the dethronement of speculative intellect or pure reason:

> What was named speculative intellect, now is merely the operations of experiencing, understanding, and judging, performed under the guidance of the moral deliberation, evaluation, decision, that selects a method and sees to it that the method is observed. The primacy now belongs to practical intellect and, perforce, philosophy ultimately becomes a philosophy of action.[87]

Lonergan himself regarded the primacy of the existential as one of the keys to the difference between *Insight* and *Method*. In an interview given in 1969, he noted that the chief difference between *Insight* and *Method* was one of emphasis: *Insight* concentrates mainly on the first three levels; *Method* uses these, but is principally concerned with the fourth. Since, however, this level is the most fundamental, it follows that *Method* puts the whole of *Insight* into a fuller, more basic context.[88]

3.4 The New Notion of Faith

The affirmation of the primacy of the existential leads quite naturally to the situation of the gift of God's love on the highest level of conscious intentionality. Thus, religion is described in 1968 as complete self-transcendence.[89] It is not this or that act of loving but rather a radical being-in-love, a first principle of all one's thoughts, words, deeds, omissions.[90] Whatever its degree, it is unconditional, unrestricted,[91] and so otherworldly. It actuates to the full 'the dynamic potentiality of the human spirit with its unrestricted reach.'[92]

Further, the love of God is a gift.[93] In *Method*, being in love with God is described in terms of an exception to the Latin tag *nihil amatum nisi cognitum*. The minor exception to this adage is falling in love, for falling in love is disproportionate to its antecedent causes. The major exception, however, is God's gift of his love.[94] If this is the case, then we have here a reversal of the usual relationship between knowledge and love:

> Where before knowledge preceded, founded, and justified loving, now falling-in-love and being-in-love culminate and complete the process of self-transcendence, which begins with knowledge but goes beyond it, as Blaise Pascal saw when he remarked that the heart has reasons which reason does not know.[95]

Thus, the priority of cognitional theory established in *Insight* yields to the moral, and the moral to the interpersonal.[96] This reversal of the relationship between knowledge and love leads to a modification of the notion of faith. Faith is now conceived, not as assent to truths, but as the eye of love, grounded in God's gift of his love.[97]

> If with some contemporary thinkers one distinguishes between particular items of knowing or believing or doing and, on the other hand, the total context within which these acts occur, then, I think, one will conclude that it is being in love that determines the total context, the *Weltanschauung*, the horizon; while faith is, so to speak, the eye of love, discerning God's hand in nature and his self-disclosure in revelation.[98]

Method points out that this new notion of faith is what was earlier called the *lumen fidei* or the *lumen gratiae* or infused wisdom.[99] What instead went by the name of faith is now called belief. For the eye of love discerns God's self-disclosure in revelation. It discerns the value of believing the word of religion, of accepting its judgments of fact and of value.[100] Thus, the new notion of faith is really a modification and not an abandonment of the old notion. The real change lies in the recognition of the primacy of the existential and of love over knowledge.

The reversal of the relationship between knowledge and love is of paramount importance, for it leads to an overcoming of classicist theological foundations. It

> liberates religion and theology from rationalist tendencies, from the need or desire to prove the truths of faith simply from reason and history. For though both reason and history have their contribution to make, still that contribution is subordinate to God's gift of his love to us, to the love that discerns God's self-manifestation in nature and his self-disclosure in revelation.[101]

Again, being in love with God 'is the existential stance opening on the horizon in which Christian doctrines are intelligible, powerful, meaningful.'[102] Between traditional fundamental theology and the act of faith there used to be a leap.[103] On the new analysis, this leap remains, but is not unparalleled, for it is an instance of the relation of sublation of lower levels by higher in intelligence, reflection, deliberation, love.[104]

The new notion of faith and the distinction between faith and beliefs lead to new theological foundations, but this is a topic for later chapters.

4   Conclusion

In the Introduction to Part Two we pointed out that the context of the period under study was the search for a method in theology, and that this context was marked by three factors: (1) the challenge of the *Geisteswissenschaften*; (2) the need for a more consistent shift from faculty psychology to interiority analysis; and (3) Lonergan's attachment to the classical notion of theology.

Chapter 5 revealed a strong continuity with *Insight* in the period 1954–61. However, in 1959 the shift from faculty psychology to an analysis of consciousness is thematized, and there is presented an account of the good in human rather than cosmic terms, as well as a new notion of human development. The a priori that is relevant to general history is now given by a differentiation of the human good rather than by a differentiation of the notion of being. There is therefore a movement into a more concrete context. As far as the universal viewpoint is concerned, there is a functional persistence; but the term as such is mentioned only once, and that too only in an unpublished text. We have proposed that its absence is part of the shift away from metaphysics and faculty psychology to more concrete categories rooted in an analysis of consciousness.

Chapter 6 noted a growing dissatisfaction with the Aristotelian notion of science, the need to integrate the new empirical notion of science, and the fact that *Insight* was already the needed integration of wisdom and prudence. Still, the developments of 1959 yield a vibrant account of a general method that is squarely situated within a more concrete context, one that is able to handle all operations and all three conversions seemingly without any need for theological transformation on the pattern of *Insight*. Grappling with the *Geisteswissenschaften* leads to a differentiation of the hermeneutical method of *Insight* into a hermeneutics that is a largely commonsense affair and a history that is explanatory. Basic context replaces the universal viewpoint as the upper blade of method, the difference being that it arises upon the general method outlined earlier and so is both more concrete and less metaphysical.

Chapter 7 showed how the developments noted in chapters 5 and 6 are crystallized in the new bipolar notion of horizon of 1963. In keeping with the shift to a more concrete context, this is a more concrete variation of the old Aristotelian-scholastic notion of potency and formal object. In keeping with the shift away from faculty psychology, it is a more unified notion that clearly indicates the dethronement of metaphysics while including it as a moment within itself. The functions of the universal viewpoint are taken over by total and basic horizon or methodical horizon, and the latter notion is perhaps merely another way of speaking about transcendental method itself. At any rate, after 1963 the term that is more frequent is transcendental method rather than total and basic horizon or methodical horizon.

The present chapter asked about the fate of the theologically transformed universal viewpoint. The Georgetown course of 1964 begins to focus on foundations. The shift to the concrete subject, begun in 1959 and consolidated in the developments of 1962 and especially 1963 with the notion of horizon, finds its theological significance in the realization that the starting points of philosophy and theology are isomorphic, and that the turn of the philosophy to the concrete subject is simultaneously its return to theology.

The course of 1964 adverts both to the difference between the Greek and the modern ideals of science and to the need to make a shift to the latter; still, as far as theology is concerned, that shift is not carried out consistently in 1964. True, once the starting point of philosophy in the concrete subject is affirmed, there is no need for a deductive transition into the theological realm; accordingly, Lonergan begins to contrast his theological foundations with the traditional fundamental theology. Still, his notion of faith remains classical: as the Nottingham lecture had affirmed, faith for the Catholic includes acceptance of truths revealed by God and taught by the church. Accordingly, when method is illumined by faith, the result is that theological data is meaning as true, theological understanding is of the mysteries, and theological judgment is within the church. The problem here is neither with theological understanding nor with theological judgment, but with theological data, for as long as such data includes truths, the relationship between positive theology and the rest of theology remains somewhat obscure; and this is no minor point, for, as the 1964 Institute itself affirms, the problem of method in theology manifests itself within Catholic theology as the problem of the integration of historical studies into theology.

The breakthrough of 1965 seems to represent an attempt to overcome precisely this tension, insofar as the point of insertion of a specifically theological principle seems to be shifted from the beginning of theology to the transition from indirect to direct discourse. Still, the starting point of theology in truths continues to be affirmed, and available evidence does not reveal any qualification of this position.

Clear affirmation of the starting point of theology in data comes in 1967, with the acknowledgment of theology as a largely empirical science. In 1968 there emerges the notion of value and there is affirmed the primacy of the existential; this is yet another element in the shift away from faculty psychology to intentionality analysis. There follows the inversion of the relationship between knowledge and love, and consequently a new notion of faith, not as assent to revealed truths, but as the horizon born of the gift of God's love, which transvalues our valuing and makes it possible to discern and assent to what is proposed for belief. With the achievement of the new notion of faith, we might say that theological foundations have become properly methodical; but the full implications of this achievement can be grasped only through the consideration of the functional specialties dialectic and foundations, in Part Three.

PART THREE

Method in Theology

9

Transcendental Method

In Part Two we have seen how the universal viewpoint is replaced by the basic context of 1962, and then how its functions are taken over by the total and basic horizon or methodical horizon of 1963. Subsequently, we saw that the notion of horizon seemed to become marginal, while transcendental method gained ascendancy. In the present chapter we will ask about the precise relationship between the methodical horizon of 1963 and transcendental method, and we will do this by following the vicissitudes of the term horizon, first in the (mostly unpublished) material of the years 1964–67, and then in the course Transcendental Philosophy and the Study of Religion of 1968.

1 The Need for a New Horizon for Theology

1.1 The Method of Theology (1964)

As we noted in chapter 8 above, the term that comes to the fore in the Georgetown course of 1964 is foundations,[1] while the term horizon instead is much less frequent. However, the Wilker notes declare that the key word in the discussion of foundations is horizon. There follows a discussion of the meaning of horizon, and of relative and absolute horizons. Relative horizons are described in terms of psychological, social, and historical differences. Absolute horizons instead involve the normative subject, deviations from the normative subject, the truncated, the actual, and the existential subject.[2]

Horizon also enters into the discussion of positive theology. This 'functional part' of theology yields a genetic and organic interlocking of meaning that is quite independent of *Fragestellung*. This does not mean that interpretation is independent of relative and absolute horizons, but only that persevering study will reveal the need to expand one's relative horizon, and dialectical criticism will reveal the problem of mistaken absolute horizons.[3] As far as expression of one's understanding of a text is concerned, there are 'divisions which exclude expression.' Statements have different meanings within different absolute horizons. 'The idealist and the realist have no direct communication; their positions are incommensurable. No absolute horizon can be demonstrated.'[4]

1.2 'MiT 1965' (Batch V.10)

Among the topics discussed in Batch v.10 are dimensions of meaning, 'two apprehensions of man,' the old theology, the new theology, transcendental method, operations, and 'the theologian as a man.' Our aim is to discover whether the term horizon enters into this discussion, but let us begin by asking about the connection between meaning, the 'new apprehension of man,' the new theology, and transcendental method.

The 'new apprehension of man' is part of the shift from classical culture to historical consciousness.[5] The most fundamental difference between this new anthropology and the old classical one lies in the attention given to meaning. Meaning is a component of human reality, it is (partially) constitutive of human reality; classical thought tends to overlook this aspect, whereas modern thought tends to emphasize it.[6]

The 'new historical apprehension of man' is one of three fundamental changes in Western culture that have led to the upheaval in contemporary theology, the other two being the shift from a demonstrative to an empirical notion of science, and the demand for a shift from a logical to a methodical approach in philosophy.[7] Together with these, it enters theology through the new methods of scholarship (research, interpretation, history), and clashes with the Aristotelian notion of science implicit in traditional theology,[8] and, we might add, also with the classicist assumptions of that theology.

The papers of Batch v.10 do not make the connection between this new situation in theology and transcendental method, but they do say something about transcendental method. By grounding itself in the data of consciousness, transcendental method justifies itself and all other methods.[9] It is described in fact as concerned with the foundations of all methods, and as a new type of control over meaning, through *Existenz* or authenticity of the subject.[10] Now the subject is discussed in terms of horizon, authenticity, and transcendental method.[11] Under 'horizon' there is mention of relative and absolute horizons, and of the new anthropology (which takes into account meaning and history as constitutive of the human being). It would seem that horizon is relevant both to self-knowledge and to knowledge of others.[12] The discussion of horizon naturally opens up to a discussion of authenticity: we are dependent on history, on our socio-cultural milieu; we must assume responsibility for our horizon. Further, absolute horizon supposes a normative horizon. There follows a discussion of normative horizon, unauthenticity (polymorphism, obnubilation, rationalization, the three biases), and *Existenz*.[13] In the light of this discussion, transcendental method is described as a fully deliberate quest of authenticity at a key point, knowing.[14]

1.3 'MiT 1965' (Batch V.7)[15]

We have been noting that transcendental method involves a consideration of relative as well as absolute horizons, and that it is a fully deliberate quest for authenticity at a key point, knowing. In line with this, the papers of Batch v.7 insist that science is not value-free in the sense of being valueless: at least the originating values of the science must be acknowledged. Accordingly, two conceptions of method must be distinguished: 'method as HCF' (Highest Common Factor) of what all will readily accept, and method as involved in a dialectic of values. 'In the latter case, each methodologist acknowledges originating and terminal values, and the series of different methodologies presents subsequent methodologists with the task of comparing, relating, judging the series.'[16] Further, '[t]heological method cannot prescind from values; it will be within the dialectic; it may include a dialectic as justifying the position adopted.'[17] This seems to vaguely recall methodical horizon, which is a transcendental horizon dealing with all transcendental horizons,[18] and also transcendental method as justifying itself and all other methods.[19]

Method continues to be associated with foundations. Thus, a discussion about method is found under the heading 'Foundations,' together with the remark 'foundations as foundations of method'; and the topics discussed are logic and method, transcendental and special methods, science and value (HCF vs Dialectic).[20]

The course of 1964 had said that horizon was a key notion in foundations; the present set of papers sheds some light on this connection. The fourth operational specialization is named 'conversion' in one place and 'Horizon, development, conversion' in another.[21] Development and conversion are allusions of course to relative and absolute horizons, and in fact on a subsequent page there is mention of relative and absolute horizons.[22] Now there is a close relationship between the fourth operational specialization, conversion, which is a question of an 'existential interpersonal decision,'[23] and the fifth specialization, foundations, which is described as 'decision made thematic – positions and counterpositions.'[24] Thus foundations are an objectification of absolute horizons.[25] Further, as we have seen above, method is not only involved in a dialectic of values, but also continues to be associated with foundations.

1.4 The Material of 1966–67

We have been saying that the papers of 1965 do not indicate clearly the link between the new situation of theology and transcendental method. Such a link comes to light instead in the articles of 1966–67. Thus, 'Transition from a Classicist World-View to Historical-Mindedness' of 1966 describes the 'new apprehension of man' as a 'historicist' horizon or viewpoint[26] that deals with the differentiation and dialectic of meaning (read 'relative and absolute horizons').[27] Most significantly, it says that the foundations of this apprehension are given by transcendental method: '[T]he more concrete and historical apprehension of man provides itself with its appropriately concrete foundations in structural features of the conscious, operating subject, by a method that has come to be named transcendental.'[28]

Where the article of 1966 speaks of the 'new apprehension of man' in terms of horizon, there is also the article of 1967 mentioned earlier, which speaks in terms of context, and is in fact entitled 'Theology in Its New Context.'[29] Corresponding to this is an early draft of the chapter 'Method' that bears the title 'The New Context.' This draft speaks about the strength, suppleness, and power of the old Aristotelian context: even disagreements among theologians took place within this context. Once a context has been established, it can be expelled only by creating a new context. But what is this new context? It will arise through a transition from logic to method, from the notion of science contained in the *Posterior Analytics* to the modern notion of science, from human nature to human history, from soul to subject, from first principles to transcendental method.[30] The suggestion is that transcendental method will provide the new context, the new horizon, the methodical horizon called for by contemporary theology.

We might mention here also a chapter III entitled 'Horizons.'[31] The contents of this chapter reflect the earlier discussions of relative horizons, and in fact the chapter itself gives rise to the 1968 chapters 'The Human Good' and 'Meaning.'[32] This suggests that the *Method* chapters 'The Human Good' and 'Meaning' deal largely with relative horizons or development. We may recall that the 1959 lectures on the philosophy of education had presented both a new non-metaphysical analysis of development and an account of the human good.

Thus, the Georgetown course of 1964 reveals that horizon is a key notion in foundations, and therefore in method. Batch v.10 (1965) casts further light on this when it speaks of transcendental method as a new control over meaning through the authenticity of the subject, and defines the authenticity of the subject in terms of a coincidence between absolute and normative horizons. Batch v.7 (1965) echoes methodical horizon in its description of method as involved in a dialectic of values, and as justifying itself and judging the series of methods. It also reiterates the link between method and foundations in various ways. Thus, for example, the fifth operational specialization, foundations, is a thematization of the decision reached in the fourth operational specialization, conversion; but that decision is about absolute horizons. Finally, the articles of 1966–67 throw up the suggestion that it is transcendental method that will provide the new context, the new horizon, the methodical horizon called for by contemporary theology.

2 Transcendental Method as Horizon

The text of the 1968 course Transcendental Philosophy and the Study of Religion is the first relatively substantial draft of *Method in Theology*, though as yet it contains only six chapters.[33] In our effort to follow the term 'horizon,' we will study the first and the third chapters of this course.

2.1 'Ch. 1: Method' (1968)[34]

This text repeats earlier themes. Thus, echoing transcendental method as foundation for all other methods, the text observes that transcendental method provides a rock and a basis for methods in any area of knowledge.[35] Transcendental method may be latent and operative or else explicit and thematized. As latent it is the basic pattern of operations that is operative in every human being. As thematized through self-appropriation, it provides a basis for all other methods.[36]

Again, among the many functions of transcendental method are the critical, the dialectical, and the foundational functions. In its critical function, transcendental method handles the philosophical scandal. This is a question of reducing differences in metaphysics to differences in epistemology, and differences in epistemology to differences in cognitional theory, and finally applying dialectical method, as described in chapter 14 of *Insight*, to this last set of differences.[37] In its dialectical function, transcendental method applies such a critique to every cognitional theory, thus determining the series of basic positions and counterpositions.[38] In its foundational function, transcendental method provides common norms; these function

156   Part Three: *Method in Theology*

as a basis for interdisciplinarity.[39] This interdisciplinary aspect is related to what was said above about transcendental method as providing the basis for all sectorial methods. Thus transcendental method offers a key to unified science[40] and this is of capital significance, insofar as it thus becomes possible to integrate quite disparate disciplines, such as research, interpretation, and history, into theology. Transcendental method is therefore the key to theological integration.

2.2 'Ch. III: *Horizons and Categories*' (1968)

Section 1 above ended with the suggestion that transcendental method provides the new horizon for contemporary theology. Chapter III of the 1968 course, entitled 'Horizons and Categories,' provides the necessary substantiating evidence. The first section of this chapter discusses the meaning of horizon, and links horizon to context.[41] The second section is entitled 'Method as Horizon,' immediately recalling the methodical horizon of the course of spring 1963. Our conception of method in theology, it says, determines a horizon in theology. This horizon differs from the old one based on the Aristotelian notion of science.[42] The third section bears the title 'Old and New,' referring to the old and the new context of theology. The old context of theology drew up its basic set of categories, or its *Begrifflichkeit* (conceptuality), by borrowing and modifying Aristotle. Now, however, there is a need for a new context, a new *Begrifflichkeit*, a new set of categories.[43]

The fourth section tells us that the categories relevant to a religion such as Christianity must be somehow transcultural; and the possibility of such transcultural categories lies in linking them to transcendental method.[44] Transcendental method provides the basic set of categories, the basic set of terms and relations: in fact, the earlier chapter on method had offered precisely such a set of categories. Now the categories relevant to theology may be divided into general and special. This division corresponds to the Thomist distinction between natural and supernatural categories,[45] to the 1963 fall distinction between *communia* and *propria*,[46] and to the distinction between common and proper norms in the chapter 'Method.'[47] The basis of general categories is intellectual and moral self-appropriation, while the basis of special categories is religious and Christian self-appropriation.[48]

General categories may be derived by complicating the basic structure, turning to concrete instances of it (individual, social, historical), filling in or extending the basic set, differentiating it in terms of authenticity and unauthenticity, and setting it in motion.[49] Special categories may also be derived in the same way.[50]

The chapters that follow, 'The Human Good' and 'Meaning,' are really sets of general categories derived from the basic set by filling in or extending it in interaction with data from the human sciences.[51] The chapter 'Religion' instead is a set of special categories derived from an appropriation of religious and Christian interiority.[52] We might add that the earlier chapter 'Functional Specialties' is itself a set of special theological categories derived by complicating the basic structure of conscious intentionality.[53]

The eighth section is entitled 'Theologians and Scientists,' and the reason for this section is that the determination of the categories will draw on the sciences, especially the human sciences and the science of religion.[54] Conflicts are possible between theologians and scientists, and these may be rooted either in lack of sufficient development, or in failure in human or Christian authenticity.[55] The remedy for failure in human authenticity is transcendental method. While this may appear idealistic, still there are grounds for hope, for not only is transcendental method conceived on the analogy of science, not only does it spring from the human mind in its operation, but also it is not just another philosophy but essentially an attempt to rise above the many philosophies.[56]

Method drops the chapter 'Horizons and Categories,' and also changes the order of the chapters: 'Method' first, followed by 'The Human Good,' 'Meaning,' 'Religion,' and 'Functional Specialties.' 'Horizons and Categories' is absorbed into chapters 10 and 11, 'Dialectic' and 'Foundations,' respectively. This makes it more difficult to see that chapters 2 to 5, 'The Human Good,' 'Meaning,' 'Religion,' and 'Functional Specialties,' are really sets of general and special theological categories, but that is what they are, and the particular structure of the 1968 course serves to make this point very clearly. Chapters 2 to 5 of *Method* are really extensions of transcendental method, models constructed on the basic set of categories presented in chapter 1, 'Method.'

The fact that 'Horizons and Categories' is absorbed into foundations is rather significant, for this chapter establishes the link between horizons, categories, and method, and so its absorption into the functional specialty foundations confirms the links we have been noting between method and foundations.[57]

To summarize, the first chapter of the course of 1968 reiterates the critical, dialectical, and foundational functions of transcendental method. The really significant chapter in this course is the third one, 'Horizons and Categories.' Its description of transcendental method as an attempt to rise above the many philosophies[58] recalls the philosophy of philosophies mentioned in *Insight*,[59] and hence the universal viewpoint.[60] Again, its description of method as horizon recalls the methdical horizon of spring 1963, and reveals that the transcendental method of fall 1963 and later is indeed linked to methodical horizon. Finally, it gives a very clear indication of the link between the new theology and transcendental method: theology needs a new context, *Begrifflichkeit*, conceptuality, categories; the possibility of this lies in transcendental method; and chapters 2 to 5 of *Method* are really sets of categories derived from transcendental method. Thus, transcendental method provides the new horizon or set of categories for contemporary theology. This conclusion is confirmed by an article of 1970, 'Philosophy and Theology,' which says that the current crisis is 'a shift in horizon,' that '[t]he earlier horizon was a basic outlook in terms of logic and of eternal truths, with the consequence that serious change of context was assumed to be impossible and so its possibility was not investigated,' that '[t]he current horizon is a basic outlook in terms of method and developing doctrines,' and, finally, that a philosophy relevant to this shift of horizon 'is one that centers on three questions: (1) What am I doing when I am knowing? (2) Why is doing that knowing? and (3) What do I know when I do it?'[61]

That there is a link between the methodical horizon of 1963 and transcendental method is therefore quite clear. But what exactly is the nature of this link? Should we say that methodical horizon is the upper blade of transcendental method? Or should we identify the two, following the clue given in the title of the second section of 'Horizons and Categories': method as horizon? The matter will be taken up in chapter 12 below. Before that, however, we must examine the relationship between transcendental method and the various functional specialties. Now Lonergan himself points out that the first five functional specialties form a unit: together they are 'a more concrete expression' of 'the third section of chapter seventeen on truth of interpretation.'[62] Within these five functional specialties there is a further division between the first three specialties – research, interpretation, and history – and the fourth and fifth specialties – dialectic and foundations. As will become evident as we go along, these two groups of specialties are related as lower blade to upper blade of a single method. In the chapters that follow, we will take up in a special manner the first five functional specialties, contenting ourselves with passing remarks about the remaining three. Thus, the extension of transcendental method to the field of scholarship will be discussed in chapter 10, while dialectic and foundations will be taken up in chapter 11. By chapter 12 we should be in a position to say a final word about the fate of the universal viewpoint in *Method in Theology*.

10

Research, Interpretation, History

By 1969, the 'Background' chapters of *Method in Theology* are stable, except for the position of the chapter on functional specialties, which will shift in 1970 from chapter 2 to chapter 5. The 'Foreground' is presented for the first time, though as yet the chapters 'Doctrines,' 'Systematics,' and 'Communications' have not appeared. 'Horizons and Categories' is moved from the 'Background' to the 'Foreground,' and is now chapter XI.

1   1969: 'Ch. VI: Research'

An early draft of the chapter on research may be found in a text entitled 'MiT VII: The Tasks of Theology.'[1] 'Ch. VI: Research' (1969) is practically identical to this text.

Lonergan is very brief on research because, together with communications, its 'extreme concreteness does not lend itself to general treatment.'[2] The purpose of research is indicated in the chapter 'Functional Specialties': to make available the data relevant to theological investigation.[3] Of interest to us are the remarks on the openness of the position taken. This has to do with the new conception of theology as 'a type of religious study,' the empirical conception of theology as beginning from data and not from truths.[4] The difference is that, in contrast to other religious study that is content with research, interpretation, and history, theology goes on to add dialectic, foundations, doctrines, systematics, and communications.[5]

A further implication of the new conception of theology is that, since research is complemented by dialectic, theology can become comprehensive as well. It can be the theology, not merely of a single religious group, but of 'a dialectically related set of distinct religious groups.'[6] Moreover, such comprehensiveness need not be restricted to the Christian religions alone.[7]

From elsewhere we learn that the new conception of theology also ensures proper independence of the first phase.[8] The first phase must reach its results not by an appeal to the magisterium but by an appeal to data. Yet again, when true believers are left to themselves, they inevitably tend to make things too easy for themselves and so avoid the difficult questions. An open theology will have the advantage of not only drawing upon the expertise of all competent persons regardless of religious affiliation but also of centering attention quickly on the most difficult questions.[9]

The possibility of this openness and comprehensiveness, we are told, 'arises from the transition from the ideals set by deductive logic to the ideals set by method.'[10] A deductivist approach instead 'has to have at the very outset the premises from which all conclusions can be reached and so, from the very outset, there are bound to be as many distinct and irreconcilable sets of premises as there are differing religions and even differing theologies.'[11] Drawing on our chapters 7 and 8, we can say that such openness and comprehensiveness is made possible by the shift from the classicist to the properly methodological viewpoint, from the old Aristotelian context to the new horizon fixed by method, and by the discovery of the new notion of faith that allows theology to take its stand not on truths but on religious conversion. In other words, the openness of research is made possible by its being a functionally specialized part of a theological method that is an extension of transcendental method.

In the course given on *Method in Theology* in 1970, the chapter on research seems to have been absorbed, for some (probably minor) reason, into the chapter on interpretation.[12] In the final draft of *Method*, however, an independent chapter on research reappears. The significant difference is that the discussion of the openness of the new conception of theology is dropped, probably because it pertains to the method as a whole rather than to research in particular.[13] Instead, there is advertence to the problem of differences among Christian theologians about the areas of theological research. How should this problem be handled? By means of the functional specialty dialectic, of course. But how are we to manage till then? The solution is to let each theologian begin from where he/she is; the method is designed to take care of the problem. In fact, the problem affects not only research but also interpretation and history. The chapters on dialectic and foundations will indicate 'how these differences can be brought out into the open so that men of good will can discover one another.'[14]

Clearly, then, there is a vital and organic interdependence between the functional specialty research and the later specialties dialectic and foundations.

2   1969: 'Ch. VII: Interpretation'

2.1 Interpretation as Functional Specialty

Functional specialization implies a decompression of the enormously complex hermeneutical method of *Insight*. Thus the functional specialty interpretation is content to ascertain the meaning of an author in a commonsense way; it does not claim to be scientific hermeneutics. Instead, we are told that what in chapter 17 of *Insight* was termed a universal viewpoint is now realized by advocating a distinct functional specialty, dialectic.[15] We postpone the exegesis of this remark to our chapter on dialectic and foundations.

Like the hermeneutical method of *Insight*, contemporary hermeneutics is also very complex. In addition, it is also affected by issues rooted in cognitional theory and epistemology. The problem can be met only by the development and application of theological method. Thus, where contemporary hermeneutics would tend to treat everything as hermeneutical, Lonergan would distinguish and keep separate questions of hermeneutics and questions of history, dialectic, foundations, doctrines, systematics, communications.[16] As the text of 1962 observes, what contemporaries call hermeneutics, Lonergan would deal with under the rubric method.[17]

A lecture of 1969, Hermeneutics and the Philosophy of Religion, points out that this account of hermeneutics is underpinned by a general theory of meaning. The reference is probably to the earlier chapter entitled 'Meaning.'[18] At any rate, the theme of carriers of meaning enters into the discussion about the type of texts that call for interpretation: interpretation deals not with systematic but with commonsense texts, and these have strange intersubjective, artistic, symbolic components.[19] This must be linked to the discussion about the limitations of a scientific treatise in *Insight*.[20] Again, stages of meaning are relevant to statement of interpretation: they serve as an upper blade.[21] Further, as the lecture Merging Horizons (1970) reveals, Lonergan's account of interpretation itself presupposes the distinction between three differentiations of consciousness: commonsense, systematic, and scholarly. Interpretation belongs to the scholarly differentiation of consciousness. Like the systematic, and in contrast to the commonsense, it goes beyond immediate practical relevance when it tries to understand some distant horizon. Unlike the systematic differentiation and like common sense, scholarship is not interested in universal and abstract laws, but deals with the intelligibility of the concrete. In the language of Gadamer, scholarship is a matter of *Horizontsverschmelzung*, a merging or fusing of horizons.[22]

2.2 Understanding the Text

As already in 1962, the understanding of a text in the functional specialty interpretation is a largely commonsense affair. There is presupposed a knowledge of the object (*die Sache*)[23] of the text. Through the self-correcting process of learning, in the manner of common sense, one understands the words. When this procedure is not successful, one needs an understanding of the author, his/her culture, and his/her times. Such understanding is attained through a more prolonged use of the same self-correcting process of learning, for it is through the self-correcting process that we understand not only other people's common sense, but also how it differs from ours. Such is scholarship.[24] As we have noted above, Merging Horizons does not hesitate to appropriate Gadamer's terminology at this point: scholarship involves a *Horizontsverschmelzung*, a fusion of horizons, the need to gradually expand one's horizon until it coincides in some way with the horizon of the text.[25]

There are times, however, when the understanding of a text demands not merely the broadening of the interpreter's initial horizon, but even a radical revolution, a conversion.[26] With this mention of conversion, of the existential dimension of the task of understanding a text, we are up against the question of absolute horizons, as becomes quite evident by the subsequent mention of the perennial divisions regarding reality, morality, and religion.[27]

Connected with the existential dimension of interpretation is the question of the tradition that has formed the mind and heart of the interpreter. For tradition is a prerequisite for interpretation: it produces in the interpreter the *Vorverständnis* necessary for understanding a text.[28] An authentic tradition facilitates understanding of the text, whereas an unauthentic tradition distorts such understanding.

2.3 Judging the Correctness of the Understanding of the Text

A point to be noticed is that whereas judgment normally follows upon formulation, in the case of the functional specialty interpretation, judgment precedes statement of the meaning of the text. This has probably to do with the fact that understanding and judging the meaning of a text are commonsense activities. For common sense is not articulate; and if at all it does formulate, its formulations are very different from the technical formulations of the theoretical disciplines.[29] The point is that commmonsense judgment functions perfectly well on the basis of the non-articulateness or non-technical articulateness of commonsense understanding. Thus, it is not surprising that Lonergan places statement of the meaning of the text after judgment.

However, this seems to call for a distinction between judgment of understanding and judgment of statement. Is there ground for such a distinction? Merging Horizons speaks of understanding and interpretation in terms of *Verstehen* and *Auslegen*: *Verstehen* is the accumulation of insights that fits the data like a glove; *Auslegen* is the expression of that understanding.[30] It goes on to hint at a distinction between judgment of understanding and judgment of statement or interpretation: 'Finally, both the understanding and the interpretation are distinct from the judgment that one's understanding and interpretation are correct.'[31] However, such a distinction is not quite drawn. But perhaps the lecture in question does not need to draw such a distinction, for it contains neither a section on statement of meaning nor a treatment of dialectic and foundations. Since it speaks of interpretation as a scholarly enterprise, it is content to speak very simply of (a scholarly) judgment of interpretation: 'We now must ask how one can tell whether or not one's interpretation is correct,' etc.[32] What about the text of 1969? Does it give basis for a distinction between two types of judgment? I would say it does. Where then does judgment of interpretation occur? We could say that it occurs through dialectic and foundations, which have the task of generating, selecting, and purifying the categories relevant to scientific statement of interpretation.

Judging the correctness of one's understanding of a text is a commonsense affair. The criterion is the absence of all further relevant questions. Which are the relevant questions? Not usually the ones that inspired the investigation. There is a shift of *Fragestellung* as one progresses, a reconstruction[33] of the context of the author.

At the beginning of one's investigation, context has a heuristic meaning; as one moves from one's own initial horizon to the fuller view that includes more and more of the author's horizon, 'context' acquires a more and more actual meaning.[34] Heuristically, the context keeps expanding: the context of the word is the sentence, that of the sentence the paragraph, chapter, or book, that of the book the *opera omnia*, that of the *opera omnia* the life and times.[35] Actually, however, a context is a nest of related questions and answers unified around a single topic. It thus presents the possibility of closure, of the petering out of further relevant questions. The point is that the interconnection of questions and answers 'comes in limited blocks': it is this that allows one to arrive at a margin where there are no further questions relevant to a given topic, and so to recognize one's task as completed.[36]

The text of 1969 is content with this analysis of judgment in terms of the cessation of further relevant questions. Merging Horizons of 1970 instead distinguishes between a proximate and a remote criterion. The proximate criterion is the absence of further relevant questions that we have been discussing above. The remote criterion instead is twofold authenticity: 'the authenticity of the tradition one has inherited and the authenticity of one's own assimilation of it.'[37] This criterion is therefore linked to the existential dimension of interpretation. Understanding oneself raises the question of authenticity, both one's own and that of one's tradition, and the problem is how such twofold authenticity is to be assured. The lecture goes back to the distinction between systematic, commonsense, and scholarly developments of understanding. In the systematic, there are controls over thinking and all assumptions are in the open. In the commonsense development, instead, one has neither inventory of contents nor precise control over process. What controls exist are implicit: they are immanent in our being attentive, intelligent, reasonable, responsible. What if either our tradition or our assimilation of it has been less than genuine? There is only one real solution: 'to accept ourselves as we are and by dint of constant and persevering attention, intelligence, reasonableness, responsibility, strive to expand what is true and force out what is mistaken in views that we have inherited or spontaneously developed.'[38] Now scholarship is really an extension of the commonsense mode of understanding. Still, in contrast to common sense, it has the advantage of being withdrawn from everyday life and so detached from its passions; its results can be checked not only by peers but also by successors; above all, it is open to the challenge of the past: both the scholar and his/her tradition are challenged by the past to criticize the present and to initiate a renewal. It is through such renewals that the remote criterion of truth is to be met.[39]

Scholarship, then, does have a way of handling the remote criterion of truth, but this is a 'non-technical' solution.[40] The 'technical' solution would be 'through self-appropriation, distinction of positions and counterpositions ..., dialectic.'[41] Accordingly, to the scholarly solution of the functional specialty interpretation, *Method* adds the technical solution of the functional specialties dialectic and foundations. If then in *Insight* the remote criterion was handled by the upper blade of hermeneutical method, which included the notion of the universal viewpoint, and if in 1962 this seems to have been handled by a history that was explanatory, now it is dialectic and foundations that serve as the upper blade for interpretation. It goes without saying of course that neither the non-technical nor the technical solutions pretend to be automatic solutions to the question of the remote criterion, for objectivity is the fruit of authentic subjectivity, and there are no criteria of truth that prescind from the authenticity of the subject.

2.4 Statement of Interpretation

The 1962 lecture Hermeneutics had distinguished a commonsense and a scientific communication of a commonsense understanding of a text. In 1969 the task of communication undergoes a still further differentiation. In the first place, the expression that is proper to the functional specialty interpretation is to be distinguished from communication with people in general.[42] Such communication is a complex and extremely important task whose execution will vary with variations in classes and cultures, but it is a task that Lonergan would keep distinct from hermeneutics: '[T]here are those that extend hermeneutics to include the problem of communications, but I think this leads, at least in theology, to a process of telescoping that omits several crucial steps from original texts down to what I tell Ted and Alice what precisely it means in their lives.'[43] Second, expression of the meaning of a text by the exegete qua exegete[44] is to be distinguished from the expressions that occur in the functional specialties history, dialectic, doctrines, and systematics.[45]

The differentiation of the task of communication and the distinction between the functional specialties interpretation and communications sets Lonergan apart from contemporary thinking in hermeneutics. It might be objected, however, that the remark about the omission of several important steps makes sense only within Lonergan's method, for the majority of exegetes do not make the distinction between interpretation, history, doctrines, and communications. But that is precisely the problem, according to Lonergan: the failure to make such distinctions makes interpretation an enormously complicated task,[46] and such complication easily leads to the omission of crucial steps. To jump from scriptural exegesis to communication amounts to ignoring the Fathers, the councils, and the theologians; but that amounts to a neglect of the *Wirkungsgeschichte* of the biblical texts. On the other hand, no single specialist can hope to handle the entire *Wirkungsgeschichte* even of a single text. Here is where Lonergan's theological method comes in: it seeks to overcome 'totalitarian ambitions'[47] as well as the fragmentation of specializations. Communication must be done; it is the real aim of all theology; and yet it must be neither underestimated nor overly simplified. There must be no overlooking of the necessary intermediate steps.

Now the communication proper to the functional specialty interpretation itself varies, for the exegete must communicate not only to colleagues in his/her own field, but also to his/her pupils, to colleagues in different but related fields, and to the theological community in general. Expression to colleagues in one's own field is done through specialized notes, articles, monographs, and commentaries; it is named technical insofar as it 'puts to full use the instruments for investigation provided by research' and insofar as it is 'functionally related to previous work in the field.'[48] Expression to pupils is done primarily in the classroom and during seminars.[49] Expres-

166 Part Three: *Method in Theology*

sion to colleagues in related fields and to those engaged in other functional specialties is somewhat more complex, and will be discussed under the topic supplementary expression.

2.4.1 A Supplementary Mode of Expression

The lecture of 1962 had presented A. Descamps as the champion of the commonsense mode of expression, but had gone on to demand a scientific mode of expression. In a similar vein, the text of 1969 observes that, as far as expression to the theological community is concerned, this basic mode of expression has to be supplemented.[50] It goes on to present Lonergan's solution: if people were to be shown how to identify the elements of meaning in their own experience and how to assemble these elements into various historical modes of meaning, 'they would find themselves in possession of a very precise tool, they would know it in all its suppositions and implications, they could form for themselves an exact notion and they could check just how well it accounted for the foreign, strange, archaic things presented by the exegetes.'[51]

An example of this supplementary mode of expression may be found in the stages of meaning set forth in the chapter 'Meaning.' This is to be taken precisely as a model, an illustration of the type of thing Lonergan has in mind.[52] In *Insight*, Lonergan had insisted that what was important was not so much the actual classification of modes of expression as the operators of development that are at the root of all such modes.[53] Here he says: 'If transcendental method coupled with a few books by Cassirer and Snell could make this beginning, why might not transcendental method coupled with the at once extensive and precise knowledge of many exegetes in many fields not yield far more?'[54]

This invitation is rather cautious and circumspect; Lonergan's intention is perhaps revealed more directly by a text that has been crossed out:

> What is needed, is not mere description but explanation, and by that I mean an intelligent construction of stages of meaning in human development, such as I attempted in chapter five, and further developments and corrections of that construction by exegetes that both understand the method we are proposing and can implement it still further by drawing on the treasures of their extensive and precise knowledge.[55]

The reason for the deletion would seem to be Lonergan's desire to keep his theological method open to all comers. Full understanding of transcendental method, while certainly not to be despised, is not a prerequisite for engaging in the functional specialties. The hermeneutical canon of relevance is not operative at the beginning of theological method.

Subsequent courses and lectures shed light on various aspects of this proposal. During question periods at the 1969 course on method in theology, Lonergan connects basic expression with the artistic or literary interpretation of chapter 17 of *Insight*,[56] and supplementary expression with the levels of expression of the same chapter. The books of Snell and Cassirer, he says, corroborated his thinking that, besides employing literary interpretation, one should try to account for differences in mentality and expression by constructing the possibilities in which people think. The idea is to find some function with many variables to enable the assembly of different ways in which people think. Cognitional analysis alone is not enough; it must be put together with detailed expertise on the development of languages and expression, and such expertise is had by the exegetes.[57] The article 'Philosophy and Theology' of 1970 mentions the contributions of scholars as well as the books of Snell and Cassirer, and then says:

> But something more is wanted. It is not supplied either by Aquinas' interpretation of Scripture in Aristotelian terms or by Bultmann's interpretation of the New Testament in terms of the early Heidegger. Rather what is wanted is a coming together of the fruits of historical expertise and, on the other hand, of models derived from the data of consciousness, from the different types of its differentiation and specialization, from the various structures that result from differentiation and specialization. From the interaction of detailed research, overall views, and the construction of models there would gradually emerge a phylogenetic set of schemata that would provide socio-cultural expertise with a first approximation to the notions it has to express and, on the other hand, would provide students both with an initial access to alien cultures and with an overall view of the stages and variations of human meanings, values, structures.[58]

Neither the preparatory drafts nor the final text of the chapter on interpretation raise the question of the foundations of scientific communication or of supplementary expression, but the reason for this is simple: the necessary foundations are provided by transcendental method. Transcendental method determines the basic context or methodical horizon and provides the necessary categories.

It is to be noted that the basic elements involved in supplementary expression were in place already in *Insight*: the genetic and dialectical sequences of viewpoints, the genetic sequence of modes of expression, and the combination of these that are the explanatory differentiations of the protean notion of being.[59] One major difference is that *Method* postpones the dialectical element to the fourth functional specialty. The stages of meaning of *Method* are exemplifications of the explanatory differentiations called for by *Insight*: they are the alternatives to occult entities such as Hebrew and Greek mentalities.[60] They are models or constructs arising from a scissors-like interaction between transcendental method and data provided by socio-cultural studies; and in turn they function as an upper blade in the statement of the meaning of a text.

What, then, of pure formulations? Since the functional specialty interpretation does not require operation from the universal viewpoint, the effort to grasp the meaning of texts will yield formulations, and the effort to apply transcendentally based categories would yield 'explanatory' formulations, but there is now no guarantee that these will be *pure* formulations. Dialectical considerations enter not on the level of the second functional specialty but of the fourth, and so pure formulations emerge only in the fifth functional specialty, doctrines. Accordingly, there is no mention of pure formulations in the *Method* chapter 'Interpretation.'

Still, these remarks on supplementary expression must be taken, not in isolation, but in the broader context of the functioning of theological method. Though the constructs or models or categories relevant to expression are generated seminally in dialectic and with explicit commitment in foundations,[61] there is, as will be seen in the next chapter, a scissors type of interaction between such categories and data.[62] But this means that the categories generated in dialectic and foundations will be available for subsequent interpretation, and in the measure that such categories are expressions of positions and not of counterpositions, in the measure that one is operating on the basis of transcendental method, supplementary expression will be equivalent to the scientific interpretation of *Insight*.

The position of 1962 on interpretation is, therefore, repeated in 1969 with a few significant differences. Thus, the technical handling of the remote criterion of judgment is done not by explanatory history as in 1962, but by the specialties dialectic and foundations. Again, scientific statement calls for an upper blade of explanatory categories; but these categories are generated seminally in dialectic and with explicit commitment in foundations. Accordingly, the specialty interpretation needs to be complemented by the further specialties dialectic and foundations.

3   1969: 'Ch. VIII: History'

At least since the acknowledgment of the distinction between the natural and the human sciences in 1962, history has been recognized as a species of scholarship. Still, while hermeneutics was acknowledged to be largely a commonsense affair, history was regarded as operating on the basis of common sense mediated by the upper blade of an ongoing philosophy, other human sciences, and other ordinary and extraordinary developments of common sense. It was even specified that the upper blade of history included comparative, genetic, and dialectical methods. The inclusion of dialectical method had the effect of making history the true successor of the methodical hermeneutics of *Insight*.[63] Again, we have seen that the breakthrough of 1965 resulted in a history that was *in oratione obliqua*;[64] nevertheless, as we have had occasion to mention already, dialectic continues to remain part of history;[65] it emerges as a distinct functional specialty only around 1968.[66] With this differentiation the functional specialty history loses its similarity to the methodical hermeneutics of *Insight*. In 1969 there appear two chapters on history: chapter VIII, entitled 'History,' and chapter IX, entitled 'History and Historians.' In the present section, we will discuss chapter VIII.

The aim of chapter VIII is to formulate the set of procedures that, other things being equal, yield historical knowledge.[67] The chapter falls into three sections. In the first, history is contrasted with the natural and the human sciences. In the second, there is a clarification of the terms historical experience and historical knowledge. In the third, finally, there is formulation of the set of procedures that, *caeteris paribus*, yield historical knowledge. This set of procedures is named critical history.

Now written history may be precritical, and then the community written about is one's own, the vehicle is narrative, and the function is a practical one, the survival and functioning of the community. Such history is artistic, ethical, explanatory, apologetic, and prophetic.[68] The functional specialty history instead is critical. Its aim is not edification, not communication, but judgment regarding what really happened. It may be described as heuristic, ecstatic, selective, constructive, and critical, where 'critical' means, not that one has tested the credibility of one's witnesses, but that 'one has shifted data from one field of relevance to another.'[69] Its distinguishing mark is that this process occurs twice: first with respect to sources, and next with respect to the object of history itself, what was going forward in the community.[70] The process is also reflective and judicial, and the criterion, as already mentioned above, is the absence of further relevant questions.[71]

We have said that the functional specialty history is a set of procedures that, other things being equal, yields historical knowledge. But why the proviso 'other things being equal'? Because history conceived as a functional specialty omits consideration of the problems of historical relativism, *Weltanschauung, Fragestellung, Standpunkt*. These problems are handled, not by the functional specialty history, but by the functional specialty dialectic.[72]

Still, historical procedures do effect a partial elimination of the problem of standpoints. Saying that a historian cannot escape his/her background does not mean that he/she cannot overcome individual, group, or general bias, or that he/she cannot undergo intellectual, moral, and religious conversion. There is an ecstatic character to developing historical insight. The historian can move out of the viewpoint of his/her place and time and come to understand that of another place and time.[73]

Like interpretation, then, history disposes of a proximate criterion of judgment.[74] Since further, like interpretation, history is an extension of commonsense procedures, it cannot objectify and so control its assumptions and procedures completely. Still, it has a non-technical way of handling the remote criterion, for it does ensure a partial elimination of standpoints. But the technical solution to the problem of standpoints consists in the addition to history of the functional specialties dialectic and foundations. For a more adequate discussion of the remote criterion we must turn to the chapter 'History and Historians.'

4   1969: 'Ch. IX: History and Historians'

A first question naturally is, Why this additional chapter on history? While we will not attempt to answer this question in an exhaustive manner, we must point out that, whereas 'Ch. VIII: History' was concerned with formulating the nature of historical knowledge, 'Ch. IX: History and Historians' is concerned with the dialectic of accounts of historical knowledge. This becomes evident also from the constantly changing titles given to this chapter: 'Historians and Cognitional Theory' (c. 1968), 'History and Dialectic' (1968 or 1969), 'History and Historians' (1969), 'From History to Dialectic' (1970, 1971).[75]

'Ch. VIII: History' had pointed out that critical history involves a double process. This double process, it would seem, is what 'Ch. IX: History and Historians' calls, with Droysen, Bernheim, Langlois, and Seignobos, criticism and interpretation, or the critical and the constructive process.[76] The critical process begins from historical experience, which consists of 'the fragments, the bits and pieces, that have caught the attention of diarists, letter-writers, chroniclers, newsmen, commentators.'[77] This first process yields facts, but these facts are merely data for the constructive process. It is only the facts resulting from the second process that may be called historical facts or historical knowledge in the proper sense of the word.[78]

Now there seem to be two types of accounts of history, the positivist and the idealist. The former tends to restrict itself to the critical process; but this yields merely fragmentary facts, merely critical editions of texts, rather than a knowledge of what was going forward.[79] The second, constructive process is necessary if the intelligible interconnectedness (*Zusammenhang*) of these facts is to be grasped. However, acknowledgment of this second process lands one into problems of idealism, as may be seen in the case of Becker and Collingwood.[80] Lonergan believes that such idealism may be offset by introducing a satisfactory theory of objectivity and of judgment.[81]

If the discussion of Becker and Collingwood gives Lonergan the opportunity to insist on understanding against the positivists and on judgment against the idealists, the discussion of perspectivism allows him both to reaffirm this position and to acknowledge that the problem of standpoints cannot be completely handled by the methods of historical scholarship. Against Heussi, Lonergan grants the premise of *Historismus* that the object of history is stably given and unequivocally structured.[82] With Heussi and against *Historismus*, however, he would hold that the past that is so fixed and unequivocal 'is the enormously complex past that historians know only incompletely and approximately.'[83] He would note further that, while mathematicians and scientists are able to objectify and so control their assumptions and procedures, and while philosophers can appeal to transcendental method, the development of historical understanding does not leave room for systematic objectification.[84] Since Lonergan rejects both the naive realism of *Historismus* and the idealist tendency of Heussi, he is able to affirm a perspectivism that is not a relativism. Such a perspectivism refers neither to genetic nor to dialectical differences in history, but to those differences that result from the finiteness of the historian, the inevitable selection that he/she makes, and the variability of selection.[85]

What then about dialectical differences among historians? For if historians are unable to objectify and control their assumptions and procedures, then such differences cannot be excluded. Thus, Becker points out that preconceived ideas of historians, derived from some contemporary horizon or climate of opinion, modify their writing of history.[86] How is this problem to be handled? Lonergan's solution is to let historians begin from where they are.[87] Each historian will write from his/her own standpoint; to eliminate the standpoint would be to eliminate the education of the historian and so his/her very capacity to carry out his/her work.[88] This means, however, that the possibility of irreconcilable histories has to be recognized. The point, then, is 'to seek methods that will help historians from the start to avoid incoherent assumptions and procedures, and ... to develop further methods that will serve to iron out differences once incompatible histories have been written.'[89] The prior methods are exemplified by the accounts of the functional specialties research, interpretation, and history. The further methods are the functional specialties dialectic and foundations. But such a distinction between methods tallies with what chapter VIII has been saying, that the functional specialty history is a set of procedures that, *caeteris paribus*, yield historical knowledge.[90] Considerations of historical relativism and the influence of the historian's views on possibility, of his/her value-judgments, his/her *Weltanschauung, Fragestellung,* or *Standpunkt,* are omitted simply because they are handled, not by the techniques of critical history, but by dialectic.[91]

Again, the dialectical confrontation of contradictory histories needs a basis that is generally accessible. 'The basis we would offer would be transcendental method extended into the methods of theology and history by constructs derived from transcendental method itself. In other words, it would be the sort of thing we have been working out in these chapters.'[92]

Finally, there is the question of value judgments in history. History is value-free in the sense that it is not directly concerned with social and cultural goals, which is the concern of the functional specialty communications. Again, history is value-free in the sense that it aims at settling matters of fact by appeal to evidence, and value judgments neither settle matters of fact nor constitute empirical evidence. But history is not value-free in the sense that the historian refrains from all value judgments. He/she cannot refrain from all value judgments, for history is selective, and value judgments influence selection. Still, the point is that making value judgments is not his/her specialty; that belongs to the specialties dialectic and foundations.[93]

It is, therefore, abundantly clear that the functional specialty history disposes of both a proximate and a remote criterion of truth. The proximate criterion is of course the commonsense criterion of the absence of further relevant questions. As for the remote criterion, we must distinguish between a technical and a non-technical handling; while the latter is done in history, the former is reserved to the specialties dialectic and foundations. History deals with what was going forward, where 'what was going forward' is understood in the generalized sense that includes not only progress but also decline, not only development but also breakdowns. Still, the method of history is designed to be able to handle only relative horizons; absolute horizons, while certainly not absent in the field of history, are left to the further specialties dialectic and foundations.

5 Conclusion

The functional specialty research is both open and comprehensive, and this openness and comprehensiveness is made possible by the shift to the properly methodical viewpoint. Thus, it begins from data rather than from revealed truths, and differences about the starting point are handled by the functional specialty dialectic.

The functional specialty interpretation is, as in 1962, a largely commonsense affair. The understanding of a text occurs through a fusion of horizons, but sometimes there is demanded not merely a development but also a revolution in the horizon of the interpreter. Judging the understanding of a text involves a proximate and a remote criterion; while scholarship disposes of a non-technical handling of the remote criterion, the technical handling is postponed to dialectic and foundations. Statement of the understanding of a text is not problematic when addressed to colleagues and to pupils, but this basic mode needs to be supplemented when it comes to colleagues in different but related fields, and to the theological community in general. This supplementary mode is another way of speaking about the 'scientific statement of a commonsense understanding of a text.'[94] This is a question of replacing merely descriptive terms such as the Hebrew mind and Hellenism with explanatory categories such as the stages of meaning sketched in the earlier chapter on meaning. As in 1962, such categories are derived from transcendental method in interaction with the expertise of the human sciences and of scholarship. The issue of the foundations of such a supplementary mode of expression is not raised, first because transcendental method has already been discussed earlier, and second because explicit commitment to method and therefore to foundations is required only in the fifth functional specialty. In sum, the functional specialty interpretation has to be complemented by dialectic and foundations as regards both judgment and expression.

Unlike the explanatory history of 1962, the functional specialty history of 1969 and subsequent years is a scholarly affair that yields historical knowledge only under the proviso, 'other things being equal.' History involves critical process, which begins from the fragmentary evidence of historical experience to arrive at a set of facts. Against the positivists, however, Lonergan insists that these facts are not yet historical knowledge; they merely provide the data in which a second, constructive process must grasp their intelligible interconnectedness. Given a proper theory of objectivity and judgment, this constructive process can avoid idealism and arrive at historical knowledge. Like interpretation, then, history disposes of a proximate criterion. It also has a non-technical way of handling the remote criterion, for it is able to achieve a partial elimination of differences in standpoints. But the technical handling of the remote criterion is reserved to dialectic, and hence the proviso 'other things being equal.'

Thus, the accounts of the functional specialties research, interpretation, and history are derived from transcendental method; they are the 'prior methods' that need to be complemented by the upper blade of dialectic and foundations.

11

Dialectic and Foundations

1   1966–68: The Comprehensive Viewpoint as Goal of Dialectic

We may recall that in 1965, while the fifth specialty was foundations, the fourth specialty was not dialectic but conversion, and dialectical method formed part of the functional specialty history. A chapter 11 entitled 'The Tasks of Theology,' dated probably 1966 or 1967, indicates that this situation remains unchanged, but also reveals that the fourth functional specialty, conversion, is itself somehow concerned with dialectic.[1] The text speaks of 'a single if dialectical view' or 'a comprehensive view' of different types and measures of conversion; such a comprehensive view would provide foundations for theology that would be ecumenical and not merely sectarian.[2]

A distinct functional specialty dialectic emerges with all probability only in 1968, and our evidence for this comes from the 1968 summer course Transcendental Philosophy and the Study of Religion. This course does not as yet contain a separate chapter on dialectic, but it does contain one on functional specialties, and the fourth functional specialty here is not conversion but dialectic.[3] This replacement of 'conversion' by 'dialectic' may perhaps be linked to the distinction between religion and theology achieved in 1967–68. For the 1967 article 'Theology in Its New Context' describes religion as 'conversion in its preparation, occurrence, development, and consequents,' and theology as reflection on religion;[4] and again an article of 1968 clearly distinguishes religion from theology: '[T]heology pertains to the cultural superstructure, while religion pertains to its day-to-day substance.'[5] But conversion taken as personal, communal, and historical coincides with living religion,[6] and so cannot be part of theology;

hence the replacement of the functional specialty conversion by the functional specialty dialectic.

If the text of 1966/67 spoke of 'conversion' as being concerned with a comprehensive view, the 1968 course describes the fourth functional specialty, dialectic, as aiming at a comprehensive viewpoint. Like the ideal of complete explanation of empirical science, such a goal is high and distant. It would be an understanding of the character, oppositions, and relations of the many viewpoints exhibited in conflicting Christian movements, histories, interpretations. Now dialectic seeks some single base or single set of related bases from which it can proceed to such a unified understanding.[7] The precise nature of the single base is not identified; still, the mention of the single base recalls chapter 17 of *Insight*,[8] and the course of 1969 makes it clear that dialectic is grounded in transcendental method.[9] Further, where the text of 1966/67 had spoken of ecumenical foundations for theology, the present text speaks of dialectic as a generalized apologetic conducted in an ecumenical spirit.[10] It is an apologetic insofar as it is a question of giving reasons for one's position; it is generalized insofar as it can be envisaged as being performed by different groups; and it is ecumenical insofar as it is conducted in an irenic rather than a polemical spirit.

At this point the question naturally arises: the comprehensive viewpoint is obviously related to the universal viewpoint, but why the change in name, and what is the precise relationship between the two?

A first reason for the change in name would seem to be the developments of the preceding years: given the fact that the notion of the universal viewpoint has been replaced by transcendental method, another name is called for. A second reason is that, unlike the universal viewpoint, the comprehensive viewpoint is not both high and distant goal as well as heuristic structure; it is clearly only the goal of dialectic; the base of dialectic, as we have seen, is transcendental method. A third reason is that, unlike the universal viewpoint, which encompassed all viewpoints, the comprehensive viewpoint is described in terms of the totality of Christian viewpoints.

Must we conclude then that the universal viewpoint is more extensive than the comprehensive viewpoint? The matter is complex. For the context of the comprehensive viewpoint is general history, and general history not only recalls the 'universal history' mentioned in chapter 17 of *Insight*,[11] but also could be taken as another way of speaking about the universal viewpoint as ideal goal. In fact, general history is described as an *ideal*, for it would offer 'the *total view* or some approximation to it.'[12] Again, the functional specialty dialectic deals with radical differences and is an evaluative history;[13] but general history is described as involving not only understanding and judgment but also evaluation of the sum of cultural, institutional, and doctrinal movements in their concrete setting; and 'it is only within the full view that can be grasped the differences between the Christian churches and sects, the relations between different religions, and the role of Christianity in world history.'[14] The comprehensive viewpoint is then quite intimately connected with general history. It might be said in fact that, considered precisely as ideal goals, the two coincide; and given the connection between general history and the universal viewpoint as ideal goal, it might be said further that the comprehensive viewpoint coincides with the universal viewpoint precisely as ideal goal. However, if the two viewpoints coincide in extension, they do not coincide in intension, for the former is more specific and concrete than the latter, just as the theologically transformed universal viewpoint was more specific and concrete than the universal viewpoint.

2   1969: Dialectic and Foundations

2.1 Dialectic

Before coming to the course of 1969,[15] a word might be said about a fragment entitled 'MiT VII. 4. Dialectic.'[16] This is probably an early attempt to expand on the relatively brief description of dialectic found in the chapter 'Functional Specialties.' Very significantly, the description of dialectic in the chapter on functional specialties speaks in terms of viewpoints, but the present text describes dialectic in terms of horizon: it involves 'advertence to differences of horizon, analysis of the consequences of such differences and, consequently, a presentation to attentive, intelligent, reasonable, and responsible subjects of the issues involved.'[17] While such advertence, analysis, and presentation will inevitably occur within some particular horizon, still dialectic is not useless:

> For while advertence, analysis, presentation of issues will occur from within some horizon, it is not true that all horizons are equally capable of adverting to the issues, analyzing them successfully, and presenting them clearly. On the contrary, the mere fact that an honest attempt at dialectic is made will result in the elimination of not a few horizons, and the further the task is pushed the larger will be the number of casualties.[18]

Coming to the course of 1969,[19] we note two things. First, we find for the first time separate chapters dedicated to the functional specialties, and among these a chapter dealing with dialectic and foundations. This fact is rather significant from the point of view of the close relationship between these specialties, a relationship that continues to be maintained even in the final text of *Method*.[20] In fact, the primary function of these two specialties is to effect the transition from mediating to mediated theology, both by addressing the open-endedness of the first three specialties and by introducing a specifically theological principle. Second, the chapter 'Functional Specialties' remains unchanged, with its description of dialectic as moving towards the high and distant goal of the comprehensive viewpoint on the basis of some single base or set of related bases. However, there is absolutely no mention of the comprehensive viewpoint later in the text, not even in the chapter on dialectic and foundations.

The papers of 1965 had described transcendental method as a deliberate search for authenticity.[21] The present text notes that, while there is truth in the assertion that science is value-free,[22] still, the notion of a science as a purely intellectual pursuit is too simplistic.[23] There is need of a method that can handle values. Such is dialectic: it is a systematic and critical strategy for controlling values.[24] It is concerned to promote authenticity.[25]

Since dialectic is a strategy for controlling values, it is the technical way of handling the existential factor or the question of standpoints. It does this by identifying and making explicit radical differences between interpretations and histories, by relating them in historical series, and by distinguishing positions and counterpositions.[26] By making conflicts explicit and revealing their roots, dialectic moves them out of their original context into a new and higher context.[27] The possibility of this procedure is transcendental method;[28] in fact, the description of transcendental method here bears an astonishing similarity to the basic context of 1962. Like the basic context that is 'at once factual and normative,'[29] transcendental method is 'a normative pattern that relates and directs the recurrent operations of human intentional consciousness.'[30] Like the basic context that is not only in the mind of the upper-blade historian but also in the minds of authors,[31] transcendental method not only 'exists and functions in the methodical theologian' but also 'has existed and functioned well or ill in all men down the ages.'[32] Like the basic context that is the ground of both genetic and dialectical relationships, so the proper functioning of transcendental method generates positions and its malfunctioning generates counterpositions.[33] Still, given the links we have established between the basic context of 1962, the methodical horizon of 1963, and transcendental method as providing a new horizon or context for contemporary theology, these similarities should not be surprising.

The strategy of dialectic, then, is 'to bring out into the open all relevant philosophic presuppositions and value-judgments ... to use their oppositions both to clarify the past and to challenge contemporary theologians to self-understanding and self-criticism.'[34] Dialectic 'invites the critical exegete and historian to advance from the critique of others to the critique of himself.'³⁵ By such an invitation to self-understanding and to self-criticism, it does what can be done, 'if not to remove disagreement, at least to liberate it from the pride and disdain that ill accord with human limitations.'³⁶

In *Insight*, the hermeneutical canon of relevance had demanded operation from the universal viewpoint; in similar fashion, the present text makes cognitional and moral self-appropriation the first condition of dialectical theology.³⁷ Again, in what clearly recalls the universal viewpoint as involving grasp of the protean notion of being, such self-appropriation demands familiarity not only with one's own conscious and intentional operations, but also 'with all the oversights and over-emphases that result in mistaken cognitional theories, inadequate epistemologies, faulty or nonexistent ontologies.'³⁸ This dialectical function of transcendental method is echoed also in the dialectic of other strategies. This dialectic, by its mention of pre-methodical everyday traditionalism, rationalism, and the rejection of all presuppositions, recalls section 3.5 of chapter 17 of *Insight*, 'Interpretation and Method.'³⁹

Despite the demand for self-appropriation, however, the text does not take for granted that authenticity is achieved at a single stroke. It is only through one's own movement towards cognitional and real self-transcendence that one can hope to discern the ambivalence at work in others.⁴⁰ Further, knowledge and appreciation of others itself leads to an increase in our own knowledge of and appreciation of values. Thus dialectic involves a reciprocal interaction, and hence an encounter with the past, an encounter between persons.⁴¹ We might recall that already in the concluding section of Hermeneutics (1962), entitled 'The Logic of Basic Context,' Lonergan had cited Ebeling on the need for a living personal encounter with history.⁴²

Since dialectical theology is based on the theologian's self-appropriation, it cannot be philosophically or morally neutral.⁴³ But is dialectic religiously neutral? The answer is complex. First, dialectic does not exclude religious people. In fact, 'very many theologians must pursue the attainment of holiness if theology is to discern, appreciate, judge religious values and communicate such discernment, appreciation, judgment to others.'⁴⁴ Second, dialectic 'occurs principally, not within some one religion, but between many religions.' It is ecumenist, for it operates not by appeal to authority but by means of dialogue.⁴⁵ Third, dialectic need not be confined to Christian religions, for theologians recognize that God's grace is given to all.⁴⁶ Fourth, dialectic takes into account non-religious and anti-religious viewpoints as well, attempting to discover the truth or value that underlies such viewpoints, and asking whether their opposition is to religion as such or to the defects of religious people and organizations.⁴⁷ Dialectic therefore excludes neither religious nor non-religious nor anti-religious people; in such a sense it may claim to be religiously neutral.

The religious neutrality of dialectic throws light on the observation in the 1969 chapter on research that it is the existence of the specialty dialectic that enables theology 'to be more comprehensive, to be the theology of a dialectically related set of distinct religious groups.'[48] But the radical possibility of such openness is the shift to method:

> The possibility of the foregoing openness and comprehensiveness arises from the transition from the ideal set by deductive logic to the ideal set by method. Religions are empirical facts that offer data for classification and scientific investigation and method guides the course of the investigation. In contrast, the deductivist approach has to have, at the very outset, the premises from which all conclusions can be reached, and so, from the outset, there are bound to be as many distinct and irreconcilable sets of premises as there are differing religions and differing theologies.[49]

We noted earlier that the chapter 'Functional Specialties' of 1968 described the comprehensive viewpoint in terms of the totality of Christian movements. That chapter remains unchanged in 1969; however, it must be admitted that the affirmation of the religious neutrality of dialectic represents an advance over the position of 1968. Still, the new position may be seen as implicit in the old one. For while the comprehensive viewpoint was described in terms of the totality of Christian movements, we have seen already that its context is general history, and that therefore it coincides with the universal viewpoint considered as ideal goal.[50]

2.2 Foundations

The theme of horizons continues to play a role in the account of foundations. Thus conversion is entry into a new horizon, and while the event of conversion is not a part of method, the objectification of conversion (and so of horizon) yields foundations.[51] The objectification of conversion may be spontaneous or reflective. Spontaneous objectification is a changed way of thinking and speaking, judging and acting. Reflective objectification on the other hand may be total or partial. Total reflective objectification sets forth not only foundations but also doctrines, systematics, communications. Partial reflective objectification sets forth only foundations, which is the key that conditions the remainder. The foundations of theology are therefore the horizon fixed by intellectual, moral, and religious conversion.[52]

Now if dialectic brings conflicts of interpretations and histories to

180   Part Three: *Method in Theology*

light,[53] it is foundations that resolves them. It does so by providing the criterion for such resolution, and this criterion is the reflective objectification of triple conversion.[53] On the basis of this objectification foundations distinguishes positions and counterpositions.[55] Further, it issues the twofold precept of developing positions and reversing counterpositions; the implementation of this precept belongs, however, to the specialties doctrines, systematics, and communications.[56]

Strangely, while cognitional and moral self-appropriation was a condition of dialectic, foundations is itself described as objectifying all three conversions. On the other hand, we are told that its principal element is the reflective objectification of religious horizon; accordingly, it might be said that in 1969 foundations concentrates on the introduction of the specifically theological principle.[57]

2.3 Horizons and Categories

The 1968 'Ch. III: Horizons and Categories' is shifted in 1969 from the 'Background' to the 'Foreground,' and finds a place immediately after the chapter 'Dialectic and Foundations' that we have been discussing. The topics discussed remain unchanged: the old and new context in theology; the need for a new horizon for contemporary theology, one that can deal with values and with authenticity;[58] method as providing this new horizon; the new horizon as a new set of basic categories; and so forth. The reason for the shift is not indicated, but will emerge when we consider the Method course of 1970.

3   1970: Dialectic and Foundations

In the 1970 course Method in Theology,[59] dialectic and foundations emerge with separate chapters of their own, and the treatment of each functional specialty is considerably more sophisticated. There is no chapter 'Horizons and Categories' anymore: it has been absorbed into the discussions of dialectic and foundations. Thus, the first section on the meaning of horizon may be found in the opening section of the chapter 'Dialectic.'[60] We may note here that the distinction between genetically related horizons and dialectically differing horizons is equivalent to the distinction between relative horizons rooted in development and absolute horizons rooted in conversion or lack of it, and that dialectic concentrates principally on dialectically related horizons. Again, sections 4 to 7 on categories may be found in the chapter on foundations. However, the second section ('Method as Horizon') and the third section ('Old and New') are dropped, as also the eighth and ninth sections ('Theologians and Science'

Dialectic and Foundations 181

and 'Pluralism'). The most obvious meaning of all this is that dialectic and foundations deal with horizons and categories. Dialectic distinguishes relative and absolute horizons, and moves towards a genetic and dialectical unification of horizons; that is, towards a comprehensive viewpoint. But perhaps there is a deeper significance to be discovered: that foundations yields a methodical horizon or basic context, and this despite the omission of the important section on method as horizon. To these points we will return later.

3.1 Dialectic

As far as dialectic is concerned, the major development in 1970 is that self-appropriation is no longer affirmed as a condition for dialectic; it is shifted instead to foundations. On the other hand, the twofold precept of developing positions and reversing counterpositions is anticipated to dialectic.[61] Correspondingly, we note the absence of the discussion about the philosophic, moral, and religious neutrality of dialectic.

Dialectic remains religiously neutral in the sense already explained. Religious conversion and horizon operate in the first phase, but as a concrete fact, not as a criterion.[62] Again, the position on philosophical neutrality does not change, for the dialectic of 1970 remains an extension of transcendental method.[63] This is clear also from Lonergan's response to papers at the 1970 International Lonergan Congress:

> While then I think the method possesses considerable theological neutrality, it is not methodically neutral and it is not philosophically neutral. It cannot be methodically neutral, for if one proposes a method, one means what one says and not something else. It is not philosophically neutral for it evaporates into thin air when rather firm positions on cognitional and moral operations, on their objectivity, and on the corresponding reality either are not grasped or are abandoned.[64]

The real effect of the shift of self-appropriation to foundations is that method becomes open not merely in a religious sense but also in an intellectual and moral sense. For in 1969 dialectic was religiously open, but it was not likewise philosophically open, for intellectual and moral self-appropriation was demanded as a prerequisite for the practice of dialectic; in 1970, instead, the latter demand is dropped, and dialectic becomes completely open.

Further, the shifting of self-appropriation to foundations renders the text more harmonious, for though the 1969 text had demanded self-appropriation, still it had spoken of a movement towards self-transcendence through encounter and of the precariousness of human achievement of authenticity.[65] The 1970 text presses forward in this direction: self-appropriation is not so much a condition for dialectic, as the ideal towards which dialectic tends.

Dialectic in fact does effect a partial self-appropriation, insofar as it involves a partial objectification of horizon. Such objectification of horizon is the function of the twofold precept of developing positions and reversing counterpositions, anticipated from foundations to dialectic.[66] This precept functions as an upper level of operators to the lower level of data. The procedure consists in assembling the results of research, interpretation, and history; completing them with evaluative interpretation and history; comparing, picking out affinities and oppositions; and identifying and selecting those affinities and oppositions that have roots in dialectically opposed horizons.[67] Once the basic affinities and oppositions have been identified, one applies the precepts: one develops what one considers positions, and reverses what one considers counterpositions. The point is to exaggerate: 'manifest to the full where you stand – gathering or scattering.'[68]

Such a procedure is by no means automatic. The definitive identification of positions and counterpositions remains the task of foundations. All that dialectic does is to provide the possibility of 'bringing to a head the divisions to which theology is subjected.'[69] *Method in Theology* compares this to the crucial experiment:

> Such an objectification of subjectivity is in the style of the crucial experiment. While it will not be automatically efficacious, it will provide the open-minded, the serious, the sincere with the occasion to ask themselves some basic questions, first, about others but eventually, even about themselves. It will make conversion a topic and thereby promote it.[70]

The omission of self-appropriation from dialectic constitutes an important departure from the hermeneutical canon of relevance that demanded operation from the universal viewpoint. How is this difference between *Insight* and *Method* to be interpreted? Relevant here is the 1973 interview in which Lonergan says that, whereas *Insight* was concerned with a 'systematic presentation of the problems of interpretation,' *Method* presents 'an orderly set of directions on what is to be done towards moving to the attainment of universal viewpoint.'[71] Chapters 7 to 11 of *Method*, he says, are a more concrete expression of the third section of chapter 17 of *Insight*.[72] I would suggest that the contrast here is not between static system and method but rather between a presentation of problems and a methodical proposal. For chapter 17 of *Insight* had concentrated on the problem of interpretation and on its solution; on its own account, what it had to say about method was only a sketch.[73] Again, we had been told that no effort would be made 'to specify the numerous and complicated techniques of the lower blade of a methodical hermeneutics.'[74] The problem is that prescinding from the lower blade results in a tendency to prescind from the actual process of interpretation.[75] A useful analogy here is the distinction in *Method* between being in love in an unrestricted manner as defined and as achieved. As defined, being in love is 'the habitual actuation of man's capacity for self-transcendence,' but 'as it actually is achieved in any human being, the achievement is dialectical. It is authenticity as a withdrawal from unauthenticity.'[76] In some similar way, chapter 17 of *Insight* with its emphasis on the upper blade of interpretation tends to concentrate on the ideal at the expense of the actual. Thus, the hermeneutical canon of relevance demands attainment of the universal viewpoint.[77] But the concrete subject is usually only on the way, not only towards the universal viewpoint as high and distant goal, but also towards the notion of the universal viewpoint itself. The functional specialty dialectic takes into account this movement towards the ideal, and is thus a more practical version of the solution to the problem of interpretation outlined in chapter 17 of *Insight*. The point we have been making in this section is that one of the key steps towards this more practical way is the 1970 shift of intellectual, moral, and religious self-appropriation to the functional specialty foundations.

3.2 Foundations

We have noted above that the section 'Method as Horizon' of the 1969 chapter 'Horizons and Categories' does not find a place in the 1970 text.[78] However, some echo of it is to be found in the chapter 'Foundations' when it indicates that, if one desires foundations for ongoing process, one must move from the static, deductive style to the methodical style. What is important is control of the process, and such control is, as in 1965, through authenticity or threefold conversion.[79]

Foundations still has the task of distinguishing positions and counterpositions, but now the positive function of foundations is given greater relief. It is described as concerned with the basis not of the whole of theology but only of doctrines, systematics, and communications. Again, it seeks not the whole foundation of these specialties – for they depend also on the first four specialties – but only the added foundation needed to move from indirect to direct discourse.[80]

Transcendental method itself continues to play, as in 1964, the basic foundational role.[81] But with the shifting of cognitional and moral self-appropriation to the functional specialty foundations, the relationship between transcendental method and foundations is rendered more complex. A clue to this is given by Lonergan's answer to M. Vertin in 1975: 'Foundational theology is *A*. Method (Back- and Foreground) *B*. The specialty that applies conversions to dialectical options.'[82] Foundations now generates not only special but also general categories. Now general categories are the *communia* of the course of fall 1963, which constituted heuristic structures for the investigation of the *propria*. But this means that general categories are really the upper blade of transcendental method, that they are the objectification of the horizon determined by transcendental method. We might say therefore that foundations yields a methodical horizon. We can also say that, while foundations is an extension of transcendental method, transcendental method is itself ratified in foundations. But this subtlety is really the key to the openness of theological method.

Since the ongoing process of derivation of the categories has been adequately clarified by Hefling,[83] we need not enter into details. The genesis of the special categories occurs in the first four specialties, but they emerge most clearly in dialectic,[84] with explicit commitment to them occurring in foundations.[85] *Method* speaks of the genesis of the special categories as occurring 'seminally in dialectic,' alluding once again to the dependence of dialectic on the previous three specialties.[86] Further, method is a question of a scissors movement, with the lower blade in data and the upper blade in heuristic structures or categories. The categories are constantly challenged by the data, and become more and more refined and differentiated through such interaction. Thus, the categories derived in foundations through cognitional, moral, and religious self-appropriation function as an upper blade for subsequent investigation,[87] and through such interaction with historical data they are subjected to a process of ongoing clarification and further determination.[88] Theology 'can be neither purely *a priori* nor purely *a posteriori* but only the fruit of an ongoing process that has one foot in a transcultural base and the other on increasingly organized data.'[89]

4   1971: The Collaborative Dimension of Dialectic

Since the position on foundations is stable by 1970, the present section deals only with the further refinement that dialectic undergoes in 1971, illuminating it with insights from the post-*Method* years. One of the most important points introduced into the 1971 text is what we may refer to as the double application of dialectic. It is observed that the work of assembly, completion, comparison, reduction, classification, and selection will be performed by different investigators operating from within different horizons; the results accordingly will not be uniform. The source of this lack of uniformity will be brought out (1) when the investigator distinguishes positions and counterpositions, (2) when, further, he/she develops positions and reverses counterpositions, and (3) when, finally, the results of the foregoing steps 'are themselves regarded as materials, when they are assembled, completed, compared, reduced, classified, selected, when positions and counter-positions are distinguished, when positions are developed and counter-positions are reversed.'[90] It is the third step above that I refer to as a 'second application' of dialectic. *Method* itself notes elsewhere that 'the functional specialty, dialectic, assembles, classifies, analyzes the conflicting views of *evaluators*, historians, interpreters, researchers.'[91] Again, among notes for the Summer School at the University of San Francisco (1972) there may be found the following remark:

> This work of assembly completion ... will be performed by different theologians / A second level dialectic will examine their results for compl[etion] compar[ison] red[uction] class[ification] s[e]lec[tion] ...[92]

Further, a paper of 1977 notes: 'But the very people that investigate the dialectic of history also are part of that dialectic and even in their investigating represent its contradictories. To their work too the dialectic is to be applied.'[93]

The double application of dialectic is an extremely important innovation. Transcendental method and functional specialization already make theology a collaborative enterprise within a common framework. Further, the first application of dialectic is already an encounter with the history-making persons of the past.[94] But the second application amounts to encounter between the history-writing persons of the present, and so the communitarian dimension of knowledge is integrated even more explicitly into method. Through the first application of dialectic, dialectical oppositions in the past are brought to light; through the second application of dialectic, dialectical oppositions in the present are brought to light.

The double application of dialectic is completed and crowned by a notion that becomes thematic only in the post-*Method* period: dialogue. The point is that even the second application may be done in two manners, one of which deals with subjects as objects, and the other with subjects as subjects. The latter possibility is dialogue. The 1976 paper 'The Ongoing Genesis of Methods' describes it thus:

> Finally, besides the dialectic that is concerned with human subjects as objects, there is the dialectic in which human subjects are concerned

186   Part Three: *Method in Theology*

with themselves and with one another. In that case dialectic becomes dialogue. It is particularly relevant when persons are authentic and know one another to be authentic yet belong to differing traditions and so find themselves in basic disagreement. It may be illustrated by the ecumenical movement among Christians and by the universalist movement set forth by R.E. Whitson in his *The Coming Convergence of World Religions*, by Raymond Panikkar's diacritical theology and by William Johnston's Christian monks frequenting Zen monasteries in Japan.[95]

Again, the 1977 article 'Natural Right and Historical Mindedness' speaks of the application of dialectic to investigators themselves, and then adds:

But it can be more helpful, especially when oppositions are less radical, for the investigators to move beyond dialectic to dialogue, to transpose issues from a conflict of statements to an encounter of persons. For every person is an embodiment of natural right. Every person can reveal to any other his natural propensity to seek understanding, to judge reasonably, to evaluate fairly, to be open to friendship. While the dialectic of history coldly relates our conflicts, dialogue adds the principle that prompts us to cure them, the natural right that is the inmost core of our being.[96]

An example of how dialogue might be expected to function may be found in the discussions at the 1977 Lonergan Workshop:

Now, the difference between Dialectic and Dialogue is that everyone has his own little self-starter of asking further questions ... And if you bring that self-starter into the picture, actually operating, you get dialogue ... The difference between dialogue and dialectic is that you have as many sources, principles of direction, of elimination of bad judgments, of value judgments, operative in the discussion, as there are persons there, or at least as there are genuine persons there.[97]

If already dialectic is encounter, dialogue is encounter with the living persons of the present. It represents the culmination of the collaborative enterprise that is theological method. It is through dialectic and ultimately through dialogue that there occurs the movement towards the comprehensive or universal viewpoint.

We may note that the notion of dialogue is not without its antecedents in Lonergan's thinking: there was, for example, the Greek propensity for dialogue and the scholastic disputation mentioned in *De constitutione Christi* ... (1956) as indirect means to conversion.[98] Again, Lonergan was not unaware that in its historical origins dialectic itself was communitarian. If in Aristotle it was an individual art, in Plato it was the art of philosophic dialogue.[99] But as inserted within theological method, dialogue becomes the full flowering of the shift from science as an individual habit to community as the carrier of science, the crowning point of the fact that progress in knowledge is properly attributed to the human species rather than to the human individual.[100]

5 Conclusion

The goal of dialectic is distinguished from its base: the goal is named the comprehensive viewpoint, and the base is transcendental method. The change in name is accounted for not only by this distinction, but also by the fact that the notion of the universal viewpoint has been replaced by transcendental method. We note that the term comprehensive viewpoint occurs only in the chapter 'Functional Specialties' of 1968 and persists into the published text of *Method*; thus it would seem to be a carry-over from earlier drafts.

In 1969, dialectic is religiously neutral and open to all religious, anti-religious and even non-religious viewpoints. It is not philosophically and morally neutral, nor is it open to just any philosophical or moral viewpoint: cognitional and moral self-appropriation is a prerequisite for engaging in dialectic. Foundations, by contrast, while being described as objectifying triple conversion, is concerned principally with religious conversion and the introduction of a specifically theological principle into theology. The religious neutrality and openness of dialectic is a step beyond the comprehensive viewpoint as totality of Christian viewpoints; however, since the context of the comprehensive viewpoint is general history, we may regard the comprehensive viewpoint as coinciding with the universal viewpoint as ideal goal.

In 1970, the requirement of self-appropriation is dropped and dialectic becomes open to every sort of philosophical, moral, and religious persuasion. The chapter 'Horizons and Categories,' shifted in 1969 to the 'Foreground,' is now absorbed into 'Dialectic' and 'Foundations.' Some echo of the section 'Method as Horizon' may be found in the description of the new type of foundations required for a methodical type of theology. At any rate, it is clear that dialectic and foundations deal with horizons and categories: dialectic lines up horizons, while foundations selects between them; categories are generated seminally in dialectic, while commitment to them occurs in foundations.

The collaborative dimension of dialectic may be seen as a consequence of the new notion of habit that transcends the restrictions of individual faculties as well as of particular minds. Dialogue itself may be seen as the culmination of the openness of dialectic. Thus, the comprehensiveness and universality of the goal of dialectic is matched by the complete openness of the method itself.

12

The Universal Viewpoint in *Method in Theology*

1   The Universal Viewpoint and Transcendental Method

1.1   Method as Horizon

The relationship of the universal viewpoint to transcendental method depends on the relationship between methodical horizon and transcendental method. But the latter relationship is not yet clear, for chapter 7 suggested a link between methodical horizon and transcendental method and chapter 9 confirmed that link but was unable to clarify its exact nature. A first task is, therefore, to clarify the link between methodical horizon and transcendental method.

We begin by clarifying the meaning of transcendental method in *Method in Theology*. The first chapter of *Method* describes transcendental method thus:

> [I]t is a heightening of consciousness that brings to light our conscious and intentional operations and thereby leads to the answers to three basic questions. What am I doing when I am knowing? Why is doing that knowing? What do I know when I do it? The first answer is a cognitional theory. The second is an epistemology. The third is a metaphysics where, however, the metaphysics is transcendental, an integration of heuristic structures.[1]

The close relationship between cognitional theory, epistemology, and metaphysics has been affirmed as early as 1962. Thus, the Regis course of 1962 notes that meeting the critical exigence involves doing, in a single leap as it were, psychology, epistemology, and metaphysics.² Again, in conversations with G.B. Sala in 1965, Lonergan insists that metaphysics is for him only one part of the transcendental unity composed of cognitional theory, epistemology, and metaphysics. There is no knowing without objects; there is no cognitional theory without metaphysics; the three cannot be separated.³ The papers of 1965 indicate the meaning of 'transcendental': for scholastics it is a property of terms or objects; for Kant it means conditions of possibility of knowing objects insofar as that knowledge is a priori; but for Lonergan, transcendental method is a question of operations given in experience (cognitional theory), in their relations (epistemology) to the totality of objects (heuristic structures – metaphysics, methods).⁴ If that is not enough, there is 'Philosophy and Theology' of 1970, which is explicit on the matter: 'There is the question of cognitional theory: What precisely is one doing when one is knowing? There is the question of epistemology: Why is doing that knowing? There is the question of metaphysics? [*sic*] What does one know when one does it? When the foregoing questions are answered with philosophic generality, one is already in possession of a transcendental method.'⁵

Now it is possible to show that such a transcendental method coincides with total and basic horizon or methodical horizon. In its chapter on doctrines, *Method* calls for a general science that will be first cognitional theory, then epistemology, and in the third place metaphysics.⁶ I suggest that the 'general science' mentioned here is a translation of the *Gesamt- und Grundwissenschaft* mentioned in the review article 'Metaphysics as Horizon' of 1963.⁷ If this is true, it follows that 'general science' is a reference to the total and basic horizon of 1963. This interpretation finds confirmation in the 'Questionnaire on Philosophy' of 1976, which speaks of philosophy precisely as the *Gesamt- und Grundwissenschaft*, the total and basic science that includes cognitional theory, epistemology, metaphysics as well as existential ethics,⁸ and goes on to identify this total and basic science with total and basic method⁹ and indeed with 'the generalized empirical method born of the reflective interplay between acting out the operations of the particular disciplines and thematizing the operations one is acting out.'¹⁰

In the light of the subject-object polarity of methodical horizon and of method itself, the later descriptions of transcendental method are very significant. Thus a paper of 1975 says that the term transcendental 'would refer not only to objects (one, true, real, good) and not only to the *a priori* of the subject but to both together, to the *a priori* of the subject's questions and to the range of objects disclosed in answers.'¹¹ Similarly, a paper of 1976 observes that generalized empirical method operates 'on a combination of both the data of sense and the data of consciousness: it does not treat of objects without taking into account the corresponding operations of the subject; it does not treat of the subject's operations without taking into account the corresponding objects.'[12] Very interestingly, a note distinguishes three meanings of the term transcendental: 'the most general and all-pervasive concepts, namely, *ens, unum, verum, bonum,* of the Scholastics; the Kantian conditions of the possibility of knowing an object *a priori*; Husserl's intentionality analysis in which *noêsis* and *noêma*, act and object, are correlative.'[13]

Again, if transcendental method coincides with methodical horizon, it should not be surprising that at times Lonergan speaks of transcendental method itself as an upper blade. Thus a paper of 1977 observes: 'Just as mathematics provides the theoretical underpinning of the exact sciences, so there is a generalized empirical method or, if you prefer, a transcendental method that performs a similar role in human studies.'[14] The *Method* course of 1969 is even more explicit because it speaks of the three parts of method, gnoseology, epistemology and metaphysics, as standing to the human sciences as mathematics stands to the natural sciences.[15] This position is repeated during the question periods, when Lonergan compares method and data to the scissors structure of the method of physics and then adds: 'Similarly you[r] method and your data generally are a pair of scissors and part of this upper blade, all of it is transcendental method.'[16]

The description of transcendental method itself as an upper blade is significant because it implies that the upper blade is not merely the integral set of heuristic structures but also cognitional theory and epistemology. In *Insight*, both genetic method and hermeneutical method were formulated in an explicitly metaphysical context; in *Method*, instead, the basic set of categories is psychological; metaphysics is explicitly and deliberately tertiary. Thus, we are told that in the measure that transcendental method is objectified, 'there are determined a set of basic terms and relations, namely, the terms that refer to the operations of cognitional process, and the relations that link these operations to one another. Such terms and relations are the substance of cognitional theory. They reveal the ground for epistemology. They are found to be isomorphic with the terms and relations denoting the ontological structure of any reality proportionate to human cognitional process.'[17] It was the priority of metaphysics in the Aristotelian tradition that led to a faculty psychology; the overcoming of the priority of metaphysics leads instead to a shift from faculty psychology to intentionality analysis.[18]

We have been establishing that transcendental method does indeed coincide with methodical horizon, and already we can say something about the universal viewpoint in the context of *Method*. In contrast to the universal viewpoint that was formulated in a metaphysical context, and which indeed coincided with the integral heuristic structure that was dialectical metaphysics, transcendental method is primarily cognitional theory, then epistemology, and only in the third place metaphysics. Thus, its basic set of categories is psychological; metaphysical categories are derived from these; the upper blade therefore need not necessarily be the integral set of heuristic structures that is metaphysics. In this sense, transcendental method is 'less metaphysical and more concrete' than the universal viewpoint.

It is equally clear, however, that metaphysics does form part of method. But this means that the universal viewpoint as heuristic structure is not completely abandoned in *Method*. This, I would suggest, is in fact the significance of the mention of the universal viewpoint in the list of derived general categories.[19] But more of this below.

1.2 Method as 'General Dynamics': The Shift from Faculty Psychology

We have been saying that while transcendental method coincides with methodical horizon, it is less metaphysical and more concrete than the universal viewpoint of chapter 17 of *Insight*. We must now add that it is also more flexible. In contrast to *Insight*'s reluctance to speak of the universal viewpoint as including the level of doing, *Method* does not hesitate to describe transcendental method as a question of appropriating operations on four levels. This is perfectly in keeping with the general method of 1962 with its ability to handle all three conversions, with the recognition of method as 'unpleasantly existential' in 1964, and with the emergence of the notion of value and the affirmation of the primacy of the existential in 1968. Yet the chapter ends with the description of method as a question of answering three basic questions, with no mention of the ethical or existential dimension.[20]

One option here would be to speak of an inconsistency or, more benignly, of a lag: while method is able to handle the existential level of consciousness, the description of method has not been adjusted correspondingly. Such an interpretation would find some support in the fact that the 'Questionnaire on Philosophy' of 1976 comes round to including 'existential ethics' within the total and basic science that is philosophy.[21] The problem is that even here the list of three basic questions is not expanded to include a fourth question about existential ethics. Further, a paper of 1977 returns once again to the description of generalized empirical method in terms of raising and answering the three basic questions.[22] The 'Questionnaire on Philosophy' of 1976 remains in fact the only place in which Lonergan includes existential ethics explicitly within what he understands by philosophy.

It would, therefore, seem obligatory to seek some other explanation about the relationship between transcendental method and the fourth level of consciousness. Now there exists an interview of 1975 in which precisely this question was put to Lonergan: why is transcendental method confined in *Method* to answering the three basic questions, thus omitting the moral aspect? Lonergan's reply was as follows:

> I am inclined to omit the term, philosophy, as misleading.
> With regard to the world mediated by meaning, I would distinguish:
> a) meaning organized by logic: Aristotle, Aquinas, Kant,
> b) meaning organized by methods of Natur- u. Geisteswissenschaften
> Hegel's logic-in-motion as transitional phase with its antithesis in contingent and irrational factors in nature and in human affairs
> c) transcendental foundations of methods logics ethics [*sic*].[23]

This cryptic reply calls for some comment, and we may do this by asking about (1) the way in which the term 'philosophy' is misleading, (2) the meaning of 'Hegel's logic-in-motion as transitional phase,' and (3) just how transcendental foundations of methods, logics, and ethics would overcome the disadvantages of the term 'philosophy.'

The first point is illuminated by discussions at the Lonergan Workshop of 1976:

> [W]hat I have to say about bias in *Insight* chapter seven would be an expression of originated original sin ... And its theological source is my dissertation on *Grace and Freedom, gratia operans* and moral impotence. Is it a philosophical explanation? Well, really I would drop the word philosophy from my vocabulary. What the theologian needs is method based on an understanding, a formulation and an acceptance of what goes on in his 'black box.'[24]

The reason for such a position follows. 'To speak of philosophy in the traditional sense is to accept the Aristotelian conception of the hierarchy of the sciences'; but this, in Lonergan's opinion, leads to all sorts of puzzles.[25] Pressed on the point, Lonergan brings in the topic of the overcoming of speculative intellect in modern philosophy: the age of innocence is over, and the fundamental issue is conversion.[26] Method instead, or answering the three basic questions, is just as relevant to the natural as to the supernatural order;[27] it both cuts free from the puzzles arising from the Aristotelian hierarchy of the sciences, and is able to handle the fundamental issue, conversion.

The discussion goes on to mention Hegel's logic-in-motion, and so we come to our second point. Hegel, though rightly concerned with movement, wrongly placed it within logic.[28] Lonergan, by contrast, feels that such a logic of movement does not solve the problem. He would leave logic to its traditional tasks and maintain instead that '[t]he guide of philosophy and science over time is method.'[29] The point, says Lonergan, has been made already in the 1970 paper 'Philosophy and Theology,' and in the 1972 lectures on philosophy of God and theology.[30] But perhaps an even clearer expression is the paper 'The Ongoing Genesis of Methods,' read at the 1976 Lonergan Workshop itself.[31] This paper notes that there has to be a shift 'from statics to dynamics,'[32] and that the dynamism must be placed not in the conceptual realm but in the methodical:

> For a quite static view of the nature of the sciences and of their relations to one another can be had from Aristotelian analysis in terms of material and formal objects. In contrast, a quite dynamic view of the same matter is had when sciences are conceived in terms of method and field, and methods are not fixed once for all but keep developing, differentiating, regrouping as the exigences of advance may demand.[33]

Hence the title of the paper, 'The Ongoing Genesis of Methods.' A paper of 1980 in fact refers to method itself as general dynamics, and this in explicit contrast to Hegel's necessitarian and dialectical logic.[34] It could be said, therefore, that Lonergan's method is not only post-Aristotelian and post-Kantian,[35] but also explicitly and consciously post-Hegelian.

If we ask, further, about the relevance of the shift from statics to dynamics, we will have indicated how method overcomes the disadvantages of 'philosophy,' and how this constitutes a reply to Vertin's question. The basic discussion here is to be found in *Philosophy of God, and Theology*. Thus:

> If the viewpoint is static, then from the very start everything really is settled. Nothing new can be added at any point after one has started. On the other hand, if the viewpoint is dynamic, then there can be added any number of reflections and discoveries that at the start were not included in one's assumptions.
>
> The static viewpoint is the ideal of deductivist logic ...
>
> The dynamic viewpoint, on the contrary, is a moving viewpoint. One starts from what one already knows or thinks one knows. One advances by learning what others have discovered and, perhaps occasionally, one may discover something for oneself.[36]

Now the context of this discussion is the relationship between philosophy of God and the functional specialty systematics, but its import is, I think, much larger, so that it is relevant to the question why Lonergan's description of transcendental method does not seem to include the existential aspect. For once the shift has been made to a dynamic viewpoint, it would seem that the important thing is the establishment of the basic nucleus of operations; all other methods arise from the adaptation of this nucleus to particular fields.[37] If transcendental method is able to provide the nucleus of all methods, whether or not it includes the question of value is quite secondary. What is important is method as 'transcendental foundations of methods logics ethics,' and this is a question of moving to a new organization of meaning or to a new control of meaning through the self-appropriation of one's conscious and intentional operations.

We must add that the basic solution has been adopted already in *Insight*: the epilogue notes that it is the moving viewpoint or the inner dynamism of inquiry that provides the solution to the methodological problem 'of the reconciliation of the independence of other fields and of the universal relevance of theology.'[38] However, the level of doing was never included within the universal viewpoint, not even in the epilogue, where the moving viewpoint is abandoned in favor of the terminal viewpoint of the believer. The point is that the universal viewpoint of *Insight* seems to be in some way still bound by the limitations of faculty psychology, and that these limitations were overcome only subsequently with the new notion of habit worked out with help from Piaget and group theory. Once again, then, the difference between the universal viewpoint and transcendental method is a difference arising from consistent application of the shift from faculty psychology to intentionality analysis. Once this shift has been consistently carried out, there is no difficulty in conceiving method as arising from an appropriation, not only of the integral heuristic structure of knowing, but also of the deeper structure that arises from the addition of the level of doing.

1.3 Method as Contemporary Stage of the Ascent to the Universal Viewpoint

Like the universal viewpoint, transcendental method amounts to the achievement of a new control over meaning, or the achievement of control over emergent probability in the properly human realm. We may approach this point by examining the rest of Lonergan's reply to Vertin:

> I agree with Butterfield that modern science is the biggest thing in human affairs since advent of Xtianity [*sic*]
>
> I add that only in the XXth century does the nature of modern science come adequately to light.[39]

Once again, this is cryptic, but not really difficult. For Lonergan has distinguished three broad stages in the organization of meaning: the logical, the methodical, and the stage of transcendental foundations of methods.[40] The mention of Butterfield is related to the second stage, where meaning is organized by the methods of the natural and the human sciences.[41] The final remark takes up a point that Lonergan makes repeatedly elsewhere, that despite the shift to method, the necessitarian ideal continued to lurk within the natural sciences, and that it was finally exorcised only in the twentieth century by the relativization of Euclidean geometry, the acceptance of Einsteinian relativity, and the advent of quantum mechanics.[42] Thus, it is only in the twentieth century that there has become possible the formulation of transcendental foundations of methods, logics, and ethics.

Method is, therefore, the contemporary stage of the ascent to the universal viewpoint. This may be further illuminated by adverting to two observations, both made in the context of Rahner's remarks on theological method:

> For Fr. Rahner's puzzlement over the swarm of disparate theologies that resist precise classification and so escape theological judgement, we may offer a set of larger containers, namely, the ordered multiplicity of differentiations of consciousness and their diversification by the presence or absence of religious, moral, or intellectual conversion. Such broad genetic differences can serve to mark off frontiers that contain conceptually disparate views.[43]

> For if one understands by method ... a framework for collaboration in creativity and, more particularly, a normative pattern of related and repeated operations with ongoing and cumulative results, then I believe one will find ways to control the present uncontrollable pluralism of theologies, one will cease to work alien, alone, isolated, one will become aware of a common site with an edifice to be erected, not in accord with a static blueprint, but under the leadership of an emergent probability that yields results proportionate to human diligence and intelligence.[44]

The links with the notion of the universal viewpoint could not be clearer: method provides a framework for collaborative creativity precisely because it envisages an ordered totality of genetically and dialectically ordered differentiations of consciousness. Further, the second remark cited here confirms the point that method is itself a continuation of emergent probability. Confirmation from other sources is not lacking. In the interview given at the 1970 Florida Congress, Lonergan agrees that the shift to interiority is axial, in Jaspers's sense.[45] But method is the mediation of theory and common sense by interiority, and so it is a new stage in the ascent to the universal viewpoint. Elsewhere, method is described as a differentiation of consciousness to deal explicitly with differentiations of consciousness.[46] Further, it presupposes a multiple differentiation of consciousness.[47] Still again, the *Method* chapter on doctrines indicates quite clearly that determination of the legitimacy of any particular doctrinal development is a question of evaluational history, but that evaluational history itself presupposes an answer to the more general question as to how developments are possible; and the answer to that question lies in the differentiations of consciousness.[48] There follows a list of differentiations of consciousness, culminating in the interior differentiation of consciousness.[49] This last is described as offering 'an invariant basis for ongoing systems and a standpoint from which all the differentiations of human consciousness can be explored.'[50] The next section opens with the remark that the differentiations 'also characterize successive stages in cultural development,' which may be named 'the ongoing discovery of the mind.'[51] There may be no need to belabor the point: the formulation of transcendental method is the contemporary stage of the ascent to the universal viewpoint.

2   The Universal Viewpoint and Theological Method

The philosophy of *Insight* was already methodical, having made the shift from objects to operations (it begins not with metaphysics but with cognitional theory). The problem was that the 'theology' of *Insight* was not adequately methodical, first insofar as the entry into the theological realm was through the deduction of God's existence, and second inasmuch as *Insight* ignored religious experience and conversion and so neglected the concrete subject.[52]

In *Method in Theology* we have a new and properly methodical notion of theology. At its root, this is the result of the achievement within theology of the shift from the Aristotelian to a properly methodical viewpoint. We have studied this shift in the previous chapter, and in the present chapter itself we have spoken of method as general dynamics, but we may adduce here a very accurate summary from Lonergan himself:

> [A]s long as one remains within the Aristotelian orbit, one conceives theology in terms of its material and formal objects and, indeed, of its *formale quod* and *formale quo*. On the other hand, when one adopts a strictly methodological viewpoint, the emphasis shifts from objects to operations and operators. In terms of functional specialties theology is an eightfold set of interdependent normative patterns of recurrent

and related operations with progressive and cumulative results. Where formerly a discipline was specifically theological because it dealt with revealed truths, now it is authentically theological because the theologian has been converted intellectually, morally, and religiously.[53]

On the deductivist notion, theology is distinguished from other disciplines insofar as it takes its premises from revelation. Within such a context, the integration of historical scholarship into theology remains a problem; disciplines such as research, interpretation, and history remain at most auxiliary. On the methodological viewpoint, the important point is not whether one is doing philosophy or theology; the point is to discern whether or not there obtains conversion.[54] Accordingly, there can be included within theology disciplines that were formerly considered auxiliary.

Once the shift to method has been achieved consistently, the distinction between philosophy and theology does not vanish, but the separation between them is overcome.[55] This relationship is perhaps best crystallized in the late notion of the two vectors of human development.[56] Human development occurs in two modes. Both begin from infancy and are interdependent. Such interdependence supposes distinction but opposes separation. In philosophy the emphasis is on self-appropriation, while in theology the emphasis is on the Christian tradition.[57] Differences in emphasis do not necessitate separation; such separation is less the product of Christian wisdom or prudence than of Cartesian universal doubt and of the Enlightenment identification of tradition with prejudice.[58] The 'theoretical shift is from philosophy as it would be worked out by men *in statu naturae purae* to philosophy that along with modern science is concerned not with abstract universals but with concrete realities.'[59] There is, in other words, no such thing as pure reason; every action is performed under the guidance of one's commitments, within some horizon.[60] Both philosophy and theology begin from the concrete subject, and this subject is open to a conversion that is not only intellectual and moral but also religious.

In the light of these observations, let us attempt to determine what happens to the theological transformation of the universal viewpoint in *Method*. It would be helpful to distinguish here (1) the transition from natural to supernatural; (2) the transition from the universal viewpoint to the theologically transformed universal viewpoint; (3) the extension of transcendental method to the field of theology; and (4) the transition from the first phase to the second phase in the theological method of 1972.

It cannot be said that *Insight* was worked out in the context of the separation between natural and supernatural, for not only did metaphysics take as its starting point the concrete subject,[61] but also the epilogue reveals explicit awareness of the issue, for it notes that the empirical human sciences, and philosophy insofar as it becomes existential, deal with human beings in the concrete, and that human beings in the concrete are in need of grace and receive, accept, or reject it.[62] Still, it remains that the key moment in the transition from the universal viewpoint to the theologically transformed universal viewpoint was the deduction of God's existence.[63] This in fact constituted the tension within *Insight*, for it embodied a concern with objects and with proofs that contrasted with the concern with operations and with the concrete subject embodied in the first part of *Insight*. *Method*, by contrast, is clearly worked out within the properly methodical context, and acknowledges the full implications of the fact that there is no starting point *in statu naturae purae*. Accordingly, it recognizes there is no need for a deductive transition into the theological realm. Theological foundations are a question of thematizing religious horizon and using it as a criterion for judgment, rather than proving the existence of God and of the divine solution to the problem of evil.

Accordingly *Method* speaks, not of the theological transformation of transcendental method, but rather of an extension of transcendental method to theology. This is a question of working out accounts of the human good, of meaning, and of religion on the basis of transcendental method; of setting up foundational accounts of scholarship, of doctrines, systematics, and communications; and of adding to these the further functional specialties needed to effect the transition from the indirect discourse of scholarship to the direct discourse of doctrines, systematics, and communications.[64]

In the context of such a theological method, the shift from indirect to direct discourse is not a shift from pure reason or historical reason to the supernatural realm,[65] but rather from what is spontaneous and *vécu* to what is deliberate and *thématique*. For if transcendental method begins from the concrete subject that each one actually is, then the first phase of method is carried out not in some hypothetical state of pure nature, but on the basis of the concrete subject that one is. The difference between the first and second phase is then a difference between conversion as functioning spontaneously and conversion as thematized and used explicitly as a theological criterion.[66] But this means (1) that *Method* is similar to the first part of *Insight*, where one moves through dialectic to cognitional foundations, rather than to the final part of *Insight*, where the transition to the theologically transformed universal viewpoint is initiated through the deduction of God's existence; (2) that like the first part of *Insight*, theological foundations – both general and special categories – are generated through self-appropriation in interaction with data, and are further clarified and determined through subsequent interaction.

There is, therefore, no theological transformation of the universal viewpoint in *Method*. In its place there is an extension of transcendental method into theology; and within the resulting theological method, the transition from indirect to direct discourse is a transition from what is *vécu* and spontaneous to what is *thématique* and deliberate. Something similar to the moving viewpoint of *Insight* is therefore to be found in *Method*: one begins with cognitional theory, moves on to epistemology and metaphysics, through accounts of the human good and meaning, to a philosophy of religion and to an account of functional specialties.

3   The Universal Viewpoint and the Functional Specialty Dialectic

We turn now to the relationship between the universal viewpoint and the functional specialty dialectic. We recall that the term universal viewpoint appears only twice in *Method*, both times in reference to *Insight*. The first occurrence is in a footnote which tells us that the universal viewpoint is now realized through dialectic: 'For instance, what there [in *Insight*] is termed a universal viewpoint, here [in *Method*] is realized by advocating a distinct functional specialty named dialectic.'[67] The second occurrence is in the section on general theological categories in the chapter 'Foundations': 'The problems of interpretation bring to light the notion of a potential universal viewpoint that moves over levels and sequences of expression.'[68]

From our previous chapter we bring forward the conclusions (1) that the comprehensive viewpoint mentioned in chapter 5 of *Method* coincides, in extension if not in intension, with the universal viewpoint as goal, and (2) that a distinction is to be drawn between the goal of dialectic, which is the comprehensive viewpoint, and the base of dialectic, which is transcendental method.

In the light of these conclusions, we propose that the universal viewpoint mentioned in the footnote in chapter 7 of *Method* is the high and distant goal of dialectic. But in what sense is it a high and distant goal? Hefling distinguishes between the universal viewpoint and the comprehensive viewpoint: the latter, he says, seems to correspond to the theologically transformed universal viewpoint. In *Insight*, the theological component in the latter is derived from the magisterium; in *Method*, instead, this component – the special theological categories – has itself to be generated in the ongoing historical process of the self-constitution of the Church. It is this difference, according to Hefling, that accounts for Lonergan's reference to the universal or comprehensive viewpoint as a high and distant goal in *Method*.[69]

However, there is another sense in which the universal or comprehensive viewpoint might be a high and distant goal, for it can be regarded also as the as yet unachieved dialectical unification of viewpoints. In this sense, the universal viewpoint – and the theologically transformed universal viewpoint as well – is a high and distant goal already in *Insight*.

What then are we to say? We might put the matter as follows. In chapter 17 of *Insight* we have movement towards the universal viewpoint on the basis of a notion of the universal viewpoint: the goal is high and distant, but the heuristic notion itself is 'proximate achievement.' Attainment of the notion of the universal viewpoint is by no means equivalent to attainment of the actual totality of viewpoints; and the movement towards such attainment is, as later in *Method*, through the scissors-interaction between a priori and a posteriori components, between upper blade and data. In the epilogue of *Insight*, we have movement towards the goal of the universal viewpoint on the basis of the heuristic structure that is the theologically transformed universal viewpoint. If the notion of the universal viewpoint might be regarded as providing general theological categories, the theologically transformed universal viewpoint here includes special theological categories, insofar as faith is an assent to truths revealed by God and defined by the magisterium. In *Method*, instead, the starting point of theology is neither the notion of the universal viewpoint nor the theologically transformed universal viewpoint, for there is presupposed neither cognitional and moral self-appropriation nor assent to revealed truths. Theology begins from data and moves towards the appropriation of foundations. Both general and special theological categories are generated in the functional specialty foundations. Further, there is the ongoing process of purification and determination of the categories through interaction with data. But this amounts to saying that theology moves first towards the universal viewpoint as heuristic structure – or more precisely, towards transcendental method or the set of general and special categories – and then towards the universal or comprehensive viewpoint as high and distant goal. The foundations of theology – both general and special categories – are themselves generated in the process of theologizing.

Coming to the second reference to the universal viewpoint in the list of derived general categories in the chapter on foundations, the reference here is clearly to the universal viewpoint as heuristic structure, for the text speaks about 'the notion of a potential universal viewpoint that moves over levels and sequences of expression.'[70] Given that the term occurs in a list of derived general theological categories, it is not quite possible to brush this off as a mere reference to *Insight*. What then? Drawing together the conclusions we have arrived at we might say the following. First, the functions of the notion of the universal viewpoint are taken over by transcendental method. Second, the universal viewpoint was a heuristic structure that was a corollary of the metaphysics of *Insight*; it was therefore somehow a set of metaphysical categories. Third, in transcendental method, metaphysical categories are tertiary and psychological categories are primary; and the latter set arises from the appropriation of cognitional as well as existential consciousness. In this sense, transcendental method is 'less metaphysical and more concrete' than the universal viewpoint. Fourth, however, since metaphysics does form part of method, the universal viewpoint as heuristic structure is not completely abandoned in *Method*. The text in question refers therefore to the universal viewpoint as heuristic structure in the sense of chapter 17 of *Insight*. In *Method*, then, the universal viewpoint forms part of the set of derived general theological categories. The universal viewpoint, therefore, does continue to function as heuristic structure in *Method*; only the more basic upper blade is given by the basic set of general categories that are the terms and relations constitutive of cognitional theory.

Now chapter 5 of *Method* tells us that dialectic seeks 'some single base or some single set of related bases' from which it can proceed to a unified understanding of the many conflicting viewpoints exhibited in history, and we have seen that this base is transcendental method. But if the universal viewpoint is included within transcendental method, it follows that dialectic operates upon a basis that may include the universal viewpoint. This conclusion may be supported by further considerations. First, dialectic and foundations between them generate both general and special theological categories. Second, these categories are objectifications of the horizon rooted in intellectual, moral, and religious conversion. Third, these categories function as an upper blade for interpretation and history. Thus we are told that dialectic, when transcendentally grounded, is able 'to provide interpretation and history with heuristic structures, much as mathematics provides the natural sciences with such structures.'[71] Again, chapter 9, 'History and Historians,' speaks of two types of method: those methods 'that will help historians from the start to avoid incoherent assumptions and procedures,' and 'further methods that will serve to iron out differences once incompatible histories have been written.'[72] A similar observation may be found in Lonergan's response to papers at the Florida Congress of 1970. If the first five functional specialties are to be performed properly, he points out, certain requirements must be met:

> The first is that one's idea of interpretation and of critical history must not be distorted either by the abundant supply of mistaken and misleading theories of knowledge or by the widespread and abominable practice of those that are convinced that an academic discipline must be this or that because of the analogy of some other academic discipline. The second is that one must find a methodical way of handling the problem of divergent value-judgments.[73]

Clearly, the first requirement is met by the functional specialties research, interpretation, and history, while the second is met by the functional specialties dialectic and foundations.[74] Dialectic and foundations, in other words, handle not only relative but also absolute horizons.

Thus, the universal viewpoint not only continues to function as the high and distant goal, but also it remains part of the upper blade of the functional specialty dialectic.

4   Wisdom and Theological Method

Part One of our study had made use of wisdom as a key to the interpretation of the universal viewpoint, and so observations on the relationship of wisdom to theological method will serve to bring our inquiry full circle.

Part One noted that Thomist wisdom had an epistemological aspect in addition to the metaphysical aspect. Corresponding to these in *Insight* were generalized empirical method and metaphysics conceived as the integral heuristic structure of being: generalized method was the 'prior wisdom' that was needed for the foundation and construction of metaphysical wisdom. Part Two followed the replacement of the universal viewpoint by the broader and more concrete notion of methodical horizon. However, the relationship between transcendental method and methodical horizon was not clear, leading to lack of clarity regarding the relationship between wisdom and method itself.[75] In Part Three, however, we have shown that method coincides with methodical horizon. Lonergan has arrived at a more nuanced understanding of the aspects of wisdom. Where before he spoke of the two aspects of wisdom, or of the prior wisdom that grounded metaphysical wisdom, he now speaks of method as including within itself cognitional theory, epistemology as well as metaphysics. We may therefore say that it is method itself that inherits the complex role of Thomist wisdom. The 'viewpoint of the wise man' is in fact replaced by the total and basic horizon of the philosopher practicing general method.[76] In place of Coreth's 'Metaphysics as Horizon' we may therefore speak of 'Method as Horizon.'[77]

What Lonergan has achieved is, therefore, a shift from a metaphysical wisdom to a methodical wisdom, from metaphysics as the highest, architectonic science[78] to method as critical architectonic.[79] Where the former was an individual habit, the carrier of the latter is a community. Since, further, any community is inserted into a tradition and a history, there results a wisdom that is not only methodical but also communitarian and historical.

But if general method is a new form of wisdom, theological method is equally a new form of wisdom. In fact, *De Deo trino: I* speaks of method as the sapiential part of theology, since its prime function is to order the whole that is theology, determining the functions of each part and governing the collaboration of all the parts.[80]

In the light of our considerations of new theological foundations, there becomes evident a clear parallel between cognitional and theological wisdom. The upper blade of knowing is initially the inchoate wisdom that is the notion of being, and later the habit of wisdom. The upper blade of transcendental method is the reality and self-knowledge of concrete subjects in community. The upper blade of theological method is the reality and self-knowledge of concrete subjects in community as undergoing or refusing to undergo intellectual, moral, and religious conversion.[81]

When faith is taken as assent to revealed truths, then the upper blade includes truths and theology remains classicist. When instead a distinction is drawn between faith as the *lumen fidei* and beliefs as truths to be apprehended, then the upper blade of theology is generated through the theological process itself.

In the case of both transcendental method and theological method, the upper blade is generated through self-appropriation or objectification of conversion. In each case the transition is from *vécu* to *thématique*. In each case, both the derivation of categories and the passing of judgments involves interaction between upper and lower blades. In each case, the interaction between upper and lower blades is at once also an interaction between the tradition that is handed down and the appropriation of that tradition.

All this amounts to saying that theological method characterized by a scissors-action finds its antecedents in wisdom and in heuristic notions and structures, and that like them it brings together a priori and a posteriori elements, the transcendental base and historical data, the individual and the community.

Such interaction, as well as the fundamental continuity between classicist and methodical theology, might be clarified by appealing to the lecture 'Variations in Fundamental Theology' of 1973/74.[82] In this lecture, Lonergan notes that fundamental theology involves two distinct components, which are the two divine missions: God's love for us, revealed in his sending of his Son, and the love that God bestows on us, the Holy Spirit.[83] The precise character of these two components varies with the historical unfolding of Christianity and the personal development of inquirers. In the early church the two came together: one was baptized in the name of Jesus, and received the Spirit. Later, greater learning or else greater perversity made necessary a more complex account. Thus, in Vatican I the two components appear as (1) the signs of revelation, the prophecies and miracles, and (2) the help of the Holy Spirit. In our own time, instead, the first is engulfed 'in the mountainous extent and intricate subtlety of biblical studies and critical history'; the second, God's gift, 'is as frequent, as powerful, but also as silent and secret as ever'; and our efforts to recognize it are perturbed by psychology, linguistic analysis, phenomenology, existentialism, social reformers, ecumenists, and universalists.[84]

It is not difficult to relate these observations to *Method*. Corresponding to the two divine missions are *fides ex auditu* and *fides ex infusione*.[85] In Lonergan's method, these would be the a posteriori and the a priori elements of theological process. Appeal to the prophecies and miracles is replaced by the first phase of hearkening to the word or appropriation of the tradition, while foundational reality would be threefold conversion rooted ultimately in the gift of God's love that is the Spirit poured forth into our hearts. The difference between the two approaches would be that between the deductivism and individualism of the old fundamental theology, and the methodical, ongoing, and collaborative nature of the new proposal.[86]

Again, the scissors-action of method is an instance of the two vectors of human development: both *fides ex infusione* and the handing on of tradition (or announcing of the word) pertain to the way down, while *fides ex auditu* or appropriation of the tradition belongs to the way up.[87] Corresponding to *fides ex auditu* and the way upwards is the first phase or mediating theology: appropriating the tradition, hearkening to the word. Corresponding to *fides ex infusione* and the way down is the second phase or mediated theology: handing on the tradition, witnessing to the word, or announcing the word.[88]

The interaction between transcendental and historical and between individual and community, contained in germ in the notion of wisdom, is thus explicitly integrated, on a level of enormous sophistication, into theological method. Such a theological method clearly does not come under the strictures extended by F. Fiorenza against those 'nineteenth- and twentieth-century idealist-influenced theologians' who place foundations in 'explicated transcendental structures of human subjectivity' and consequently 'make no reference to the actual history of Christian belief and practice.'[89] Lonergan's transcendental or generalized empirical method, we have said, consists of an explicit and ongoing interaction between object and subject.[90]

In conclusion, it might be said that, if in *Verbum* Lonergan had reconstructed a genetic wisdom from elements found in Aquinas, and if that reconstruction was expanded and put on a new basis in *Insight*, it is only in *Method* that he achieves a similar dynamic wisdom in the realm of theology.

Conclusion

Our aim has been to study the development of Lonergan's notion of the universal viewpoint in the period extending from *Insight* to *Method*, and at this point our conclusions might be summed up in terms of (1) an interpretation of the notion of the universal viewpoint that upholds Lonergan's self-interpretation through the simple expedient of a better grasp of the notion of heuristic structures and of its roots in wisdom; (2) an outline of the development of the notion of the universal viewpoint, which also illuminates several points of detail such as the fate of scientific interpretation in *Method*, the precise relationship between the hermeneutics of chapter 17 of *Insight* and that of *Method*, and the transformation undergone by the theologically transformed universal viewpoint itself. Research, we have said in the Introduction, was divided on the former question, and had not pronounced itself extensively on the latter. The present conclusion will attempt to say something on each of these two points.

The interpretation

Already in the conclusion to Part One we have noted that the key to understanding the notion of the universal viewpoint is the Thomist notion of wisdom that Lonergan appropriated in his *Verbum* articles. The notion of the universal viewpoint shares in the paradox of wisdom. Perfect wisdom is something that we do not possess, and yet we move towards that perfection. The key to the solution is the recognition that our movement towards wisdom is not from a complete absence of wisdom but rather from the inchoate and rudimentary wisdom or view of the whole that we already possess in the pure desire to know. Now this insight into the genesis of wisdom is embodied by Lonergan in his notion of heuristic structures, in his notion of metaphysics as integral heuristic structure, and in the notion of the universal viewpoint as the unrestricted viewpoint of such a metaphysics. Accordingly, the universal viewpoint is, like perfect wisdom, a 'high and distant goal'; but that goal is also an operative component in our progress towards it.

The universal viewpoint, then, is a high and distant goal. We do not possess this goal, this ordered totality of viewpoints, just as we do not possess that understanding of everything about everything that would be the idea of being. But we do possess a notion of the universal viewpoint, just as we possess a notion of being. In fact, the notion of the universal viewpoint is merely a further specification of the notion of being. The notion of being is spontaneous; the heuristic notion of being is this spontaneous notion made explicit; the notion of the universal viewpoint is the grasp of the spontaneous notion as undergoing objectification, differentiation, and integration. For the spontaneous notion of being undergoes objectification and differentiation in the course of history; such objectifications and differentiations may be either positions that develop or counterpositions that head for a reversal; and the notion of the universal viewpoint is the grasp of the integration of these differentiations. Insofar as the universal viewpoint of *Insight* is already a high and distant goal, there is no discrepancy between the comprehensive viewpoint of *Method* and the universal viewpoint of *Insight*. Movement towards that goal is normally spontaneous, but it can also be deliberate and methodical. The notion of the universal viewpoint is the spontaneous movement made deliberate and explicit and so methodical.

The Development

Turning now to the question of the development, we might begin by noting that our effort to establish this development has drawn both upon the transcripts of courses, institutes, and lectures available at the various Lonergan centers, and upon unpublished archival material. In a special way there might be mentioned here (1) the handwritten notes for the *De methodo theologiae* course of spring 1963, containing the analysis of transcendental horizon and methodical horizon; (2) the archival file marked 'Various Papers' containing, among other things, the autograph typescript of Hermeneutics 1962 (with the interesting 'alternative ending'), and five items pertaining to the otherwise poorly documented 1964 Institute at Georgetown University; (3) 'MiT II. The Tasks of Theology,' an early version of the *Method* chapter on 'Functional Specialties,' which speaks of the functional specialty conversion as concerned with a comprehensive view, or a single if dialectical view; and (4) 'MiT VII. The Tasks of Theology,' an early draft of what became the chapters on the individual functional specialties in *Method.*

The *Gratia Operans* introduction offers the 'pure form of speculative development' as an a priori or upper blade for the interpretation not of any text whatsoever but precisely of a speculative development. The basic inspiration for this technique is the pincer movement of physics that moves from data upwards towards the discovery of laws and from mathematical considerations downwards towards data.

In the *Verbum* articles the technique of psychological introspection results in a self-knowledge that serves as an upper blade in the interpretation of psychological texts. This upper blade is synchronic, in contrast to the diachronic character of the pure form of speculative development. Like the pure form, however, it is not yet a generalized hermeneutical tool, restricted as it is to the interpretation of psychological texts. The content of the study is also significant because of its discovery of the Thomist notion of wisdom: wisdom is the original upper blade that sets up a pincer movement in all knowledge.

Insight carries out a transposition of Thomist wisdom. Generalized method takes the place of psychological introspection. This is a genetic and epistemological wisdom that, through appropriation of intellectual and rational consciousness, gives rise to a metaphysical wisdom that is not only 'scientific' but also dialectical, and that therefore includes the heuristic structure for meaning that is the universal viewpoint. Such a universal viewpoint can serve as a generalized upper blade for any interpretation whatsoever, for it is a heuristic integration of the differentiations of the notion of being, while the data of interpretation are themselves determinate differentiations of the notion of being. Thus, while the pure form of speculative development was a diachronic upper blade, and psychological introspection yielded a synchronic upper blade, the universal viewpoint is synchronic as well as diachronic.

While the universal viewpoint is relevant to the level of doing, *Insight* hesitates to expand its base of operations to include this level; such hesitation, we have suggested, is due to the fact that the universal viewpoint is metaphysical, presupposing as it does the ontological analysis of development in chapter 15. But this means that in some way the universal viewpoint is still involved in faculty psychology. Significantly, generalized method does not manifest any such limitations: with equal ease it yields both a method of metaphysics and a method of ethics.

Again, the universal viewpoint undergoes an expansion to the level of general metaphysics as well as a transformation into a theological viewpoint, but the key moment in this expansion and transformation is a deduction of God's existence, and the pattern of the transformation is that of classical fundamental theology or apologetics. Finally, given this classicist element and the traditional Catholic notion of faith as assent to revealed truths, the upper blade of theological method consists of a theologically transformed universal viewpoint that includes revealed truths.

We have been noting certain problems and tensions inherent in the notion of the universal viewpoint, but we must add that these come to light not so much in *Insight* as in the post-*Insight* period, when Lonergan begins working more explicitly towards a theological method. These tensions arise concretely in the form of the need to integrate historical scholarship into theology. Immanent in this problem are the three components to be mastered on the way towards theological method: the hermeneutical, the existential, and the theological.

As far as mastery over the hermeneutical component is concerned, there is the appropriation of the distinction between the *Geisteswissenschaften* and the *Naturwissenschaften* in 1962, which leads to a modification of the hermeneutical method of *Insight*: that method is now distinguished into a hermeneutics based on common sense and a history based on common sense mediated by ongoing philosophy and human sciences. Still, since there is a shift towards system even in the commonsense realm, history may be said to be 'explanatory' in the manner of the hermeneutical method of chapter 17 of *Insight*.

Mastery over the existential component is a question of a complete shift from faculty psychology to intentionality analysis and a complete appropriation of the existential level of human consciousness. The courses of 1959 thematize the shift from faculty psychology to intentionality analysis and work out a new notion of habit (which is restricted neither to some single faculty nor to a single mind), a new functional analysis of development (in contrast to the ontological analysis of chapter 15 of *Insight*), and a 'human' account of the good (in contrast to the cosmic and intellectual account of chapter 18 of *Insight*). These developments are crystallized in the general method of 1962, which defines the methodological viewpoint as one that deals with objects only through operations and through the subject, and similarly transcendental method as moving from the structured operations of human consciousness to the isomorphically structured objects of these operations. There arises a new notion of formal object as fixed by operations; this differs from the traditional notion in which objects defined acts, acts defined potencies, and potencies defined the essence of the soul. In 1963 there is worked out a new notion of horizon in place of the Aristotelian-scholastic pair potency and formal object. The subject pole of this horizon is not an abstract potency but the concrete subject, and the object pole is not the object considered from a particular angle, but some concrete totality of objects attained by the concrete subject. Total and basic horizon or methodical horizon deals with transcendental horizons, and since these horizons are rooted in presence or absence of intellectual, moral, as well as religious conversion, methodical horizon is already theological. Like the general method of 1962, it is able to deal with religious conversion without need of a deductive transition into the theological realm. But the complete appropriation of existential consciousness is achieved only with the emergence of the new notion of value in 1968, and with the affirmation of the primacy of the existential.

Mastery of the theological element consists in the attainment of new theological foundations, and we might go into this aspect in somewhat greater detail. The attainment of new theological foundations is intimately linked to full mastery of the non-theological element. *Insight* achieves mastery of the methods of the natural sciences, but theological foundations are still partially classical. It is only with the mastery of the methods of the human sciences as well as of the existential level of consciousness that there emerges the new notion of faith, and consequently new theological foundations. Thus, the question of theological foundations comes up in 1959, but is not as yet conceived radically. The question of the foundations of theology as a whole begins to come up in 1963, once the contribution of the *Geisteswissenschaften* has been appropriated; it comes to a focus in the Institute of 1964; the fundamental breakthrough occurs in February 1965; the starting point of theology is placed in data in 1967; but achievement of new theological foundations occurs only in 1968, upon acknowledgment of the primacy of the existential. The basic moment in these new theological foundations is the reversal of the relationship between knowledge and love. The love of God is a gift; it is not the product of our knowing and choosing. Faith is to be distinguished from beliefs; faith is the eye of love, fruit of the gift of God's love, the horizon within which religious doctrines are found to be meaningful. Theology had of course always regarded the *initium fidei* as supernatural, but it had felt the need of adding on a fundamental theology carried out in the light of pure reason. New theological foundations recognize that pure reason does not exist, and that what is needed in the first place is not so much a proof of God's existence as a bringing to light of one's ongoing response to the gift of God's love. New theological foundations are, in other words, a question of thematization of religious conversion.

Against this background, we may note that the universal viewpoint is mentioned only once in this period, in an unpublished text, and that too in the context of an upper blade for the history of philosophy. In the years 1954–61, there is strong continuity with *Insight* as well as an ongoing concern with an upper blade for history. In 1962 the universal viewpoint is replaced by basic context, the difference being that the latter presupposes the less ontological analysis of development crystallized in the general method of 1962, as well as the shift to the 'larger and more concrete context'[1] that includes not only knowing but also doing, not only intellectual but also moral and religious conversion, not only being but also the good. This shift from faculty psychology to intentionality analysis results in a major development in 1963: the total and basic horizon, the 'horizon of the wise man,' is no longer identified with metaphysics, but rather with the horizon of the philosopher practicing transcendental method. Metaphysics coincides with the object pole but not with the subject pole of such a horizon. Total and basic horizon or methodical horizon also takes over the functions of the universal viewpoint or basic context, and like the latter it is broader, less ontological, and more concrete than the former. After 1963, however, the term that is more common is transcendental method, and it turns out that this is another way of speaking about methodical horizon.

Coming finally to *Method*, the universal viewpoint mentioned in the footnote in the chapter on interpretation coincides in extension if not in intension with the comprehensive viewpoint mentioned in the chapter on functional specialties as the high and distant goal of dialectic. The universal viewpoint as heuristic structure instead is mentioned in the chapter on foundations, as part of the set of derived general theological categories. The basic set of general categories is clearly psychological. But general theological categories (and this includes basic as well as derived categories) are merely transcendental method as objectified; and so the notion of the universal viewpoint remains part, but not the basic part, of method. From another angle too we can come to the same conclusion: transcendental method consists of cognitional theory, epistemology, and metaphysics; but the universal viewpoint is part of explicit metaphysics; and so the universal viewpoint remains part of transcendental method. In this sense, then, it might be said that transcendental method is less ontological than the universal viewpoint. It is also more concrete: it arises from the appropriation not merely of cognitional but also of existential consciousness. Thus, the universal viewpoint does not disappear completely in *Method*, but, given the shift from faculty psychology, method is dominant. Method takes over the functions of the universal viewpoint while including it in the way we have been describing. Since, further, the base of dialectic is transcendental method, we may say that, in the measure that transcendental method is objectified, the base of dialectic may include the universal viewpoint.

We must also note a certain circularity that characterizes the method: transcendental method grounds dialectic and foundations, and dialectic and foundations in turn objectify transcendental method. Method both reveals the nature of the heuristic function and, in the measure that it is objectified, provides sets of basic terms and relations relevant to both human subjects and to objects proportionate to human cognitional process.[2] Again, the first phase of method is open to all comers, whether or not they subscribe to or are familiar with transcendental method. But this means that there is a sense in which method may be described as moving first towards the objectification of itself and then towards the high and distant goal of the universal viewpoint.

Research, interpretation, and history are sets of special theological categories, where special categories are themselves generated on the basis of an extension of general categories as well as appropriation of religious interiority. In addition, these three specialties are commonsense affairs and so they cannot handle the problem of standpoints or of dialectically different horizons. The equivalent of the scientific interpretation of *Insight* arises only when these specialties are complemented by the upper blade of dialectic and foundations. Nevertheless, some echo of chapter 17 of *Insight* may be found in the account of statement of interpretation. While a commonsense statement of interpretation is possible, in certain cases a supplementary mode becomes necessary, in which merely descriptive categories are replaced by categories that are properly explanatory. Such categories are provided by transcendental method in combination with the expertise of human studies; examples are the stages of meaning or explanatory differentiations of consciousness worked out in the *Method* chapter on meaning.

In *Verbum*, it was wisdom that was basic, and this wisdom was primarily metaphysical, while having also an epistemological aspect that we had identified with the method of psychological introspection. In *Insight* we still find these two aspects, for there is a metaphysics that is explicitly dialectical and a generalized empirical method with a dialectical upper blade; the difference is that metaphysics is now fruit of the method. In *Method*, instead, it is clearly generalized empirical method that is basic; metaphysics is a tertiary part in a dynamic unity that begins in cognitional theory. Further, this generalized method is easily extended into foundations or methods of ethics and theology. All this is the result of a complete shift from faculty psychology to intentionality analysis, as well as the replacement of classical fundamental theology and the overcoming of the classical notion of theology. With a clarity that was not possible in *Insight*, generalized empirical method now incorporates within itself the duality of wisdom. It is, therefore, generalized method that takes the place of Thomist wisdom. Where Thomist wisdom principally regarded the objective order of reality,[3] generalized empirical method overcomes the priority of metaphysics by including it within a dynamic unity.[4] In place of the architectonic science that is Thomist wisdom,[5] we have the critical architectonic of generalized method.[6] In place of metaphysics as horizon we now have method as horizon. It is this shift that explains the fate of the universal viewpoint in *Method*: while it remains the high and distant goal of method, as heuristic structure it is reduced to being merely a part, and that too not a primary part, of method itself.

Relevance

We might turn finally to the question of relevance. A first point is Lonergan's contribution to the contemporary hermeneutical debate. The universal viewpoint and generalized empirical method arise from an appropriation both of tradition and of contemporary developments. Not only is the universal viewpoint rooted in the Aristotelian-Thomist notion of wisdom, but also it has evolved in interaction with the modern ideal of science, the emergence of historical consciousness, and contemporary developments in philosophy. In turn, there are important contributions that Lonergan can make to the contemporary discussion of hermeneutics and method. Thus, for example, if Lonergan has no hesitation whatsoever in admitting the role of pre-understanding in interpretation, he would propose the possibility of a somewhat more methodical use of such pre-understanding. Thus, he would agree with Ricoeur that all interpretation begins as intelligent guesswork; but he would add that such guesswork can be made a bit more systematic with the help of categories generated through the appropriation of interiority. Again, there is the question of judgment on the correctness of interpretations. In consonance with the contemporary emphasis on authenticity, Lonergan develops a position that begins in Aristotle and goes on through Augustine and Aquinas to Newman. The result is a brilliant phenomenology of judgment and a dialectical method that may well be described as the direction towards which contemporaries like Gadamer and Ricoeur have been moving. The complexity of Lonergan's thinking on this point is summed up in the lapidary phrase, 'objectivity is the fruit of authentic subjectivity.' In human judgment there come together subject and object, individual and community, tradition and history, a priori and a posteriori, for the authentic subjectivity in question is the fruit of a minor as well as a major authenticity, the authenticity of the individual as well as the authenticity of his/her tradition.

A second point is the relevance of Lonergan's method to a postmodern age that is not only keenly aware of distinct universes of discourse and of cultural differences but also is marked by a growing desire for dialogue. A method that not only respects differences but is also intrinsically dialogical and world-ecumenical is therefore more than topical. But a method that rests upon a long and laborious effort at appropriation of intellectual, moral, and religious interiority brings an added contribution, for it is normative and critical as well. Thus, Lonergan's differentiations of consciousness and stages of meaning provide models for an understanding of cultures, and the functional specialties dialectic and foundations make sure that questions of judgment and decision are not overlooked or evaded, while recognizing at the same time that neither judgments nor decisions are automatically correct.

Theologizing in India in particular might find relevant the idea of differentiations of consciousness and stages of meaning. For inevitably in the course of such theologizing there arise questions about Indian culture, Eastern culture, Western culture; and here Lonergan's work can provide models. The function of a model is to raise questions, direct attention to aspects that might have been overlooked, and enable description of realities that are often very complex. Thus, it might be asked, Are we to think in terms of a global and indistinct entity named Indian culture, or should we not recognize further differentiations within this culture? How do such differentiations relate to human history, for presumably India forms part of the evolution of human meaning in general? And if we are ready to recognize cultural and genetic differentiation, what of dialectical diversification of such differentiations, arising from presence or absence of what Lonergan refers to as intellectual, moral, and religious conversion? These are not of course questions that admit of simplistic answers. Neither is it to be presumed that Lonergan provides all the answers. But the notion of the universal viewpoint can, at the very least, help us raise the questions and avoid the creation of vague entities or easy generalizations such as 'Indian culture' and 'Western culture.'

It should be stressed that the construction of a generalized empirical method constitutes an abandonment of the supremacy of logic. This is a conscious and deliberate cutting-free from conceptualism and nominalism in favor of what is truly fundamental: understanding, wisdom, and love. It also implies a shift from the primacy of metaphysics to the primacy of cognitional theory, and ultimately to the primacy of the existential. The implications of this shift for contemporary theology are expressed aphoristically in a comment found in Lonergan's *De methodo theologiae* course of spring 1963: if in the New Testament the question was 'aut Judaeus aut Graecus,' if the technical formulations of the conciliar and medieval period were a question of 'neque Judaeus neque Graecus,' now it is possible to be 'et Judaeus et Graecus e methodo.'[7] If reflection on the faith had to pass through a theoretical phase, if it had to make the ascent to the *priora quoad se* and to universal formulations, the emergence of historical consciousness and the discovery of the plurality of cultures makes necessary, and method makes possible, a return to the concrete. Lonergan does not of course dictate the form that contemporary theology must take in India or in China or in Japan; he is concerned with the conditions for collaboration and for dialogue.

The shift from logic to method results also in the centrality of experience, whether cognitional, moral, or religious, and this without falling into the subjectivist bog. Such an emphasis on experience should not fail to evoke an echo in the Indian theologian who is aware of the centrality of *anubhava* (experience) in Indian thinking. Further, it is this placing of foundations in experience that allows method to break free from imprisonment in a sterile conceptualism and so to be intrinsically dialogical.

I have been arguing that Lonergan's method can be a useful tool for theologizing in India, but I am also aware of the diffidence that will be felt by many an Indian theologian to take over yet another Western achievement. Still, I am not convinced that Eastern and Western are adequate and ultimate criteria of selection. The adequate criterion is simply authenticity on every level, and such authenticity is not limited to any one culture. I would argue for the appreciation of particularity without the sacrifice of universality; and besides, this seems to me to be the genuine direction of dialogue: not a new closure but a new openness.

Finally, there is something to be learned from Lonergan's own slow development on the question of method. His final position is the fruit of a lifetime of stubborn wrestling with fundamental questions and a refusal to indulge in half-measures. One of the roots of this phenomenal ability to 'withdraw from the chase' is indicated by a little word that surfaces time and again in Lonergan's writings: providence. Lonergan's work is in fact suffused with a hope born of faith, with the confidence that it is God who works through history. This, I think, is a salutary attitude, especially for those who work on the frontiers; and besides, as we will perhaps realize through the ongoing dialogue, such an attitude is not completely unrelated to the *anattā* (selflessness) of the Buddhists and the *niṣkāma karma* (desireless action) of the *Gītā*.

Appendix A

Archival Material: Chronology

Note: The following is an attempt to date the undated archival material used in this study.

1 'Radix dialecticae' (single handwritten page). Batch IX.7.c.

This jotting is found in the same folder as the autograph of Philosophy of History, the lecture of 23 Sept. 1960 (Batch IX.7 a). Further, the contents are related to section 3.b' (pp. 5–6) on Dialectic of the same lecture: note especially the mention in both texts of Moreau on Blondel, of *Insight*, of Plato's dialectic as dialogue (opposed to eristic), of Aristotle's dialectic as review of opinions, and of the dialectic of history. It is probable therefore that the two items are contemporaneous.

2 'Problematik' (7 typed pp.). Found in LRI Archives file entitled 'Various Papers.'

This almost certainly pertains to MoT 1962, and the reasons are as follows: (1) 'Problematik' 1 speaks of the 'dogmatico-theological context' as 'what is taken for granted among Catholics / what is taught and learnt in seminaries'; MoT 1962 29 speaks of the dogmatic-theological context as 'what is taught and learnt at seminaries and in theological schools. It is what is assumed by Catholics.' (Cf. also *analogia fidei, sensus ecclesiae, consensus Patrum, consensus theologorum*. Again, for the dogmatico-theological context, cf. also MoT 1962 255, 285, 288, 290–95.) (2) Context is described as a 'remainder concept' ('Problematik' 1; MoT 1962 29, 312; Hermeneutics 13). (3) Both texts draw a distinction between hermeneutics as a common-sense task and history as explanatory ('Problematik' 7; cf. our chapter 6 above). (4) Both texts mention the visible world (the life of community) and the inner life ('Problematik' 6; cf. MoT 1962 62–78). KL 1963 speaks in terms of horizons, not of worlds. (5) There is mention of a '"Problematik" of Development' in what seems to be a prospectus (2 pp.) of MoT 1962, found in LRI Library file 301, 'The Meth. of Theology Inst. Regis College 1962.'

3 Five texts (items 3–7) in the LRI Archives folder entitled 'Various Papers': (1) Method in Theology. The Problem. External Factors (pp. 1–14); (2) Method in Theology – Internal Problems (pp. 1–5); (3) Positive Theology (1 p.); (4) Dogmatic Theology (pp. 1–2); (5) Development of Dogma (1 p.).

These five items are almost certainly (part of) Lonergan's own notes for MoT 1964. (1) The prospectus of MoT 1964 as well as the Wilker notes (and Crowe's index to them) indicate that the course had discussed among other things, 'The Contemporary Problem. Factors external to theology. The internal situation,' 'Positive Theology,' 'Dogmatic Theology,' as well as 'The Development of Dogma.' (2) There is a close correspondence in structure as well as contents between these texts and the Wilker notes. (3) The bibliographical list on Method in Theology – Internal Problems 5 contains several items of 1964, excluding therefore a 1963 date. (4) DDT-II is mentioned in Method in Theology – Internal problems 2, and in Dogmatic Theology 1; both DDT-I and DDT-II are added in pen on p. 5 of the former. (5) Method in Theology – Internal Problems is found also on the reverse of Batch v.7 a, and this latter is clearly of 1965, since it is a handwritten scheme of the eight functional specialties *in fieri*.

4 'MiT II. The Tasks of Theology' (pp. 1–14, with pages missing; a total of 45 pages with all the repetitions and false starts). Batch x.5.

This is clearly pre-1968: (1) In TPSR of 1968, chapter 2 is named 'Functional Specialties,' not 'The Tasks of Theology.' (2) The TPSR chapter 2 is identical to 'Functional Specialties in Theology' of 1969 and to the *Method* chapter on 'Functional Specialties,' but differs significantly from the present text. (3) In TPSR the fourth functional specialty is 'dialectic' (cf. TPSR chapt. 2), whereas in the present text it is 'conversion.'

5 'MiT III Horizons' (pp. 1–79). Batch VI.1.b.

This pre-dates TPSR of 1968, which has a chapter 3 entitled 'Horizons and Categories' and a chapter 4 entitled 'The Human Good, Values, Beliefs,' both of which contain material from 'MiT III Horizons.' Probably circa 1967.

6 'MiT III Horizons and Categories' (pp. 1–37). Batch VI.6.

This is related to but also significantly dissimilar to TPSR 1968 chapter 3, 'Horizons and Categories.' Further, it does not contain the matter on values that was present in 'MiT III Horizons' (Batch VI.1 b). Seeing that in 1968 there was a chapter 'The Human Good, Values, Beliefs,' it would seem that the present text would post-date 'MiT III Horizons' but pre-date chapter 3, 'Horizons and Categories,' of 1968. It would seem then that 'MiT III Horizons' gave rise to two chapters, which in 1968 are chapter 3, 'Horizons and Categories,' and chapter 4, 'The Human Good, Values, Beliefs.'

7 'MiT VII. The Tasks of Theology' (pp. 1–62.) Batch VI.2.

This seems to have been an early attempt at a more extensive treatment of individual functional specialties. Thus, section 1 (pp. 1–3) discusses research, section 2 (pp. 3–30) interpretation, and section 3 (pp. 31–62) history. From a reference to a chapter 5 entitled 'Meaning' (cf. p. 30), the present text pre-dates MiT 1969, where 'Meaning' is chapter 4. TPSR instead has a chapter 5 entitled 'Meaning,' and so the present text was composed after that chapter. A probable date is therefore 1968.

8 'MiT VII. 4. Dialectic' (fragment, pp. 63–65). Batch VIII.17.e.

Probably a part of 'MiT VII. The Tasks of theology' (Batch VI.2), especially since this latter consists of pp. 1–62, and ends with a section 3 on history. Accordingly, it would share the 1968 dating of the latter.

9 Horizons and Categories (14 pp.). LRI Archives Lonergan Papers 307, 'MT Boston Summaries.'

Tallies closely with the chapter of the same name in TPSR 1968 held at Boston College, so that these might have been Lonergan's lecture notes.

10 List of chapters found in Lonergan Papers 307, 'MT Boston Summaries' (Part I: The Hermeneutic Circle. 1. Method. 2. Functional Specialties. 3. Horizons and Categories. 4. The Human Good, Values, Beliefs. 5. Meaning. 6. Religion. II: The Expansion. 7. Research. 8. Interpretation. 9. History. 10. Dialectic. 11. Foundations. 12. Doctrines. 13. Systematics. 14. Communications).

This list may be dated 1968 because (1) it is found in a file entitled 'MT Boston Summaries'; (2) the item 'Horizons and Categories' found in the same file is almost certainly dated 1968 (cf. above); (3) Part I of the list

220   Appendix A

matches perfectly the order of the chapters in TPSR 1968, but not that of MiT 1969.

11 'MiT VII' (44 pp., beginning with p. 13). Batch XI.11.

This is a version of 'MiT VII. The Tasks of Theology.' The earlier pages discuss interpretation. Pp. 63–82 instead deal with history: cf. below, 'Ch. IX. Historians and Cognitional Theory.' Date: circa 1968, or at any rate pre-dating MiT 1969, where there are already separate chapters for various functional specialties.

12 'Ch. IX. Historians and Cognitional Theory' (pp. 63–82). Batch XI.11. The title has been added in pencil on one of the p. 63's.

The text is an early version of MT chapter 9. It may be dated 1968; at any rate it pre-dates MiT 1969. In the list of chapters found in Lonergan Papers 307, 'MT Boston Summaries' (1968), there is no second chapter on history, and in MiT 1969, chapter 9 is 'History and Historians.'

13 'Ch. IX: History and Dialectic' (pp. 1–32). Batch X.12.

Note that (1) 'History and Historians' of MiT 1969 is structurally almost identical to MT chapter 9, except that the last section, 'Science and Scholarship,' is missing; (2) the topics discussed in the present text (Three Handbooks, Verstehen, Dialectic: The Problem, Horizons) are in MT found in two different chapters, 9 ('History and Historians') and 10 ('Dialectic'). The text therefore pre-dates chapter 9, 'History and Historians' of MiT 1969. It would at the same time post-date 'Ch. IX. Historians and Cognitional Theory,' Batch XI.11. Accordingly, there would be indicated a 1968 or early 1969 dating.

14 'MiT x. Chapter Ten. Dialectic and Foundations' (pp. 1–15). Batch VI.5.

This is identical to the first four sections (dealing with the functional specialty dialectic) of MiT 1969 chapter 10, 'Dialectic and Foundations,' except for matter on p. 14 that is developed at greater length in the Regis course. This would make the present text an earlier version of the MiT 1969 chapter, and indicate a late 1968 or early 1969 dating.

Appendix B

A Note on the Emergence of Chapters 7–11 of *Method in Theology*

Among the drafts of *Method* there may be found a chapter II entitled 'The Tasks of Theology' as well as a chapter VII of the same name. The first (Batch x.5) is an earlier version of what was published in 1969 as 'Functional Specialties in Theology' in *Gregorianum*.[1] The second (Batch VI.2), instead, seems to have been an early attempt at a more extensive treatment of the individual specialties. Existing drafts of this latter chapter indicate a section 2 dealing with interpretation and running to some thirty pages,[2] a section 3 entitled 'History' and running to another thirty odd pages,[3] and a section 4 entitled 'Dialectic' of which we have three pages.[4] An autograph of *Method in Theology* reveals that this chapter VII was split up to yield the chapters on interpretation[5] and history.[6]

In addition, there is another set of pages bearing the header 'MiT VII,' but entitled in pencil 'Ch. IX. Historians and Cognitional Theory.'[7] Given that sections 1–3 of Batch VI.2 are numbered pp. 1–62, it would seem that we have here a continuation of 'MiT VII. The Tasks of Theology.' We might surmise that the section 4 entitled 'Dialectic' was substituted by 'Historians and Cognitional Theory,' and that we have here the origin of the present chapter 9 of *Method*, entitled 'History and Historians.' Batch x.12 contains a chapter 9 entitled 'History and Dialectic.'[8] The 1969 Method course contains a chapter 9 entitled 'History and Historians'; the contents here are far more developed than in the text of Batch x.12, and in fact are substantially equivalent to the *Method* text.[9] In 1970 this becomes chapter 8, with the title 'From History to Dialectic.'[10] In the 1971 Autograph of *Method* (Batch XII) this becomes chapter 9 once again, and the title is changed back to 'History and Historians.'[11]

It would seem then that 'MiT VII. The Tasks of Theology' was a chapter of at least 82 pages, which included sections on research, interpretation, history, and dialectic; and that the section on dialectic was later substituted with what became the chapter 'History and Historians.' This chapter VII was probably composed as a sequel to chapter VI, 'Religion,' of the 1968 Boston course. In MiT 1969 we already have chapters 'Interpretation,' 'History,' and 'History and Historians' that correspond substantially to the text of *Method*.

Coming to the emergence of an independent chapter on dialectic, we may recall that in 1965, while the fifth specialty was foundations, the fourth specialty was not dialectic but conversion, and dialectical method formed part of the functional specialty history. 'Ch. II. The Tasks of Theology' indicates that this situation remains unchanged, but also reveals that the fourth functional specialty, conversion, is itself somehow concerned with dialectic, for it seeks to achieve a dialectical unity between various types of conversion.[12]

The functional specialty dialectic emerges with all probability in 1968. The main argument for this is the mention of 'dialectic' instead of 'conversion' as the fourth functional specialty in the 1968 chapter 'Functional Specialties.'[13] But there is also section 4 of 'MiT VII. The Tasks of Theology' which is entitled 'Dialectic' and not 'Conversion.'[14] Again, the section on interpretation of the same text speaks of the functional specialty interpretation opening out upon history and *dialectic*.[15]

We have suggested above that this section 4, 'Dialectic,' was substituted with 'Ch. IX. Historians and Cognitional Theory,'[16] which itself subsequently became 'Ch. IX. History and Dialectic.'[17] However, it might be more exact to say that the section 'Dialectic' evolved into 'Historians and Cognitional Theory,' or 'History and Dialectic,' for the latter text contains a section 4 entitled 'Dialectic: The Problem' and also a discussion of the dialectic of methods.[18]

'Ch. IX. History and Dialectic' must be assigned a 1968 or else early 1969 dating, since in the Method course of 1969 the sections on dialectic are dropped, the title is changed to 'History and Historians,' and the chapter attains a structure that corresponds substantially to that of *Method*.[19]

If the sections on dialectic are dropped from the chapter 'History and Historians' in 1969, there is as yet no sign of an independent chapter on dialectic. The 1969 Method course contains instead a chapter X entitled 'Dialectic and Foundations.'[20] It is only in 1970 that there emerges a separate chapter on dialectic.[21] This chapter is substantially identical to the *Method* text, except for the fact that in 1971 there was added a section 10 entitled 'A Supplementary Note.' This is matched by the emergence of a separate chapter on foundations, also corresponding substantially to the *Method* text. This chapter takes over sections from the 1969 chapter X 'Dialectic and Foundations,'[22] as well as from the chapter XI 'Horizons and Categories' of the same year.[23]

Notes

Introduction

1 B. Lonergan, *Insight: A Study of Human Understanding*, Collected Works of Bernard Lonergan 3, ed. Frederick E. Crowe and Robert M. Doran (Toronto: Lonergan Research Institute of Regis College and University of Toronto Press, 1992). First published in 1957 (London: Longmans, Green).
2 INCW 587.
3 INCW 18.
4 INCW 762.
5 Hermeneutics 1962 13–15.
6 Lonergan, 'Functional Specialties in Theology,' *Gregorianum* 50 (1969) 489–90.
7 Lonergan, *Method in Theology* (London: Darton, Longman & Todd, 1972). The edition used here will be *Method in Theology* (Toronto: University of Toronto Press for the Lonergan Research Institute of Regis College, 1990).
8 MT 153, note 1; 288.
9 MT 153, note 1.
10 MT 129–30.
11 Terry J. Tekippe, 'The Universal Viewpoint and the Relationship of Philosophy and Theology in the Works of Bernard Lonergan,' unpublished doctoral dissertation, Fordham University, New York, 1972. Director: Gerald McCool.
12 Ibid. 88. By 'generalized universal viewpoint' Tekippe means 'a viewpoint – based unrevisably on cognitional analysis – in aid of understanding and judging any human meaning, whether past, present or future, whether written, spoken or acted out, by ascertaining the basic viewpoint of the author of the meaning' (ibid. 73).

13 Ibid. 122.
14 Ibid. 97.
15 Ibid. 125.
16 Ibid. 128.
17 Cf. note 6 above.
18 Cf. Tekippe 165–66.
19 Ibid. 164. From an independent transcription of the discussions, we report here Tekippe's question: 'In *Insight* you spoke of a universal viewpoint as proximate achievement, the upper blade of an actual method of hermeneutics, but in dialectic you speak of a comprehensive viewpoint in terms of aspiration towards a "high and distant goal." Does this signify a softening of a perhaps overly ambitious claim to a universal viewpoint, or is there some other reason for this discrepancy?' (MiT 1971 596, question no. 133).
20 Tekippe had forwarded a written presentation to Lonergan, comparing texts on the universal viewpoint and the comprehensive viewpoint. This presentation is reproduced in the appendix to his dissertation, 164–66.
21 Ibid. 166 (brackets in Tekippe's text). MiT 1971 639 reads: 'but to state it would have been to write a Hegelian treatise, and I never aimed at rivalling Hegel. And I am still of that position: that it is a matter of experience, understanding and judgment, and a matter of dialectic, to arrive at an account of all the different positions that different people have held.'
22 Tekippe 163 note 1. For the technical precision, cf. ibid. 28.
23 Ibid. 163 note 1.
24 Ibid. 168–70.
25 Ibid. 168 note 1.
26 Lonergan, '*Insight* Revisited' 2C 276.
27 Ibid. 275–76.
28 Charles C. Hefling, Jr, 'Lonergan on Development: *The Way to Nicea* in Light of His More Recent Methodology,' unpublished doctoral dissertation, Andover Newton Theological School – Boston College, Boston, 1982. Director: Fred Lawrence.
29 Ibid. 370 n. 14, emphases in text. It might be noted that this echoes Lonergan's own position reported earlier.
30 Ibid. 164–65.
31 Ibid. 121, cf. 119–31.
32 Ibid. 172.
33 Ibid. 166.
34 Ibid. 171.
35 Ibid. 166–68.
36 Ibid. 169–70.
37 MT 153.

38 The theologically transformed universal viewpoint of *Insight* includes 'the older notion of foundations as a set of doctrines' (Hefling 181).
39 MiT 1971 596.
40 Robert M. Doran, *Theology and the Dialectics of History* (Toronto: University of Toronto Press, 1990) 563.
41 Doran, 'Psychic Conversion and Lonergan's Hermeneutics,' in Sean E. McEvenue and Ben F. Meyer, eds, *Lonergan's Hermeneutics: Its Development and Application* (Washington: Catholic University of America Press, 1989) 217.
42 Doran, *Theology and the Dialectics of History* 589.
43 Ibid. chapter 19, The Ontology of Meaning.
44 Philip McShane, 'Psychic Differentiations and Systematic Heuristics' (Response to Robert Doran's paper 'Psychic Conversion and Lonergan's Hermeneutics') in McEvenue and Meyer, eds, *Lonergan's Hermeneutics* 210, 214–16.
45 Frederick E. Crowe, 'The Exigent Mind: Bernard Lonergan's Intellectualism,' in Frederick E. Crowe, ed., *Spirit as Inquiry: Studies in Honor of Bernard Lonergan, S.J.* (Chicago: Saint Xavier College, 1964) 27.
46 Crowe, 'Lonergan's Search for Foundations: The Early Years, 1940–1959,' in P. McShane, ed., *Searching for Cultural Foundations* (Lanham, MD: University Press of America, 1984) 136.
47 Ibid. 117, 119, 125, 127, 133.
48 Ibid. 114–15. For the 'Introduction' to Lonergan's doctoral dissertation, cf. Lonergan, 'The *Gratia Operans* Dissertation: Preface and Introduction,' *Method: Journal of Lonergan Studies* 3:2 (1985) 9–46.
49 Lonergan, 'The Concept of *Verbum* in the Writings of St. Thomas Aquinas,' *Theological Studies* 7 (1946) 349–92, 8 (1947) 35–79, 404–44, 10 (1949) 3–40, 359–93. The articles have since been published in book form under the title *Verbum: Word and Idea in Aquinas*, ed. David M. Burrell (Notre Dame: University of Notre Dame Press, 1967), and recently as *Verbum: Word and Idea in Aquinas*, Collected Works of Bernard Lonergan 2, ed. F.E. Crowe and R.M. Doran (Toronto: University of Toronto Press, 1997). Our references will be to the 1967 edition.
50 Given the variety of meanings currently given to the name 'transcendental method,' and given the fact that Lonergan himself ultimately abandoned this name in favor of 'generalized empirical method' (cf. 3C 140–44, 150, 'Questionnaire' 26, 3C 177, 180, etc.) or 'foundational methodology' (3C 76, 149, etc.), I have thought it best to avoid the word 'transcendental' in the title of this study.
51 INCW 605.
52 Cf. MT 156–62.
53 MT 137.
54 Cf. below, chapter 6, section 2.

55 For this hint, I am indebted to Fr Carlo Huber, SJ. Cf. in fact F. Crowe, *Lonergan* (Collegeville, MD: Liturgical Press, 1992) 17.

Chapter 1

1 Lonergan's doctoral dissertation was entitled 'GRATIA OPERANS: A Study of Speculative Development in the Writings of St. Thomas of Aquin,' Gregorian University, Rome, 1940. The director was Charles Boyer SJ. The main body of the dissertation was published in the form of four articles: 'St. Thomas' Thought on *Gratia Operans*,' *Theological Studies* 2 (1941) 289–324; 3 (1942) 69–88, 375–402, 533–78. It was later published in book form under the title *Grace and Freedom: Operative Grace in the Thought of St. Thomas Aquinas*, ed. J. Patout Burns (London: Darton, Longman & Todd, 1971), and is now published as CWL 1. The 'Introduction' to the dissertation remained unpublished during Lonergan's lifetime. It is now available under the title 'The *Gratia Operans* Dissertation: Preface and Introduction,' in *Method: Journal of Lonergan Studies* 3:2 (1985) 9–46. What we refer to as the 'Introduction' really consists of the preface, the introduction, and chapter 1 of the dissertation. However, as Crowe notes [cf. 'Lonergan's Search for Foundations: The Early Years, 1940–1959' in Philip McShane, ed., *Searching for Cultural Foundations* (Lanham, MD, and London: University Press of America, 1984) 187], it has become customary to refer to the whole as the 'Introduction.'
2 'The Concept of *Verbum* in the Writings of St. Thomas Aquinas,' *Theological Studies* 7 (1946) 349–92, 8 (1947) 35–79, 404–44, 10 (1949) 3–40, 359–93. Our references will be to the book form of these articles published under the title *Verbum: Word and Idea in Aquinas*, ed. David M. Burrell (Notre Dame: University of Notre Dame Press, 1967).
3 GOI 10–11, 16.
4 GOI 11.
5 GOI 16.
6 GOI 12.
7 GOI 11.
8 GOI 10, 12.
9 F. Crowe, '"All my work has been introducing history into Catholic theology" (Lonergan, March 28, 1980),' in Fred Lawrence ed., *Lonergan Workshop* (Boston: Boston College, 1994) 10:55. Cf. GOI 32–33.
10 That the pincer movement is a military metaphor is indicated by Lonergan himself: 'what strategists term a "pincer" movement' (GOI 13). For another well-known Lonerganian military metaphor, cf. breakthrough, encirclement, confinement: INCW 508–509, 545–46, 537, 576, 593.
11 In the particular argument at hand the movement unfolds in five stages; but this is merely due to the fact that the complexity of the issue necessitates two

subordinate stages or inquiries; the fifth stage is the return to the original problem.
12 GOI 13.
13 Ibid.
14 Ibid.
15 Ibid. In the review article 'On God and Secondary Causes' (1946) Lonergan affirms that interpretation is a question of making a hypothesis, working out presuppositions and implications, and verifying these in the text. The hypothesis here is the particular hypothesis that is the interpretation; there is no reference to the pure form (1C 60). INCW 616 instead distinguishes between general and particular hypotheses, the difference being that a general hypothesis 'has general presuppositions and implications, and so it can be tested in many ways,' but a particular hypothesis 'is an ad hoc construction.' In this light, it would seem that the pure form of speculative development is a general but not a particular hypothesis.

We note further that Lonergan admits the possibility of the scheme being mistaken. The point to using the scheme is that it makes the process of interpretation accountable, for the scheme is neither a habit of mind prejudicing the issue nor merely an intuition, but rather something tangible that can be refuted (GOI 34).
16 GOI 12.
17 Cf. e.g. INCW 601.
18 Cf. INCW 588: 'It is simply a heuristic structure that contains virtually the various ranges of possible alternatives of interpretations.'
19 Cf. INCW 38–39.
20 GOI 12.
21 Ibid. This is echoed in *Grace and Freedom*, when Lonergan observes that the most legitimate commentary on Augustine's initial speculation on grace and freedom is the history of subsequent speculation, because that is the best way to keep oneself free from the vice of anachronism, or the tendency to read into Augustine ideas from the contemporary theological context (GF 5).
22 GOI 9, 10, 11. This again is echoed in *Grace and Freedom*: the interpretations of Bañez and Stufler are examples of logical interpretation, because they are efforts to bring logical unity into a text or texts, without adverting to the fact that the problem may be historical (GF 76).
23 VB 10–11.
24 VB 215.
25 VB 11.
26 Cf. VB 217.
27 VB 95. Cf. also VB vii.
28 VB 11.

29 VB 79. Cf. VB 12: the thesis is 'that we must begin by grasping the nature of the act of understanding, that thence we shall come to a grasp of the nature of inner words, their relation to language, and their role in our knowledge of reality.' Cf. also the introduction (written some fifteen years after the articles): without such grasp, 'one is in the unhappy position of the blind man hearing about colors and the deaf man reading about counterpoint' (VB xii).
30 VB 95. Cf. also VB xi–xii.
31 VB 94.
32 VB 94; cf. also 11, 12, 47. Cf. VB xi–xii: '[I]t is only by introspection that one can discover what an introspective psychologist is talking about.'
33 Cf. VB 33–34, 35–37, 140, 190 (note 28).
34 VB 75.
35 VB 61–66.
36 VB 60–61.
37 VB 61–65.
38 VB 66.
39 VB 68.
40 Ibid.
41 VB 67.
42 Cf. VB 68.
43 VB 71.
44 VB 71, 72–73.
45 VB 71–72.
46 VB 71.
47 VB 72.
48 VB 73.
49 Ibid.
50 Ibid.
51 VB 73–74.
52 VB 74.
53 *De Veritate*, q. 1, a. 9 c.; VB 74.
54 VB 74–75. *Summa theologiae*, 1, q. 16, a. 2: 'Et propter hoc per conformitatem intellectus et rei veritas definitur. Unde conformitatem cognoscere est cognoscere veritatem. Hanc autem nullo modo sensus cognoscit; licet enim visus habeat similitudinem visibilis, non tamen cognoscit comparationem quae est inter rem visam et id quod ipse apprehendit se ea ... Et ideo bene invenitur quod sensus est verus de aliqua re, vel intellectus cognoscens quod quid est; sed non quod cognoscat aut dicat verum.'
55 VB 75.
56 Ibid.
57 Cf. VB 76.

58 VB 76–78.
59 VB 79.
60 VB 80.
61 VB 80.
62 Ibid.
63 Cf. VB 80.
64 VB 79.
65 VB 83–84.
66 VB 84.
67 Cf. VB 75, 74.
68 VB 84–85.
69 On the difference between reasoning and deduction, cf. VB 55.
70 VB 85.
71 Ibid.
72 Cf. VB 85–86.
73 VB 86–87.
74 VB 87.
75 Ibid.
76 Cf. Ibid. Also TE 149. PTP 67: every judgment has to take into account everything of relevance; and this wisdom can do, because it orders all things. The Nottingham lecture 12 = PTP 40: any single judgment requires a context of other judgments, because any single item of knowledge is really only an increment in the whole that can be known; and the universal principle of good judgment is wisdom.
77 IM 1959 Student Notes 21. TE 151. Cf. also VB 90.
78 VB 87. IM 1959 Student Notes 20.
79 VB 87.
80 TE 151. IM 1959 Student Notes 20: wisdom grows by fuller orderings in each division of being.
81 TE 152: the other possibility in the development of wisdom is the role of the educator.
82 IM 1959 Student Notes 20, 21.
83 VB 88.
84 Ibid.
85 VB 79.
86 VB 75. Cf. also VB 92: '[A]part from prying introspection, self-knowledge within rational consciousness is neither a *discernere*, nor a *cogitare*, nor an *intelligere* with a fixed object.'
87 Cf. VB 74, which speaks of critical reflection as the highest point in rational reflection. The same point is made in *De intellectu et methodo* (1959). The question of possibility of some knowledge is always a much more difficult question than that of the actual possession of that knowledge. This question cannot

therefore be the first question. We must proceed from what is to what is possible. Thus, the first thing is to know, then to know that we know (gnoseology), and only then to inquire into the possibility of our knowing (epistemology). The question of the possibility of knowledge is last and most fundamental (IM 1959 Student Notes 22).

88 VB 90–91.
89 VB 90.
90 VB 90–91.
91 VB 91.
92 Cf. the section 'The Unity of Wisdom,' esp. VB 88–91.
93 VB 88.
94 Ibid.
95 VB 90.
96 VB 88.
97 VB 87. Cf. TE 151: if the universal scheme in question is a rudimentary view of the whole, we move towards detailed knowledge of this whole by a process of dichotomy: we divide being into material and non-material, subdivide the material into the living and the non-living, and so on.
98 VB 64, 80.
99 DSH 9.
100 Cf. VB 87.
101 DMT 1962 Student Notes 49.
102 VB 90.
103 VB 216.
104 VB 216–17.
105 VB 1.
106 VB 215–16.
107 VB 216.
108 VB xi–xii.
109 VB 216.
110 VB 76.
111 VB 90.
112 VB 58.
113 GOI 15. Cf. also Crowe, '"All my work has been introducing history into Catholic theology" (Lonergan, March 28, 1980)' 56.

Chapter 2

1 Cf. F.E. Crowe, 'Transcendental Deduction: A Lonerganian Meaning and Use,' *Method: Journal of Lonergan Studies* 2:1 (1984) 34.
2 INCW 588.
3 Cf. Crowe, 'Transcendental Deduction' 34: '[E]xcept perhaps in the intro-

ductory pages of his doctoral dissertation, the term, *a priori*, is not by any means a favorite of Lonergan. Already, by the time *Insight* was written, it had yielded to the much more characteristic term, heuristic.'
4 INCW 5.
5 INCW 128.
6 UB 159. For the paragraph, cf. UB 159–60.
7 He further distinguishes between the way the exercise of inquiry involves experience, and the way insight involves experience; in the former, experience is merely an occasion; in the latter, images are not merely the occasion but the object of insight (UB 164–65).
8 UB 169. Cf. INCW 356 on the spontaneous dynamism of knowing as the ultimate foundation of knowing.
9 UB 170.
10 Cf. e.g. Lonergan, *Topics in Education* (1959), which refers to the upper blade of specialized and of generalized history as an a priori (TE 237, 250 n. 26, 251, 255); Lonergan, 'Horizons and Categories' 11 (LRI Archives, Lonergan Papers file 307, probable dating 1968, cf. appendix A) 11 again refers to the upper blade as an a priori: categories derived through self-appropriation serve as an a priori for the understanding of other men, their history, etc.; even in *Method* this reference to the upper blade as relatively a priori is maintained: cf. e.g. MT 293.
11 Lonergan, 'Mission and the Spirit' 3C 28. Cf. also Crowe, 'Transcendental Deduction,' 34.
12 Lonergan, 'Christology Today: Methodological Reflections' 3C 87.
13 Cf. KL Laporte, 3: heuristic structure is the *intentio entis intendens* as specified by data; it is the particularized intention that is the heuristic structure.
14 GOI 13.
15 INCW 67–68; cf. 60.
16 INCW 63.
17 INCW 64–67.
18 INCW 337–38.
19 INCW 337. Cf. also INCW 87 and 486.
20 INCW 126.
21 INCW 707: Understanding 'arises in intelligent and rational consciousness but, before it arises, it is anticipated, and that anticipation is the spontaneous ground that, when reflectively enucleated, becomes the methods of science and the integral heuristic structure implemented in the metaphysics of proportionate being.' INCW 708: '[T]he method of the empirical sciences rests on the heuristic structure of man's desire and capacity to understand data correctly.'
22 Cf. Conversazioni con Bernard Lonergan, transcripts of interviews with Lonergan conducted by G.B. Sala, 1965, 41–42: 'S. [= Sala] "Ora, la riflessione su

queste strutture euristiche ..." / L. [= Lonergan] "Sull'uso, sull'operazioni scientifiche, *rivela* le strutture che si adoperano nelle scienze; e così si arriva alle strutture euristiche. E conoscendo le strutture euristiche si possono dare precetti riflessi per le operazioni scientifiche stesse." / S. "E questo secondo sarebbe il metodo." / L. "Sì. Prima c'è la scienza, poi la conoscenza della scienza"' (emphasis in text).

23 INCW 93.
24 INCW 127: 'Of themselves, heuristic structures are empty. They anticipate a form that is to be filled. Now, just as the *form* can be anticipated in its general properties, so also can the *process* of filling be anticipated in its general properties. There exist, then, canons of empirical method' (emphases mine).
25 INCW 128.
26 Cf. INCW 91.
27 UB 196.
28 INCW 380. Cf. INCW 707: 'But the fundamental anticipation is the detached, disinterested, unrestricted desire to understand correctly.' Cf. also DMT Fall 1963 Daly 7: 'Ens est prima notio heuristica, et fundamentale.'
29 INCW 69.
30 INCW 378–79.
31 VB 47, 79–88.
32 INCW 380.
33 UB 67: 'Besides the movement upwards from the data ... there is also a downward movement that is operative in the sciences, and that downward movement is partly illustrated by the anticipation of "a nature of ..." Again, the idea that similars are similarly understood, and the idea that the relevant similarities in science are not similarities of things in their relations to us but rather in their relations to one another, pertain to the downward movement on the data.'
34 Cf. chapter 1, section 2.2 above.
35 INCW 86.
36 INCW 417: Prior to the understanding that issues in answers, there are the questions that anticipate answers; such anticipation can be used to fix the characteristics of the answers not yet known; 'for while the content of a future cognitional act is unknown, the general characteristics of the act itself not only can be known but also can supply a premise that leads to the act.'
37 INCW 417.
38 Ibid. For examples of heuristic notions, cf. INCW 380: the notion of the intelligible, and the notion of the grounded. For an example of heuristic structure, cf. INCW 417: the definition of proportionate being. It must be noted, however, that Lonergan does not always maintain this distinction rigorously, and tends to use the two terms interchangeably. Thus, for example, the universal viewpoint is regularly referred to as a notion, but INCW 588 is not

Notes to pages 35–38   233

averse to describing it as 'a heuristic structure that contains virtually the ranges of possible alternatives of interpretations.'
39 UB 341–44.
40 INCW 759.
41 VB 87, and cf. above, chapter 1, note 97.
42 INCW 256.
43 INCW 54; cf. 721. Note that a theorem does not add anything new to the data, but is only a new organization of data: cf. GOI 19, and GF 13–14, 88. Also GF 143: 'Thus, to St. Thomas cooperation was a theorem, something known by understanding the data already apprehended and not something known by adding a new datum to the apprehension, something like the principle of work and not something like another lever, something like the discovery of gravitation and not something like the discovery of America.' The dialectical theorem is therefore a particular organization of data, resulting from the identification of two opposed principles in the unfolding of the social situation, the pure desire to know on the one hand, and human sensitivity and intersubjectivity on the other.
44 INCW 242.
45 INCW 268–69.
46 INCW 268.
47 INCW 269.
48 Ibid.
49 INCW 278.
50 INCW 293.
51 Ibid.
52 INCW 401. The matter is less clear in *Verbum*. *Verbum* notes in several places that the real problem, the critical point in philosophy, is the meaning that one assigns to 'real' (VB 7, 179 note 200). Still, it seems to retain also the standard meaning of the phrase 'critical problem,' even though only in contexts where it adverts to its overcoming once the true meaning of 'real' is grasped (VB 88).
53 Quite clearly the meaning one assigns to the word 'real' is more fundamental than the 'critical question' in the standard sense, for such meaning determines one's formulation of the 'critical question' itself. For Lonergan, the real is what is known through understanding and judgment; on this position, the standard problem simply disappears, for both knowledge of objects and knowledge of oneself is a question of understanding correctly.
54 Cf. UB 146: 'But is that final object, known through the concept and judgment – is that really what is real? That is the critical question, and it begins to arise in chapter 14 of *Insight*. Metaphysical analysis presupposes an answer to both this critical question and the cognitional question of objectivity.' Again, UB 149: 'One may have critical difficulties at once and say, "That being is

being in quite a different sense from what I understand; that isn't the being that really is." Such critical difficulties are considered in chapter 14 of *Insight*, where we turn to metaphysics.'
55 INCW 355–56.
56 INCW 358–60. Cf. Crowe, 'Lonergan's Search for Foundations' 123: The critical problem 'in the standard sense' emerges in chapter 11 'to receive ... quick riddance'.
57 INCW 401.
58 INCW 384–85.
59 INCW 545.
60 INCW 408.
61 INCW 408–409.
62 INCW 508–509.
63 INCW 293.
64 INCW 410.
65 INCW 411.
66 Cf. INCW 410–11.
67 INCW 412.
68 Ibid. For an explanation of this principle, cf. INCW 412–13.
69 INCW 414.
70 Once this distinction is adverted to, it becomes possible to understand why Lonergan constantly keeps repeating the phrase 'mistaken formulations of genuine discoveries,' or 'dialectical formulations of discoveries.' Cf. INCW 415, 443–44, 531, 549.
71 INCW 412–13.
72 INCW 301–302.
73 INCW 301–302, 310–11.
74 INCW 302. Cf. also INCW 582–83: Appropriation of truth demands not only a process of learning and of identification, but also the maintenance of the orientation towards truth.
75 Cf. the Nottingham lecture 12 = PTP 40.
76 INCW 416.
77 INCW 422.
78 INCW 421, 423.
79 INCW 423.
80 INCW 426.
81 INCW 413.
82 INCW 426.
83 INCW 753.
84 INCW 22, 769, and cf. 13–17.
85 INCW 11.
86 INCW 13.

87 VB 81, 185.
88 VB 90–91.
89 INCW 268–69, cf. 260–61.
90 INCW 331.
91 Ibid.
92 INCW 432.
93 INCW 446.
94 INCW 432.
95 INCW 432–33.
96 INCW 446.
97 Ibid.
98 INCW 448; emphasis mine.
99 TE 149–50.
100 Wisdom for us is a foundation that lies ahead (TE 150). But how is it then that we can make judgments at all? The solution as in *Verbum* is that from the beginning we have a rudimentary view of the whole, inasmuch as our pure desire to know asks about everything. As St Thomas said, all knowledge is virtually given us in the light of intellect, and we move towards detailed knowledge of that whole by a process of dichotomy (TE 152–53). There is also mentioned the role of the educator in the development of wisdom (TE 152); this takes up a point made already in *Insight* (INCW 311). Cf. also IM 1959 Student Notes 17–22: Wisdom, though a foundation that lies ahead, is also a foundation that is always with us. The progress of the mind is not from the unknown to the known, but from being as somehow known, towards an explicit and ever fuller knowledge of it.
101 TE 157.
102 The 1957 lectures on mathematical logic confirm that *Insight* was an attempt to work out 'a genetic account' of wisdom: cf. Lonergan, Mathematical Logic, lectures at Boston College, 8–12 July 1957, V/1, as cited by Crowe, 'Lonergan's Search for Foundations' 127.
103 Cf. INCW 424.
104 INCW 424–25.
105 F.E. Crowe, 'Transcendental Deduction' 35: '[T]ranscendental deduction, though it is valid *a priori* for every logical exercise of conscious intentionality, is nevertheless valid only in virtue of a premise which was itself formed *a posteriori*.'
106 Ibid. 36.
107 INCW 456, 512–13.
108 Cf. INCW 424–25.
109 Cf. INCW 503.
110 Cf. UB 224: '[S]elf-appropriation enables us ... to grasp proportionate being as a whole: on the less than human levels, I did it in terms of emer-

Notes to pages 45–46

gent probability; and on the human level, the categories of a scientific hermeneutics.'
111 INCW 553.
112 INCW 553–54. Cf. in this connection the apology proffered in the introduction (INCW 24): '[S]cattered throughout this work there occur bold statements on the views of various thinkers. May I express the hope that they will not cause too much annoyance? As the lengthy discussion of the truth of interpretation in chapter 17 will reveal, they can hardly pretend to be verdicts issued by the court of history ... Their primary significance is simply that of an abbreviated mode of speech ... And perhaps ... there could be added a suggestion that, in the measure that the principles of this work are accepted, the significance that we happen to have underlined may provide a starting point for further inquiry.'
113 INCW 554. Cf. also UB 222.
114 Cf. INCW 554: '[W]e propose to ask whether there exists a single base of operations from which any philosophy can be interpreted correctly, and we propose to show that our cognitional analysis provides such a base.'
115 INCW 416.
116 Cf. INCW 588.
117 INCW 510. Cf. also INCW 510–11: 'From the structural unification of the methods by generalized emergent probability, there follow the structural account of the explanatory genera and species and the immanent order of the universe of proportionate being.'
118 INCW 235. Cf. INCW 235–37, 252–53.
119 INCW 236.
120 INCW 252–53. INCW 261 calls upon human science to drop 'the nineteenth-century scientific outlook of mechanist determinism in favor of an emergent probability' and to 'profit by the distinction between the intelligible emergent probability of prehuman process and the intelligent emergent probability that arises in the measure that man succeeds in understanding himself and in implementing that understanding.'
121 INCW 261.
122 INCW 268–69.
123 Robert Doran has shown that chapter 17 of *Insight* may be cast in terms of emergent probability on the lines of the account of genetic method in chapter 15: cf. his *Theology and the Dialectics of History* (Toronto: University of Toronto Press, 1990) chapter 19: The Ontology of Meaning.
124 INCW 268.
125 Philip McShane, 'Psychic Differentiations and Systematic Heuristics,' in Sean E. McEvenue and Ben F. Meyer, eds, *Lonergan's Hermeneutics: Its Development and Application* (Washington: Catholic University of America Press, 1989) 215. Cf. also ibid. 210: 'The metaphysics of *Insight* ... twists into a founda-

tional task of conceiving, affirming, and valuing concretely implementable categories within a perspective of emergent probability.'
126 INCW 554–72.
127 INCW 554–55.
128 INCW 557.
129 INCW 558. Cf. INCW 560: As metaphysics is not unconcerned with its own genesis, it cannot prescind entirely from the historical phenomena of mysteries and myths.
130 INCW 566. INCW 565: Myth and magic are necessary factors in the dialectical unfolding of human intelligence.
131 For the discussion of truth, cf. INCW 572–85.
132 In an earlier draft of chapter 17 of *Insight*, this section 3, The Truth of Interpretation, was section 2.6, and therefore part of section 2, The Notion of Truth. Cf. LRI Archives Batch IV.11, version of chapters 16 and 17.
133 INCW 532.
134 Cf. section 3 above.
135 Cf. VB xiii: 'For performance must precede reflection on performance, and method is the fruit of that reflection. Aquinas had to be content to perform.'
136 INCW 553, 617, and Doran, *Theology and the Dialectics of History* 592. Recall also the mention of Hegel in chapter 8 of *Insight*, precisely in the context of a philosophy of philosophies (INCW 293).

Chapter 3

1 INCW 616.
2 VB 12.
3 VB 153.
4 The reason for this position is the Platonic problem, What are we talking about when we speak of 'man' or 'triangle'? Directly, we mean objects of thought, inner words, and only indirectly, insofar as our inner words have objective reference, are we talking about real things. 'Because outer words may be abstract, and true or false, because real things are neither abstract nor true nor false, the immediate reference of their meaning is to an inner word' (VB 2–3).
5 VB 152–53. Lonergan cites the example of the names of God: since we have no knowledge of the essence of God, we cannot use names to express the essence of God.
6 INCW 4–5, 6.
7 Cf. INCW 412–13.
8 INCW 451. This is connected of course with the fact that wisdom selects basic terms, and especially the meaning of being. 'There is no first principle that does not attain a different meaning according to the different meaning you

238 Notes to page 50

give being.' (TE 156–57). Cf. also 3C 156: 'Philosophic differences affect the very meaning of meaning.'
We might note the rather restricted idea of language here: it has a purely cognitive and communicative function.

9 Cf. INCW 530: Metaphysical equivalence provides a critical technique for the precise control of meaning. The Nottingham lecture 22 = PTP 52 mentions a 'semantics or metaphysics of meaning.' Again, IM 1959 4: 'Unde semantica, metaphysica: distinctio inter entia realia et rationis, inter distinctiones reales et rationis; et harum ad omnia applicatio systematica.' Further, IM 1959 Student Notes 6: For a system to have real meaning, it must go beyond logic to metaphysics or semantics.

10 INCW 381, 592.

11 INCW 592; cf. 381.

12 Among concepts are to be included heuristic concepts as well as common-sense concepts. Thus, DMT 1962 Student Notes 20: From the act of understanding proceeds a non-complex inner word, which can be either a scientific definition of something, having full universality, or else an expression that suffices for immediate consideration and use, which is the case in ordinary everyday knowledge. Again, *Insight* tells us that commonsense concepts are more a question of an understanding of verbal usage than an understanding of what names denote: '[I]t is one thing to understand in a concrete, commonsense fashion, and it is quite another to be able to formulate one's understanding coherently in general terms' (INCW 565). Commonsense concepts are really a heuristic anticipation of insight (INCW 565). Cf. also INCW 35–36 on nominal definitions as insights into the use of language, etc. Note then that commonsense concepts are concepts, but are often merely names of things, and so represent heuristic rather than actual understanding. Further, they are not adequate formulations: they lack full universality.

13 INCW 381–82: 'Formal terms of meaning are what is conceived, thought, considered, defined, supposed, formulated.' Cf. also INCW 330. It might be noted that formal acts and terms of meaning correspond to *dicere* and the non-complex inner word of definition. It would seem that the act of defining and the definition are not really distinct. This is affirmed explicitly in the 1945 course Thought and Reality, which says that the act of meaning is the definition proceeding from the insight, and that, since defining and definition are related as action and passion, they are the same thing regarded from two different points of view (cf. Lonergan, Thought and Reality, the Daly typescript of the O'Hara notes 17). It is implied in the way *Verbum* uses interchangeably the terms inner word, definition, inner word of defining: cf. VB 198: '[T]he inner word is to our intelligence in act as act to act, perfection to proportionate perfection; in us the process is *processio operati*; in us *dicere* is

Notes to pages 50–52   239

producere verbum.' Again, VB 199: 'The inner word of defining not only is *caused by* but also is *because of* the act of understanding' (emphases in text). Further, VB 200: 'In us inner word proceeds from act of understanding by a *processio intelligibilis* that is also a *processio operati*, for our inner word and act of understanding are two absolute entities really distinct.'

14 INCW 382, 330.
15 MT 75; cf. Doran, *Theology and the Dialectics of History* 573.
16 *Intelligere, dicere,* and inner word are related as act, act proceeding from act, and term of act (VB 167, 178, 126–27, etc). *Intelligere* is distinct from *dicere*, and the distinction between the two is a distinction between two meanings of action, operation: *intelligere* is action in the sense of act, while *dicere* is action in the sense of operating an effect (VB 139). Further, at least as far as human knowing is concerned, the distinction is real and not merely notional: 'In us there are two acts, first an act of understanding, secondly, a really distinct act of defining or judging. In God there is but one act' (VB 198; cf. also the argument of VB 190). Again, cf. UB 282, where Lonergan speaks of the distinction between insight and concept, and refers to his discussion of apprehensive and formative abstraction in VB 151–68. To this he adds that, from a metaphysical point of view, the 'systematic proof of the distinction between insight and concept, between *intelligere* and *dicere*, is from objects.'
17 VB 178–79. A clear grasp of the relations between *intelligere* and *dicere*, between potential and principal acts of meaning, between apprehensive and formative abstraction, is of some importance for a theory of interpretation. For besides understanding there is the identification that makes teaching and communication possible, and identification is possession of insight or formative abstraction. More precisely, it is perhaps a type of formative abstraction that goes beyond merely commonsense formulations.
18 INCW 330.
19 INCW 381.
20 INCW 296.
21 INCW 611.
22 Cf. INCW 579, 586.
23 INCW 381.
24 INCW 381–83.
25 INCW 576.
26 INCW 576–77.
27 INCW 577.
28 Ibid. Distinguish, however, expression for oneself and expression for others. The latter has to take into account the habitual intellectual development of the audience, and may be named communication.
29 Cf. INCW 611–12: '[O]nce any stage in the development of meaning has

become propagated and established in a cultural milieu, there will result an appropriate mode of expression to bear witness to its existence.'
30 INCW 610.
31 VB 9–10.
32 INCW 610.
33 Ibid.
34 INCW 577.
35 INCW 560, cf. 554: A contemporary metaphysics cannot be unconcerned with its own origins. INCW 555: Myth and mystery seem to be cognate to earlier stages in the development of metaphysics.
36 Cf. note 9 above.
37 INCW 560.
38 INCW 560–66.
39 INCW 565.
40 INCW 566–67.
41 Cf. the subsection 'Myth and Allegory,' INCW 567–69.
42 INCW 571.
43 For 'the insights and judgments of the individual can be communicated successfully and permanently to others only in the measure that the community has accumulated the prior, presupposed insights and has developed the techniques for their dissemination and preservation' (INCW 561).
44 INCW 568. Thus, it is the discussion of myth and allegory rather than that of mythic consciousness that speaks clearly of the development of meaning: '[T]he transformations of meanings that change the reference of words' (INCW 568), the 'series of discoveries of new meanings' that might be 'expansions of existing viewpoints' but also 'new viewpoints' (INCW 569). The connection with the discussion of mythic consciousness is, however, clearly indicated: the problem of expression arises 'inasmuch as the mythmaker is endeavoring to transcend the counterpositions, inasmuch as he is trying to turn attention from the sensible to the intelligible, inasmuch as he has reached a viewpoint that current modes of expression cannot convey' (INCW 569).
45 INCW 567.
46 Cf. INCW 616, 572–73.
47 Cf. Lonergan, Mathematical Logic, Graham transcript 51, for a clear distinction between definition and criterion of truth. Truth is defined as 'adaequatio intellectus ad rem,' but the criterion of truth is commonly expressed as 'perspicientia evidentiae sufficientis qua sufficientis.' Lonergan remarks that this is a rather woolly notion, and that chapter 10 of *Insight* was an attempt to clarify it.
48 INCW 575; cf. text for greater detail.
49 INCW 573.

50 Ibid.
51 INCW 576–81.
52 INCW 581–85.
53 INCW 585.
54 INCW 582–83.
55 INCW 573.
56 INCW 585.
57 INCW 608.
58 INCW 582.
59 VB 216; cf. INCW 769.
60 INCW 582.
61 Ibid.
62 INCW 588.
63 INCW 590. Cf. also INCW 601 and 588.
64 'Orientations' is another name for patterns of experience. Both the intellectual and the biological patterns are described as orientations: cf. INCW 378, 529, 584 for the intellectual pattern; INCW 410 for the biological pattern; INCW 598, which speaks of both patterns as orientations. But the clearest indications are on INCW 589, 590, and 602, which speak interchangeably of patterns and orientations. Cf. also INCW 205: There is, immanent in experience, 'a factor variously named conation, interest, attention, purpose,' and ibid.: The stream of consciousness involves 'not only the temporal succession of different contents but also direction, striving, effort.'
65 A habitual orientation is the context formed by previous insights and judgments. Cf. INCW 302: '[P]ast judgments remain with us. They form a habitual orientation, present and operative ... Previous insights remain with us ... Hence, when a new judgment is made, there is within us a habitual context of insights and other judgments.'
66 INCW 582–83. Cf. also INCW 404.
67 INCW 563.
68 INCW 564.
69 INCW 587; cf. INCW 314–24.
70 INCW 301–302, 382.
71 Cf. here the discussion of the source of commonsense judgments: INCW 314–16; also the analysis of belief and of the human collaboration in knowledge: INCW 725–35.
72 INCW 402–405.
73 INCW 573–75. The proximate criterion of truth is the grasp of the virtually unconditioned (INCW 310–12). The connection between normative objectivity and the remote criterion is quite evident. Thus INCW 404: 'The ground of normative objectivity lies in the unfolding of the unrestricted, detached, disinterested desire to know ... Because it is detached, it is opposed to the inhibi-

tions of cognitional process that arise from other human desires and drives. Because it is disinterested, it is opposed to the well-meaning but disastrous reinforcement that other desires lend cognitional process only to twist its orientation ...' And INCW 573: '[T]he remote criterion is the proper unfolding of the detached and disinterested desire to know. In negative terms this proper unfolding is the absence of interference from other desires that inhibit or reinforce, and in either case distort, the guidance given by the pure desire.'

74 INCW 564.
75 INCW 585.
76 INCW 568.
77 INCW 579–80.
78 INCW 579.
79 INCW 586.
80 INCW 586–87.
81 INCW 587: Since neither common sense nor historical sense can analyze or criticize themselves or arrive at an abstract formulation of their central nucleus, 'both are far more likely to be correct in pronouncing verdicts than in assigning exact and convincing reasons for them.'
82 INCW 587.
83 There may be found other more partial statements of the problem, which emphasize the aspect of appropriation. Thus the title of section 3 is 'The Truth of Interpretation' (INCW 585). Again, the subsection 'Interpretation and Method' speaks of the problem of relativism caused by the lack of an appropriate upper blade for interpretation, goes on to insist that correct interpretation is possible, but fails to mention the problem of communication (INCW 600). Further, it would seem to be this same relativism and absence of an appropriate upper blade that is referred to when the conclusion of chapter 17 observes that 'the present account of insight into the insights of others possesses peculiar relevance at a time when theoretical differences of a philosophic character so frequently constitute the principal cause of divergence not only in the conclusions reached but also in the methods employed by otherwise competent investigators' (INCW 616).
84 INCW 600, 602.
85 INCW 600: Presuppositionless interpretation is quite impossible.
86 INCW 564.
87 Ibid.
88 Ibid.
89 INCW 558.
90 INCW 23.
91 INCW 600.
92 INCW 564: 'As the data assembled by historical research accumulate, insights are revised continuously in accord with the concrete process of learning.'

93 This point is especially well expressed in Paul Swartzentruber, 'The Development of an Approach to Hermeneutic Method in the Work of Bernard Lonergan, s.j.: From *Insight* to *Method in Theology*,' master's thesis, University of St Michael's College, Toronto (1981) 29–30.
94 Cf. above, section 1.2 and chapter 2, section 4.
95 INCW 587.
96 INCW 588. Cf. UB 222: 'Again, as it is not deducing in the ordinary sense of the word, so it is not deducing in the Hegelian sense of the word, namely, in the precise form of the Hegelian dialectic.' Cf. also MiT 1971 639, where Lonergan insists that he is not doing universal history or attempting to rival Hegel.
97 INCW 446–47.
98 Cf. INCW 588. For a contrast between the Kantian and the Lonerganian sense of the *a priori*, cf. above, chapter 2, section 1.1.
99 INCW 588.
100 Cf. Lonergan, Mathematical Logic, Graham transcript 56.
101 Cf. above, chapter 2, section 1.2.
102 INCW 39. Cf. also VB 3–4: Correspondence of realities to inner words is 'like the correspondence between a function and its derivative; as the derivative, so the inner word is outside all particular cases and refers to all from some higher view-point.' Again, VB 10: The more perfect a single act of understanding, the more numerous the inner words it embraces in a single view.
103 INCW 22.
104 Cf. INCW 5–6.
105 Cf. INCW 590: '[I]n the measure that one grasps the structure of this protean notion of being, one possesses the base and ground from which one can proceed to the content and context of every meaning.'
106 INCW 600.
107 Corresponding to the protean notion of being there is a universe of meanings: 'There is, then, a universe of meanings, and its four dimensions are the full range of possible combinations (1) of experiences and lack of experience, (2) of insights and lack of insight, (3) of judgments and of failures to judge, and (4) of the various orientations of the polymorphic consciousness of man' (INCW 590). Cf. also INCW 590: 'Being is (or is thought to be) whatever is (or is thought to be) grasped intelligently and affirmed reasonably.'
108 Cf. INCW 589.
109 Cf. INCW 590.
110 INCW 591. Cf. also ibid.: '[T]he potential totality of all viewpoints lies in the dynamic structure of cognitional activity.' It is to be remembered that this dynamic structure includes also the various patterns in which human consciousness flows. Thus INCW 422: 'They may be unable to discover in them-

selves other equally dynamic structures that can interfere with the detached and disinterested unfolding of the pure desire to know.'

111 Cf. INCW 591.
112 Cf. above, Introduction.
113 INCW 587; emphasis mine.
114 INCW 588. 'Insights and judgments' here would seem to refer to formal and full acts of meaning rather than to direct and reflective acts of understanding, which, as we saw above (cf. section 1.1) are merely potential acts of meaning.
115 Cf. INCW 399: Human knowing is cumulative, 'not only in memory's store of experiences and understanding's clustering of insights, but also in the coalescence of judgments into the context named knowledge or mentality.' Again, ibid.: the principal notion of objectivity is contained within a patterned context of judgments. Cf. also INCW 301–303: past judgments remain with us, they form a habitual orientation. Previous insights remain with us. Hence when a new judgment is made, there is within us a habitual context of insights and other judgments. Again, INCW 573: '[W]hile the content of the judgment is grasped as unconditioned, still that content either demands or rests on the contents of experiences, insights, and other judgments for its full clarification. This concrete inevitability of a context of other acts and a context of other contents is what necessitates the addition of a remote to a proximate criterion of truth.'
116 INCW 602–603.
117 Hermeneutics 1962 13–15. There is further the use of the term 'upper context' in *Insight* itself, but this demands separate treatment (cf. below, chapter 4, section 1.3).
118 It is a question of reaching 'a concrete presentation of any formulation of any discovery through the identification in personal experience of the elements that, as confused or as distinguished and related, as related under this or that orientation of polymorphic consciousness, could combine to make the position or counterposition humanly convincing' (INCW 589).
119 INCW 611.
120 Cf. above, chapter 1, section 2.3.
121 The universal viewpoint 'has its base in an adequate self-knowledge and in the consequent metaphysics' (INCW 588).
122 It is a question of an ability to distinguish and recombine elements in one's own experience, an ability 'to work backwards from contemporary to earlier accumulations of insights in human development,' an ability 'to envisage the protean possibilities of the notion of being' (INCW 588).
123 Cf. UB 219–24.
124 Cf. above, chapter 2, section 3.
125 INCW 588–89.

126 INCW 493–94.
127 INCW 589.
128 INCW 592.
129 INCW 615, cf. 611. INCW 613: '[T]he fields of meaning, of expression as related to meaning.' INCW 615: '[E]xpression bears the signature ... of the controlling meaning.'
130 INCW 568.
131 INCW 611–12.
132 INCW 595.
133 Cf. ibid.
134 INCW 601: '[T]he possibility of connecting possible meanings with particular documents lies in the genetic sequence that extrapolates from present to past correlations between meaning and mode of expression.' Cf. INCW 87: '[C]lassical inquiry evolves practical techniques of curve fitting to aid the transition from measurements to functional relations.' Again, ibid.: '[C]lassical inquiry proceeds not only from below upwards from measurements through curve fitting but also from above downwards.'
135 INCW 592; cf. text for details.
136 INCW 592–93.
137 INCW 594.
138 Cf. INCW 579–80, and above, section 2.1.
139 INCW 594. The point is stressed in the subsection 'Limitations of the Treatise': perfect treatises do not exist; most texts do not stand unambiguously upon a single level of expression, and are not free from relativity to some audience (INCW 596).
140 INCW 595; cf. INCW 568–69. Lonergan's personal discovery of this lag is recorded in the *Verbum* articles: Aquinas was struggling to express his grasp of psychological facts in metaphysical categories (cf. VB 94–95).
141 INCW 595; cf. VB 23–24.
142 The latter conclusion at least is supported by Hefling: '[S]ince insight into insight is insight into the sources of meaning, and since these sources are prior to the instrumental acts that express them, an understanding of levels and sequences of expressions is likewise possible.' Cf. Charles Hefling, Jr, 'On Understanding Salvation History,' in Sean McEvenue and Ben F. Meyer, eds, *Lonergan's Hermeneutics: Its Development and Application* (Washington: Catholic University of America Press, 1989) 260.
143 Note that this sketch includes the three final subsections of the third section of chapter 17, and not merely the subsection entitled 'The Sketch.'
144 INCW 609, 602. The striking similarity of expression between the canon of relevance and the discussion of pure formulations is to be noted.
145 INCW 602, cf. 609.
146 There is possibly an allusion here to the pure desire to know. Pure formula-

tions are those that are formulated within the purely intellectual pattern of experience, and that are not distorted by interference from other desire.

147 INCW 602.
148 Ibid.; cf. 609.
149 For the canon of parsimony, cf. INCW 612–13, and also the fourth principle of criticism of the canon of successive approximations (INCW 612). On pure formulations as hypotheses, cf. INCW 612.
150 INCW 603.
151 Relevant to the type of control made possible by the universal viewpoint is the distinction between general and particular hypotheses: the universal viewpoint is a general hypothesis that has 'general presuppositions and implications' and can therefore 'be tested in a variety of manners' (INCW 616). It might be recalled that we had identified the pure form of speculative development as a general hypothesis: cf. above, chapter 1, section 1, note 15.
152 INCW 609. INCW 604: '[I]nterpretation aims at differentiating the protean notion of being by a set of genetically and dialectically related set of terms.' And again, ibid.: '[T]he position calls for determinations of being by an explanatorily related set of terms.' INCW 608: 'A scientific interpretation is concerned to formulate the relevant insights and judgments, and to do so in a manner that is consonant with scientific collaboration and scientific control.'
153 INCW 609.
154 INCW 610–12.
155 'Hence certitudes may be strengthened by the agreement of others, and this strengthening will vary with the numbers of those that agree, the diversity of their circumstances, the consequent virtual elimination of individual and group bias, and the absence of any ground for suspecting general bias' (INCW 574).
156 INCW 575.
157 INCW 612; emphasis mine.
158 INCW 575.
159 Crowe notes that 'differentiation' is used in a variety of ways in *Insight*, and that the word has not yet acquired its technical meaning: cf. '"All my work has been introducing history into Catholic theology" (Lonergan, March 28, 1980),' *Lonergan Workshop* 10:77.
160 INCW 609–10. Elsewhere, 'the transition from one differentiation to another' is described as 'the quite determinate and determinable process of changing patterns of experience, accumulations of insights, and sets of judgments' (INCW 608). This description includes the genetic and the dialectical sequences of meanings, but not the genetic sequence of expressions. Still, what we have here is not a description of explanatory differentiations but an effort to explain transitions over differentiations.

161 Cf. INCW 609.
162 A more adequate exploration of this topic would require investigation of genetic method. Cf. especially the remark on INCW 223, which indicates that the first section of chapter 17 (which discusses the earlier stages of metaphysics or the genesis of self-knowledge) is made possible by the 'earlier exploration of genetic method.' Note also that the discussion of genetic method speaks often of stages (INCW 491, 495) and of differentiation (ibid.).
163 INCW 611.
164 Ibid.
165 INCW 611–12.
166 INCW 612.
167 INCW 560: 'Just as an explicit and adequate metaphysics is to be reached by grasping and formulating the integral heuristic structure of our knowing and its proportionate known, so the hypothetical introduction of blind spots into the structure has the interesting consequence of revealing the categories not only of inadequate philosophies but also, in the limit, of mythic consciousness.' Compare INCW 591: '[F]or there is a particular philosophy that would take its stand upon the dynamic structure of human cognitional activity, that would distinguish the various elements involved in that structure, that would be able to construct any philosophic position by postulating appropriate and plausible omissions and confusions of the elements.'
168 In this connection it may be interesting to note that MiT 1971 223–24 observes that the *Method* chapter 'Meaning' had carried out reconstruction of the mentalities of myth and magic. Recall also that chapter 17 of *Insight* describes latent and problematic metaphysics as earlier stages of metaphysics, and asks whether mystery and myth 'are cognate to these earlier stages and whether they vanish in the measure that the earlier stages are transcended' (INCW 555).
169 INCW 611; emphasis mine. Note that this phrase is missing in earlier editions of *Insight*: cf. ed. note cc, INCW 803.
170 INCW 588: The universal viewpoint 'has a retrospective expansion in the various genetic series of discoveries through which man could advance to his present knowledge.' INCW 589: 'What is ordered is itself advancing from the generic to the specific, from the undifferentiated to the differentiated.'
171 INCW 588, 590, and esp. 558: '[S]uch adequate self-knowledge can be reached by man only at the summit of a long ascent.'
172 INCW 703.
173 INCW 471: '[S]ince cognitional activity is itself but a part of this universe, its striving to know being is but the intelligent and reasonable part of a universal striving towards being.' INCW 501: 'Unconsciously operative is the finality that consists in the upwardly but indeterminately directed dynamism of all proportionate being. Consciously operative is the detached and disinterested

desire raising ever further questions.' Cf. also INCW 235–37, 253, 261, and chapter 2, section 4 above.
174 INCW 261.
175 INCW 252–53.
176 INCW 560–66.
177 INCW 558–59.
178 INCW 590.
179 INCW 588.
180 INCW 591.
181 INCW 18.
182 INCW 593.
183 INCW 602.
184 INCW 595.
185 INCW 593.
186 Lonergan, 'The Original Preface of *Insight*,' ed. F.E. Crowe, *Method: Journal of Lonergan Studies* 3:1 (1985) 3–7. This preface was ready by August 1953; it was subsequently discarded in favor of the one actually published in 1957: cf. Crowe, 'A Note on the Prefaces of *Insight*,' *Method: Journal of Lonergan Studies* 3:1 (1985) 2.
187 Lonergan, 'The Original Preface of *Insight*' 5.
188 Ibid. 5–6.
189 Ibid.
190 Ibid. 6.
191 INCW 415.
192 INCW 418–19.
193 MiT 1971 631.
194 INCW 592.
195 INCW 494: '[T]he higher system of intellectual development is primarily the higher integration, not of the man in whom the development occurs, but of the universe that he inspects.'
196 Apart from the reappearance of the universal viewpoint in the final chapters of *Insight*, Tekippe contends that it is operative also in the context of a dialectical history of philosophy, of philosophical method, and of cosmopolis. Cf. Tekippe, 'The Universal Viewpoint' 58.
197 Cf. Swartzentruber, 'The Development of an Approach' 58–59; Hefling, 'Lonergan on Development' 369–70, note 14; Lonergan, 2C 275–76.

Chapter 4

1 INCW 647, 650–56.
2 Cf. INCW 654.
3 INCW 655–56, and cf. also INCW 263–67 on cosmopolis.

4 INCW 655–56.
5 Cf. INCW 413, and also 508–509, 545–46, 665.
6 Cf. INCW 701.
7 INCW 665.
8 INCW 666.
9 INCW 666–67.
10 Cf. INCW 701.
11 INCW 698.
12 Ibid.
13 INCW 761.
14 INCW 703.
15 Ibid.
16 INCW 688.
17 INCW 702.
18 INCW 703.
19 Ibid.
20 INCW 704.
21 INCW 704–705.
22 Ibid.
23 INCW 705.
24 Cf. above, chapter 2, section 1.2, and also INCW 386–87 and 388–89.
25 Cf. above, chapter 2, section 1.2.
26 Cf. VB 90: 'The basic duality of our wisdom is between our immanent intellectual light and the uncreated Light that is the object of its groping and its straining ... Between these poles, the highest in us and in God the most like us, our wisdom moves to knowledge of itself and of its source.'
27 Cf. INCW 656.
28 Cf. INCW 718.
29 INCW 718–19.
30 INCW 761.
31 INCW 763.
32 INCW 723–24.
33 INCW 724.
34 INCW 725. For a discussion of belief, cf. INCW 725–40. The analysis of the process of believing (cf. esp. INCW 728–32) is similar in structure to the analysis of the process leading to the assent of faith in *Analysis fidei* of 1952 (cf. Lonergan, *Analysis fidei*, The Early Latin Works of Bernard J.F. Lonergan, ed. F.E. Crowe, assisted by C. O'Donovan and G. Sala, Regis College, Toronto, 1973). *Analysis fidei* consists of class notes prepared by Lonergan in 1952; if therefore the final chapters of *Insight* were composed in early 1953 (cf. Editors' Preface, INCW xii), *Analysis fidei* belongs to their immediate history.

35 This also follows from the fact that the solution is a harmonious continuation of the actual order of the universe, and so a new and higher integration (INCW 719); but higher integrations leave intact the functioning of the lower levels, and we are intelligent, rational, and free; hence, the solution will not come to us without our apprehension and consent (INCW 720).
36 INCW 741.
37 INCW 741-42.
38 INCW 742.
39 Ibid.
40 Cf. above, note 34.
41 *Analysis fidei* speaks of a *logical process* and a *psychological process* leading to faith. The logical process consists of two syllogisms (cf. AF 1-2). The psychological process divides into a remote and a proximate part. In the *remote* part there are distinguished the *principal acts*, which are the four judgments by which the four premises of the logical process are affirmed, and the *secondary acts*, which are all those acts that lead to the principal acts. The *proximate* part consists of six acts: the reflective act grasping the sufficiency of evidence for eliciting the next five acts (this is the beginning of supernatural faith), the practical judgments of credibility and of credendity, the will of the end, the will of the means, and finally the assent of faith itself. (Cf. AF 2-3, corrected by AF 4.) It should be noted that the logical process corresponds to a part of the remote process.
42 INCW 724.
43 INCW 743.
44 INCW 761: The universal viewpoint 'receives further determinations from our final chapters on transcendent knowledge.'
45 We might stress once again that the acknowledgment of the divine solution follows from the affirmation of the existence of God: since God is good, and since he exists, there exists not merely a problem of evil but also a divine solution to it (cf. INCW 709).
46 This might be the place to note that Tekippe's solution (cf. Tekippe, 'The Universal Viewpoint' 125, and also above, Introduction) about the relationship between the universal viewpoint and the 'theological viewpoint' is basically correct: the difference between them is that between lesser and greater determination of a heuristic structure. Only, it must be recognized that this solution follows quite simply once the notion of heuristic structures is properly grasped.
47 INCW 746.
48 INCW 749.
49 INCW 750.
50 INCW 749.
51 Cf. INCW 647-49.

52 INCW 649.
53 INCW 498.
54 INCW 502.
55 1C 198.
56 'Universal willingness' is mentioned about four times in chapter 18: cf. INCW 647, 648, 651.
57 INCW 646.
58 INCW 647.
59 INCW 651.
60 INCW 647, 648.
61 INCW 646; cf. INCW 621–22.
62 INCW 622. Compare George P. Klubertanz, *The Philosophy of Human Nature* (New York: Appleton-Century Crofts, 1953) 282: 'A wise man ... is a man who judges correctly of the reality, *significance, and value* of the things which he knows; he can locate them correctly in the order of being, and he knows, at least in general, how they are related to the ultimate end. Hence, *though wisdom is essentially a habit and virtue of the speculative intellect, its influence overflows into the order of action. Clearly, if a man knows the order and value of things, he would be acting very irrationally if he did not measure his actions by that knowledge.* That is why it is sometimes said that wisdom, though it is a speculative virtue, is *eminently practical*' (emphasis added).
63 INCW 626.
64 Ibid.
65 INCW 630.
66 INCW 626; cf. 630.
67 INCW 629–30.
68 INCW 766–67; cf. also INCW 768.
69 INCW 54.
70 INCW 242.
71 INCW 754.
72 Ibid.
73 INCW 702; and cf. sections 1.1 and 1.2 above.
74 Even the acknowledgment and acceptance of the divine solution seems not so much to expand this base as to make it de facto possible.
75 Cf. INCW 18–20.
76 INCW 18: '[I]t must begin from a minimal viewpoint and a minimal context; it will exploit that minimum to raise a further question that enlarges the viewpoint and the context; it will proceed with the enlarged viewpoint and context ... [T]his device can be repeated ... as often as may be required to reach the universal viewpoint and the completely concrete context that embraces every aspect of reality.'
77 INCW 19–20: '[T]here also is the *noêsis* or *intentio intendens* or *pensée pensante*

that is constituted by the very activity of inquiring and reflecting, understanding and affirming, asking further questions and reaching further answers.' INCW 20: 'Moreover, if it can be shown that the upper context is invariant, that any attempt to revise it can be legitimate only if the hypothetical reviser refutes his own attempt by invoking experience, understanding, and reflection ... then it will appear that ... the immanent and recurrently operative structure of the *noêsis* or *intentio intendens* or *pensée pensante* must always be one and the same.'

78 Cf. INCW 743, and above, section 1.2.
79 INCW 754.
80 INCW 755. On the humanist viewpoint, cf. INCW 749, 753.
81 INCW 753.
82 AF 14: 'Secundarii sunt qui in principales ducunt, puta, philosophia sana et theologia fundamentalis.'
83 Cf. above, note 41.
84 AF 14–15. Cf. also AF 21: 'Per preambula intelligimus illa fidei fundamenta quae certo sed non fide divina cognoscuntur.'
85 AF 22. Compare a typical text from the beginning of the twentieth century, Eugenio Duplessy, *Apologetica*, 3 vols. (Rome: Francesco Ferrari Editore; Turin: Soc. Edit. Internazionale, 1929): the first volume establishes that a religion is necessary for human beings, and that this religion should have been revealed by God; the second volume goes on to identify which among the various existing religions is revealed, by applying to them various criteria, especially that of the miracle; the third volume goes on to identify the true church. It is clearly indicated that apologetics is the work of pure reason: cf. ibid., 3:277: 'Quello che abbiamo stabilito fin qui, l'abbiam fatto seguendo unicamente i dati di una saggia ragione.' Again, cf. ibid., 3:286, which raises the question of the transition from the act of pure reason to that of faith.
86 INCW 750–51.
87 AF 15: 'existentia Dei quae est totius negotii fundamentum (DB 1806).' Cf. also Hefling, 'Lonergan on Development' 119–25, and esp. 125.
88 Cf. Lonergan, 'Variations in Fundamental Theology,' *Method: Journal of Lonergan Studies* 16 (1998) 8: 'A natural theology established the existence of God. A natural ethics established the obligation of worshiping God.'
89 INCW 742–43.
90 INCW 744.
91 Cf. 1C 129. The terminal viewpoint (cf. INCW 754, 766), by contrast, on the other hand would seem to be the viewpoint of the believer, the viewpoint of faith. It need not include the universal viewpoint, for operating from the universal viewpoint is not an intrinsic part of believing.
92 INCW 417.
93 Cf. INCW 417–18.

94 INCW 559.
95 Cf. above, chapter 3, section 3.5.
96 Cf. esp. INCW 680–92.
97 Cf. INCW 685–86 on divine efficacy and the *scientia media*; and INCW 687 on how God applies every contingent agent to its operation.
98 Cf. INCW 687, note 1.
99 2C 224–25.
100 INCW 743, and above, section 1.2.
101 Cf. INCW 761.
102 INCW 761.
103 Ibid.
104 INCW 762.
105 Ibid.
106 Ibid.
107 Hefling, 'Lonergan on Development' 118. Hefling goes on: 'The alternative I have just stated appears to be real. But it is not. The theologically transformed universal viewpoint does away with it. A theological interpreter is both an interpreter and a theologian; his or her base of operations is a viewpoint that is "broader and firmer" owing to the theological transformation; and ... one result of the transformation, though not the only one, is assent to dogma' (Ibid.).
108 INCW 761.
109 F.E. Crowe, *Lonergan* (Collegeville, MN: Liturgical Press, 1992) 83, notes that the analytic-synthetic pair is to be found already in *De ente supernaturali: supplementum schematicum* (1946), which are a set of notes prepared by Lonergan for a course on divine grace.
110 INCW 756. The 'Vatican Council' here is of course the First Vatican Council.
111 INCW 762.
112 It is to be noted that *Insight* was completed in 1953.
113 1C 126–27.
114 INCW 762.
115 INCW 761.
116 Ibid.
117 Cf. INCW 761.
118 INCW 760.
119 Cf. INCW 761.
120 INCW 759.
121 INCW 760; and cf. above, chapter 2, section 1.2.
122 INCW 759–60, and 417: An explicit metaphysics would be progressive.
123 INCW 760.
124 INCW 760–61.
125 Ibid.

254 Notes to pages 94–102

126 IM 1959 Student Notes 67: 'Theologus credit Deum revelasse, atque modo providentiali conservare verum revelatum per Ecclesiam suam. Quivis theologus ipsam fidem ex Deo habet atque directionem circa fidem ex Magisterio Ecclesiae; Tamen [*sic*] debet et ipse propria facere iudicia. Theologia, enim, non est aliquod exercitium repetitionis, sed intelligentia augetur per saecula ...' Again, ibid. 64: 'Utique, sine theologia positiva, theologia speculativa poterit inniti super magisterium ecclesiasticum. Sic demonstrare poterit quid sit de fide, quid non, quid sit theologice certum, quid probabile aut tutum, quid non, quid temerarium ... At hoc modo iudicium dabitur tantum de fide, seu de eo quod est credendum, non illius *intelligentia* obtinebitur.' Cf. also the Nottingham lecture 22–23 = PTP 53.
127 Cf. IM 1959 Student Notes 52–63, but esp. 61–62: 'Circa hunc transitum historicus theologiae duo praesertim debet facere: intelligibilitatem diversarum positionum et transitus ab una ad aliam obtinere, atque deinde iudicium ferre atque rationem reddere harum diversarum tendentiarum.' The critical principle here is dialectical: cf. ibid. 62. Note also the theological significance assigned in the epilogue of *Insight* to the opposition between positions and counterpositions: the revolt against dogma is rooted in the counterpositions; again, the solution of disputed questions in metaphysics by dialectical technique is an at least indirect contribution to the demise of disputed questions in theology; a grasp of the role of understanding in knowledge is very relevant to the imperfect but fruitful understanding of the mysteries promoted especially by Vatican I (INCW 756).
128 On this point, cf. Charles Hefling, Jr, 'Redemption and Intellectual Conversion: Notes on Lonergan's "Christology Today,"' *Lonergan Workshop*, ed. Fred Lawrence (Chico, CA: Scholars Press, 1985) 5:232.
129 INCW 765.
130 INCW 765–66. Cf. INCW 766: 'So it is that we have endeavored to promote the fruitful interaction of subject and object by inviting subjects to a personal appropriation of their own rational self-consciousness.'
131 UB 97.

Chapter 5

1 In the application here of the metaphor of breakthrough and encirclement, I am following F.E. Crowe, *Lonergan* (Collegeville, MN: Liturgical Press, 1992) 95.
2 INCW 761.
3 1C 128–29.
4 1C 129.
5 Ibid.
6 1C 127.

7 Ibid.
8 Ibid.
9 Lonergan, Review of P. Vanier, SJ, *Théologie trinitaire chez saint Thomas d'Aquin*, in *Gregorianum* 36 (1955) 705.
10 INCW 607–608.
11 INCW 608.
12 DP 19.
13 DP 29.
14 DP 29–30.
15 DP 30–31.
16 DP 31. References are given to the following sections: contrast with relativist analysis (IN 342–47 = INCW 366–71); the problem of internal and external relations (IN 493–95 = INCW 517–19); the truth of interpretation (IN 562–94 = INCW 585–617).
17 UB 217.
18 UB 219.
19 UB 220–21, 222.
20 UB 222–24.
21 1C 127: 'If Aristotelian and scholastic notions of science seem to me to be adequate for a formulation of the nature of speculative theology both in itself and in its relations to revelation, to philosophy, and to the teaching authority of the church, still I should avoid the appearance of making exaggerated claims, and so I should acknowledge the existence of contemporary methodological issues that cannot be dispatched in so expeditious a fashion.'
22 IM 1959 Student Notes 16.
23 Ibid.
24 IM 1959 Student Notes 13 (Shields translation). Cf. also ibid.: 'The problem of historicity seems to knock the foundation out from under speculative theology, leaving it without direction, form, purpose, or solidity.'
25 IM 1959 Student Notes 14.
26 Cf. IM 1959 Student Notes 70.
27 On the link between foundations based on wisdom and method, cf. IM 1959 Student Notes 16 (Shields translation): 'In fact, these three problems are but three logically distinct aspects of *one* real problem, that of *method*.' There follows the discussion of foundations based on wisdom, and also a preliminary adumbration of the way in which such foundations can resolve the three problems. The whole discussion is later taken up in the chapter on method, though the connections are not so evident.
28 IM 1959 Student Notes 37.
29 Ibid.: Reasons belong properly in a theory of knowledge. IM 1959 Student Notes 1 (Shields translation): 'Presupposing what is explained in *Insight: A Study of Human Understanding* ... our next step now is to throw some light on

the problem of *method*.' The point becomes especially clear in the course of the explanation of the second precept, Understand systematically: understanding must aim at the ideal goal of complete explanation (IM 1959 Student Notes 40); this ideal goal 'is not just a standard by which we know how far we have to go,' but also 'an operative component in our progress' (PTP 35 = The Nottingham lecture 8); and while this goal is spontaneously employed as an implicit premise in our efforts to understand, method is a question of making it 'an explicit and consciously exploited premise' (PTP 35 = The Nottingham lecture 8; cf. IM 1959 Student Notes 40).

30 IM 1959 Student Notes 41–43.
31 PTP 39 = The Nottingham lecture 11.
32 PTP 41 = The Nottingham lecture 13.
33 Ibid.
34 INCW 610.
35 PTP 47 = The Nottingham lecture 17: 'The rules seem immanent in history. I have illustrated the first rule from the twelfth century, the second from the thirteenth, the third from the fourteenth, the fourth from a subsequent and still expanding inquiry.' Cf. also IM 1959 Student Notes 54.
36 PTP 37 = The Nottingham lecture 9.
37 Ibid.
38 IM 1959 Student Notes 65–66.
39 IM 1959 Student Notes 64.
40 IM 1959 Student Notes 65.
41 In 1959, theology is faith seeking *systematic* understanding: IM 1959 Students Notes 55.
42 IM 1959 Student Notes 55–56.
43 IM 1959 Student Notes 56.
44 IM 1959 Student Notes 59.
45 IM 1959 Student Notes 56.
46 IM 1959 Student Notes 58–59. Cf. chapter 2, 'The Two Modes of Human Thought,' which calls for a shift from merely descriptive to explanatory categories. These result from an examination of the two modes of human thought, the symbolic and the theoretic. Dialectical interaction between these yields three 'steps' or stages: symbolism, the use of language (realization of the opposition between *mythos* and *logos*), and methodical scientific intelligence. IM 1959 Student Notes 31ff.
47 IM 1959 Student Notes 65.
48 PTP 47 = The Nottingham lecture 17.
49 PTP 47–49 = The Nottingham lecture 18–19.
50 IM 1959 Student Notes 65.
51 TE 255.
52 PTP 109.

53 Cf. TE chapters 2–4.
54 Cf. INCW 618, 628–30. Note, however, that chapter 18 had itself formulated the ontological account by extrapolating from the human account of the good: cf. INCW 628.
55 TE 73–78.
56 Cf. TE chapter 2.3, 'The Invariant Structure of the Human Good,' and chapter 3.1, 'The Differentials of the Human Good.' Note that chapters 2–4 of TE bring together in a synthetic way what had been discussed in *Insight* under different headings: cf. chapters 6 and 7 on common sense, chapter 18 on ethics, and chapter 20 on the divine solution to the problem of evil.
57 TE 82–85: 'There is nothing wrong with faculty psychology, but it is not enough for our present purposes, because it does not take us near enough to the concrete. You have to be in the concrete if you wish to study development.'
58 DSH 16. PTP 62.
59 '[T]he introduction of an upper blade does not escape relativism in other fields/history of philosophy: there is one mathematics but there are many philosophies; hence many upper blades/Cassirer, Erkenntnisproblem [*sic*]/Gilson, Spirit of Middle Ages, Being and Some Philosophers [*sic*]/question, universal viewpoint, Insight 17, [*sic*] philosophy of philosophies/no question that issue seems to be much more philosophic than historical.' Lonergan, Philosophy of History (autograph typescript of notes for the lecture of 23 September 1960) LRI Archives Batch IX.7 item a.2. There exists also a transcript of the lecture (cf. Lonergan, The Philosophy of History, Montreal, 23 September 1960, 5), which does not contain this reference to the universal viewpoint. Unfortunately, for some reason the reference is omitted also from the recently published version in the Collected Works (cf. PTP 62).
60 DSH 16–17.
61 This text probably belongs to the 1959 *De systemate* course itself. Cf. SH item l. The 'circle of operations' mentioned here may possibly be the Latin for the notion of 'group of operations' developed in the 1959 lectures (cf. TE 127–32).
62 SH l.6.
63 Ibid.: '[S]cientia esse potest quae tanta est ut tota in unius hominis mente non contineatur.'
64 Lonergan reports here that Joseph Moreau's book on idealism and realism in Plato (*Réalisme et idéalisme chez Platon* [Paris: Presses Universitaires de France, 1951]) ends with a quote from Blondel's *L'Action* (1893), to the effect that a fully coherent idealism ends by eliminating all the differences that separate it from realism. This, says Lonergan, is what he himself is trying to say by his positions and counterpositions (PTP 74). The fragment 'Radix dialecticae' (LRI Archives Batch IX.7.c, to be dated probably 1960, cf. appendix A) says that positions express the pure desire to know in accord with the norms and

exigences of the pure desire, while counterpositions express the de facto subject. Counterpositions tend to their elimination, because the de facto subject is in conflict with the original norms and exigences. The elimination of counterpositions and expression of positions is not solely a question of logic, but basically is a *transformation of the subject*.

65 *De constitutione Christi* ... mentions the Greek use of conversation or dialogue as one of the indirect natural means towards conversion: cf. DCC 16.

66 PTP 75–76. The fragment 'Radix dialecticae' contrasts Plato with Aristotle. In Plato, dialectic is dialogue: a concrete situation favoring the development of positions. In Aristotle, instead, dialectic is a question of *the purified subject* reflecting on the sequence of opinions. The latter, we might note, would be very much the position of chapter 17 of *Insight*, which calls for interpretation from the universal viewpoint. The former instead seems to have contributed something to the functional specialty dialectic of *Method in Theology*, which not only does not exclude the unconverted, but also is decisively and intrinsically collaborative. Cf. below, chapter 11, section 4.

67 PTP 77. 'A third notion is stages. Most of you are familiar, from the study of the New Testament and the Old Testament, with the difference between the Greek and Hebrew mentality.' Cf. also Lonergan, 'Critical Realism and the Integration of the Sciences,' lectures at University College, Dublin, 23–25 May 1961 (LRI Library File 253) 38: The spontaneous subject and the theoretic subject have different languages. 'The clearest examples of that appear when you compare a pre-theoretic culture with a theoretic culture. Both the HEBREWS and the GREEKS knew they talked and they learned. But the same words have different meaning in Hebrew and Greek.'

68 PTP 77. Note the reference to 'the mythical type of consciousness,' PTP 78. Note also the reference to the human good, which links up to the analysis of the human good in the 1959 lectures.

69 DDTPA 13: 'Antequam ipsas theses dogmaticas aggrederemur, praemittenda esse duximus quae respiciunt tum (1) *symbolicam* SS. Trinitatis repraesentationem, tum (2) haereses paulo accuratius formulatas, tum (3) imperfectionem qui dicitur *concipiendi et loquendi modum* a scriptoribus christianis et antenicaenis adhibitum' (emphases mine).

70 DDTPA 86–87.

71 Cf. e.g. DDTPA 33–34.

72 DDTPA 39.

73 Ibid. (translation from WN 49). Cf. the reference to Moreau on Blondel, note 64 above.

74 Ibid.: 'Eiusdem terminus aut est haeresis aut theologiae profectus: haeresis quidem ubi solo naturali rationis lumine proceditur, theologiae autem profectus ubi naturale lumen per fidem illustratur atque confortatur.'

75 Ibid.

Chapter 6

1 DMT 1962 1 = DMT 1962 Student Notes 1.
2 DMT 1962 9 = DMT 1962 Student Notes 7.
3 A fragment entitled 'Problematik' (LRI Archives file 'Various Papers,' cf. appendix A below) notes that a problematik 'is concerned with locating, ordering, the types of questions to be raised.' IM 1959 spoke of orderings of questions.
4 DMT 1962 1 = DMT 1962 Student Notes 1.
5 Note once again the conception of theology here: theology is theory or speculative systematic theology.
6 DMT 1962 10 = DMT 1962 Student Notes 7–8. The Augustinian-Aristotelian controversy in the Middle Ages was about the necessity of a *Begrifflichkeit*, a coherent set of basic terms, if theology was to be a proper science. Aquinas drew his *Begrifflichkeit* by adopting and adapting Aristotle, but others opposed this vehemently. Historically, the verdict has been in favor of Aquinas, but questions remain about the limitations of the Aristotelian approach (MoT 1962 102–105.)
7 DMT 1962 1 = DMT 1962 Student Notes 1.
8 DMT 1962 10 = DMT 1962 Student Notes 8. This problem is related to the familiar one that has been mentioned since 1954: studies in positive theology have been flourishing; the theologian is overwhelmed by a huge flood of monographs, periodicals, etc.; theology students are submerged in a whole series of new specializations; and new philosophies give rise to doubts about the usefulness of dogmatic theology (DMT 1962 9 = DMT 1962 Student Notes 7; cf. MoT 1962 102–105.)
9 Cf. DMT 1962 Batch v.4, item 6. I am indebted to Robert Doran and Michael Shields for bringing this item to my notice and for suggesting that it pertains to the second problematic of the 1962 course.

For the Regis course of 1962, I will depend largely on the Graham transcript (The Method of Theology, Summer Institute at Regis College, Toronto, 9–20 July 1962, transcribed by N. Graham, unpublished. Abbreviation: MoT 1962). The editor tells us, however, that he has not only 'relied heavily' on existing tape-recordings, transcripts, and notes, but also 'endeavoured to improve' the text 'by deletions and additions of our own,' and further that he has 'added headings and sub-titles and made general improvements with the intention of moving this manuscript closer to the stage of printing' (cf. Editor's Note, MoT 1962 viii). Graham's division of the text between an analytic and a synthetic part does not seem to coincide with the first and second problematic mentioned above. In my reading, the first problematic should end with Graham's 'Chapter VI: From Faith to Theology,' and the second problematic should begin with 'Chapter VII: Meaning,' and go on to include 'Chapter VIII: Hermeneutics' and 'Chapter IX: History.'

10 Cf. above, chapter 5, section 3.
11 DMT 1962 Student Notes 2. MoT 1962 9.
12 MoT 1962 10.
13 DMT Student Notes 6.
14 DMT Student Notes 45.
15 Cf. the Index of *Insight*, s.v. 'subject' and 'genuineness.'
16 Cf. esp. TE chapter 8.
17 DMT 1962 Student Notes 2.
18 Ibid.; cf. MoT 1962 7–8.
19 Cf. above, chapter 5, section 5.
20 MoT 1962 27–28.
21 MoT 1962 28. Cf. also MoT 1962 31: 'From a methodological viewpoint, one can define the formal object of a science by defining the group of operations through which it is reached' (spelling corrected). Again, DMT 1962 Student Notes 25: 'Quae tamen inter se differunt, quatenus logica de cognitione in facto esse tractat, methodologia autem de cognitione in fieri.'

It may be recalled that a heuristic notion is a question of determining an unknown object by anticipating the operations through which it becomes known. It is this idea that is now expressed in terms of 'the methodological viewpoint' or of the '*de facto* formal object' defined by some particular group of operations. Subsequently, Lonergan will abandon even the term '*de facto* formal object,' and will speak simply of the shift from logic to method, from objects (formal as well as material) to operations, from the Aristotelian to the modern notion of science.
22 Cf. MoT 1962 1, where Lonergan cites Charles Journet to the effect that the dimension of time had to be added to medieval theology.
23 MoT 1962 28. Cf. also MoT 1962 35: The methodological consideration is necessary insofar as the sciences are developing.
24 DMT 1962 Student Notes 4.
25 MoT 1962 28–30.
26 MoT 1962 28. It might be noted how the methodological viewpoint is intrinsically dynamic. Recall that *Insight* had not only concentrated on operations, but had also employed the moving viewpoint.
27 DMT 1962 Student Notes 5.
28 MoT 1962 35–39.
29 MoT 1962 228–29.
30 DMT 1962 Student Notes 5. MoT 1962 39.
31 Cf. here the theological problematic arising from the existence of antithetical worlds, which is a problem of the relation between objective theory, the interior subject, and the visible world (DMT 1962 Student Notes 19).
32 DMT 1962 Student Notes 14: 'Ulterius, non tam ipsi mundi quam complexiones operationum subiecti sunt integrandae.'

33 MoT 1962 10.
34 Cf. above, chapter 5, section 3.
35 DMT 1962 Student Notes 19.
36 DMT 1962 Student Notes 15.
37 DMT 1962 Student Notes 21. MoT 1962 138, 139–40.
38 DMT 1962 Student Notes 21–22. MoT 1962 141.
39 DMT 1962 Student Notes 22–38, but esp. 22 and 36.
40 DMT 1962 Student Notes 27–28.
41 The decision to use this name seems to have been influenced by Lonergan's reading of Coreth (cf. Crowe, ed. note d, 1C 297). Note the reference to Coreth in DMT 1962 Student Notes 6.
42 The term 'transcendental method' seems to occur only once: in the course of the discussion whether method is transcendental (cf. DMT 1962 Student Notes 6). Elsewhere, Lonergan continues to speak of 'method in general' (ibid. 1), or about general method in contrast to special methods (ibid. 25), or simply of method.
43 MoT 1962 40.
44 Cf. F.E. Crowe, 'Transcendental Deduction: A Lonerganian Meaning and Use,' *Method: Journal of Lonergan Studies* 2:1 (1984) 21–40.
45 DMT 1962 8 (Shields translation) = DMT 1962 Student Notes 6. MoT 1962 40–41 points out that the correspondence may be between subject and object, or else between subject and thinking of another subject.
46 On the a priori, cf. above, chapter 2, section 1.1.
47 DMT 1962 8 (Shields translation) = DMT 1962 Student Notes 6.
48 These points are: (1) that immediate objectivity is only through *Anschauung*, (2) that human intuition is knowledge of appearances only, (3) that hence every valid human judgment is a judgment about appearances only, and (4) that the obvious openness of the mind is only a transcendental illusion (DMT 1962 Student Notes 6).

On the relationship between Kant and Lonergan, cf. G. Sala, *Lonergan and Kant: Five Essays on Human Knowledge* (Toronto: University of Toronto Press, 1994).
49 DMT 1962 Batch v.5 (folder containing mostly handwritten material related to DMT 1962), h.1: '[O]biectum scientiae naturalis non constituitur per actus humanos intentionales (intelligendi, concipiendi, significandi)/obiectum scientiae humanae (Geisteswissenschaften) vel partim vel totaliter constitutiur [*sic*] per actus humanos intentionales.' Also PTP 203–205.
50 MoT 1962 257–58.
51 DMT 1962 Batch v.5, h.1: '[A]ctus humani intentionales et obiectorum constitutivi sunt actus intelligentiae non scientificae sed vulgaris (sensus communis).' Scientific and commonsense understanding differ on the side of the object as well as on the side of the subject. They differ on the side of the

object, for scientific understanding aims at system, at universal definitions, divides terms and principles into primitive and derived, and accepts all that the system presupposes or implies; commonsense understanding instead does not aim at system; it tries to understand what is to be done and said in any of a range of particular situations; it regards anything else as superfluous, useless, dangerous. They differ on the side of the subject: in scientific understanding, the intellectual pattern dominates totally; in the dramatico-practical pattern instead, intellect is only a part of a whole, and is subordinated to the task of living (ibid.).

52 DMT 1962 Batch v.5, d.2, cf. e.3.
53 DMT 1962 Batch v.5, b.6.
54 DMT 1962 Batch v.5, h.1 (typed page). An example of such a shift is the theory of war: 'Notate theoriam puram bellicam esse ortam non ante omnia proelia sed post permulta, eamque etiam ex subsequentibus perfici' (ibid.).
55 The 'genetic and dialectical statement of explanation of differences revealed by comparative method/is an explanatory account of the history of doctrine.' Lonergan, 'Problematik' (typescript pertaining with all probability to MoT 1962; cf. appendix A below), LRI Archives, folder entitled 'Various Papers' 7.
56 As far as hermeneutics is concerned, we are fortunate to have the autograph of the lecture (Hermeneutics 1962 MS), the transcript of the lecture (MoT 1962 369–422), as well as a copy of the autograph made at the Thomas More Institute, Montreal, in 1963 (Hermeneutics 1962).
57 MoT 1962 376; cf. Hermeneutics 1962 MS 2 = Hermeneutics 1962 2.
58 MoT 1962 377 = Hermeneutics 1962 MS 3 = Hermeneutics 1962 3.
59 MoT 1962 378 = Hermeneutics 1962 MS 3 = Hermeneutics 1962 3.
60 MoT 1962 379 = Hermeneutics 1962 MS 3 = Hermeneutics 1962 3.
61 MoT 1962 379; cf. Hermeneutics 1962 MS 3 = Hermeneutics 1962 3–4.
62 MoT 1962 380; cf. Hermeneutics 1962 MS 4 = Hermeneutics 1962 4.
63 INCW 609–10.
64 INCW 609.
65 Hermeneutics 1962 MS 7 = Hermeneutics 1962 7.
66 MoT 1962 394 = Hermeneutics 1962 MS 7 = Hermeneutics 1962 7.
67 MoT 1962 395–96 = Hermeneutics 1962 MS 7–8 = Hermeneutics 1962 7–8. Cf. the repeated references to *Wirkungsgeschichte* in the archival texts: DMT 1962 Batch v.5, c.3, d.3, g.1–2.
68 MoT 1962 410; cf. Hermeneutics 1962 MS 11 = Hermeneutics 1962 10.
69 Hermeneutics 1962 MS 12–13 = Hermeneutics 1962 11–13. Since basic orientations are expressed in original texts, in interpretations, as well as in the way the human sciences are conceived, they are the basic meanings of all texts.
70 Cf. Hermeneutics 1962 MS 12 = Hermeneutics 1962 11.
71 INCW 602–603.
72 Hermeneutics 1962 MS 14 = Hermeneutics 1962 13.

73 Ibid.
74 Hermeneutics 1962 MS 15 = Hermeneutics 1962 14.
75 Hermeneutics 1962 MS 14 = Hermeneutics 1962 13.
76 Hermeneutics 1962 MS 14 = Hermeneutics 1962 13.
77 Hermeneutics 1962 MS 14 = Hermeneutics 1962 14.
78 Hermeneutics 1962 MS 14 = Hermeneutics 1962 14.
79 Hermeneutics 1962 MS 14 = Hermeneutics 1962 13.
80 Cf. Hermeneutics 1962 MS 15 = Hermeneutics 1962 14. Cf. also Hermeneutics 1962 MS 15 = Hermeneutics 1962 15: '[I]t is content to select in the light of its own principles (usually unknown to the author) significant if very brief points; e.g., prove Tertullian had two distinct modes of thinking about the divinity of the Son.'
81 Hermeneutics 1962 MS 15 = Hermeneutics 1962 14.
82 Hermeneutics 1962 MS 6 = Hermeneutics 1962 6. Cf. also DMT 1962 Batch v.5, b.3: Romanticism asserts that there is a series, a spectrum, of modes of thinking and of speaking, or *Denkformen*: '[D]atur series, spectrum, modorum cogitandi loquendi a ... mythis, per poemata, orationes, ... ad tract. scientificum.' Again, ibid. b.6: Romanticism is correct regarding the existence of *Denkformen*, but there is in addition *die Wendung zur Idee*, which is to be studied by comparative, genetic, and dialectical methods.
83 Hermeneutics 1962 MS 14 = Hermeneutics 1962 14.
84 INCW 754. Cf. above, chapter 4, section 1.3.
85 Hermeneutics 1962 MS 15 = Hermeneutics 1962 14.
86 Here we draw not only on the Graham transcript of the Regis course of 1962 (= MoT 1962), but also on two items from the LRI Archives. The first is a single typed page entitled 'History' (Batch IX.7, e = 'fair copy' of Batch VIII.17, a, first unnumbered page), the contents of which correspond to 450–51 of MoT 1962. The second consists of 19 numbered typed pages, again entitled 'History' (Batch IX.7, f = 'fair copy' of Batch VIII.17, a.1–20), the contents of which correspond to the chapter on History in MoT 1962. The abbreviation 'History 1962' refers to the latter (i.e., to Batch IX.7, f).
87 History 1962 19.
88 Ibid.
89 History 1962 9–10. Common historical research operates on the basis of contemporary common sense and of generally accepted methods to develop a participation in the common sense of other times and places in order to determine elementary matters of fact (Did Brutus kill Caesar?), elementary interdependences, and elementary developments of interdependences (History 1962 6). 'The field of common historical research is the field in which universal agreement is easily reached and doubt about that agreement is extremely difficult' (History 1962 6). Uncommon historical research instead would seem to include (1) historical essays that operate on the basis of a spe-

cially qualified common sense, and (2) specialized histories (history of particular sciences, of scientific method, of philosophy, of theology) that proceed not from ordinary or exceptional developments of common sense but from scientific knowledge in its current state (History 1962 6–7).

90 MoT 1962 461–65.
91 History 1962 8.
92 Ibid.
93 Hermeneutics 1962 14.
94 MoT 1962 347–48.
95 MoT 1962 348; cf. 348–68.
96 MoT 1962 368.
97 Hermeneutics 1962 13.
98 Hermeneutics 1962 14.
99 PTP 94.
100 PTP 94–95.
101 PTP 95.
102 PTP 108.
103 PTP 108–109.
104 PTP 117.

Chapter 7

1 Lonergan, Existentialism, notes for lectures at Boston College, 15–19 July 1957, mimeographed edition (Thomas More Institute, Montreal, 1957) 19–28.
2 MoT 1962 18. Note that the habits in question are groups of operations.
3 1C 198.
4 Horizon is concrete because in place of the potency and the *ratio sub qua obiectum attingitur*, there is the concrete subject and the concrete totality of objects (KL 1). Cf. ibid.: Formal object is the object under the aspect under which it is attained, but field is a concrete totality of objects. Again, habit is first act, from which second act springs easily and promptly, but pole is the concrete subject that operates in this way. Cf. also DMT Spring 1963 item l.
5 Cf. above, chapter 5, section 5, and chapter 6, section 1.
6 Cf. above, chapter 6, section 1.
7 1C 198.
8 1C 198–99.
9 1C 204.
10 Ibid.
11 Ibid.
12 Ibid.

13 Recall the ease with which dialectical method is extended into the realm of ethics: cf. INCW 626–28.
14 1C 204.
15 Cf. 2C 228: The good is beyond the intelligible, the true, the real, but it is not beyond being.
16 1C 204.
17 MiT 1971 481–82.
18 2C 276–77.
19 2C 276–77. Cf. 2C 222–23.
20 1C 299, ed. note l.
21 'Questionnaire' 5.
22 DMT Spring 1963 items p, r. Cf. also KL 2.
23 DMT Spring 1963 item r. Cf. KL 2: 'Development, on the other hand, is psychological, social, and historical. It occurs in the way we operate (psychological) with others (social) within a tradition (historical).'
24 DMT Spring 1963 item r. Cf. also the undated text 'History' (LRI Archives, file entitled 'Various Papers'), which speaks of relative and absolute horizons (a.2), and a little later of relative and transcendental horizons (b.3).
25 Ibid. Cf. also KL 8: 'To consider conversion is to move beyond relative to absolute horizon; it introduces absolute oppositions.'
26 Lonergan's Latin term here is *polus originarius*.
27 DMT Spring 1963 item r.
28 Ibid.
29 Ibid.
30 DMT Spring 1963 item p.
31 Ibid.
32 Clearly it is methodical horizon, and not transcendental horizon, that is related to the notion of the universal viewpoint. All comprehensive philosophies and theologies are instances of transcendental horizon, for any of them would have an originary pole and an existential pole, and an implicit as well as an explicit field; but obviously not all philosophies and theologies coincide with methodical horizon.
33 Cf. e.g. DMT Spring 1963 item t. The summer course of 1963, Knowledge and Learning, clearly states that since conversion is triple, operations and habits may pertain not merely to the cognitional but also to the moral and religious dimensions (KL 8).
34 DMT Spring 1963 item z.
35 Ibid.
36 DMT Spring 1963 item z+1.
37 The term is used only once; cf. DMT Spring 1963 item h.3.
38 DMT Spring 1963 n.1, z.2, z+1.1–6.
39 DMT Spring 1963 z+1.5–6; also n.1.

40 DMT Fall 1963 m.1. Cf. DMT Fall 1963 Daly 27.
41 DMT Fall 1963 l.3.
42 DMT Fall 1963 Daly 22. Cf. ibid. 24, and also DMT Fall 1963 l.7 bis: The heuristic structure develops with time, according to fuller reflection on the mind and on its operations, according to fuller understanding of things, and according as fuller reflection and understanding either lead to conversion or else hide more skillfully the lack of conversion.
43 Note that it is the process of objectification that is dialectical; this is another way of saying that counterpositions are not plain mistakes or errors, but rather mistaken formulations of genuine discoveries.
44 DMT Fall 1963 l.6–7.
45 DMT Fall 1963 l.3. Such a distinction between common and proper principles is of course another way of stating the distinction between transcendental and particular methods.
46 DMT Fall 1963 Daly 27, 33, 38; DMT Fall 1963 m.1, p, s.2.
47 DMT Fall 1963 Daly 38.
48 DMT Fall 1963 Daly 41.
49 DMT Fall 1963 Daly 45.
50 DMT Fall 1963 Daly 45–46.
51 Cf. above, section 1.

Chapter 8

1 F.E. Crowe, 'Lonergan's Search for Foundations: The Early Years, 1940–1959,' in Philip McShane, ed., *Searching for Cultural Foundations* (Lanham, MD: University Press of America, 1984) 130.
2 Ibid. 131. The 'orderings' of doctrines here are, for example, the analytic and the synthetic orderings. The former is an ordering that proceeds from what is first for us to what is first in itself. The latter begins from the first in itself and comes back to what is first for us.
3 Ibid.
4 PTP 51 = The Nottingham lecture 21.
5 PTP 52 = The Nottingham lecture 22.
6 DMT Student Notes 3; Hermeneutics 1962 MS 14 = Hermeneutics 1962 14.
7 Cf. DDT-II 20; MoT 1964 Wilker 6; MiT 1965 Batch v, c.11.
8 We have seen (cf. above, chapter 7, section 1) that 'Metaphysics as Horizon' (1963) speaks of the incarnate subject as being 'open to a theology that Karl Rahner has described as an *Aufhebung* of philosophy' (1C 204). *Aufhebung* later becomes Lonergan's notion of sublation. Thus, the relationships between levels of consciousness 'are best expressed as instances of what Hegel named sublation, of a lower being retained, preserved, yet transcended and completed by a higher,' though Hegel's view that the higher

reconciles a contradiction in the lower is to be omitted (cf. 2C 80). The transition to faith is thus parallel (though not identical) to other transitions such as that from experience to understanding, or from understanding to reflection: cf. below, section 3.4.

9 DMT 1962 Student Notes 29.
10 DMT Spring 1963 z+1. On transcendental horizon, cf. above, chapter 7, section 2.
11 MoT 1964, Method in Theology. The Problem. External Factors, 14.
12 Cf. 2C 277. F.E. Crowe, '"All my work has been introducing history into Catholic theology" (Lonergan, March 28, 1980),' *Lonergan Workshop* 10:60 lists also the following references: Lonergan, 'Time and Meaning,' in R. Eric O'Connor, ed., *Bernard Lonergan: 3 lectures* (Montreal: Thomas More Institute for Adult Education, 1975) 30 [= PTP 95]; 2C 220; *Caring about Meaning: Patterns in the Life of Bernard Lonergan*, ed. P. Lambert, C. Tansey, and C. Going (Montreal: Thomas More Institute, 1982) 105.
13 Cf. above, chapter 6, section 2.
14 *De methodo theologiae* (1962) explicitly remarks on the differentiation of tasks: 'Quo magis contextus biblicus et contextus theologicus distinguuntur atque separantur, eo magis distinguuntur et separantur scientia biblica et theologia dogmatica. Qua distinctione et separatione peracta, interpretatio scripturae ad exegetam pertinet, neque plus facit dogmaticus quam *usum* scripturae interpretatae' (DMT 1962 Student Notes 56; emphasis in text). Cf. also DMT 1962 Batch v.5 b.1, which speaks explicitly of hermeneutics: '*Hermeneutics* is concerned to clarify, understand, the original question and its context / Systematic *Theology* employs original answers to meet later questions that arise in later contexts' (emphases in text).
15 DMT 1962 81: 'Theologia positiva dogmatica praecipue occupatur circa ipsas transformationes ex alio in alium contextum; theologiae positivae et specializatae praecipue occupantur circa ipsos contextus particulares.' There follows a reference to the discussion of the truth of interpretation in chapter 17 of *Insight*. Further, a marginal note reads: 'axes, groups of transformation, series of geometric transformations' (DMT 1962 81).

It may be noted that Lonergan's terminology is in flux. In my judgment, 'specialized positive theologies' is equivalent to 'exegesis.'
16 DMT 1962 Student Notes 54–56, 58–59.
17 This may be gathered from the preface and introduction of *De Deo trino: I* (DDT-1 3–14). Lonergan does not himself draw attention to a shift in terminology in his own work, but cf. DDT-1 7, n. 4, which speaks of a historical shift in terminology. At the end of the sixteenth century, theology was called dogmatic insofar as it was distinct from moral theology, whereas it was called positive insofar as it was distinct from scholastic, speculative, or systematic theology. This positive theology was not adequately distinguished from dog-

matic theology, and it pursued a dogmatic or else an apologetic end. The twentieth century instead saw a flourishing of theological investigations that were neither dogmatic nor systematic but rather positive in the strict sense. Because, however, things change faster than their names, there is often confusion regarding things or about their names. Thus, some want to reject all positive studies on the grounds that they are not dogmatic, whereas others would like dogmatic study to follow a positive method. But all these fail to grasp that development consists of differentiation and integration; that from a common dogmatic-positive root there could have arisen two distinct types of discipline, one strictly dogmatic and the other strictly positive; that development precedes exact distinction, and that differentiation precedes integration.

18 DDT-I 5, n. 1.
19 DDT-I 5.
20 DDT-I 7–8, 12.
21 DDT-I 7–8, 10.
22 DDT-I 8.
23 DDT-I 10. For the expressions '*in oratione obliqua, in oratione recta,*' cf. DMT Spring 1963 item z+7, and PTP 207. Cf. also DMT Fall 1963 Daly 10.
24 DDT-I 11–12.
25 DDT-I 12. Such a systematic distinction between dogmatic and positive theology results in the fact that *De Deo Trino: I*, which is a reworking of *De Deo Trino: Pars analytica*, bears the subtitle '*Pars dogmatica.*' Again, *Divinarum personarum* ... had spoken of theology as moving towards its end through the *via analytica*, the *via synthetica*, and a third, superadded historical process (DP 28). *De Deo trino: Pars analytica* had identified the *via analytica* with the historical process, indicating that it could therefore be referred to also as the *via historica* (DDTPA 5–6). *De Deo Trino: II* (which is a reworking of *Divinarum personarum* ...) accordingly speaks of a twofold process by which theology moves towards its end, but now the *via historica* is also referred to as the *via dogmatica* (DDT-II 36).
26 DDT-I 5, n. 1.
27 Ibid.: 'Quibus multis praeesse oportet sapientialem seu methodicam quae partes distinguat, munera et officia singulis attribuat, mutuam omnium opitulationem dirigat.' The foundational part is named already in a discussion of 1961: 'I would like to suggest that there is a sense in which a fundamental theology is needed, namely, in the same sense as physicists speak of the foundations of physics, and as mathematicians speak of the foundations of mathematics; it is implicit in the nature of theology as grounding the method of theology' (intervention in a discussion, reported in John V. Wildeman and Charles M. Murphy, 'Some Directions for Theology,' *Roman Echoes* [1961] 39). Again, it is mentioned in discussion following the 1963 lecture 'The

Analogy of Meaning': 'You can have a fundamental basis of method, the grounds of method – fundamental in that sense – in which one moves from the objects of theology to the theologian ... The study of the theologian as a subject in his operations gives you a fundamental theology' (PTP 208–209).
28 DMT Fall 1963 Daly 9.
29 Ibid.
30 Crowe, 'Lonergan's Search for Foundations,' in McShane, ed., *Searching for Cultural Foundations* 130.
31 Institute on The Method in Theology, Georgetown 1964. For our account we will draw upon three sources: (1) the notes taken by Sr Rose Wilker, (2) four pages of jottings by F.E. Crowe, made (we are told by Crowe) probably from Lonergan's own lecture notes, and (3) various items that are part of Lonergan's own notes for the Institute, found in the LRI Archives in the file entitled 'Various Papers.' These items are entitled 'Method in theology. The Problem. External Factors' (14 pp.), 'Method in theology – internal problem' (5 pp.), 'Positive theology' (1 p.), 'Dogmatic theology' (2 pp.), and 'Development of Dogma' (1 p.).
32 MoT 1964, Method in theology – internal problem, 1.
33 MoT 1964 Wilker 1.
34 MoT 1964 Wilker 4. MoT 1964, Method in theology – internal problem, 1.
35 MoT 1964, Method in theology – internal problem, 3.
36 Ibid. 4–5.
37 Cf. MoT 1964, Method in Theology. The Problem. External Factors, esp. 1–3.
38 Ibid. 12.
39 Ibid. Such foundations go against the extrinsicist demand for foundations 'out there.' 'The ultimate criterion lies in the "for intérieur", in the immediacy and ultimacy of das Sein in seiner Gelichtetheit, in the utterly private realm in which man saves his soul or loses it' (ibid. 13).
40 Ibid. 12.
41 Other occurrences: MoT 1964, Method in Theology. The Problem. External Factors, 9: '[T]o confront the problem of historicity is (1) to know the fact of that freedom and (2) to exercise it responsibly'; ibid. 11: 'The proper subject in a world constituted by meaning is a self-orientating, self-constituting subject: ... individually we are responsible for the lives we lead, and collectively we are responsible for the world in which we live them.' Again, ibid. 12 speaks of the normative reality of one's own being 'in its intellectual, rational, moral luminousness.' Cf. also ibid. 13, which deals with objections against critical foundations placed 'in the subject's empirical, intelligent, rational, responsible consciousness.' Cf. also the 1964 article '*Existenz* and *Aggiornamento*,' where the theme of the self-constituting subject responsible for his own life and for that of his world is dominant (1C 222–31).
42 MoT 1964, Method in Theology. The Problem. External Factors, 12.

43 Ibid.
44 MoT 1964, Method in theology – internal problems, 1.
45 MoT 1964, Method in Theology. The Problem. External Factors, 14.
46 Cf. MoT 1964 Wilker 10.
47 Cf. F.E. Crowe's report of a conversation with Lonergan in 'BL's Georgetown U. Lectures: 1964,' notes (4 handwritten pp.) taken by Crowe. Cf. also MoT 1964 Wilker 7: 'Foundations: *not* Fundamental Theology.'
48 MoT 1964, Method in theology – internal problem, 1; emphasis mine.
49 MoT 1964 Wilker 4.
50 Recall 'Theology and Understanding,' 1954 (1C 129): '[S]ince method is simply reason's explicit consciousness of the norms of its own procedures, the illumination of reason by faith implies an illumination of method by faith.'
51 MoT 1964 Wilker 7. Though the diagram mentions just 'being,' Lonergan's notes for the Fall 1963 course indicate that transcendental method is related to the *intention* of being: cf. DMT Fall 1963 m.1.
52 MoT 1964, Method in theology – internal problem, 1. Also ibid.: The foundational part of theology is concerned with 'the divisions of theology, their respective methods, the integration of the separate parts.'
53 MoT 1964 Wilker 6–7.
54 MoT 1964 Wilker 6.
55 MoT 1964, Dogmatic Theology, 2.
56 Lonergan did not offer any course on method in 1965. In February 1965 he began what was to be a sabbatical year. In the summer of 1965 he was diagnosed with cancer and had to undergo two major surgical interventions (Crowe, *Lonergan* [Collegeville, MN: The Liturgical Press, 1992] 106–107). 'Dimensions of Meaning' was delivered on 12 May 1965, probably therefore before the diagnosis. The first paper after the surgery seems to have been 'Transition from a Classicist World View to Historical Mindedness,' delivered on 10 September 1966. What we know about 1965 is from notes extant in the Archives, and from Lonergan's own reports – one of the most important being surely that about his 'breakthrough' to eight functional specialties in February 1965 (cf. *Caring about Meaning: Patterns in the Life of Bernard Lonergan*, ed. P. Lambert, C. Tansey, and C. Going [Montreal: Thomas More Institute, 1982] 59). The archival notes contain several sketches of the 'breakthrough,' as well as typewritten attempts revealing that work on the book on theological method had begun in earnest.
57 Cf. above, section 1.2.
58 MoT 1964 Wilker 4; cf. also 5.
59 Cf. ibid. 7.
60 Cf. MiT 1965 Batch v.7, item b: 'Be attentive, intelligent, reasonable, responsible.' Item c.11 (ibid.) speaks of experience, understanding, judgment, and decision as four levels.

61 MiT 1965 Batch v.7 item a.
62 Handwritten notes pertaining to the *De methodo* course of spring 1963 reveal that Lonergan had toyed already then with the idea of distinguishing dialectic from history. The notes speak of an explanatory history that includes comparative, organic, and genetic methods, but not dialectical method (DMT Spring 1963 item i). Dialectical method is the task of what is named *critica major*, which examines not only the historical process, texts, interpretations and histories, exegetes and historians (ibid. item j), but also *critica major* as practiced by other investigators (ibid. item k). In *De Deo trino: I*, however, composed probably during the same spring semester, dialectic remains clearly part of the *via historica* (cf. e.g. DDT-1 49). This suggests that proper differentiation of tasks is achieved only on the basis of the notion of operational or functional specialization.
63 MiT 1965 Batch v.7, c.12. Compare this with the Nottingham lecture 13 = PTP 41: method does not give a watertight solution. Rather, it aids the personal task of judging by illuminating the alternatives and thus heightening the responsibility involved.
64 Cf. MiT 1965 Batch v.7 item c.12–14.
65 MiT 1965 Batch v.7, c.13. Cf. ibid. c.14: 'positions and counterpositions regarding rel[igious], mor[al], int[ellectual] conversion = foundations.'
66 One listing of the operational specializations speaks of 'Categories – recurrent qq [= questions] in their roots' instead of Foundations (MiT 1965 Batch v.7, c.1). The next page speaks once again of Foundations, but describes it as dealing with 'categories, roots of recurrent questions' (ibid. c.2).
67 MiT 1965 Batch v.7, c.11: 'Data: as given (natural science), as possessing meaning (human science), as conveying truth and inviting to personal decision and commitment (theology).'
68 Cf. Crowe, *Lonergan* 95: In February 1965 there was the breakthrough, 'but there was not yet the encirclement that only a whole new set of categories would make possible.'
69 Lonergan, 'Theology in Its New Context,' 2C 55–67.
70 2C 58.
71 2C 58–60.
72 2C 63–64. Cf. 2C 161: '[T]he *deductivist approach* of the past was possible only as long as accurate and detailed knowledge was lacking' (emphasis mine).
73 2C 67. Cf. Lonergan, Dialogue at the Lonergan Workshop, Boston College, 1976, transcript 6–7: '[I]n so far as by fundamental theology you mean the old treatises on the true religion, on the divine [legate], on the church, on the inspiration of Scripture, you're talking about doctrines and they are determined in the same way as any other doctrine. They have no logical precedence because your theology is no longer deductivist, you have moved out

of the Aristotelian deductivism, it has become a quasi empirical science vis. a human science working with past history into the present to the illumination of the future.'

74 2C 197.

75 Jan Walgrave, *Concilium* 46 (1969) 82, cited by Lonergan in 'Variations in Fundamental Theology,' *Method: Journal of Lonergan Studies* 16 (1998) 9. Cf. p. 10 of the same text by Lonergan: Even if fundamental theology were scientific, it would not reach its goal, for at most it can set forth prolegomena; and these 'are only *remotely relevant* to an encounter, an act of adoration, and in the adoration an act of faith' (emphasis mine). It is likely that 'remotely relevant' here echoes the fact that fundamental theology used to be part of the remote process leading to the faith: cf. AF 14, and above, chapter 4, section 2.1.

76 Cf. above, chapter 4, section 2.1.

77 Lonergan, 'Variations in Fundamental Theology' 8–9; cf. 12.

78 2C 64–65.

79 2C 67.

80 Cf. above, chapter 4, section 2.1. Also PGT 11–12.

81 Lonergan, Dialogue at the Lonergan Workshop, Boston College, 1976, transcript 96.

82 We must note that *Insight* had first outlined the proportionate good (INCW 626) or the good in a human sense (INCW 628) and had then gone on to extrapolate it to the cosmic or ontological account of the good (INCW 618). However, it still remains that *Insight* did not distinguish the notion of value from the notion of being.

83 2C 81–84. The LRI Archives contain a 'Ch.III Horizons' (Batch x.6; probable date 1967), which contains a section on values, in which a discussion of the transcendental notion and the definition of value (pp. 2–27) is followed by a discussion of religion (28–35).

For further details on the notion of value, cf. the article 'An Exploration of Lonergan's New Notion of Value,' in F.E. Crowe, *Appropriating the Lonergan Idea*, ed. M. Vertin (Washington: Catholic University of America Press, 1989) 51–70.

84 2C 84.

85 2C 80, 84.

86 Lonergan, 'Since Writing *Insight*. Extract from a Lecture by Bernard Lonergan Followed by an Interview. In the Course, *The Alerted Mind*, TMI, February 25, 1969,' in Eric O'Connor, *Curiosity at the Center of One's Life* (Montreal: Thomas More Institute, 1987) 371.

87 Lonergan, *Doctrinal Pluralism* (Milwaukee: Marquette University Press, 1971) 31–32. Cf. also 2C 223, 236–37, 242; 3C 160, 246.

88 Lonergan, 'Since Writing *Insight*' 371. In this connection we must perhaps

recall that *Insight* itself had promised a 'far larger' work set in a 'larger and more concrete context,' which would include, for example, personal relations (INCW 754).
89 2C 129. A lecture of 1970 notes that ordinary human beings seriously and perseveringly transcend themselves when they fall in love (2C 170). An article of 1968 had observed that being-in-love is of three kinds: being-in-love with the domestic community, with the civil community, with God (2C 145). The lecture of 1970 calls these love of intimacy, love of one's fellow men, love of God (2C 171).
90 2C 129. Cf. 2C 145.
91 2C 129. Cf. 2C 145: All authentic being-in-love is total self-surrender, but the love of God is not restricted to particular areas of human living.
92 2C 129. Cf. also 2C 145, 171.
93 The word 'gift' seems to be first used in the article of 1969 entitled 'The Future of Christianity': cf. 2C 162. Cf. also 2C 153, 172.
94 MT 122.
95 2C 161–62.
96 Lonergan, 'Variations in Fundamental Theology' 12. Cf. Lonergan, Dialogue at the Lonergan Workshop, 1976, transcript 98–100: One reaches the functional specialties and praxis only by going beyond the generalized empirical method of *Insight*, sublating the cognitional operations by responsibility and all of these by love.
97 'Being in love with God grounds faith.' In 1968 being-in-love with God 'is the eye of faith that discerns God's hand in nature and his message in revelation.' (Cf. the article 'Natural Knowledge of God,' 2C 129.)
98 The 1969 article 'The Future of Christianity,' 2C 154.
99 MT 118.
100 Ibid.
101 2C 162.
102 Ibid.
103 Cf. above, section 3.1.
104 Lonergan, 'Variations in Fundamental Theology' 12–13.

Chapter 9

1 Cf. above, chapter 8, section 1.2.
2 MoT 1964 Wilker 7–10.
3 Lonergan, Positive Theology (notes [1 p.] pertaining to the summer Institute on The Method in Theology, Georgetown University, Washington, 13–17 July 1964) LRI Archives, folder entitled 'Various Papers.' These notes speak of 'RH' and 'TH,' which I take to be relative and transcendental or absolute horizons.

4 MoT 1964 Wilker 12. Cf. 1C 199 and also Hermeneutics 1962 MS 11, 'Alternative ending.'
5 Cf. esp. 'Dimensions of Meaning,' 1C 235-44.
6 MiT 1965 Batch v.10 c.36-37. Cf. 2C 61.
7 MiT 1965 Batch v.10 a.1.
8 MiT 1965 Batch v.10 g.3-4.
9 MiT 1965 v.10 d. MiT 1965 v.10 l: Transcendental method grounds all methods and also itself.
10 MiT 1965 Batch v.10 j.
11 MiT 1965 Batch v.10 l. Cf. 'Theologian as a Man.'
12 Ibid.
13 Ibid.
14 Ibid.
15 The papers of Batch v.7 contain, among other things, a very early draft of a chapter on method (MiT 1965 v.7 3.1-9), pages indicating the breakthrough to the eight functional specialties, here referred to as operational specializations (MiT 1965 v.7 a, c.1.2.6.8.12-15), and even an outline of the *Method* chapter on functional specialties (MiT 1965 v.7 c.12-13).
16 MiT 1965 Batch v.7 b.
17 Ibid.
18 Cf. above, chapter 7, section 3.
19 Cf. above, note 9.
20 MiT 1965 Batch v.7 c.15.
21 MiT 1965 Batch v.7 c.1.6; cf. also c.2.
22 MiT 1965 Batch v.7 c.14.
23 MiT 1965 Batch v.7 c.13.
24 Ibid.
25 MiT 1965 Batch v.7 c.1-2.
26 2C 2-3.
27 2C 5-6.
28 2C 6.
29 2C 55-67.
30 LRI Archives Batch VI.1 a.1-3.
31 LRI Archives Batch x.6. Also Batch VI.1 b.
32 Batch x.6 contains two items. The contents of the first item are as follows: psychological development; self-transcendence; order and efficiency; mediation of society; faith; conversions and breakdowns. The contents of the second item, entitled 'Values': the transcendental notion; definition of value; question of mind; question of value.
33 We have two transcripts of the lectures, one by Timothy Fallon and the other by N. Graham. There are also fragments of Lonergan's own notes: cf. e.g. Lonergan Papers 307 in the LRI Lonergan Archives, item entitled 'Horizons and Categories.'

34 If the papers of 1965 contain an early draft of a chapter on method, in 1968 the chapter on method is already relatively stable. Structurally, it corresponds to chapter 1 of *Method*. Cf. the Table of Contents in TPSR Graham.
35 TPSR Graham 39, 40.
36 TPSR Graham 31–40.
37 TPSR Graham 41–42.
38 TPSR Graham 43.
39 TPSR Graham 46–47. The critical and foundational functions (especially the mention of proper and common norms) recall elements of DMT Fall 1963.
40 TPSR Graham 47.
41 TPSR Graham 96.
42 TPSR Graham 97–99.
43 TPSR Graham 109–18.
44 TPSR Graham 118–19; cf. LRI Archives Batch VI.6 15.
45 TPSR Graham 120.
46 DMT Fall 1963 l.3–7 = DMT Fall 1963 Daly 22–24; cf. chapter 7, section 2 above.
47 TPSR Graham 46.
48 TPSR Graham 136; cf. LRI Archives Batch VI.6 22–23.
49 TPSR Graham 121 = LRI Archives Batch VI.6 17.
50 TPSR Graham 137–38 = LRI Archives Batch VI.6 23.
51 Cf. TPSR Graham 123, 153; cf. LRI Archives Batch VI.6 17–18.
52 Cf. TPSR Graham 136, 138 = LRI Archives Batch VI.6 22–23.
53 Cf. TPSR Graham 138.
54 TPSR Graham 142.
55 TPSR Graham 145.
56 TPSR Graham 146–49.
57 Cf. chapter 8, section 1.2 above.
58 TPSR Graham 148.
59 INCW 293.
60 Cf. above, chapter 2, section 4 and chapter 5, section 5.
61 2C 206. The article makes it clear that the method in question is transcendental method. Besides, *Method* describes transcendental method in precisely these terms: cf. MT 24–25.
62 Cf. 2C 275.

Chapter 10

1 Cf. LRI Archives Batch VI.2. Abbreviation: 'MiT VII.'
2 'MiT VII' 1 = MiT 1969 256.
3 Cf. Lonergan, 'Functional Specialties in Theology,' *Gregorianum* 50 (1969) 487 = MT 127.
4 Cf. chapter 8, section 3.1 above.

5 'MiT VII' 1–2 = MiT 1969 257.
6 'MiT VII' 2 = MiT 1969 257.
7 Ibid.
8 Lonergan, 'Functional Specialties in Theology' 502–503 = MT 143.
9 Cf. MiT 1969 'Question Periods, Seminar on Method in Theology' 105: 'We want everyone to put in their oar because if you only pay attention to the converted you very easily move into an ivory tower and avoid the more difficult questions and reduce religion to as [*sic*] state that will ultimately be defenseless.'
10 'MiT VII' 2 = MiT 1969 258.
11 'MiT VII' 2–3 = MiT 1969 258.
12 Cf. MiT 1970 231–33.
13 Since the 1971 text is the final draft of *Method in Theology*, my references will be to the text of the latter.
14 MT 151.
15 'MiT VII' 3 = MT 153, n. 1. The footnote is already present in MiT VII. The Graham transcript reveals that only a part of it was read out.
16 'MiT VII' 5 = MiT 1969 262 = MT 154–55.
17 Hermeneutics 1962 MS 2 = Hermeneutics 1962 2.
18 Lonergan, Hermeneutics and the Philosophy of Religion (lecture at the Catholic University of America, 21 November 1969) LRI Archives Lonergan Papers 616, Hermeneutics and The Philosophy of Religion (a C.U.A. Seminar) 1.
19 'MiT VII' 3bis–4 = MiT 1969 259–60.
20 INCW 595–600.
21 'MiT VII' 30 = MiT 1969 295.
22 Lonergan, Merging Horizons: System, Common Sense, Scholarship, lecture given at the University of Toronto in series on Hermeneutics, 3 November 1970. My references will be to the article form published in 1973: Lonergan, 'Merging Horizons: System, Common Sense, Scholarship,' *Cultural Hermeneutics* (Boston College) 1 (1973) 89.
23 MoT 1962 376.
24 'MiT VII' 6–13 = MiT 1969 264–72.
25 Lonergan, 'Merging Horizons' 89.
26 'MiT VII' 13 = MiT 1969 273.
27 'MiT VII' 14 = MiT 1969 274.
28 Ibid. Cf. Lonergan, Hermeneutics and the Philosophy of Religion 8, where the existential aspect of interpretation is discussed under the title *Wirkungsgeschichte*.
29 INCW 200–201: '[I]t would be an error for common sense to attempt a systematic formulation of its completed set of insights in some particular case; for every systematic formulation envisages the universal, and every concrete

situation is particular. It follows that common sense has no use for a technical language and no tendency towards a formal mode of speech ... [I]ts correspondence between saying and meaning is at once subtle and fluid ... [T]he elliptical utterances of common sense have a deeper ground than many logicians and practically all controversialists have managed to reach.'

30 Cf. Lonergan, 'Merging Horizons' 92.
31 Cf. ibid.
32 Ibid. 95.
33 Reconstruction is to be distinguished from the *Reproducieren* of Romantic hermeneutics, which, as the text of 1962 points out, is excessive. 'Finally, the criterion of Reproducieren is excessive. It means that one not only understands the author but also can do what the author himself could not do, namely, explain why he wrote in just the way he did. Common sense understands what is to be said and what is to be done; but common sense does not understand itself and much less does it explain itself' (Hermeneutics 1962 7).
34 'MiT VII' 16 = MiT 1969 277 = MT 163.
35 'MiT VII' 16 = MiT 1969 277 = MT 163.
36 Lonergan, 'Merging Horizons' 97.
37 Ibid. 98–99.
38 Ibid. 98. The solution here is the same as that for the critique of belief: cf. INCW 737–39.
39 Ibid. 98–99.
40 Cf. Hermeneutics 1962 MS 11. (This page bears the header 'Hermeneutics – alternative ending.' It seems to have been used, not in the Regis course of 1962 but in the 1964 Georgetown Institute: cf. MoT 1964 Wilker 12.) The 1954 article 'Theology and Understanding' already hints at such a solution: speaking of the challenge presented to speculative theology by the methods of scholarly research, it says: 'No doubt, the issue admits a *solvitur ambulando*' (1C 129).
41 Hermeneutics 1962 MS 11.
42 MiT 1969 287–89 = 'MiT VII' 24–25 = MT 168–69.
43 Lonergan, Hermeneutics and the Philosophy of Religion 11.
44 MiT 1969 285, 288, 290 = 'MiT VII' 23, 24, 26 = MT 167, 169, 170.
45 Lonergan, notes for the Dublin Institute on Method in Theology, 1971 (LRI Archives Lonergan Papers 122). Cf. also the discussion of Bultmann and of Denzinger theology in MiT 1969 289 = 'MiT VII' 25 = MT 169–70.
46 Cf. 'MiT VII' 3 = MT 153, n. 1.
47 MT 137. Cf. MiT 1969 288 = 'MiT VII' 24 = MT 169.
48 MiT 1969 290 = 'MiT VII' 26 = MT 170.
49 Cf. MiT 1969 290–91 = 'MiT VII' 26–27 = MT 170–71.
50 MiT 1969 294 = 'MiT VII' 29 = MT 172. Note that what has here been called

278   Notes to pages 166–69

'supplementary expression' is sometimes also referred to as 'technical expression': cf. e.g. Lonergan, Hermeneutics and the Philosophy of Religion 10.

51 MiT 1969 295 = 'MiT vii' 30 = MT 172–73.
52 Ibid. Cf. 1970 MiT 1970 274–75: 'I reconstructed the mode of apprehension in primitive language by noting that primitive language rests on insight into sensible presentations, that it doesn't work much from linguistic feedback.' Again, MiT 1971 223–24 alludes to chapter 17 of *Insight* on myth and magic, when it says that the chapter 'Meaning' had carried out reconstruction of the mentalities of myth and magic. Neither of these illustrations is present in the *Method* text.
53 INCW 595.
54 MiT 1969 295 = 'MiT vii' 30 = MT 173. The 1969 lecture Hermeneutics and the Philosophy of Religion (10) points out that technical expression is a question of setting up a system of meanings and showing how one may transpose from the language of the texts to the language of the system, and notes that this is not unrelated to Aquinas's use of Aristotle or to Bultmann's use of Heidegger, but is more empirical and less abstract. The basic idea is to combine scholarly studies of language and of development such as Bruno Snell's *Discovery of Mind* with philosophical work. Thus, Cassirer's *Philosophy of Symbolic Forms* seems to use such scholarly work to reveal the underlying determinants. (Cf. also the Graham transcript of the lecture, LRI Library file 542, 8.)
55 'MiT vii' 29. The 'chapter five' refers to the chapter 'Meaning,' which was chapter 5 in TPSR 1968. Cf. also MiT 1971 224: '[I]f people doing work such as Cassirer and Snell did were to work from the basis of a transcendental method and its extensions, it would be possible to proceed systematically towards the reconstruction of mentalities.'
56 INCW 608, cf. 602.
57 MiT 1969 'Question Periods, Seminar on Method in Theology,' 83–85.
58 2C 205–206.
59 INCW 609–10.
60 MT 172 mentions the need to avoid occult entities such as the Hebrew mind and Hellenism.
61 MT 292.
62 MT 293.
63 Cf. chapter 6, section 2 above.
64 Cf. chapter 8, section 2 above.
65 Ibid.
66 Cf. chapter 11, section 1 below.
67 'MiT vii' 60.
68 'MiT vii' 45–46.

69 The former would be the procedure of precritical history; the latter is the procedure of critical history. 'MiT vii' 51, note.
70 'MiT vii' 47–52.
71 'MiT vii' 55. 'Reflective and judicial' here must be carefully distinguished from 'critical' in the sense explained above, which is a question of shifting data from one field of relevance to another.
72 'MiT vii' 60.
73 'MiT vii' 61.
74 MT 191–92. It must be added that history, unlike interpretation, is complicated by perspectivism: cf. MT 192 and also the discussion below.
75 For more details cf. appendix B.
76 MiT 1969 361–62.
77 MiT 1969 357.
78 MiT 1969 355–58.
79 MiT 1969 352–55. Langlois and Seignobos seem to be representatives of historical positivism.
80 This is the upshot of the section 'Three Historians.' Cf. MiT 1969 358–66.
81 MiT 1969 358–63.
82 MT 214, and MT 220: 'The past is fixed and its intelligible structures are unequivocal.'
83 MT 220.
84 MT 216.
85 MT 218.
86 MT 221.
87 MT 224.
88 MiT 1969 'Question Periods, Seminar on Method in Theology,' 94 = MT 223.
89 MT 224.
90 MT 195.
91 Ibid.
92 MT 227.
93 MiT 1969 408–10.
94 Cf. Hermeneutics 1962 MS 11 = Hermeneutics 1962 10–11.

Chapter 11

1 LRI Archives, Batch x.5, one of several p. 13's. For the dating of the text, cf. appendix A. The chapter speaks of history as comparing and relating interpreted data; such comparison leads to determining organistic, genetic, and dialectical relationships (Batch x.5, one of several p. 6's). This chapter is an early version of the 1969 article on functional specialties and chapter 5 of *Method*.
2 'Contemporary developments seem to require that conversion be considered

both from a confessional and from an oecumenical viewpoint. From a confessional viewpoint [...]. The oecumenist, however, while respecting all instances of such existential commitment, is concerned to go beyond them, to list their similarities and differences, to uncover their roots, and so to place all of them within a single if dialectical view' (Batch x.5 13, first of three attempts). 'But if a given type and measure of conversion is basic to a given type of confession religious confession, [sic] it follows that a comprehensive view of all types and measures would provide oecumenical foundations for theology' (Batch x.5 13, second of three attempts). 'The oecumenist, however, seeks a more basic position that will include, dialectically, all the confessional positions in their similarities and their differences. This position he will relate to the similarities and differences brought to light by the study of history and, further, to the theological foundations that are our next topic' (Batch x.5 13, third of three attempts).

3 TPSR Graham 52–92. As far as the emergence of the functional specialty dialectic is concerned, there is also the archival text 'MiT VII. 4. Dialectic' (cf. note 16 below). This, however, belongs with all probability to 'MiT VII.'
4 2C 67.
5 2C 97.
6 2C 66–67.
7 TPSR Graham 60.
8 INCW 554.
9 MiT 1969 413. We may recall also that the generally accessible basis for the dialectical confrontation of contradictory histories is transcendental method: cf. chapter 10, section 4 above, and MiT 1969 399 = MT 227.
10 TPSR Graham 62.
11 INCW 588.
12 TPSR Graham 58; emphasis mine.
13 Cf. MT 312.
14 TPSR Graham 59.
15 Lonergan, Method in Theology, Institute at Regis College, Toronto, 7–18 July 1969. Abbrev.: MiT 1969.
16 Lonergan, 'MiT VII. 4. Dialectic,' LRI Archives Batch VIII.17, item e. Cf. also appendix B.
17 Ibid. 63.
18 Ibid. Cf. the Nottingham lecture 13 = PTP 41 (cf. also above, chapter 5, section 3).
19 MiT 1969.
20 The two specialties are often mentioned together in *Method*: cf. MT 142, 268–69, 298, 299, 336, 349, 355.
21 MiT 1965 Batch v.10 l; cf. above, chapter 9, section 1.
22 MiT 1969 423–26.

23 MiT 1969 433.
24 MiT 1969 423–26.
25 MiT 1969 431.
26 MiT 1969 413–14.
27 MiT 1969 413.
28 Ibid.: 'The possibility of this procedure is transcendental method.'
29 Hermeneutics 1962 14.
30 MiT 1969 413.
31 Hermeneutics 1962 14.
32 MiT 1969 414.
33 Ibid.
34 MiT 1969 419.
35 Ibid. Note the echo here of INCW 23.
36 MiT 1969 418.
37 'The first condition the dialectic[al] theologian must fulfil is self-appropriation.' MiT 1969 414; cf. Lonergan, 'MiT x. Chapter Ten. Dialectic and Foundations,' LRI Archives Batch VI.5, 2.
38 MiT 1969 415. It might be recalled that UB had spoken of self-appropriation as the upper blade in interpretation (cf. UB 222–24 and also above, chapter 5, section 2).
39 MiT 1969 419ff.
40 MiT 1969 416.
41 MiT 1969 416–17. Cf. also ibid. 436: 'The first phase of theology – the phase of research, interpretation, history, and dialectic – is an encounter with the religious past. The encounter rises from the data, gathered by research, through the meanings revealed by interpretation and through the facts of history, to a meeting with the originating values that are persons and to an appreciation of the values they effected.' It might also be noted that in 1965 the 'object' of the fourth operational specialization was 'encounter' (MiT 1965 Batch V.7 item a). The theme of encounter is an important aspect of the functional specialty dialectic in *Method*, but is perhaps not adequately thematic, and consequently easily missed. In this connection, cf. also section 4 below.
42 Hermeneutics 1962 15; cf. G. Ebeling, 'Die Bedeutung der historisch-kritischen Methode,' *Zeitschrift für Theologie und Kirche* 47 (1950) 33.
43 MiT 1969 433: '[D]ialectic was not philosophically neutral, for it rested on the theologian's self-appropriation, and that implies a determinate gnoseology, epistemology, and metaphysics. Similarly, ... dialectic was not morally neutral: it has to break with bias of every kind.'
44 MiT 1969 433.
45 MiT 1969 434.
46 MiT 1969 434–35.

47 MiT 1969 435.
48 MiT 1969 257.
49 MiT 1969 258.
50 Cf. section 1 above.
51 MiT 1969 437.
52 MiT 1969 437–38.
53 MiT 1969 452.
54 MiT 1969 450.
55 MiT 1969 452.
56 Ibid.
57 MiT 1969 443–44: 'That religious horizon, not as constituted, not as spontaneously objectified, but as reflectively objectified, is the principal element in our fifth functional specialty, foundations.'
58 Cf. TPSR 107.
59 Lonergan, Method in Theology, Institute at Boston College, 15–26 June 1970. Abbrev.: MiT 1970.
60 MiT 1970 399–402.
61 MiT 1970 419–20.
62 MiT 1970, McShane transcript of the discussions following the lecture of 26 June 1970, 20.
63 Cf. 2C 204-205. Appeals to transcendental method are not lacking in the 1970 chapter on dialectic itself: cf. the sections on the dialectic of methods, MiT 1970 424–35.
64 Lonergan, 'Bernard Lonergan Responds,' in P. McShane, ed., *Foundations of Theology: Papers from the International Lonergan Congress, 1970* (Dublin: Gill and Macmillan, 1971) 232–33.
65 MiT 1969 416–17, 436.
66 MiT 1970 419.
67 MiT 1970 419–20.
68 MiT 1970 420.
69 MiT 1970 423–24.
70 MT 253. Compare MiT 1971 298: Dialectic aims at being a methodical equivalent in the realm of value judgments to the crucial experiment in science. It aims at being methodical in a very delicate area – that of value judgments. Lonergan, 'Philosophy and the Religious Phenomenon,' *Method: Journal of Lonergan Studies* 12 (1994) 137–38 refers to this procedure as a 'projective test' in which investigators will reveal their own notions of authenticity and unauthenticity both to others and to themselves. Cf. also Lonergan, 'Method Theology Seminar 1980' (LRI Archives Lonergan Papers 776), 8 of the handwritten notes on chapter 10, Dialectic: 'objectification of subjectivity: method in human studies / crucial experiment: method in natural sciences.'
71 2C 275–76.

72 2C 275.
73 INCW 601.
74 INCW 609.
75 It must be said, however, that the canon of successive approximations does envisage such a process (INCW 610–12). Despite this, the problem we have been adverting to remains.
76 MT 283–84.
77 INCW 609.
78 Cf. section 3 above.
79 MT 269–71; cf. above, chapter 9, section 1.
80 MT 267.
81 Cf. above, chapter 8, section 1.2.
82 Lonergan, 'August 26, 1975: Prof. Vertin's Questions' (LRI Library file 855).
83 Cf. above, Introduction.
84 MiT 1970 466: '[T]heir genesis is in dialectic – well, in the first four. But they come out clearly in dialectic.' Recall also Hermeneutics 1962 13–14: basic context as the statement of the foundations of basic orientations and attitudes.
85 MiT 1970 466.
86 MT 292. Cf. MiT 1971 359–60: Genesis of the special theological categories 'occurs in the dialectic as assembling and comparing, and reducing, and classifying the terms of conflicts.'
87 MiT 1970 467. Note that, while the 1970 text speaks of the derivation of the categories in terms of self-appropriation but does not mention use (MiT 1970 465), still, already from 1968 the texts speak of the interaction between upper and lower blades (TPSR Graham 141).
88 Ibid.
89 MT 293.
90 MT 250. Given that the text of 1971 is identical with *Method*, our references will be to the latter.
91 MT 331; emphasis mine.
92 Lonergan, handwritten notes for lectures on *Method in Theology* at the University of San Francisco, 1972 (LRI Archives Lonergan Papers 502) 3.
93 Lonergan, 'Natural Right and Historical Mindedness,' 3C 182.
94 Cf. above, section 2.1.
95 Lonergan, 'Third Lecture: The Ongoing Genesis of Methods,' 3C 159. Cf. also Dialogue at the Lonergan Workshop, 1976, transcript 48: 'Dialectic becomes dialogue in the limit.' Again, ibid. 57: Dialectic on a more personal level becomes dialogue. Further, ibid. 61: dialectic deals with subject as object: you talk about Aristotle, Marx, Hegel, etc. But in dialogue, 'it is the people that differ talking to one another and respecting one another and there you are getting much closer to the issue.'

Lonergan notes that Ricoeur's hermeneutic of suspicion and of recovery, as well as his own article 'The Origins of Christian Realism' (and *The Way to Nicea*) are instances of the dialectic that deals with subjects as objects (3C 157, 165 note 5).

96 3C 182. Cf. Lonergan, Dialogue at the Lonergan Workshop, 1977, transcript 36–37: 'Another approach to it is dialogue which is better ... [It] is a step beyond dialectic. Dialectic is an objective approach: A says this and B says that and C says the other; ... But in the Dialogue they are talking to one another. One says not that you are wrong, but I'm not too sure of that.'

Cf. Lonergan, 'Method Theology Seminar 1980' (LRI Archives Lonergan Papers 776) 7 of the handwritten notes on *Method* chapter 10, Dialectic: '[Dialectic is] performed by different operators with radically opposed horizons ... / results not uniform / ask divergent to formulate their criteria of / int[ellectual] conversion / mor[al] conversion / rlg. [religious] conversion / explain how they went about developing positions reversing c-p's [counterpositions] / *if confrontation* profitable / repeat method on their results explanations / *better if dialectic yields to dialogue*' (emphases in text).

97 Lonergan, Dialogue at the Lonergan Workshop, 1977, transcript, 92. Cf. also Lonergan, Dialogue at the Lonergan Workshop, 1976, transcript 57: The more personal approach of dialogue is needed simply because value judgments are personal judgments, and it is by bringing persons together that one gets some way to handle value judgments.

98 Cf. DCC 16.

99 INCW 242. Cf. PTP 75: The dialogues of Plato are in fact an instance of the concrete group use of dialectic in the individual sense. Also 'Radix dialecticae' (Batch IX.7, item c), and above, chapter 5, section 5, note 66: in Aristotle, dialectic is a question of the purified subject reflecting on the sequence of opinions.

100 Cf. Lonergan, '*Pantôn Anakephalaiôsis*,' *Method: Journal of Lonergan Studies* 9:2 (1991) 144: 'It is to be noted that this progress [i.e., of human thought] from potency through incomplete act to perfect act is to be predicated not of the individual but of humanity.'

Chapter 12

1 MT 25. Cf. also Lonergan, 'MiT III: Horizons and Categories,' LRI Archives Batch VI.6 15: 'That method [i.e., transcendental method] brings to light (1) attending to data and questioning for intelligence, for reflection, and for deliberation, (2) the operations that follow upon attending and questioning, (3) the structure in which these operations occur, and (4) the objects correlative to the operations and structure and specified, not by their own qualities, but only by their correlativity. These four may be referred to

more briefly as (1) the *a priori* or, with Karl Rahner, the *Vorgriff* as distinct from the *Begriff*, (2) the operations, (3) the structure, and (4) the objects.' For some further references to the three questions, or to the triad cognitional theory, epistemology, metaphysics, cf. DMT 1962 34; MoT 1964, Method in Theology. The Problem. External Factors, 5; MiT 1965 Batch v.10 item i; PGT 7–8, 39–40.
2 MoT 1962 199.
3 Conversazioni con Bernard Lonergan (transcript of interviews conducted by G.B. Sala, January and June 1965, unpublished) 18; cf. also 52.
4 MiT 1965 Batch V.10 i.
5 2C 203. Cf. also 3C 76.
6 MT 316.
7 Cf. 1C 204.
8 'Questionnaire' 3ff.
9 'Questionnaire' 23–24.
10 'Questionnaire' 26.
11 3C 76; cf. also 79, 82, 87.
12 3C 141.
13 3C 145. Cf. also Lonergan, Dialogue at the Lonergan Workshop, 1976, unpublished transcript 96, which notes that the change of terminology from generalized empirical method to transcendental method was not an altogether happy one. Husserl's meaning is closer to Lonergan's own, though Lonergan does not share Husserl's notion of the subject.
14 3C 180.
15 MiT 1969 422–23.
16 'Question Periods, Seminar on Method in Theology' (Graham transcript of the question sessions at the 1969 course), LRI Library file 515 80.
17 MT 21.
18 Lonergan, 'Philosophy and the Religious Phenomenon,' *Method: Journal of Lonergan Studies* 12 (1994) 129.
19 MT 288.
20 MT 25.
21 'Questionnaire' 5–7.
22 3C 177. The paper is 'Natural Right and Historical Mindedness.'
23 Lonergan, 'August 26, 1975: Prof. Vertin's Questions' LRI Library file 855. Vertin's question runs as follows: 'Frequently (e.g., METHOD, p. 25) you speak of transcendental method as coincident with the basic part of what has been considered philosophy, and you note that it comes to light in the answers to the three basic questions ... In such contexts, why do you not also indicate one or more basic questions of *ethics*? I.e., besides the basic COGNITIONAL aspect of transcendental method, is there not also a basic MORAL/ETHICAL aspect, or is the latter simply derivative from the former?'

24 Lonergan, Dialogue at the Lonergan Workshop, Boston College, 1976, transcript 32, with slight corrections to the text.
25 Ibid. 32.
26 Ibid. 37–38.
27 Ibid. 38.
28 Cf. ibid. 40.
29 Lonergan, 'Philosophy and the Religious Phenomenon' 128. Lonergan does not mention here that Hegel's option leads to an 'immanental dialectic,' but we have already examined the contrasts drawn between such a dialectic and Lonergan's own normative and open-ended dialectic (cf. INCW 446–47 and chapter 3, section 3.1 above.). Cf. also the reference to 'the Hegelian dialectical deduction of the universe through an interplay of opposed *Begriffe*' in 3C 221.
30 Lonergan, Dialogue at the Lonergan Workshop, 1976, transcript 32–33. 'Philosophy and Theology' makes the point that the key shift in contemporary Catholic theology is the transition from eternal truths to developing doctrines (2C 193), and that the contribution of philosophy is 'to replace the shattered thoughtforms associated with eternal truths and logical ideals with new thoughtforms that accord with the dynamics of development and the concrete style of method' (2C 202).
31 Lonergan, 'The Ongoing Genesis of Methods,' 3C 146–65.
32 3C 146.
33 Ibid.
34 This explicit contrast is indicated not only in the opening section of the paper (3C 202), but also and especially in the title: 'A Post-Hegelian Philosophy of Religion.' On method as general dynamics, cf. sections 1 and 2 of the paper (3C 204–15). Note also the reference to 'The Ongoing Genesis of Methods' in note 4 (3C 222).
35 On transcendental method as post-Kantian, cf. 3C 82.
36 PGT 45–46.
37 PGT 49: 'The basic discipline sets up a transcendental method, a manner of proceeding in any and every cognitional enterprise. The other disciplines add to transcendental method the categorial determinations appropriate to their specific enterprise.' 3C 150: '[U]nderpinning special methods there is what I have named generalized empirical method.' 3C 204: 'For methods and procedures are dynamic, and all share a common dynamism that is proper to our common humanity.' 3C 209: '[W]e turn from the core of methods generally to the differentiation of that core.' 'Questionnaire' 25: 'In this fashion a philosophic theory of knowledge is attained and from it one moves with relative ease to an epistemology, a metaphysics of proportionate being, and an existential ethics.'
38 INCW 765–66. The problem here arises from the development of the empirical human sciences. There is first the universal relevance of theology. For the

empirical human sciences consider man in the concrete, and man in the concrete is in need of grace, receives grace, and either accepts or rejects that grace; but such data cannot be mastered without an appeal to theology. There is on the other hand the autonomy of the sciences. Lonergan notes that this problem has in a large measure 'dictated the structure of the present work' (INCW 765).

39 Lonergan, 'August 26, 1975: Prof. Vertin's Questions,' LRI Library file 855.
40 Ibid.
41 The reference is to H. Butterfield, *The Origins of Modern Science, 1300–1800* (New York: Free Press, first published 1949). Cf. also e.g. 3C 147.
42 Cf. e.g. 3C 63–64, 137–40, 149, 178–79.
43 Lonergan, 'Variations in Fundamental Theology,' *Method: Journal of Lonergan Studies* 16 (1998) 24. This remark is from the conclusion of the 1973 version of the paper; the 1974 version contains a different conclusion. The 'Original Conclusion, 1973' has been included as an appendix in the published text.
44 Lonergan, 'A Response to Fr. Dych,' in *Theology and Discovery: Essays in Honor of Karl Rahner*, ed. W.J. Kelly (Milwaukee: Marquette University Press, 1980) 55. It might be noted that, while taking issue with Rahner's pessimism here, Lonergan also observes that what Rahner calls 'indirect method' is closely related to his own method (ibid.). The point being made here is the centrality of discernment in theological method (cf. ibid. and also 3C 195); the differences regarding transcendental method observed earlier remain.
45 2C 226–27.
46 2C 29.
47 PGT 57.
48 MT 302.
49 MT 302–305.
50 MT 305.
51 Ibid.
52 Cf. PGT 12–13.
53 Lonergan, 'Bernard Lonergan Responds,' in P. McShane, ed., *Foundations of Theology: Papers from the International Lonergan Congress, 1970* (Dublin: Gill and Macmillan, 1991) 224.
54 Lonergan, Dialogue at the Lonergan Workshop, 1976, transcript 32–33, 37–38.
55 PGT 15, cf. x. Note that there is implied here a correction of the statement in 'Dimensions of Meaning' (1C 245) that 'once philosophy becomes existential and historical ... the very possibility of the old distinction between philosophy and theology vanishes.'
56 For an account of this notion, cf. F.E. Crowe, *Appropriating the Lonergan Idea*, ed. M. Vertin (Washington: Catholic University of America Press, 1989) 344–59.
57 'Questionnaire' 10. Again, Lonergan, 'Philosophy and the Religious Phe-

nomenon' 127: '[T]his shift from the priority of a metaphysics of objects to the priority of a theory of cognitional operations has an interesting implication for a philosophy of religion. For the distinction between naturally known objects and supernaturally known objects can now both retain all of its validity and, at the same time, lose the rather absolute priority it enjoyed in scholastic thought.'

58 'Questionnaire,' 10–11. Cf. also Lonergan, Horizons and Transpositions (lecture at the Lonergan Workshop, with the theme Crisis of Liberal Education, Boston College, 21 June 1979; unpublished), LRI Library file 963-2a 24: 'Aquinas sharply distinguished between philosophy and theology, yet he did not separate them ... But the separation of philosophy and theology was brought about very effectively by Descartes with his doctrine of methodic doubt.'

59 'Questionnaire' 11.

60 Cf. above, chapter 8, section 3.3.

61 INCW 421, 426.

62 INCW 765.

63 Cf. above, chapter 4, section 2.1.

64 Cf. 2C 203–206.

65 Cf. 2C 162.

66 This is later expressed in terms of praxis: first-phase theology is praxis in the weak sense, whereas second-phase theology is praxis in the strong sense. Cf. Lonergan, Dialogue at the Lonergan Workshop, 1976, transcript 6–7, 22. On praxis as method, cf. 3C 147, 160–61.

67 MT 153, n. 1. Cf. also the paper of 1973 '*Insight* Revisited' (2C 275–76), when it speaks of *Method* as being 'an orderly set of directions on what is to be done towards moving to the attainment of universal viewpoint.'

68 MT 288.

69 Cf. Charles C. Hefling, Jr, 'Lonergan on Development: *The Way to Nicea* in Light of His More Recent Methodology,' doctoral dissertation (Andover Newton Theological School – Boston College, Boston, 1982) 164–74.

70 MT 288.

71 MT 141.

72 MT 223–24. Cf. History 1962 8: 'A critical philosophy provides the foundations for historical method and fully conscious historical operations ... As it grounds and directs historical method and operations, so also a critical philosophy provides an ultimate basis for a critique of the results of historical work.'

73 Lonergan, 'Bernard Lonergan Responds' 229–30. Again, 2C 203–205: On the basis of cognitional theory, epistemology, and metaphysics, there has to be worked out a foundational account both of hermeneutics and of critical history. Cognitional theory, epistemology, and metaphysics in turn have to be subsumed under operations on the fourth level of consciousness

Notes to pages 203–205   289

so as to yield a historical theology. Such historical theology will yield a dialectic. Cf. also 2C 191: The relevant philosophy would follow the transcendental turn: it would bring to light the conditions of possibility of religious studies and their correlative objects; it would survey the areas studied and the methods used; it would ground appropriate methods as well as justify or criticize accepted ones.

74 Cf. also 2C 275–76, where Lonergan indicates that the hermeneutical method of chapter 17 of *Insight* is realized through the first five functional specialties of *Method*.

75 Cf. chapter 7, section 3 above.

76 1C 198–99, and cf. chapter 7, section 1 above.

77 It is quite possible that the title of section 2 of the 1968 chapter 'Horizons and Categories' (cf. chapter 9, section 2 above) is an allusion to Coreth's position and to the 1963 review article.

78 VB 68.

79 3C 76.

80 DDT-I 5, n. 1, and above, chapter 8, section 1.1.

81 Cf. Lonergan, 'Problematik,' typescript found in LRI Archives in folder entitled 'Various Papers' (pertaining with all probability to MoT 1962: cf. appendix A) 7, which observes that the possibility of positive theology passing into systematic theology 'lies in the transcendental implications of (a) the reality and (b) the self-knowledge of the believer' and adds that such self-knowledge provides the upper blade of positive theology and grounds judgments, for 'sapientia omnia ordinat.'

82 Lonergan, 'Variations in Fundamental Theology' 5–24.

83 Ibid. 14.

84 Ibid. 14–15.

85 3C 32.

86 The scissors movement, the correspondence between the inner and outer words, is not a theme that is peculiar to Lonergan; he himself finds it in Bouillard (Lonergan, 'Variations in Fundamental Theology' 16), Fries (ibid. 16), Walgrave (ibid. 16–17), and Geffré (ibid. 17-18).

87 3C 32 relates the two divine missions not only to *fides ex auditu* and *fides ex infusione*, but also to the two ways. Further, in 'The Human Good,' *Humanitas* (Duquesne University) 15 (1979) 120, Lonergan links the transmission of tradition to the way downwards: development from above downwards is described as 'the benefits of acculturation, socialization, education, the transmission of the position.'

88 Cf. Lonergan, Dialogue at the Lonergan Workshop, 1976, transcript 6–7. Note the sequence: love, response, judgment, understanding, experience. Cf. also Crowe, *Appropriating the Lonergan Idea* 350.

89 F. Fiorenza as reported by M. Vertin, 'The Resurrection, Reconstructive

Hermeneutics, and Foundational Theology,' *Proceedings of the Catholic Theological Society of America* 40 (1985) 181.
90 Cf. above, section 1.1.

Conclusion

1 INCW 754.
2 MT 21-22.
3 VB 67.
4 3C 76.
5 VB 68.
6 3C 76.
7 Cf. DMT Spring 1963 item z+7, p. 3.

Appendix B

1 Lonergan, 'Functional Specialties in Theology,' *Gregorianum* 50 (1969) 485-504.
2 Batch VI.2 3-30. This may be dated either 1968 or 1969: cf. appendix A.
3 Cf. Batch VI.2 31-62. Note the strikeout on p. 31: '© Copyright BL, 1969 3. History.'
4 Batch VIII.17 e.63-65. The header is 'MiT VII.'
5 The autograph in question (Batch XII) contains a chapter 'Interpretation.' The running head of this chapter, crossed out, is 'MiT VII'; the original pagination is pp. 1-30, which corresponds exactly to pp. 1-30 of 'MiT VII. The Tasks of Theology' (Batch VI.2).
6 Batch XII contains a chapter eight, 'History.' The running head of this chapter, crossed out in pencil, is 'MiT VII'; the original pagination is pp. 31-62; and on p. 31 there is struck out '© Copyright BL, 1969 3. History.'
7 Batch X.11 63-82.
8 Batch X.12 1-32.
9 MiT 1969 347-411.
10 MiT 1970 320-96.
11 Batch XII.9 277-330.
12 Batch X.5, one of several p. 13's. The chapter speaks of history as comparing and relating interpreted data; such comparison leads to determining organistic, genetic, and dialectical relationships. Batch X.5, one of several p. 6's.
13 Cf. TPSR chapter 2: Functional Specialties.
14 Batch VIII.17 e.63.
15 Batch VI.2 15 = Batch X.11 15.
16 Batch X.11 63-82.
17 Batch X.12 1-32.

18 Note that both these discussions are to be found in the present *Method* chapter 'Dialectic.' Note also the mention of Wittgenstein on p. 25.
19 Cf. appendix A above.
20 Cf. also Batch VI.5, 'MiT Ch. x. Dialectic and Foundations' 1–15.
21 Cf. MiT 1970, 'Ch.9 Dialectic.'
22 MiT 1969, chapter x, sections 5–8.
23 MiT 1969, chapter XI, sections 4–7, 9.

Bibliography

1 Primary Sources

The following is a list, in chronological order, of those works of Bernard Lonergan consulted for this study. Items beginning at the left margin are the original works; when indented items follow, they are editions or versions actually used in the present study. Original works are listed under the year of completion (thus, for example, since *Insight* was completed in 1953, it is listed under '1953' rather than in 1957, which is its date of publication.) The abbreviation used in the notes for each work follows the entry in brackets.

Note: 'LRI Archives' are the Archives of the Lonergan Research Institute of Regis College, 10 St Mary Street, Suite 500, Toronto, Ontario M4Y 1P9 Canada.

1935
'*Pantôn Anakephalaiôsis:* A Theory of Human Solidarity, A Metaphysic for the Interpretation of St Paul, A Theology for the Social Order, Catholic Action, and the Kingship of Christ, *In Incipient Outline.*' Dated 'Dominica in Albis' [= 28 April] 1935.

> '*Pantôn Anakephalaiôsis.*' *Method: Journal of Lonergan Studies* 9:2 (1991) 139–72. Edited by F.E. Crowe and R.M. Doran.

1940
'*Gratia Operans:* A Study of the Speculative Development in the Writings of St. Thomas of Aquin.' Thesis director Charles Boyer, SJ. Rome: Gregorian University, 1940.

> 'The *Gratia Operans* Dissertation: Preface and Introduction.' *Method: Journal of Lonergan Studies* 3:2 (1985) 9–46. [GOI]

1941

'St. Thomas' Thought on *Gratia Operans.*' *Theological Studies* 2 (1941) 289–324.

Grace and Freedom: Operative Grace in the Thought of St. Thomas Aquinas. Edited by J. Patout Burns. London: Darton, Longman & Todd; New York: Herder and Herder, 1971. [GF]

1942

'St. Thomas' Thought on *Gratia Operans.*' *Theological Studies* 3 (1942) 69–88, 375–402, 533–78.

Grace and Freedom: Operative Grace in the Thought of St. Thomas Aquinas. Edited by J. Patout Burns. London: Darton, Longman & Todd; New York: Herder and Herder, 1971. [GF]

1943

'Finality, Love, Marriage.' *Theological Studies* 4 (1943) 477–510.

'Finality, Love, Marriage.' In *Collection*, edited by Frederick E. Crowe and Robert M. Doran, 17–52. Second edition, revised and augmented. Collected Works of Bernard Lonergan 4. Toronto: University of Toronto Press, 1988.

1945–46

Thought and Reality. Series of weekly lectures at the Thomas More Institute, Montreal, from mid-November 1945 to May 1946. Notes taken by M. O'Hara, typescript by Thomas V. Daly. LRI Library file 31. Unpublished.

1946

'The Concept of *Verbum* in the Writings of St. Thomas Aquinas.' *Theological Studies* 7 (1946) 349–92.

Verbum: Word and Idea in Aquinas. Edited by David B. Burrell. Notre Dame: University of Notre Dame Press, 1967. [VB]

De ente supernaturali: Supplementum schematicum. Marianopoli: Collegium Immaculate Conceptionis, 1946. Unpublished.

De ente supernaturali: Supplementum schematicum. The Early Latin Works of Bernard J.F. Lonergan. Edited by Frederick E. Crowe, assisted by Conn O'Donovan and Giovanni Sala. Toronto: Regis College, 1973.

Review of Eduardo Iglesias, *De Deo in operatione naturae vel voluntatis operante. Theological Studies* 7 (1946) 602–13.

'On God and Secondary Causes.' In *Collection*, edited by Frederick E. Crowe and Robert M. Doran, 53–65. Second edition, revised and augmented. Collected Works of Bernard Lonergan 4. Toronto: University of Toronto Press, 1988.

1947

'The Concept of *Verbum* in the Writings of St. Thomas Aquinas.' *Theological Studies* 8 (1947) 35–79, 404–44.

Verbum: Word and Idea in Aquinas. Edited by David B. Burrell. Notre Dame: University of Notre Dame Press, 1967. [VB]

1949

'The Concept of *Verbum* in the Writings of St. Thomas Aquinas.' *Theological Studies* 10 (1949) 3–40, 359–93.

Verbum: Word and Idea in Aquinas. Edited by David B. Burrell. Notre Dame: University of Notre Dame Press, 1967. [VB]

'The Natural Desire to See God.' Paper at the Convention of the Jesuit Philosophical Association, Boston, 18 April 1949.

'The Natural Desire to See God.' In *Collection*, edited by Frederick E. Crowe and Robert M. Doran, 81–91. Second edition, revised and augmented. Collected Works of Bernard Lonergan 4. Toronto: University of Toronto Press, 1988.

1951

Intelligence and Reality. Notes for Lectures at the Thomas More Institute, Montreal, March–May 1951. Unpublished.

1952

Analysis fidei. Collegium Christi Regis Torontini, 1952. Unpublished.

Analysis Fidei. The Early Latin Works of Bernard J.F. Lonergan. Edited by Frederick E. Crowe, assisted by Conn O'Donovan and Giovanni Sala. Regis College, Toronto, 1973. Unpublished. [AF]

1953

Insight: A Study of Human Understanding. London: Longmans, Green, 1957. Though published only in 1957, the manuscript was ready in September 1953.

Insight: A Study of Human Understanding. San Francisco: Harper & Row, 1978. [IN]

Insight: A Study of Human Understanding. Fifth edition. Edited by Frederick E. Crowe and Robert M. Doran. Collected Works of Bernard Lonergan 3. Toronto: University of Toronto Press, 1992. [INCW]

Original Preface to *Insight*. This preface was ready, with the rest of the *Insight* manuscript, in September 1953. It was replaced by the existing preface at the request of the publisher.

'The Original Preface to *Insight.*' *Method: Journal of Lonergan Studies* 3:1 (1985) 3–7.

1954
'Theology and Understanding.' *Gregorianum* 35 (1954) 630–48.

'Theology and Understanding.' In *Collection*, edited by Frederick E. Crowe and Robert M. Doran, 114–132. Second edition, revised and augmented. Collected Works of Bernard Lonergan 4. Toronto: University of Toronto Press, 1988.

1955
Review of P. Vanier, *Théologie trinitaire chez saint Thomas d'Aquin. Gregorianum* 36 (1955) 703–705.

'Isomorphism of Thomist and Scientific Thought.' Paper (in absentia) at the Congressus quartus thomisticus internationalis, Rome, 13–17 September 1955.

'Isomorphism of Thomist and Scientific Thought.' In *Collection*, edited by Frederick E. Crowe and Robert M. Doran, 133–41. Second edition, revised and augmented. Collected Works of Bernard Lonergan 4. Toronto: University of Toronto Press, 1988.

1956
De Constitutione Christi ontologica et psychologica supplementum confecit Bernardus Lonergan, S.I. Rome: Gregorian University Press, 1956.

De Constitutione Christi ontologica et psychologica supplementum confecit Bernardus Lonergan, S.I. 4th edition. Rome: Gregorian University Press, 1964. [DCC]

On the Ontological and Psychological Constitution of Christ. Supplement. Translated by John Hochban, Michael Shields, and Charles Hefling Jr. Toronto: Lonergan Research Institute of Regis College, 1987. First draft of a translation of *De Constitutione Christi ontologica et psychologica*, 4th edition, Rome: Gregorian University Press, 1964. Unpublished.

1957
Divinarum personarum conceptionem analogicam evolvit Bernardus Lonergan, S.I. Rome: Gregorian University Press, 1957. [DP]

Theological Understanding. Translation of chapter 1 of the above, by Francis P. Greaney, 1966, and edited by Edmund Morton. LRI Library LB 188. Unpublished.

Mathematical Logic. Lectures at Boston College, 8–12 July 1957. Transcript from the tapes made by Nicholas Graham. Unpublished.

Existentialism. Notes for Lectures at Boston College. 15–19 July 1957. Mimeographed edition. Montreal: Thomas More Institute, 1957. Unpublished.

Existentialism. Lectures at Boston College, 15–19 July 1957. Transcript from the tapes made by Nicholas Graham. Unpublished.

1958
'Philosophic Differences and Personal Development.' *New Scholasticism* 32 (1958) 97.

'*Insight*: Preface to a Discussion.' Paper (in absentia) at the convention of the American Catholic Philosophical Association, Detroit, 9 April 1958.

'*Insight*: Preface to a Discussion.' In *Collection*, edited by Frederick E. Crowe and Robert M. Doran, 142–52. Second edition, revised and augmented. Collected Works of Bernard Lonergan 4. Toronto: University of Toronto Press, 1988.

Insight. Institute at Saint Mary's University, Halifax, 4–15 August 1958.

Understanding and Being: The Halifax Lectures on Insight. Edited by Elizabeth A. Morelli and Mark D. Morelli. Revised and augmented by Frederick E. Crowe, with the collaboration of Elizabeth A. Morelli, Mark D. Morelli, Robert M. Doran, and Thomas V. Daly. Collected Works of Bernard Lonergan 5. Toronto: University of Toronto Press, 1990. [UB]

1959
'Christ as Subject: A Reply.' *Gregorianum* 40 (1959) 242–70.

'Christ as Subject: A Reply.' In *Collection*, edited by Frederick E. Crowe, and Robert M. Doran, 153–84. Second edition, revised and augmented. Collected Works of Bernard Lonergan, 4. Toronto: University of Toronto Press, 1988.

'Method in Catholic Theology.' Lecture to the Society for the Study of Theology, Nottingham, England, 15 April 1959.

'Method in Catholic Theology.' *Method: Journal of Lonergan Studies* 10:1 (1992) 1–26. [The Nottingham lecture]

'Method in Catholic Theology.' In *Philosophical and Theological Papers 1958–1964*, edited by Robert C. Croken, Frederick E. Crowe, and Robert M. Doran, 29–53. Collected Works of Bernard Lonergan 6. Toronto: University of Toronto Press, 1996.

De intellectu et methodo. Notes taken by F. Rossi de Gasperis and P. Joseph Cahill from the course given at the Gregorian University, Rome, Spring 1959. Unpublished. [IM 1959 Student Notes]

Understanding and Method. English translation (1988) by Michael G. Shields of the student notes of *De intellectu et methodo*, 1959. Unpublished.

De intellectu et methodo. LRI Archives Batch v.2.a. Autograph typescript of chapter 1 of the course given at the Gregorian University, Rome, Spring 1959. Unpublished. [IM 1959]

The Philosophy of Education. Institute at Xavier University, Cincinnati, 3–14 August 1959.

Topics in Education: The Cincinnati Lectures of 1959 on the Philosophy of Education. Edited by Robert M. Doran and Frederick E. Crowe, revising and augmenting the unpublished text prepared by James Quinn and John Quinn. Collected Works of Bernard Lonergan 10. Toronto: University of Toronto Press, 1993. [TE]

Folder entitled 'System and History.' LRI Archives Batch v.8, 1959. The folder contains sheaves of handwritten and typed notes probably prepared for the course *De systemate et historia* given at the Gregorian University, Rome, Fall 1959. Unpublished. [SH]

De systemate et historia. LRI Archives Batch v.8.i. Autograph typescript of notes (18 pp.) for the course given at the Gregorian University, Rome, Fall 1959. Unpublished. [DSH]

System and History. English translation of *De systemate et historia* (LRI Archives Batch v.8.i) by Michael G. Shields, 1990. Unpublished.

De systemate et historia. Handwritten notes taken by F. Rossi de Gasperis from the course given at the Gregorian University, Rome, Fall 1959. LRI Archives. Unpublished.

1960

'Openness and Religious Experience.' Paper (in absentia) at the XV Convegno del centro di studi filosofici tra professori universitari, Gallarate (Milan) on Il problema dell'esperienza religiosa, 4–6 September 1960.

'Openness and Religious Experience.' In *Collection*, edited by Frederick E. Crowe, and Robert M. Doran, 185–87. Second edition, revised and augmented. Collected Works of Bernard Lonergan 4. Toronto: University of Toronto Press, 1988.

Philosophy of History. Notes for the lecture given at the Thomas More Institute, Montreal, 23 September 1960. LRI Archives Batch IX.7.a. Unpublished.

'Radix dialecticae.' (Single handwritten page.) LRI Archives Batch IX.7.c. Probable date 1960 (cf. appendix A). Unpublished.

The Philosophy of History. Introductory lecture at the Thomas More Institute for Adult Education, Montreal, 23 September 1960. Transcript from tape. LRI no. LB 160. Unpublished.

'The Philosophy of History.' In *Philosophical and Theological Papers 1958–1964*, edited by Robert C. Croken, Frederick E. Crowe, and Robert M. Doran, 54–79. Collected Works of Bernard Lonergan 6. Toronto: University of Toronto Press, 1996.

1961

De Deo trino: Pars analytica. Rome: Gregorian University Press, 1961. [DDTPA]

LRI Archives Batch v.3. The folder contains sheaves of handwritten notes prepared probably for the course *De intellectu et methodo* given at the Gregorian University, Rome, Spring 1961. Unpublished.

LRI Archives Batch v.6. The folder contains sheaves of handwritten and typed notes prepared probably for the course *De intellectu et methodo* given at the Gregorian University, Rome, Spring 1961. Unpublished.

Participation in a discussion at the North American College, Rome, reported in John V. Wildeman and Charles M. Murphy, 'Some Directions for Theology,' *Roman Echoes* (Yearbook of the North American College, Rome) (1961) 32–41.

Critical Realism and the Integration of the Sciences. Series of six lectures at University College, Dublin, 23–25 May 1961. Unpublished.

Insight. Summer course at St Mary's College, Moraga, California, 10 July–4 August 1961. Typescript made by Harry Kohls from the autograph lecture notes. Unpublished.

1962

De methodo theologiae. Autograph typescript (83 pp.) of notes for the course given at the Gregorian University, Spring semester 1962. LRI Archives Batch v.1.c. Pp. 79–83 are missing in the 'student notes' listed below. Unpublished. [DMT 1962]

The Method of Theology. English translation (1989) by Michael G. Shields of the autograph (Batch v.1.c) of the Gregorian course *De methodo theologiae*, 1962. Unpublished.

Folder entitled 'De methodo theologiae.' LRI Archives Batch v.1. The folder contains handwritten and typed material mostly related to *De methodo theologiae* of 1962. Batch v.1.c here is the autograph mentioned above. Unpublished.

LRI Archives Batch v.5. The folder contains mostly handwritten pages probably related to *De methodo theologiae* of 1962. Unpublished. [DMT 1962 Batch v.5]

LRI Archives Batch v.4. The folder contains mostly handwritten pages probably related to *De methodo theologiae* of 1962 and to the Summer Institute on The Method of Theology, Regis College, Toronto, 1962. Unpublished. [DMT 1962 Batch v.4]

300 Bibliography

De methodo theologiae. Notes taken by students (60 pp.), but almost certainly copied from Lonergan's own notes, from the course given at the Gregorian University, Spring semester 1962. Unpublished. [DMT 1962 Student Notes]

'Method of Theology. Prospectus and bibliography for 1962 Regis Course.' LRI Library file 301, 'The Method of Theology Institute Regis College 1962.' Unpublished.

'Problematik.' Typescript (7 pp.) found in LRI Archives folder entitled 'Various Papers.' Pertaining with all probability to the Institute on The Method of Theology, Regis College, 1962 (cf. appendix A). Unpublished.

The Method of Theology. Summer Institute at Regis College, Toronto, 9–20 July 1962. Edited transcript from tapes by Nicholas W. Graham. Toronto: Lonergan Centre, Regis College, 1984. Unpublished. [MoT 1962]

'*Sensus* (meaning).' Typescript (7 pp.) dated 19–20 May 1962. LRI Archives file entitled 'Various Papers.' Probably pertaining to *De methodo theologiae*, 1962. Unpublished.

Hermeneutics. Autograph typescript of the lecture during the Institute on The Method of Theology, Regis College, Toronto 1962. The typescript contains two p. 11's, the first of which bears the header 'Hermeneutics – alternative ending.' LRI Archives, file entitled 'Various Papers.' Unpublished. [Hermeneutics 1962 MS]

Hermeneutics. Notes for lecture during the Institute on The Method of Theology, Regis College, Toronto, 20 July 1962. Mimeographed edition, Thomas More Institute, Montreal, 1963. Unpublished. [Hermeneutics 1962]

'Hermeneutics.' Fragment (2 typed pp.) found on the reverse of Lonergan Papers Batch v.9.m, pp. 1–2 (= A 515 a, pp. 1–2). 1962. Unpublished.

'Hermeneutics (5).' Fragment (1 typed p.) found on reverse of a handwritten page entitled 'the task – *munus nobilissimum*' in LRI Archives file entitled 'Various Papers.' 1962. Unpublished.

'History.' Notes for lectures on history at the Institute on The Method of Theology, Regis College, Toronto, 1962. LRI Archives Batch IX.7 e, f. Typescript made probably by someone else from the autograph typescript 'History,' found in LRI Archives Batch VIII.17 a. Unpublished. [Batch IX.7 f = History 1962]

Time and Meaning. Lecture at Thomas More Institute, Montreal, 25 September 1962.

'Time and Meaning.' In *Bernard Lonergan: 3 Lectures*, edited by R. Eric O'Connor, 29–54. Montreal: Thomas More Institute for Adult Education, 1975.

'Time and Meaning.' In *Philosophical and Theological Papers 1958–1964*, edited by

Robert C. Croken, Frederick E. Crowe, and Robert M. Doran, 94–121. Collected Works of Bernard Lonergan 6. Toronto: University of Toronto Press, 1996.

1963

'Metaphysics as Horizon.' *Gregorianum* 44 (1963) 307–18.

  'Metaphysics as Horizon.' In *Collection*, edited by Frederick E. Crowe and Robert M. Doran, 188–204. Second edition, revised and augmented. Collected Works of Bernard Lonergan 4. Toronto: University of Toronto Press, 1988.

Folder entitled 'De methodo theologiae 1963.' LRI Archives Batch v.11, 1963. Handwritten notes for the course given at the Gregorian University, Spring semester 1963. Unpublished. [DMT Spring 1963]

Knowledge and Learning. Notes for the Institute in the Graduate School of Gonzaga University, Spokane, Washington, 15–26 July 1963. LRI Library file 357-1. Unpublished. [KL]

Knowledge and Learning. Institute in the Graduate School of Gonzaga University, Spokane, Washington, 15–26 July 1963. Notes made during lectures by J.M. Laporte. LRI Library file 357-2. Unpublished. [KL Laporte]

Knowledge and Learning. Institute in the Graduate School of Gonzaga University, Spokane, Washington, 15–26 July 1963. *Reportatio* by B. Tyrrell. LRI Library file 357-3. Unpublished. [KL Tyrrell]

Exegesis and Dogma. Lecture at Regis College, Toronto, 3 September 1963. Transcript, LRI Library file 371. Unpublished.

  'Exegesis and Dogma.' In *Philosophical and Theological Papers 1958–1964*, edited by Robert C. Croken, Frederick E. Crowe, and Robert M. Doran, 142–59. Collected Works of Bernard Lonergan 6. Toronto: University of Toronto Press, 1996.

The Analogy of Meaning. Lecture at the Thomas More Institute, Montreal, 25 September 1963. Transcript by Philip McShane, LRI Library file 375. Unpublished.

  'The Analogy of Meaning.' In *Philosophical and Theological Papers 1958–1964*, edited by Robert C. Croken, Frederick E. Crowe, and Robert M. Doran, 183–213. Collected Works of Bernard Lonergan 6. Toronto: University of Toronto Press, 1996.

De Deo trino: I. Pars dogmatica. Rome: Gregorian University Press, 1964. Second revised edition of *De Deo trino: Pars analytica*, 1961. The 'Imprimi potest' is dated 30 November 1963. [DDT-I]

  The Way to Nicea: The Dialectical Development of Trinitarian Theology. Translated by Conn O'Donovan. London: Darton, Longman & Todd, 1976, 1982. Trans.

of first part (pp. 17–112) of *De Deo trino: I. Pars dogmatica*, 1964.

De Deo trino: II. Pars systematica seu divinarum personarum conceptio analogica. Rome: Gregorian University Press, 1964. Third revised edition of *Divinarum personarum conceptionem analogicam* ... 1957. The 'Imprimi potest' is dated 13 October 1963. [DDT-II]

Folder entitled 'De methodo theol. 1963.' LRI Archives Batch v.9. Handwritten schematic notes pertaining to the course *De methodo theologiae* at the Gregorian University, Fall semester 1963. Unpublished. [DMT Fall 1963]

De methodo theologiae. Notes made by Tom Daly and typed by John Begley, of the course given at the Gregorian University, Fall semester 1963. Unpublished. [DMT Fall 1963 Daly]

1964

'Cognitional Structure.' In *Spirit as Inquiry: Studies in Honor of Bernard Lonergan*, edited by Frederick E. Crowe, 230–42. Chicago: Saint Xavier College, 1964.

'Cognitional Structure.' In *Collection*, edited by Frederick E. Crowe and Robert M. Doran, 205-21. Second edition, revised and augmented. Collected Works of Bernard Lonergan 4. Toronto: University of Toronto Press, 1988.

Method in Theology. The Problem. External Factors. LRI Archives, folder entitled 'Various Papers.' Notes (14 pp.) pertaining to the Summer Institute on The Method in Theology, Georgetown University, Washington, 13–17 July 1964 (cf. appendix A). Unpublished.

Method in Theology – Internal Problems. LRI Archives, folder entitled 'Various Papers.' Notes (5 pp.) pertaining to the Summer Institute on The Method in Theology, Georgetown University, Washington, 13–17 July 1964 (cf. appendix A). Unpublished.

Positive Theology. LRI Archives, folder entitled 'Various Papers.' Notes (1 p.) pertaining to the Summer Institute on The Method in Theology, Georgetown University, Washington, 13–17 July 1964 (cf. appendix A). Unpublished.

Dogmatic Theology. LRI Archives, folder entitled 'Various Papers.' Notes (2 pp.) pertaining to the Summer Institute on The Method in Theology, Georgetown University, Washington, 13–17 July 1964 (cf. appendix A). Unpublished.

Development of Dogma. LRI Archives, folder entitled 'Various Papers.' Notes (1 p.) pertaining to the Summer Institute on The Method in Theology, Georgetown University, Washington, 13–17 July 1964 (cf. appendix A). Unpublished.

The Method of Theology. Summer Institute at Georgetown University, Washington, 13–17 July 1964. Notes (16 pp.) taken by Sr Rose Wilker. Unpublished. [MoT 1964 Wilker]

BL's Georgetown U. Lectures: 1964. Notes (4 handwritten pp.) taken by F.E. Crowe from Lonergan's own lecture notes for the Summer Institute on The Method in Theology, Georgetown University, Washington, 13–17 July 1964. Unpublished.

Existenz and *Aggiornamento*. Lecture at Regis College, Toronto, 14 September 1964.

'*Existenz* and *Aggiornamento*.' In *Collection*, edited by Frederick E. Crowe, and Robert M. Doran, 222–31. Second edition, revised and augmented. Collected Works of Bernard Lonergan 4. Toronto: University of Toronto Press, 1988.

'History.' (pp. A.1–3.) LRI Archives, file marked 'Various Papers.' To be dated circa 1963–64. Unpublished.

'Historical Understanding.' (pp. B.1–4.) LRI Archives, file marked 'Various Papers.' To be dated circa 1963–64. Unpublished.

1965

'Subject and Soul.' *Philippine Studies* 13 (1965) 576–85.

Published as the introduction to *Verbum: Word and Idea in Aquinas*, edited by David B. Burrell, vii–xv. Notre Dame: University of Notre Dame Press, 1967.

Folder entitled 'MiT 1965.' LRI Archives Batch v.7. Handwritten and typed pages, 1965. Unpublished. [MiT 1965 Batch v.7]

Folder entitled 'Method in Theology 1965.' LRI Archives Batch v.10. Handwritten and typed pages, 1965. Unpublished. [Mit 1965 Batch v.10]

Conversazioni con Bernard Lonergan. Transcript of interviews conducted by G.B. Sala, January and June 1965. Unpublished.

Dimensions of Meaning. An address in the Distinguished Lecture Series at Marquette University, 12 May 1965.

'Dimensions of Meaning.' In *Collection*, edited by Frederick E. Crowe and Robert M. Doran, 232–45. Second edition, revised and augmented. Collected Works of Bernard Lonergan 4. Toronto: University of Toronto Press, 1988.

1966

The Transition from a Classicist Worldview to Historical Mindedness. Lecture for the opening of the academic year at Regis College, Toronto, 10 September 1966.

'The Transition from a Classicist Worldview to Historical Mindedness.' In *A Second Collection: Papers by Bernard Lonergan, S.J.*, edited by William F.J. Ryan and Bernard J. Tyrrell, 1–9. Philadelphia: Westminster, 1974.

1967

Verbum: Word and Idea in Aquinas. Edited by David B. Burrell. Notre Dame: University of Notre Dame Press, 1967.

Collection: Papers by Bernard Lonergan, S.J. Edited by Frederick E. Crowe. London: Darton, Longman & Todd; New York: Herder & Herder, 1967.

Collection. Edited by Frederick E. Crowe and Robert M. Doran. Second edition, revised and augmented. Collected Works of Bernard Lonergan 4. Toronto: University of Toronto Press, 1988. [1C]

'The Dehellenization of Dogma.' A review of Leslie Dewart, *The Future of Belief: Theism in a World Come of Age* (New York 1966) in *Theological Studies* 28 (1967) 336–51.

'The Dehellenization of Dogma.' In *A Second Collection: Papers by Bernard Lonergan, S.J.*, edited by William F.J. Ryan and Bernard J. Tyrrell, 11–32. Philadelphia: Westminster, 1974.

Responses to questions raised in a symposium on 'Bernard Lonergan's Theory of Inquiry vis-à-vis American Thought,' held at the University of Notre Dame, Indiana, as part of the American Catholic Philosophical Association's annual convention, 28–29 March 1967.

'Theories of Inquiry: Responses to a Symposium.' In *A Second Collection: Papers by Bernard Lonergan, S.J.*, edited by William F.J. Ryan, and Bernard J. Tyrrell, 33–42. Philadelphia: Westminster, 1974.

'Theology in Its New Context.' Paper at the Congress of the Theology of Renewal of the Church: Centenary of Canada, 1867–1967, Toronto, 20–25 August 1967.

'Theology in Its New Context.' In *A Second Collection: Papers by Bernard Lonergan, S.J.*, edited by William F.J. Ryan and Bernard J. Tyrrell, 55–67. Philadelphia: Westminster, 1974.

'Bernard Lonergan, s.j. *Theology in Its New Context.* La Théologie dans son nouveau contexte' (Participation in discussion after presentation of paper). In *Discussions. Congress on the Theology of Renewal of the Church. August 20 to 25, 1967,* edited by Laurence K. Shook, 5–8. Toronto: Pontifical Institute of Medieval Studies, 1968.

'MiT Ch. 1: The New Context.' (61 typed pp., numbered 1–61.) LRI Archives Batch VI.1.a. Probable date 1967. Unpublished.

'MiT II: The Tasks of Theology.' (45 typed pp., numbered 1–14, with repetitions, false starts, and missing pages.) LRI Archives Batch X.5. Pre-1968: either 1966 or 1967 (cf. appendix A). Unpublished.

'MiT III: Horizons.' (79 typed pp, numbered 1–79.) LRI Archives Batch VI.1.b. Probable date 1967 (cf. appendix A). Unpublished.

'MiT III: Horizons and Categories.' (Contents + 37 typed pp, numbered 1–37.) LRI Archives Batch VI.6. Probable date 1967 (cf. appendix A). Unpublished.

1968

'MiT VII. The Tasks of Theology.' (62 typed pp.). LRI Archives Batch VI.2. Probable date 1968 (cf. appendix A). Unpublished. ['MiT VII']

'MiT VII.' (44 typed pp., beginning with p. 13). LRI Archives Batch XI.11. Probable date 1968 (cf. appendix A). Unpublished.

'MiT VII.4. Dialectic.' Fragment (3 typed pp., numbered 63–65). LRI Archives Batch VIII.17.e. Probable date 1968 (cf. appendix A). Unpublished.

Horizons and Categories (14 typed pp.). Cf. LRI Archives Lonergan Papers folder 307, 'MT Boston Summaries.' 1968 (cf. appendix A). Unpublished.

'Ch. IX. Historians and Cognitional Theory.' (Pp. numbered 63–82). LRI Archives Batch XI.11. Probable date 1968 (cf. appendix A). Unpublished.

'Ch. IX. History and Dialectic.' (Pp. numbered 1–32). LRI Archives Batch X.12. Probable date 1968 or early 1969 (cf. appendix A). Unpublished.

'MiT X. Chapter Ten. Dialectic and Foundations.' (Pp. numbered 1–15). LRI Archives Batch VI.5. Probable date 1968 or early 1969 (cf. appendix A). Unpublished.

The Absence of God in Modern Culture. Lecture at the University of St. Michael's College, Toronto, 15 February 1968.

'The Absence of God in Modern Culture.' In *A Second Collection: Papers by Bernard Lonergan, S.J.*, edited by William F.J. Ryan and Bernard J. Tyrrell, 101–16. Philadelphia: Westminster, 1974.

The Subject. The Aquinas Lecture for 1968, Marquette University, Milwaukee, 3 March 1968.

'The Subject.' In *A Second Collection: Papers by Bernard Lonergan, S.J.*, edited by William F.J. Ryan and Bernard J. Tyrrell, 69–86. Philadelphia: Westminster, 1974.

The Future of Thomism. Lecture at St Paul's Seminary, Pittsburgh, Pa., 15 March 1968.

'The Future of Thomism.' In *A Second Collection: Papers by Bernard Lonergan, S.J.*, edited by William F.J. Ryan and Bernard J. Tyrrell, 43–53. Philadelphia: Westminster, 1974.

'Belief: Today's Issue.' A paper prepared for the Pax Romana Symposium on Faith. Synod Hall, Pittsburgh, 16 March 1968.

'Belief: Today's Issue.' In *A Second Collection: Papers by Bernard Lonergan, S.J.*, edited by William F.J.Ryan and Bernard J. Tyrrell, 87–99. Philadelphia: Westminster, 1974.

'Natural Knowledge of God.' Paper at the CTSA Convention, Washington, DC, June 1968.

'Natural Knowledge of God.' In *A Second Collection: Papers by Bernard Lonergan, S.J.*, edited by William F.J.Ryan and Bernard J. Tyrrell, 117–33. Philadelphia: Westminster, 1974.

Transcendental Philosophy and the Study of Religion. Institute at Boston College, Boston, 3–12 July 1968.

Transcendental Philosophy and the Study of Religion. Institute at Boston College, Boston, 3–12 July 1968. Transcript by Timothy Fallon from tapes of lectures. Unpublished.

Transcendental Philosophy and the Study of Religion. Institute at Boston College, Boston, 3–12 July 1968. Transcript by N. Graham from tapes of lectures. Unpublished. [TPSR Graham]

'Theology and Man's Future.' Paper at the 150th anniversary celebrations, St Louis University, 17 October 1968.

'Theology and Man's Future.' In *A Second Collection: Papers by Bernard Lonergan, S.J.*, edited by William F.J. Ryan and Bernard J. Tyrrell, 135–48. Philadelphia: Westminster, 1974.

1969

'Functional Specialties in Theology.' *Gregorianum* 50 (1969) 485–504.

'Religious Commitment.' In *Theological Folia of Villanova University. Speculative Studies*, II, edited by Joseph Papin, 193–217. Villanova: Villanova University Press, 1969.

History. Lecture followed by discussion at the Thomas More Institute, Montreal, 24 February 1969. LRI Library file 505, 'History.' Transcript by N. Graham of Questions and Answers. Unpublished.

The Alerted Mind: Theology and Other Disciplines. Lecture at the Thomas More Institute, Montreal, 25 February 1969.

'Since Writing *Insight*. Extract from a Lecture by Bernard Lonergan Followed by an Interview. In the course, *The Alerted Mind*, TMI, February 25, 1969.' In Eric O'Connor, *Curiosity at the Center of One's Life*, 371–84. Montreal: Thomas More Institute, 1987 (?).

Meaning as a Category for Interpretation. Lecture in the Symposium on Hermeneutics at the Catholic University of America, Washington, DC, 25–26 April 1969. LRI Library file 511. The actual topic of the lecture seems to be 'History.' Unpublished.

'MiT x. Chapter Ten. Dialectic and Foundations.' (15 pp.) LRI Archives Batch VI.5. 1969. Unpublished.

Method in Theology. Institute at Regis College, Toronto, 7–18 July 1969. Transcript by N. Graham from tapes. Unpublished. [MiT 1969]

'Question Periods, Seminar on Method in Theology.' Transcript by N. Graham of discussions at the Institute on Method in Theology at Regis College, Toronto, 7–18 July 1969. LRI Library file 515. Unpublished.

Faith and Beliefs. Lecture at the meeting of the American Academy of Religion, Baltimore, 23 October 1969. Transcript from tape, with Response by W.C. Smith and Reply by Lonergan. Unpublished.

Hermeneutics and the Philosophy of Religion. Lecture at the Catholic University of America, 21 November 1969. LRI Archives Lonergan Papers 616, 'Hermeneutics and The Philosophy of Religion (a C.U.A. Seminar).' Unpublished.

Hermeneutics and the Philosophy of Religion. Lecture at the Catholic University of America, 21 November 1969. LRI Library file 542. Transcript by N. Graham of the last part of the lecture, presumably because only this part differs from the *Method* chapter on Interpretation. Unpublished.

'The Future of Christianity.' *Holy Cross Quarterly* (Worcester, Mass.), Winter 1969: 5–10.

'The Future of Christianity.' In *A Second Collection: Papers by Bernard Lonergan, S.J.*, edited by William F.J. Ryan and Bernard J. Tyrrell, 149-63. Philadelphia: Westminster, 1974.

1970

'The Example of Gibson Winter.' *Social Compass* (1970) 280–82.

'The Example of Gibson Winter.' In *A Second Collection: Papers by Bernard Lonergan, S.J.*, edited by William F.J. Ryan and Bernard J. Tyrrell, 189–92. Philadelphia: Westminster, 1974.

Priesthood and Apostolate. Lecture at Fusz Memorial Residence, St Louis University, 6–8 February 1970.

'The Response of the Jesuit as Priest and Apostle in the Modern World.' In *A Second Collection: Papers by Bernard Lonergan, S.J.*, edited by William F.J. Ryan and Bernard J. Tyrrell, 165–87. Philadelphia: Westminster, 1974.

'Conversazioni con B.L.' Transcript of interview conducted by G.B. Sala. Regis College, Toronto, 11 March 1970. Unpublished.

'Philosophy and Theology.' Paper (in absentia) at the convention of the American Catholic Philosophical Association, San Francisco, 30 March to 1 April 1970.

'Philosophy and Theology.' In *A Second Collection: Papers by Bernard Lonergan, S.J.*, edited by William F.J. Ryan and Bernard J. Tyrrell, 193–208. Philadelphia: Westminster, 1974.

'Bernard Lonergan Responds.' In *Foundations of Theology: Papers from the International Lonergan Congress, 1970*, edited by Philip McShane 223–35, 256–57. Dublin: Gill and Macmillan, 1971.

'Bernard Lonergan Responds.' In *Language Truth and Meaning: Papers from the International Lonergan Congress, 1970*, edited by Philip McShane, 306–12. Dublin: Gill and Macmillan, 1972.

'Bernard Lonergan Comments.' Prepared for a projected third volume of papers from the International Lonergan Congress, 1970. Unpublished.

Interview at the First International Lonergan Congress, Florida, 1970.

'An Interview with Fr. Bernard Lonergan.' In *A Second Collection: Papers by Bernard Lonergan, S.J.*, edited by William F.J. Ryan and Bernard J. Tyrrell, 209–30. Philadelphia: Westminster, 1974.

Method in Theology. Institute at Boston College, Boston, 15–26 June 1970. Transcript by N. Graham, Toronto, 1984. Unpublished. [MiT 1970]

Merging Horizons: System, Common Sense, Scholarship. Lecture at the University of Toronto in series on Hermeneutics, 3 November 1970.

'Merging Horizons: System, Common Sense, Scholarship.' *Cultural Hermeneutics* (Boston College) 1 (1973) 87–99.

1971

Doctrinal Pluralism. Milwaukee: Marquette University Press, 1971.

Grace and Freedom: Operative Grace in the Thought of St. Thomas Aquinas. Edited by J. Patout Burns. London: Darton, Longman & Todd; New York: Herder and Herder, 1971. [GF]

Method in Theology. London: Darton, Longman & Todd; New York: Herder and Herder, 1972. The text was ready by March 1971.

Method in Theology. Toronto: University of Toronto Press, 1990. [MT]

Conversation with Eric O'Connor, 30 March 1971.

'With *Method in Theology* Ready to Print. In the final session of the course *The Dia-*

lectics of Reconciliation, TMI, March 30, 1971.' In Eric O'Connor, *Curiosity at the Center of One's Life*, 385–401. Montreal: Thomas More Institute, 1987 (?).

Method in Theology. Institute at Milltown Park, Dublin, 2–14 August 1971. Transcribed and edited by N. Graham, Lonergan Center, Regis College, Toronto, 1985. Unpublished. [MiT 1971]

LRI Archives Lonergan Papers 122, 'Method.' Handwritten notes pertaining to the Institute on Method in Theology, Milltown Park, Dublin, 2–14 August 1971. Unpublished.

'Grace after Faculty Psychology.' Conversation with Eric O'Connor, 30 December 1971.

'Grace after Faculty Psychology. Interview in the course, *Fields of Action*, TMI, December 30, 1971.' In Eric O'Connor, *Curiosity at the Center of One's Life*, 402–13. Montreal: Thomas More Institute, 1987 (?).

1972

LRI Archives, Lonergan Papers 502, 'USF 1972 Theology Summer School.' Notes for series of weekly lectures on Method in Theology during period as Scholar in Residence at the University of San Francisco, 1972. Unpublished.

What Are Judgments of Value? Third of three lectures in seminar on Technology and Culture, at the Massachusetts Institute of Technology, 8 May 1972. Unpublished.

'The Revolution in Catholic Theology.' Paper at the joint meeting of the CTSA and the CTS, Los Angeles, 2 September 1972.

'Revolution in Catholic Theology.' In *A Second Collection: Papers by Bernard Lonergan, S.J.*, edited by William F.J. Ryan and Bernard J. Tyrrell, 231–38. Philadelphia: Westminster 1974.

The Origins of Christian Realism. Seventeenth Annual Bellarmine Lecture, St Louis University School of Divinity, 27 September 1972.

'The Origins of Christian Realism.' In *A Second Collection: Papers by Bernard Lonergan, S.J.*, edited by William F.J. Ryan and Bernard J. Tyrrell, 239–61. Philadelphia: Westminster 1974.

The Relationship of the Philosophy of God and the Functional Specialty, Systematic Theology. 1972 Inaugural lectures in the St Michael's Lecture Series, Gonzaga University, Spokane, Washington, 8, 9, 10 December 1972.

Philosophy of God, and Theology: The Relationship between Philosophy of God and the Functional Specialty, Systematics. Philadelphia: Westminster, 1973. [PGT]

1973

'Lonergan's notion of religious experience; the possibility (or impossibility) of a philosophy of religion.' Interview at Regis College, conducted by Richard Renshaw, 18 January 1973. Unpublished.

Method in Theology. LRI Library file 745. Seminar session with professors and students of McMaster University, Hamilton, at Regis College, Toronto, 6 February 1973. Unpublished.

'*Insight* Revisited.' Paper for discussion at the thirty-fifth annual convention of the Jesuit Philosophical Association, 3 April 1973, held at Collège Jean-de-Brébeuf, Montréal.

'*Insight* Revisited.' In *A Second Collection: Papers by Bernard Lonergan, S.J.*, edited by William F.J. Ryan and Bernard J. Tyrrell, 263–78. Philadelphia: Westminster 1974.

Variations in Fundamental Theology. (19 pp.) The Larkin-Stuart Lectures at Trinity College in the University of Toronto, 13 November 1973.

Cf. 'Variations in Fundamental Theology.' *Method: Journal of Lonergan Studies* 16 (1998) 5–24. Edited by Frederick E. Crowe.

Sacralization and Secularization. The Larkin-Stuart Lectures at Trinity College in the University of Toronto, 14 November 1973. LRI Library file 779. Unpublished.

The Scope of Renewal. The Larkin-Stuart Lectures at Trinity College in the University of Toronto, 15 November 1973. LRI Library file 777.

'The Scope of Renewal.' *Method: Journal of Lonergan Studies* 16 (1998) 83–101.

1974

A Second Collection: Papers by Bernard Lonergan, S.J., edited by William F.J. Ryan and Bernard J. Tyrrell. Philadelphia: Westminster, 1974.

'Variations in Fundamental Theology.' St Thomas More Lectures 1974, Strathcona Hall, New Haven, CT. 12 February 1974. Note that the conclusion of this lecture (pp. 25–28) differs significantly from the conclusion of the 1973 version of the same lecture (pp. 18–19).

'Variations in Fundamental Theology.' *Method: Journal of Lonergan Studies* 16 (1998) 5–24. Edited by Frederick E. Crowe.

Method: Trend and Variations. A lecture to the Southwestern Regional Joint Meeting of the societies affiliated with the Council on the Study of Religion, Austin College, Sherman, TX, 15 March 1974.

'Method: Trend and Variations.' In *A Third Collection: Papers by Bernard J.F. Loner-*

gan, S.J., edited by Frederick E. Crowe, 13–22. Mahwah, NJ: Paulist Press; London: Geoffrey Chapman, 1985.

Dialogue (question sessions) at the Lonergan Workshop, with the theme Faith and the Crisis of Our Culture. Boston College, 17–21 June 1974. Transcript by Philip and Fiona McShane. Unpublished.

'Mission and the Spirit.' Paper prepared for *Concilium* and ready before November 1974. (It appears in translation in the Spanish issue of *Concilium*, Madrid, November 1974, pp. 203–15.)

'Mission and the Spirit.' In *A Third Collection: Papers by Bernard J.F. Lonergan, S.J.*, edited by Frederick E. Crowe, 23–34. Mahwah, NJ: Paulist Press; London: Geoffrey Chapman, 1985.

Aquinas Today: Tradition and Innovation. A lecture in the series A Colloquy on Medieval Religious Thought, University of Chicago, 8 November 1974.

'Aquinas Today: Tradition and Innovation.' In *A Third Collection: Papers by Bernard J.F. Lonergan, S.J.*, edited by Frederick E. Crowe, 35–54. Mahwah, NJ: Paulist Press; London: Geoffrey Chapman, 1985.

1975

'Prolegomena to the Study of the Emerging Religious Consciousness of Our Time.' Paper presented at the Second International Symposium on Belief, Baden/Vienna, January 1975.

'Prolegomena to the Study of the Emerging Religious Consciousness of Our Time.' In *A Third Collection: Papers by Bernard J. F. Lonergan, S.J.*, edited by Frederick E. Crowe, 55–73. Mahwah, NJ: Paulist Press; London: Geoffrey Chapman, 1985.

Christology Today: Methodological Reflections. A lecture at the Colloque de Christologie, Université Laval, Quebec, 22 March 1975.

'Christology Today: Methodological Reflections.' In *A Third Collection: Papers by Bernard J.F. Lonergan, S.J.*, edited by Frederick E. Crowe, 74–99. Mahwah, NJ: Paulist Press; London: Geoffrey Chapman, 1985.

Healing and Creating in History. A lecture in the series Anniversary Lectures, the Thomas More Institute, Montreal, 13 May 1975.

'Healing and Creating in History.' In *A Third Collection: Papers by Bernard J.F. Lonergan, S.J.*, edited by Frederick E. Crowe, 100–109. Mahwah, NJ: Paulist Press; London: Geoffrey Chapman, 1985.

Dialogue (question sessions) at the Lonergan Workshop, with the theme Values and Cultural Crisis. Boston College, Boston, 16–20 June 1975. Transcript. Unpublished.

'August 26, 1975: Prof. Vertin's Questions.' (1 p.) Autograph typescript of answers to questions by Michael Vertin, August 1975. LRI Library file 855. Unpublished.

Il metodo in teologia. Italian translation of *Method in Theology* by Giovanni B. Sala. Brescia: Editrice Queriniana, 1975, 1985.

1976

The Way to Nicea: The Dialectical Development of Trinitarian Theology. Translated by Conn O'Donovan. London: Darton, Longman & Todd, 1976, 1982. Trans. of first part (pp. 17–112) of *De Deo trino: I*, 1964. With 'Foreword' by Lonergan, pp. vii–viii, dated April 1976. [WN]

Reply to a questionnaire about the study of philosophy, in preparation for a Jesuit symposium on the topic. 1976.

'Questionnaire on Philosophy.' *Method: Journal of Lonergan Studies* 2:2 (1984) 1–35. ['Questionnaire']

Religious Studies and Theology. The Donald Mathers Memorial Lectures, given at Queen's University, Kingston, Ontario. Religious Experience, 2 March; Religious Knowledge, 3 March; The Ongoing Genesis of Methods, 4 March 1976.

'Preface' and 'First Lecture: Religious Experience'; 'Second Lecture: Religious Knowledge'; 'Third Lecture: The Ongoing Genesis of Methods.' In *A Third Collection: Papers by Bernard J.F. Lonergan, S.J.*, edited by Frederick E. Crowe, 113–28; 129–45; 146–65. Mahwah, NJ: Paulist Press; London: Geoffrey Chapman, 1985.

Dialogue (question sessions) at the Lonergan Workshop, with the theme Theology as Public Discourse. Boston College, Boston, 14–18 June 1976. Unpublished transcript.

'The Human Good.' Paper at the 1976 conference of the Institute of Human Values, Saint Mary's University, Halifax, 8–10 September 1976.

'The Human Good.' *Humanitas* (Duquesne University) 15 (1979) 113–26.

1977

Response to a questionnaire sent to Lonergan by Harper & Row in 1977 when they were preparing their 1978 edition of *Insight*.

'Lonergan's Own Account of Insight.' *Lonergan Studies Newsletter* 12 (1991) 22–24.

Natural Right and Historical Mindedness. A lecture at the Fifty-first Annual Meeting of the American Catholic Philosophical Association, Detroit, 16 April 1977.

'Natural Right and Historical Mindedness.' In *A Third Collection: Papers by Bernard*

J.F. Lonergan, S.J., edited by Frederick E. Crowe, 169–83. Mahwah, NJ: Paulist Press; London: Geoffrey Chapman, 1985.

Theology and Praxis. A lecture at the Thirty-second Annual Convention of the Catholic Theological Society of America, Toronto, 16 June 1977.

'Theology and Praxis.' In *A Third Collection: Papers by Bernard J.F. Lonergan, S.J.*, edited by Frederick E. Crowe, 184–201. Mahwah, NJ: Paulist Press; London: Geoffrey Chapman, 1985.

Dialogue (question sessions) at the Lonergan Workshop, with the theme New Christian Vision. Boston College, Boston, 20–24 June 1977. Transcript by N. Graham. Unpublished.

Participation in the symposium The Question as Commitment. Thomas More Institute, Montreal, 23–24 September 1977.

The Question as Commitment: A Symposium. Edited by Elaine Cahn and Cathleen Going. Montreal: Thomas More Institute, 1979.

1978

'Foreword' to Matthew L. Lamb, *History, Method and Theology: A Dialectical Comparison of Wilhelm Dilthey's Critique of Historical Reason and Bernard Lonergan's Meta-Methodology*, ix–xii. Missoula, MT: Scholars Press (for the American Academy of Religion Dissertation Series), 1978.

'Philosophy and the Religious Phenomenon.' LRI Archives Lonergan Papers 725. Early 1978 or late 1977.

'Philosophy and the Religious Phenomenon.' *Method: Journal of Lonergan Studies* 12 (1994) 121–46.

'Reality, Myth, Symbol.' Paper at Boston University, 29 March 1978, contributing to a series sponsored by the Boston University Institute for Philosophy and Religion.

'Reality, Myth, Symbol.' In *Myth, Symbol, and Reality*, edited by Alan M. Olson, 31–37. Notre Dame, IN: University of Notre Dame Press, 1980.

Dialogue (question sessions) at the Lonergan Workshop, with the theme At the Edge of Political Power. Boston College, Boston, 12–17 June 1978. Unpublished transcript.

1979

Response to William Dych's paper 'Method in Theology According to Karl Rahner,' 29 March 1979.

'A Response to Fr. Dych.' In *Theology and Discovery: Essays in Honor of Karl*

Rahner, edited by W.J. Kelly, 54–57. Milwaukee: Marquette University Press, 1980.

Horizons and Transpositions. Transcript of lecture at Lonergan Workshop, with the theme Crisis of Liberal Education. Boston College, Boston, 21 June 1979. LRI Library file 963-2a. Unpublished.

Dialogue (question sessions) at the Lonergan Workshop, with the theme Crisis of Liberal Education. Boston College, Boston, 18–22 June 1979. Unpublished transcript.

1980

Method in Theology. Course given at Boston College, Fall semester, 1979–80.

'Method Theology Seminar 1980.' Handwritten notes. LRI Archives Lonergan Papers 776.

Conversation with Lonergan, 28 March 1980.

'Bernard Lonergan in Conversation. With Eric O'Connor, Patricia Coonan, Charlotte Tansey, Roberta and Stan Machnik, Montreal. March 28, 1980.' In R. Eric. O'Connor, *Curiosity at the Center of One's Life*, 414–38. Montreal: Thomas More Institute, 1987 (?).

A Post-Hegelian Philosophy of Religion. Lecture at the seventh annual Lonergan Workshop, Boston College, June 1980.

'A Post-Hegelian Philosophy of Religion.' In *A Third Collection: Papers by Bernard J.F. Lonergan, S.J.*, edited by Frederick E. Crowe, 202–23. Mahwah, NJ: Paulist Press; London: Geoffrey Chapman, 1985.

Dialogue (question sessions) at the Lonergan Workshop, with the theme Healing and Creating in History: The New Community. Boston College, Boston, 16–20 June 1980. Unpublished.

1981

Interviews with Lonergan, 16–20 February 1981.

Caring about Meaning: Patterns in the Life of Bernard Lonergan. Transcript of above interviews edited by Pierrot Lambert, Charlotte Tansey, and Cathleen Going. Montreal: Thomas More Institute, 1982.

Pope John's Intention. A lecture given at the eighth annual Lonergan Workshop, Boston College, Boston, June 1981.

'Pope John's Intention.' In *A Third Collection: Papers by Bernard J.F. Lonergan, S.J.*, edited by Frederick E. Crowe, 224–38. Mahwah, NJ: Paulist Press; London: Geoffrey Chapman, 1985.

1982

Interview with Lonergan in 1982, conducted by Pierre Robert.

'Théologie et vie spirituelle. Rencontre avec Bernard Lonergan.' *Science et Esprit* 38 (1986) 331–41.

Interviews with Lonergan, 20 May 1982.

Caring about Meaning: Patterns in the Life of Bernard Lonergan. Transcript of above interviews edited by Pierrot Lambert, Charlotte Tansey, and Cathleen Going. Montreal: Thomas More Institute, 1982.

Unity and Plurality: The Coherence of Christian Truth. A lecture given at the ninth annual Lonergan Workshop, Boston College, Boston, 17 June 1982.

'Unity and Plurality: The Coherence of Christian Truth.' In *A Third Collection: Papers by Bernard J.F. Lonergan, S.J.*, edited by Frederick E. Crowe, 239–50. Mahwah, NJ: Paulist Press; London: Geoffrey Chapman, 1985.

Drafts of replies for discussions at the Lonergan Workshop, Boston College, Boston, June 1982. LRI Archives file 'Lonergan Workshop 82, 778b [JH], 1982. Unpublished.

1984

'Questionnaire on Philosophy.' *Method: Journal of Lonergan Studies* 2:2 (1984) 1–35.

1985

'The Original Preface to Insight.' *Method: Journal of Lonergan Studies* 3:1 (1985) 3–7.

A Third Collection: Papers by Bernard J.F. Lonergan, S.J. Edited by Frederick E. Crowe. New York/Mahwah, NJ: Paulist Press; London: Geoffrey Chapman, 1985. [3C]

1988

Collection. Edited by Frederick E. Crowe and Robert M. Doran. Second edition, revised and augmented. Collected Works of Bernard Lonergan 4. Toronto: University of Toronto Press, 1988. [1C]

1990

Understanding and Being: The Halifax Lectures on Insight. Edited by Elizabeth A. Morelli and Mark D. Morelli. Revised and augmented by Frederick E. Crowe with the collaboration of Elizabeth A. Morelli, Mark D. Morelli, Robert M. Doran, and Thomas V. Daly. Collected Works of Bernard Lonergan 5. Toronto: University of Toronto Press, 1990. [UB]

1991

'Lonergan's Own Account of Insight.' *Lonergan Studies Newsletter* 12 (1991) 22–24.

1992

'Method in Catholic Theology.' *Method: Journal of Lonergan Studies* 10:1 (1992) 1–26. [The Nottingham lecture]

Insight: A Study of Human Understanding. Fifth edition. Edited by Frederic E. Crowe and Robert M. Doran. Collected Works of Bernard Lonergan 3. Toronto: University of Toronto Press, 1992. [INCW]

1993

Topics in Education: The Cincinnati Lectures of 1959 on the Philosophy of Education. Edited by Robert M. Doran and Frederick E. Crowe, revising and augmenting the unpublished text prepared by James Quinn and John Quinn. Collected Works of Bernard Lonergan 10. Toronto: Univerity of Toronto Press, 1993. [TE]

1994

'Philosophy and the Religious Phenomenon.' *Method: Journal of Lonergan Studies* 12 (1994) 121–46.

1996

Philosophical and Theological Papers 1958–1964. Edited by Robert C. Croken, Frederick E. Crowe, and Robert M. Doran. Collected Works of Bernard Lonergan 6. Toronto: University of Toronto Press, 1996 [PTP]

1997

Verbum: Word and Idea in Aquinas. Edited by Frederick E. Crowe and Robert M. Doran. Collected Works of Bernard Lonergan 2. Toronto: University of Toronto Press, 1997.

1998

'Variations in Fundamental Theology.' *Method: Journal of Lonergan Studies* 16 (1998) 5–24. Edited by Frederick E. Crowe.

'The Scope of Renewal.' *Method: Journal of Lonergan Studies* 16 (1998) 83–101.

2   Secondary Sources

The following is largely a list of studies on Lonergan consulted for the present work, but it includes also a few of Lonergan's own sources and some items on hermeneutics.

Bonsor, Jack A. 'Irreducible Pluralism: The Transcendental and Hermeneutical as Theological Options.' *Horizons (CTS)* 16 (1989) 316–27.
Brennan, Larry. 'The Functional Specialty Dialectic: Bernard Lonergan's Method and Theological Disputes.' Doctoral dissertation, Pontifical University of St Thomas (Angelicum), Rome, 1982.
Congar, M.-J. 'Théologie.' In *Dictionnaire de théologie catholique*, 15/1: col. 341–502. Paris: Letouzey et Ané, 1946.
Conley, Peter V. 'The Development of the Notion of Hermeneutics in the Works of Bernard J. Lonergan, S.J.' Doctoral dissertation, Catholic University of America, Washington, 1973.
Crowe, Frederick E. '"All my work has been introducing history into Catholic theology" (Lonergan, March 28, 1980).' *Lonergan Workshop* 10, edited by Fred Lawrence, 49–81. Boston: Boston College, 1994.
– *Appropriating the Lonergan Idea*. Edited by Michael Vertin. Washington: Catholic University of America Press, 1989.
– 'Bernard Lonergan.' In *Modern Theologians: Christians and Jews*, edited by Thomas E. Bird, 126–51. Notre Dame, London: University of Notre Dame Press; New York: Association Press, c. 1967.
– 'But Is There a Fault in the Very Foundations?' *Continuum* 7 (1969) 323–31.
– 'Creativity and Method: Index to a Movement. A Review-Article.' *Science et Esprit* 34 (1982) 107-13.
– 'Development of Doctrine: Aid or Barrier to Christian Unity?' *Proceedings: Catholic Theological Society of America* 21 (1966) 1–20.
– 'Development of Doctrine.' *American Ecclesiastical Review* 159 (1968) 233–47.
– 'Doctrines and Historicity in the Context of Lonergan's Method.' *Theological Studies* 38 (1977) 115–24.
– 'Dogma versus the Self-Correcting Process of Learning.' In *Foundations of Theology*, edited by Philip McShane. Dublin: Gill and Macmillan, 1971.
– 'Early Jottings on Bernard Lonergan's Method in Theology.' *Science et Esprit (Sciences Ecclésiastiques)* 25 (1973) 121–38.
– 'The Exigent Mind: Bernard Lonergan's Intellectualism.' In F.E. Crowe, ed., *Spirit as Inquiry: Studies in Honor of Bernard Lonergan, S.J.* Chicago: Saint Xavier College, 1964.
– '*Insight*: Genesis and Ongoing Context.' In *Lonergan Workshop* 8, edited by Fred Lawrence, 61–83. Atlanta: Scholars Press, 1990.
– *Lonergan*. Collegeville, MN: The Liturgical Press, 1992.
– *The Lonergan Enterprise*. Cambridge, MA: Cowley, 1980.
– 'Lonergan's Early Use of Analogy. A Research Note – With Reflections.' *Method: Journal of Lonergan Studies* 1:1 (1983) 31–46.
– 'Lonergan's Search for Foundations: The Early Years, 1940–1959.' In *Searching for Cultural Foundations*, edited by Philip McShane, 113–39. Lanham, MD; London: University Press of America, c. 1984.

- *Method in Theology: An Organon for Our Time.* Milwaukee: Marquette University Press, 1980.
- 'On the Method of Theology.' *Theological Studies* 23 (1962) 637–42.
- 'A Note on Lonergan's Dissertation and Its Introductory Pages.' *Method: Journal of Lonergan Studies* 3:2 (1985) 1–8.
- 'A Note on the Prefaces of *Insight*.' *Method: Journal of Lonergan Studies* 3:1 (1985) 1–3.
- 'Pull of the Future and Link with the Past: On the Need for Theological Method.' *Continuum* 7 (1969) 30–49.
- 'St. Thomas and the Isomorphism of Human Knowing and Its Proper Object.' *Sciences Ecclésiastiques* 13 (1961) 167–90.
- *Theology of the Christian Word: A Study in History.* New York: Paulist Press, 1978.
- 'Transcendental Deduction: A Lonerganian Meaning and Use.' *Method: Journal of Lonergan Studies* 2:1 (1984) 21–40.
- 'Transcultural Process and the Structure of *Insight*: Isomorphic?' Paper delivered at the Lonergan Workshop, Boston College, 15–19 June 1992. Unpublished.

Delaney, Hubert. 'From "Viewpoint" in *Insight* to "Horizon" in *Method in Theology*.' *Milltown Studies* (1983) 11: 75–98; 12: 45–60.

De Marneffe, J. 'Lonergan's *Method in Theology* and Its Relevance for Theologizing in India.' In *Theologizing in India: Selection of Papers Presented at the Seminar Held in Poona on October 26–30, 1978*, edited by M. Amaladoss, T.K. John, and G. Gispert-Sauch, 116–33. Bangalore: Theological Publications in India, 1981.

Doran, Robert M. 'The Analogy of Dialectic and the Systematics of History.' In *Religion in Context: Recent Studies in Lonergan*, edited by Timothy P. Fallon, and Philip Boo Riley, 35–57. Lanham, MD: University Press of America, 1988.
- 'Duality and Dialectic.' In *Lonergan Workshop* 7, edited by Fred Lawrence, 59–84. Atlanta: Scholars Press, 1988.
- 'From Psychic Conversion to the Dialectic of Community.' In *Lonergan Workshop* 6, edited by Fred Lawrence, 35–107. Atlanta: Scholars Press, 1986.
- 'Psychic Conversion and Lonergan's Hermeneutics.' In *Lonergan's Hermeneutics: Its Development and Application*, edited by Sean E. McEvenue and Ben F. Meyer, 161–208. Washington: Catholic University of America Press, 1989.
- *Psychic Conversion and Theological Foundations: Toward a Reorientation of the Human Sciences.* Chico, CA: Scholars Press, 1981.
- 'Self-Knowledge and the Interpretation of Imaginal Expression.' *Method: Journal of Lonergan Studies* 4 (1986) 55–84.
- 'Subject, Psyche, and Theology's Foundations.' *Journal of Religion* 57 (1977) 267–87.
- *Theology and the Dialectics of History.* Toronto: University of Toronto Press, 1990.

Duplessy, Eugenio. *Apologetica.* 3 vols. Rome: Francesco Ferrari Editore; Turin: Soc. Edit. Internazionale, 1929.

Ebeling, Gerhard. 'Die Bedeutung der historisch-kritischen Methode für die protestantische Theologie und Kirche.' *Zeitschrift für Theologie und Kirche* 47 (1950) 1–46.
Fiorenza, Francis Schüssler. 'Theology: Transcendental or Hermeneutical?' *Horizons (CTS)* 16 (1989) 329–41.
Gaetz, Ivan. 'Methodical Hermeneutics: Bernard Lonergan's Treatment of Hermeneutics and Hermeneutical Issues in *Method in Theology*.' Master's thesis, Regis College, Toronto, 1985.
Greisch, Jean. 'Bulletin de philosophie. Herméneutique et philosophie pratique.' *Revue des sciences philosophiques et théologiques* 75 (1991) 97–128.
Harrington, Joseph Warren. 'Conversion as Foundation of Theology: An Interpretation of Bernard Lonergan's Position.' Doctoral dissertation, Fordham University, New York, 1980.
Hefling Jr, Charles C. 'Lonergan on Development: *The Way to Nicea* in Light of His More Recent Methodology.' Doctoral dissertation, Andover Newton Theological School – Boston College, 1982.
– 'The Meaning of God Incarnate according to Friedrich Schleiermacher; or, Whether Lonergan Is Appropriately Regarded as "A Schleiermacher for Our Time," and Why Not.' In *Lonergan Workshop* 7, edited by Fred Lawrence, 105–78. Atlanta: Scholars Press, 1988.
– 'On Reading *The Way to Nicea*.' In *Religion and Culture: Essays in Honor of Bernard Lonergan s.j.*, edited by Timothy P. Fallon and Philip Boo Riley, 149–66. Albany: State University of New York Press, 1987.
– 'Redemption and Intellectual Conversion: Notes on Lonergan's "Christology Today."' *Lonergan Workshop* 5, edited by Fred Lawrence, 219–61. Chico, CA: Scholars Press, 1985.
– 'Turning Liberalism Inside Out.' A review of George Lindbeck's *The Nature of Doctrine*. In *Method: Journal of Lonergan Studies* 3 (1985) 51–69.
– 'On Understanding Salvation History.' In *Lonergan's Hermeneutics, its Development and Application*, edited by Sean McEvenue and Ben F. Meyer, 221–75. Washington: The Catholic University of America Press, 1989.
Hughes, Glenn. 'A Critique of "Lonergan's Notion of Dialectic" by Ron McKinney.' *Method: Journal of Lonergan Studies* 1 (1983) 60–73.
Kidder, Paul. 'Lonergan's Negative Dialectic.' *International Philosophical Quarterly* 30 (1990) 299–309.
Lamb, Matthew. 'William Dilthey's Critique of Historical Reason and Bernard Lonergan's Meta-methodology.' In *Language, Truth and Meaning*, edited by Philip McShane, 115–66. Dublin: Gill and Macmillan, 1972.
Lapointe, Roger. 'Hermeneutics Today.' *Biblical Theology Bulletin* 2 (1972) 107–54.
Lawrence, Fred. 'Basic Christian Community: An Issue of "Mind and the Mystery of Christ."' In *Lonergan Workshop* 5, edited by Fred Lawrence, 263–88. Chico, CA: Scholars Press, 1985.

- 'Critical Realism and the Hermeneutical Revolution.' Paper at the Lonergan Workshop, Boston College, 1990. Unpublished.
- 'Elements of Basic Communication.' In *Lonergan Workshop* 6, edited by Fred Lawrence, 127–42. Atlanta: Scholars Press, 1986.
- 'The Fragility of Consciousness: Lonergan and the Postmodern Concern for the Other.' *Theological Studies* 54 (1993) 55–94.
- 'Gadamer and Lonergan: A Dialectical Comparison.' *International Philosophical Quarterly* 20 (1980) 25–47.
- 'The Human Good and Christian Conversion.' In *Searching for Cultural Foundations*, edited by Philip McShane, 86–112. Washington: University Press of America, 1984.
- 'Language as Horizon?' In *The Beginning and the Beyond: Papers from the Gadamer and Voegelin Conferences*. Supplementary issue of *Lonergan Workshop* 4, edited by Fred Lawrence, 13–34. Atlanta: Scholars Press, 1989.
- 'Lonergan as Political Theologian.' In *Religion in Context: Recent Studies in Lonergan*, edited by Timothy P. Fallon and Philip Boo Riley, 1–21. Lanham, MD: University Press of America, 1988.
- 'Method and Theology as Hermeneutical.' In *Creativity and Method: Essays in Honor of Bernard Lonergan s.j.*, edited by Matthew L. Lamb, 79–104. Milwaukee: Marquette University Press, 1981.
- '"The Modern Philosophic Differentiation of Consciousness" or What Is the Enlightenment.' In *Lonergan Workshop* 2, edited by Fred Lawrence, 231–79. Chico, CA: Scholars Press, 1980.
- 'Political Theology and "The Longer Cycle of Decline."' In *Lonergan Workshop* 1, edited by Fred Lawrence, 223–55. Missoula, MT: Scholars Press, 1978.
- 'On the Relationship between Transcendental and Hermeneutical Approaches to Theology.' *Horizons (CTS)* 16 (1989) 342–45.
- 'A Response (I) to Gerald McCool.' *Proceedings: Catholic Theological Society of America* 32 (1977) 90–96.
- 'Self-Knowledge in History in Gadamer and Lonergan.' In *Language, Truth and Meaning: International Lonergan Congress*, edited by Philip McShane, 167–217. Dublin: Gill and Macmillan, 1972.

McCool, G.A. 'Theology and Philosophy.' *Proceedings: Catholic Theological Society of America* 32 (1977) 72–89.

McEvenue, Sean, and Ben F. Meyer, eds. *Lonergan's Hermeneutics: Its Development and Application*. Washington: Catholic University of America Press, 1989.

McKenzie, John L. 'An Exegetical Answer to Lonergan's Method in Theology.' *Listening: Journal of Religion and Culture* 10 (1975) 2–12.

McKinney, Ronald. 'The Hermeneutical Theory of Bernard Lonergan.' *International Philosophical Quarterly* 23 (1983) 277–90.
- 'Lonergan's Notion of Dialectic.' *Thomist* 46 (1982) 221–41.
- 'The Role of Dialectic in the Thought of Bernard Lonergan.' Doctoral dissertation, Fordham University, New York, 1980.

McShane, Philip. 'The Arctic Grail.' Paper delivered at the Lonergan Workshop, Boston College, 15–19 June 1992. Unpublished.
- *Process: Introducing Themselves to Young (Christian) Minders*. Halifax: Mount St Vincent University, 1989.
- 'Psychic Differentiations and Systematic Heuristics.' In *Lonergan's Hermeneutics: Its Development and Application*, edited by Sean McEvenue and Ben F. Meyer, 209–16. Washington: Catholic University of America Press, 1989.

Meyer, Ben F. *Critical Realism and the New Testament*. Allison Park, PA: Pickwick Publications, 1989.

O'Callaghan, Michael. 'Rahner and Lonergan on Foundational Theology.' In *Creativity and Method: Essays in Honor of Bernard Lonergan*, edited by Matthew Lamb, 123–39. Milwaukee: Marquette University Press, 1981.

Page, Carl. 'Philosophical Hermeneutics and Its Meaning for Philosophy.' *Philosophy Today* 35 (1991) 127–36.

Putti, Joseph. *Theology as Hermeneutics: Paul Ricoeur's Theory of Text Interpretation and Method in Theology*. Bangalore: Kristu Jyoti Publications, 1991.

Rahner, Karl. 'Some Critical Thoughts on "Functional Specialties in Theology."' In *Foundations of Theology*, edited by Philip McShane, 194–96. Dublin: Gill and Macmillan, 1971.

Rasmussen, David M. 'From Problematics to Hermeneutics: Lonergan and Ricoeur.' In *Language, Truth and Meaning*, edited by Philip McShane, 236–71. Dublin: Gill and Macmillan, 1972.

Reck, Andrew J. 'Interpretation.' *Continuum* 2 (1964) 455–63.

Riordan, Patrick. 'Reconstruction, Dialectic and Praxis.' *Method: Journal of Lonergan Studies* 9:1 (1991) 1–22.

Rosen, Stanley. 'Squaring the Hermeneutical Circle.' *Review of Metaphysics* 44 (1991) 707–28.

Sala, Giovanni B. 'L'analisi della conoscenza umana in B. Lonergan.' *La Scuola Cattolica* 94 (1966) 187–213.
- 'Aspetti filosofici del "Metodo in Teologia" di Bernard Lonergan.' *La Civiltà Cattolica* 124:1 (1973) 329–41.
- 'Aspetti teologici del "Metodo in Teologia" di Bernard Lonergan.' *La Civiltà Cattolica* 124:II (1973) 553–67.
- 'B. Lonergans Methode der Theologie.' *Theologie und Philosophie* 63 (1988) 34–59.
- 'Bernard J.F. Lonergan, S.I.: Il contributo di un teologo per una filosofia cristiana.' *Rassegna di Teologia* 26 (1985) 529–52.
- 'Bernard Lonergan, SJ: Un teologo esamina la propria mente.' *La Nottola (Pergola/Perugia)* 4 (1985) 35–50.
- 'Coscienza e intenzionalità in Bernard Lonergan.' In *Studi di filosofia trascendentale*, edited by Virgilio Melchiorre, 49–99. Milano: Vita e Pensiero, 1993.
- *Lonergan and Kant: Five Essays on Human Knowledge*. Translated by Joseph Spoerl. Edited by Robert M. Doran. Toronto: University of Toronto Press, 1994.

- '"Il Metodo in Teologia" di Bernard Lonergan.' *La Civiltà Cattolica* 123:IV (1972) 468–77.
- 'Oltre la neoscolastica, verso una nuova filosofia. Quale?' *La Scuola Cattolica* 96 (1968) 291–333.

Sala, Giovanni B., G. Blandino, and P. Pellecchia. Contribution to 'Discussione sulla causalità.' *Aquinas: Rivista internazionale di filosofia* 23 (1980) 93–113.

Schindler, David L. 'History, Objectivity, and Moral Conversion.' *The Thomist* 37 (1973) 569–88.

Shea, William M. 'The Stance and Task of the Foundational Theologian: Critical or Dogmatic?' *The Heythrop Journal* 17 (1976) 273–92.

Streeter, Carla Mae. 'Religious Love in Bernard Lonergan as Hermeneutical and Transcultural.' Doctoral dissertation, Toronto, Toronto School of Theology, 1986.
- 'Theological Categories: The Transposition Needed for Comparative Theology.' In *Lonergan Workshop* 14, edited by Fred Lawrence, 265–77. Boston: Boston College, 1998.

Surlis, Paul. 'Rahner and Lonergan on Method in Theology.' *Irish Theological Quarterly* 38 (1971) 187-201.

Swartzentruber, Paul. 'The Development of an Approach to Hermeneutic Method in the Work of Bernard Lonergan, S.J.: From *Insight* to *Method in Theology*.' Master's thesis, University of St Michael's College, Toronto, 1981.

Swift, J.E. 'Bernard Lonergan on Conversion-Faith and Critical Theological Methodology.' Doctoral dissertation, Pontifical University of St Thomas Aquinas, Rome, 1988.

Tekippe, Terry J. 'The Universal Viewpoint and the Relationship of Philosophy and Theology in the Works of Bernard Lonergan.' Doctoral dissertation, Fordham University, New York, 1972.

Tekippe, Terry J., ed. *Primary Bibliography of Lonergan Sources*. New Orleans: Notre Dame Seminary, 1990.
- *Secondary Bibliography of Lonergan Sources*. New Orleans: Notre Dame Seminary, 1988.

Tracy, David. *The Achievement of Bernard Lonergan*. New York: Herder and Herder, 1970.
- 'Horizon Analysis and Eschatology.' *Continuum* 6 (1968) 166–79.
- 'Lonergan's Foundational Theology: An Interpretation and a Critique.' In *Foundations of Theology*, edited by Philip McShane, 197–222. Dublin: Gill and Macmillan, 1971.
- 'Method as Foundation for Theology: Bernard Lonergan's Option.' *Journal of Religion* 50 (1970) 292–318.

Vertin, Michael. 'The Resurrection, Reconstructive Hermeneutics and Foundational Theology: A Discussion Summary.' *Proceedings: Catholic Theological Society of America* 40 (1985) 181–83.

Index

Abstraction, apprehensive and formative, 51, 55, 239 nn. 16, 17. See also *Intelligere*; *Intelligere, dicere*, and inner word
Agent intellect, ground of intellectual light, 24
Anachronism, 227 n. 21
Anattā, 215
Animal rationale, 72
Animal symbolicum, 72
Anthropology, new: a historicist horizon, 154; and meaning, 152
Anubhava, 215
Apologetic(s): extrinsicist, 134, 138; generalized, 175; *Insight* a contribution to, 88; and theologically transformed universal viewpoint, 209. *See also* Fundamental theology
Apprehension of man, new. *See* Anthropology, new
Appropriation: in interpretation, 54–56, 58, 63 (and self-appropriation, 59); of rational self-consciousness, 72
A priori, 31–33; for general history, 108–109, 145; Kantian, 61; marginal in *Insight*, 21; universal viewpoint an, 3; upper blade of history, 231 n. 10. *See also* Heuristic; Heuristic structure(s)
Architectonic: generalized empirical method as critical a., 212–13; metaphysics as a. science, 203; ontological wisdom as a. science, 21
Aristotle, 258 n. 66, 259 n. 6, 278 n. 54, 284 n. 99; and critical problem, 21–22; and development of positions, 70; dialectic as individual art in, 110, 187; gnoseology, limitations of, 22, 24; habits, 114; judgment, 213; knowing by identity, 22; limitations of approach, 259 n. 6; meaning organized by logic, 193; potency and formal object, 146, 209; scientific ideal incomplete, 116; self-knowledge, 23; wisdom, 12, 21, 43
Audience(s): that grasps the universal viewpoint, 66; relativity of interpretation to, 57–58, 59, 75, 83
Aufhebung: of philosophy, 126; and sublation, 266 n. 8
Augustine, St, 227 n. 21; and development of positions, 70; and judgment,

213; and vision of eternal Truth, 22
Augustinian-Aristotelian controversy, 259 n. 6
Auslegen, 163
Authenticity: achieved gradually, 138, 178; as adequate criterion, 215; as coincidence of absolute and normative horizons, 155; as coincidence of existential and originary poles, 129; and critical foundations for philosophy, 137–38; and dialectic, 177; and dialogue, 186; and existential level, 143; and foundations, 183; and general method (1962), 114; and interpretation, 162, 164, 213; major and minor, 164, 213; and new control over meaning, 152; precariousness of, 182; and transcendental method, 153

Babel of philosophies, 37
Basic context, 4, 63, 120–22; and foundations, 140, 283 n. 84; and general method (1962), 121; and protean notion of being, 122; and pure desire to know, 121; a reality that develops, 123; and stages of meaning, 124; and statement of meaning, 121; and universal viewpoint, 121, 122, 132, 211; as upper blade of method, 121–22; and upper context, 121
Becker, C., 171
Begrifflichkeit, 156, 158, 259 n. 6. *See also* Conceptuality; Categories
Being: and good, coincidence of, 127–28; and knowing, de facto coincidence of, 79; in love (kinds of, 273 n. 89; total self-surrender, 273 n. 91; unrestricted, as defined and as achieved, 183); and meaning (all-inclusive term of, 51; more basic than, 73); and notion of being, 62; universe of, 73
Being, notion of. *See* Notion of being
Being, protean notion of. *See* Notion of being, protean
Belief: critique of, 277 n. 38. *See also* Faith
Bernheim, E., 170
Bias: control over, 75, 76; and hermeneutic method, 58, 68; and human sciences, 95; and simple interpretation, 56
Blondel, M., 257 n. 64
Bouillard, H., 289 n. 86
Breakthrough, to eight functional specialties, 147, 210, 270 n. 56
Breakthrough, encirclement, confinement, 38, 44, 71, 226 n. 10
Bultmann, R., 119, 120, 122, 167, 277 n. 45, 278 n. 54
Butterfield, H., 195–96, 287 n. 41

Caeteris paribus, and critical history, 169, 172. *See also* Other things being equal
Canon(s): of explanation, 67, 119; of general method (1959), 105–107; of method, a priori, 32; of parsimony, 67, 68; of relevance, 66, 106, 119, 183 (not operative at beginning of theological method, 167; not required in dialectic, 182); of successive approximations, 67, 283 n. 75
Cassirer, E., 72, 166, 167, 257 n. 59, 278 nn. 54, 55
Categories: basic set of, in theology, 156, 157; basic set psychological, in *Method*, 191–92, 211; for communication, 120; and dialectic and foundations, 180–81; derivation of, 156, 184; descriptive and explanatory, 212; and foundations, 184; function as upper blade, 184, 202; general and special

theological c., 156–57; and human sciences, 157; imposition of current, 17; natural and supernatural, 156; neutral set of, 17, 18; special theological c. (derivation of, 7; seminally generated in dialectic, 184); and transcendental method, 167, 184; transcultural, 156. See also *Begrifflichkeit*; Conceptuality

Chasm, problem of, 105, 113

Classical culture, and shift to historical consciousness, 152

Classicist: tendency in interpretation, 123; viewpoint, and shift to methodological viewpoint, 160

Cognitional theory: base of upper blade in hermeneutics, 66; priority of, 118, 127, 144

Cognitional theory, epistemology, and metaphysics, 189–90

Collaboration: conditions for, and method, 215; new and higher (in pursuit of truth, 82; and interpretation, simple and scientific, 83, 90; and universal viewpoint, 83); scientific, in interpretation, 67

Collaborative: control, and dialectical anticipation, 76; dimension of dialectic, 184–87; enterprise, theology as, 185

Collingwood, R.G., 171

Common sense: in interpretation, 56, 58, 75; shared, and communication, 57. *See also* Hermeneutics, commonsense affair; Interpretation, commonsense affair

Common vision of a common goal, 72, 73–74

Communication: cross-cultural, 10; differentiation of, 165–68; distinct from hermeneutics, 165; expression for others, 239 n. 28; foundations of scientific, 167; and level of audience, 53; and practical insight, 51; in process of interpretation, 56–58; and resources of language, 57; and viewpoint of audience, 57. *See also* Expression; Interpretation, statement of

Comprehensive: integration, 47; view (and ecumenical foundations for theology, 174; generalized emergent probability, 46; theological, 95)

Comprehensive viewpoint: change in name, 175; and general history, 175; as goal, 8, 200; goal of dialectic, 4, 174–76; theological transformation, ongoing, 7; and universal viewpoint (*see* Universal viewpoint and comprehensive viewpoint)

Concepts: changeless, and historical theology, 93; commonsense, 238 n. 12; explanatory, 93; heuristic: 93, 238 n. 12

Conceptualism: cutting free from, 214; sterile, 215

Conceptualist illusion, 29

Conceptuality, 156, 158. *See also Begrifflichkeit*; Categories

Confrontationist model of knowing, 22, 32

Consciousness: analysis of, shift to, 88, 109, 111–12, 121, 145–46; differentiations of (*see* Differentiations of consciousness); grasp of, key to universe of meanings, 4; invariant elements in, 4; mythic, 53

Context: concrete, 71, 130, 145, 146, 211; dogmatico-theological, 115; heuristic and actual, 163; influences formulation, 40; and judgment, 40; material, hermeneutic formal, historical formal, 12, 120; nest of questions and answers, 163; new, of theology, 141, 154, 158; old and new in theol-

326   Index

ogy, 156; and remote criterion of truth, 54; understanding of, 11

Continuity: in doctrines, 105; identity in difference, 12; in knowledge, and heuristic structures, 35; principle of, provided by heuristic concepts, 93; problem of, 130

Control: over bias, 75, 76; of meaning (*see* Meaning, control of); scientific, in interpretation, 67

Conversation, and shared viewpoint, 57

Conversion, 198; and basic context, 121; coincides with living religion, 142; focus on, 114; and foundations, 179, 183, 187; as functional specialty, 140, 174; and general method, 114; intellectual, and universal viewpoint, 120; as spontaneous and as thematic, 199; and theology, 198; three types of, 131, 146; and understanding a text, 162

Coreth, E., 126, 127, 261 n. 41, 289 n. 77

Cosmopolis, 248 n. 3

Counterpositions: and dogma, revolt against, 254 n. 127; elimination of, 258 n. 64; mistaken formulations of, 40, 266 n. 43. *See also* Positions and counterpositions

Criteriological question, 21, 50

Criterion of truth: as grasp of sufficiency of evidence, a woolly notion, 240 n. 47; proximate and remote, 54, 163, 172, 173; theological, conversion as thematic, 199

Criterion of truth, remote: and context, 54; in interpretation, 68; and problem of orientation, 56; proper unfolding of desire to know, 242 n. 73; technical and non-technical, 164, 170, 172, 173; twofold authenticity, 164

Critical: attitude, and dialectic, 37; distinction between types of knowing, 37; philosophy, 122; point, and meaning of 'real,' 233 n. 52; position, full, 37, 41; theory of knowledge, 37; viewpoint, general, 37

Critical problem, 50; from above downwards, 27; and Aristotle, 21–22; and dialectical theorem, 39; and philosophy, modern type of, 137; raised in chapter 14 of *Insight*, 39; reformulation of, 26, 38, 39; and self-knowledge, 23; solution to, 24 (through generalized empirical method, 42; not automatic, 138); standard meaning of, 233 n. 52; and Thomas Aquinas, 21, 23; and wisdom, 21, 40

Critica major, 271 n. 62

Crowe, F.E., 9, 17, 225 nn. 45–48, 226 nn. 55, 1, 9, 230 nn. 113, 1, 231 n. 11, 235 nn. 102, 105, 248 n. 186, 254 n. 1, 261 nn. 41, 44, 266 n. 1, 267 n. 12, 269 n. 30, 270 n. 56, 272 n. 83, 287 n. 56, 289 n. 88; analytic-synthetic pair, 253 n. 109; breakthrough of 1965, 141, 271 n. 68; critical problem in standard sense, 234 n. 56; differentiation, meaning of, 246 n. 159; explicit metaphysics, transition to, 44; foundations, first thematization of, 133; 'heuristic' preferred over 'a priori' by Lonergan, 230–31 n. 3; metaphysics and method, 127–28

Crucial experiment, 182

Culture(s): alien, initial access to, 167; differences in, 213; Indian, Eastern, Western, 214; plurality of, 214; stages of, and self-appropriation, 104

Data: in natural science, human science, theology, 271 n. 67; theological, word of God as true, 139, 147

Definition(s): and act of defining, 238 n. 13; nominal, 238 n. 12
Denkformen, 102, 108, 263 n. 82
Denzinger theology, 277 n. 45
Descamps, A., 166
Descartes, R., 288 n. 58
Development: differentiation and integration, 268 n. 17; dogmatic, 104, 110; functional analysis of, 108, 109, 111, 118, 209; historical, general notions about, 104; of meaning, 118; ontological analysis of, 108, 111, 123–24, 208; stages of, 69, 108, 110
Dialectic: and authenticity, 177; and canon of relevance, 182; collaborative dimension of, 184–87; communitarian origins of, 110, 187; and comprehensive viewpoint, 175, 181, 187; and comprehensiveness of theology, 159, 179; and confinement, 38–39; and control of values, 177; and dialogue, 185–87, 188; and dogmatic development, 111; double application of, 184–85, 271 n. 62; and elimination of horizons, 176; and encounter, 178, 185; as functional specialty, 174, 176–79, 181–83; fundamentally within individual, 110; general form of critical attitude, 37; generalized apologetic, 175; goal and base of, 200; Hegelian, 43, 60, 71, 110; and hermeneutics of *Insight*, 183; and history, 140, 271 n. 62; of history, 111; integration, tool for, 45; neutrality of, 178, 181, 187; and objectification of horizon, 182; openness of, 181, 188; in Plato, Aristotle, Hegel, Marx, 110; and positions and counterpositions, 106, 181; and research, 160; and self-appropriation, 178, 181, 182; and standpoints, technical handling of, 177; strategy of, 177; and transcendental method, 172, 175, 177–78, 187; tripolar, 84; and universal viewpoint (*see* Universal viewpoint, and dialectic); upper blade of generalized empirical method, 37

Dialectic, and foundations: circularity, 211; and horizons and categories, 181, 187; and horizons, relative and absolute, 203; and judgment and decision, 214; and remote criterion, technical solution to, 164, 170, 187; separate chapters on, 176; and transition to mediated theology, 177; as upper blade, 164, 173

Dialectical: alternatives, rooted in polymorphism, 64; analysis (and historical theology, 93; and philosophy of philosophies, 37); criticism, and absolute horizons, 152; heuristic structure, 36–40; process, grasped in series of authors, 111

Dialectical metaphysics. *See* Metaphysics, dialectical

Dialectical method: and conceptual identity in difference, 93; and critical function of transcendental method, 155; epistemological wisdom, 47; extension of, 83–84; and human level, 44–45, 46, 74, 75; and universal viewpoint, 87, 96. *See also* Dialectical analysis; Dialectical theorem; Metaphysics, dialectical

Dialectical theorem: and critical problem, 39; definition of, 36–37; empirical and critical, 37, 42; and human field, 36, 39; upper blade of generalized empirical method, 42. *See also* Dialectical heuristic structure

Dialogue, 185–87; genuine direction of, 215; growing desire for, 213; and universal viewpoint, 10

Dicere, 51, 238 n. 13

Differentiation(s) of consciousness, 109, 110, 124; dialectical, within cultures, 214; explanatory, 108–109; genetically and dialectically ordered, 196; interior, 197; and method, 197

Differentiations of protean notion of being: explanatory, 68, 103; historical, 70; and stages of meaning, 69; as upper blade for history, 103, 108

Discernment, 287 n. 44

Divine missions, 204–205

Divine solution to problem of evil: and fidelity to positions, 81–82; transmission of, 83, 90–94

Doctrinal identity, methodical solution to, 101

Doctrines, development of, 94, 104, 110

Dogmatic-speculative theology, 92

Dogmatic theology. *See* Theology, dogmatic

Doran, R.M., 8–9, 225 nn. 40–43, 236 n. 123, 239 n. 15, 259 n. 9

Droysen, J.G., 170

Duplessy, E., 252 n. 85

Ebeling, G., 119, 178, 281 n. 42

Ecumenical movement, 186

Emergent probability: generalized, 45; on human level, 70; and theology, 196; transcendental method as control over, 195; and world of meaning, 9; world-view of, 44

empirical human sciences. See *Geisteswissenschaften*; Human sciences

Encounter, 281 n. 41; with the past, 178; between persons, 178, 186

Epistemological reflection, Thomistic, 24, 26, 42, 47

Epistemology: first *quoad nos*, 27; inquiry into possibility of knowledge, 230 n. 87; and introspection, 23; in Thomas Aquinas, 22, 24

Eternal light, 22

Et Judaeus et Graecus e methodo, 214

Exegesis: concerned with particular contexts, 134–35; and positive dogmatic theology, 134

Exegetes, expertise of, 167

Existential: component, and theological method, 209; ethics, 127, 128, 192

Existential, primacy of, 7, 147, 210, 214; and difference between *Insight* and *Method*, 143; and theological foundations, 142-3

Existenz, 152, 153

Experience: centrality of, both in method and in Indian thinking, 215; historical, 170, 173; patterns of, 102

Explanatory unification, from universal viewpoint, 91

Explicitly dialectical metaphysics. *See* Metaphysics, explicitly dialectical

Explicit metaphysics. *See* Metaphysics, explicit

Expression: by exegete qua exegete, 165; and expertise in development of, 167; and inner word, 29; instrument of principal acts of meaning, 65; levels and sequences of (*see* Levels and sequences of expression); and mistaken formulations, 52; not merely logical, 123; for oneself, for others, 239 n. 28; phylogenetic set of schemata for, 167; reduction of, to knowledge, 51; and upper blade in hermeneutics, 4. *See also* Communication; Formulation(s); Meaning, statement of

Expression, modes of, 65; basic, 167; and exact communication, 52; and grasp of discovery, 52; scientific treatise as, 123; and stages of meaning, 69. *See also* Interpretation, statement of

Expression, supplementary mode of, 166–68; foundations of, 167, 173; and levels and sequences of expression, 167; and scientific interpretation, 168. *See also* Interpretation, statement of

Faculty psychology: affects universal viewpoint, 88, 96, 208; not invalid, 118; rooted in priority of metaphysics, 124, 191
Faculty psychology, shift from, 96, 143, 192–95; to analysis of consciousness, 88, 109, 111–12, 118, 121, 145–46; to intentionality analysis, 10, 127, 147, 209, 211, 212; to interiority analysis, 124, 131, 133, 136, 145, 146
Faith: assent to truths, 82, 147, 209; and belief, 82, 144; classical notion of, 107, 108, 139, 146–47; as eye of love, 144; new notion of, 144–45, 147, 210
Faith, hope, charity, 82
Fides ex auditu: appropriation of tradition, 205; and *fides ex infusione*, 205
Fides ex infusione: handing on of tradition, 205
Finality of being, 70
Fiorenza, F., 205, 290 n. 89
Formal object: Aristotelian (and static view of sciences, 194; and theology, 197); and methodological viewpoint, 115; new notion of, 209
Formulation(s): and identification, problem of, 55; mistaken, 52; pure, 63, 66, 168 (mere hypotheses, 67; and pure desire to know, 245 n. 146); universal (aim of dogmatic-speculative theology and extraordinary magisterium, 92; ascent to, 214). *See also* Expression
Foundational methodology, 225 n. 50
Foundational part of theology: coincides with method, 139; concerned with conversion, 138; and fundamental theology, 138; and intention of being, 139; transcendental method, 140
Foundation(s): and absolute horizons, objectification of, 154; and authenticity, 183; and conflicts of interpretations and histories, 179–80; and conversion, objectification of, 155, 179; differentiation of, 140; for an empirical theology, 141; focus on, 146; functional specialty, 140, 179–80, 183–84; and general and special categories, 184, 201; and horizon, 153–54, 179; of knowing, 231 n. 8; and method, 153, 157; and methodical horizon, 184; of a modern science, 142; new, and methodical theology, 187; of new anthropology, 154; for ongoing process, 183; for philosophy, 137; and positions and counterpositions, 180; and religious conversion, 187; of scientific communication, 120; theological principle, introduction of, 147, 180, 187; transcendental, of methods, logics, ethics, 193; and wisdom, 9, 43, 105
Foundations, theological, 133–34, 136, 142; classicist, overcoming of, 145; and comprehensive view, 174; in concrete subject, 136; and fundamental theology, traditional, 146; generated in process of theologizing, 201; generated through self-appropriation, 199; illumination of reason by faith, 138; new, 138, 142, 210; problem of, 105; properly methodical, 147; and thematization of religious horizon, 142, 199
Fragestellung, 163, 169, 172
Fries, H., 289 n. 86
Functional specialization: decompres-

sion of hermeneutical method, 161; emergence of idea of, 135–36; and hermeneutics of *Insight*, 158; and transcendental method, 158. *See also* Operational specializations

Fundamental critics, 131

Fundamental theology, 88–90, 138; classical, and transformation of universal viewpoint, 7; and divine missions, 204–205; and leap of faith, 142, 145; in light of pure reason, 89, 210; and objective statements, 141–42; and religious experience, 90; replacement of, 212; rhetorical, 142; and structure of final chapters of *Insight*, 89; and theologically transformed universal viewpoint, 94, 96–97, 209

Gadamer, H.-G., 119, 161, 162, 213

Geffré, C., 289 n. 86

Geisteswissenschaften, 118, 146, 193; appropriation of, 209, 210; challenge of, 145; and differentiation of hermeneutics, 146, 209; Lonergan's reading of, 12; and positive and dogmatic theology, distinction between, 134; and theological problematic, 113. *See also* Human sciences

General history: a priori for, 108, 112; and universal and comprehensive viewpoint, 175–76

Generalized apologetic, 175

Generalized emergent probability: comprehensive view, 46; and generalized empirical method, 46

Generalized empirical method, 225 n. 50; critical architectonic, 212–13; and critical problem, 42; dialectic as upper blade, 37, 42; and full critical position, 41; and generalized emergent probability, 46; and introspection, 44, 208; metaphysics as tertiary part of, 212; and method of metaphysics and of ethics, 208; and philosophic writing, 71; rooted in tradition and contemporary developments, 213; and subject-object polarity, 95, 190–91, 205; and supremacy of logic, 214 (*see also* Logic, shift from); and transition to explicit metaphysics, 44; and wisdom, 44, 48, 96, 132 (cognitional and dialectical, 43; epistemological, 40, 47, 74, 77, 132; genetic and epistemological, 96, 208; incorporates duality of, 212; new type of, 117; takes place of Thomist, 212)

Generalized universal viewpoint, 223 n. 12

General method (1959), 105–107; and ascent to universal viewpoint, 106–107; and conversions, 146; and positions and counterpositions, 106; rules of, 105–107 (encompass entire aprioristic element, 108; immanent in history, 106); theological transformation of, 107

General method (1962), 114–18, 209; and appropriation of inner world, 115; and basic context, 121; generalized empirical method, 115; new basis of, 114; and new notion of habit, 117; novelty in, 118; and three conversions, 114

Genetic and dialectical sequences, 64, 67, 68–69, 70, 74; of differentiations of consciousness, 196; identification of, 75–76

Genetic method: and dialectical method, 44–45; and stages of meaning, 247 n. 162

Genuineness, law of, 85

Gesamt- und Grundwissenschaft, 126, 127, 128, 190

Gilson, E., 257 n. 59

Index   331

Gnoseology: incomplete in Aristotle, 22; knowing that we know, 230 n. 87
Gödel's theorem, 88
God's existence: deduction of, 89–90, 97; and positions, 80
Good: cosmic or intellectual or ontological account of, 108, 111, 145; human account of, 108–109, 111, 118, 145, 209 (a priori for general history, 112; emergence of, 143); psychological notion of, 143
Graham, N., 259 n. 9
Group of operations, 114

Habit(s): acquired, 264 n. 2; Aristotle on, 114; new notion of, 111–12, 114, 131, 209, 188 (accounts better for unity, 115; and general method, 117; and horizon, 125; and interpretation, 29, 119; and universal viewpoint, 195); operational, 109; operative, 109; relation between, 88
Habitual intellectual development, 55, 58
Habitual understanding, 28–30, 55
Hefling, C., 7–8, 74, 91, 184, 200, 224–45 nn. 28–36, 38, 245 n. 142, 248 n. 197, 252 n. 87, 253 n. 107, 254 n. 128, 288 n. 69
Hegel, G.W.F., 60, 120, 237 n. 135, 266 n. 8, 286 n. 29; dialectic, 43, 109, 110; explicitly dialectical metaphysics, 48; logic-in-motion, 193–94; Lonergan never aimed to write like, 5; and Lonergan's notion of dialectic, 12; necessitarian and dialectical logic, 194; and philosophy of philosophies, 37
Heidegger, M., 120, 278 n. 54
Hermeneutical: component, and theological method, 209; debate, Lonergan's contribution to, 213
Hermeneutical method, 58–60; and bias, 68; and concrete historical process, 45; and control of meaning, 46; differentiation of, 118, 146, 209; functioning of, 66–68; of *Insight*, only a sketch, 183; and polymorphism, 45; and self-appropriation, 59; subject-object polarity in, 96; universal viewpoint as upper blade of, 3; and universe of meanings, integration of, 45
Hermeneutics: and cognitional theory and epistemology, 161; common-sense affair, 118–20, 146, 209; contemporary, and method, 161; differentiation from history, 118, 124; and general theory of meaning, 161; nonscientific, 119; theological, 90–94. *See also* Hermeneutical method
Hermeneutic of suspicion and of recovery, 284 n. 95
Heuristic: characteristic term in Lonergan, 230–31 n. 3; notion(s), 35, 76 (examples of, 232 n. 38; and structure, used interchangeably, 232 n. 38). *See also* A priori
Heuristic structure(s), 31–36, 76; a priori, 32, 34; basis for method, 34; and continuity in knowledge, 35; development in, 36, 93, 266 n. 42; differentiation of notion of being, 36; and genesis of wisdom, 36, 206–207; in human sciences, dialectical, 36; indeterminateness of, 35; intellectual light as applied, 33; and notion of being, 96; ordered set of heuristic notions, 35; and pincer movement, 33; total, 34; universal viewpoint a, 3, 60–63; upper and lower blade, 33–4. *See also* A priori
Heussi, K., 171
Historical: intelligibility, 117; investigation, descriptive and explanatory, 102–103; scholarship, integration of,

198, 209; sciences, higher-level controls in, 102; sense, and simple interpretation, 56
Historical consciousness: acknowledgment of, 118; emergence of, 214; and problem of method in theology, 136; shift to, 152
Historicity, problem of, 105
Historismus, 171
History: accounts of, positivist and idealist, 170; and criteria, proximate and remote, 170, 172, 173; critical, double process in, 169, 170, 173; dialectical differences in, 171; explanatory, 118, 119, 121, 146, 209; functional specialty, 168–72; *in oratione obliqua*, 140; methods for, 171; other things being equal, 169; of philosophy, a priori for, 112; precritical, 169; and relativism, 169–70, 171; rewriting of, 56; as scholarship, 168–69; value judgments in, 172
Horizon(s), 125; and authenticity, 153; and being in love with God, 145; categories, set of, 157; and context, 156; and dialectic, 176; and dialectic and foundations, 180–81; enlarging of, 118; and foundations, 151, 153–54, 179; fundamental heuristic notion for meaning, 131; historicist, 154; merging or fusion of, 161, 162, 173; method as, 155–58, 189–92, 213 (replaces metaphysics as horizon, 203); methodical (*see* Methodical horizon); new, in theology, 151–55; new notion of, 131, 146, 209; of the philosopher practicing transcendental method, 211; and positive theology, 151; relative (and genetic sequences of viewpoints, 128; in *Method*, 154); relative and absolute, 131, 151, 152, 154 (genetically and dialectically related, 180); subject-object polarity, 125, 132; technically simpler than notion of viewpoint, 126; total and basic (*see* Total and basic horizon); of the wise man, 126, 131, 211

Horizon(s), absolute, 130; and dialectical criticism, 152; and foundations, 154; incommensurable, 152; indemonstrable, 152

Horizon(s), transcendental, 129, 210; and dialectical sequences of viewpoints, 128; makes method automatically theological, 134; and methodical horizon, 153

Horizontsverschmelzung, 161, 162

Huber, C., 226 n. 55

Human sciences: autonomy of, 95; and dialectical heuristic structure, 36; method of, 36; and problem of theology, 94–5. See also *Geisteswissenschaften*

Humor, and universal viewpoint, 84

Husserl, E., 191, 285 n. 13

Hypotheses, general and particular, 227 n. 15, 246 n. 151

Idealism: post-Hegelian, 73; and realism, 257 n. 64

Identification, problem of: and formative abstraction, 239 n. 17; and process of interpretation, 55

Incommensurability, of absolute horizons, 152

Individual and community, interaction between, 204–205

Inner word: gives rise to expression, 29; intelligible procession of, 19, 20, 29, 49, 239 n. 13; non-complex, 238 nn. 12, 13

In oratione obliqua, 135, 140; and positive theology, 139

In oratione recta, 135, 140
Insight: and concept, 239 n. 16; practical, 51, 56, 57; relatively a priori, 31
Insight and *Method*, relationship between, 6–7, 8, 11
Integration: heuristic, 45; metaphysics as highest and most comprehensive, 73–74; metaphysics as i. of all methods, 45; in theology, 156; of universe of meanings into explicit metaphysics, 48
Intellectual light: contains virtually whole of science, 28; created participation of Eternal Light, 22; inchoate wisdom, 25, 76; introspective grasp of, 23; knowing that we reach being, 26; and knowledge of the other, 22; and pure desire to know, 36, 48; rudimentary view of the whole, 25; and self-appropriation, 41; and self-knowledge, 23; spontaneous notion of being, 35; and Thomistic epistemology, 24–25
Intelligere, 19; *dicere*, real distinction from, 239 nn. 16, 17; potential act of meaning, 51
Intelligere, dicere, and inner word, 239 n. 16
Intentionality analysis: and faculty psychology, 10; shift to, 10, 127, 131, 147, 195, 209, 211, 212 (and overcoming of priority of metaphysics, 191). *See also* Consciousness, analysis of, shift to; Interiority analysis, shift to
Interdisciplinarity, 94–95, 156, 195
Interiority analysis, shift to, 124, 131, 133, 136, 145, 146; axial, 196–97. *See also* Consciousness, analysis of, shift to; Intentionality analysis, shift to
Interpersonal, priority of, 144
Interpretation: based on historical sense, 92; circular process, 30; commonsense affair, 161, 162, 172–73; conflicting, 58, 67; and conversion, 120; correct, not automatic, 68; data of, 55; and development of understanding, 30; and dialectic and foundations, 168, 173; and differentiations of consciousness, 161; existential dimension of, 164; functional specialty, 161–68; and habits, 29; inductive procedure, 19; and judgment, 162–64, 173; logical, 227 n. 22; method of, in *Verbum*, 28–30; presuppositionless, 242 n. 85; problem of, 3, 17, 19, 58 (rooted in neglect of understanding, 29; partial statements of, 242 n. 83); process of, 29, 54–58, 74; recovery of viewpoint of past, 59; reflective, 57; as scholarship, 161, 163; second expression, 54; theological, necessarily scientific, 92; theory (in *Insight*, systematic account of, 6–7; in *Method*, orderly set of directions, 6); true (and magisterium, 91; mounts to a universal viewpoint, 92; and theologians, 91); truth of, and Catholic fact, 91; and understanding the text, 162; vicious circle in, 29
Interpretation, scientific, 58, 67; and extraordinary magisterium, 91; and transmission of divine solution, 83, 90–94; and upper blade, 59. *See also* Expression, supplementary mode of
Interpretation, simple, 57; based on historical sense, 56; and ordinary magisterium, 91; and transmission of divine solution, 83, 90–94
Interpretation, statement of, 164–68; and basic context, 120–21, 123; and basic mode, 173; commonsense, 120, 212; scientific, 173; and stages of meaning, 124; supplementary mode, 173, 212. *See also* Expression, modes

334 Index

of; Expression, supplementary mode of
Interpreter, full development of, 119
Introspection, 19–28; bridge between centuries, 20; and epistemological wisdom, 26, 28; and epistemology, 23; in interaction with texts, 30; key to Thomist psychology, 20; and meaning, theory of, 49; as method of interpretation, not yet generalized, 30; mounting up to mind of Aquinas, 30; and movement to self-knowledge, 64; a synchronic upper blade, 27, 208; and Thomas Aquinas, 20, 23, 47; and Thomistic epistemological reflection, 26; and universal viewpoint, 30; and wisdom, 20, 27. *See also* Self-appropriation
Invariants, of intellectual development, 72
Isomorphism, between knowledge and expression, 51–52

Jaspers, K., 197
Johnston, W., 186
Journet, C., 260 n. 22
Judgment: brilliant phenomenology of, 213; and decisions, not automatically correct, 214; in interpretation (a commonsense affair, 162–64; precedes statement, 162; of understanding and of statement, 163); no recipe for, 106

Kant, I., 261 n. 48; meaning organized by logic, 193; transcendental, meaning of, 190; transcendental method, 117
Klubertanz, G.P., 251 n. 62
Knowing: and being, intimate relationship, 27; as confrontation, 32; duality in, 37; by identity, 22; as ontological perfection, 32; two types of, 102

Knowledge: communitarian dimension of, 185; development of (and heuristic structures, 35; and modes of expression, 52); and expression (interpenetration of, 52, 54; isomorphism as well as distinction, 54); historical, 173; and love, reversal of relationship, 144–45, 147, 210; progress in, 187

Langlois, C., 170, 279 n. 79
Language(s): development of, 52–53; expertise in development of, 167; restricted idea of, 237–38 n. 8. *See also* Expression
Leap of faith, 142
Learning, problem of, 55
Levels and sequences of expression, 65–66, 75; lower blade, 65; and operators, 66
Literary genre, 66
Logic: necessitarian and dialectical, 194; shift from, 136, 137, 152, 179, 215 (and openness of theology, 160)
love of God, gift, 144, 147
Lumen fidei, 144
Lumen gratiae, 144

Magisterium: extraordinary (and scientific interpretation, 91; and universal formulations, 92); and historical theology, distinct tasks, 94; ordinary (and simple interpretation, 91; and true interpretation, 92); and theologians, 92
Marx, K., 110
McShane, P., 9, 46, 225 n. 44, 236 n. 125
Meaning(s): act of, and inner word, 29; all-inclusive term of, 51; of basic terms (and critical problem, 39; selection of, work of wisdom, 40, 50); carriers of, 161; component of

Index   335

hermeneutical upper blade, 4; constitutive of human reality, 118, 152; core of, 51; development of (and genesis of metaphysics, 53; genetic and dialectical, 53, 61; and mystery and myth, 46); dimensions of, aesthetic, intersubjective, symbolic, 121, 123, 161; and expression (correlations, 65; and hermeneutical upper blade, 59; recurrent gaps, 69); formal acts of, 50, 238 n. 13; formal and full acts and terms of, 50; formal terms of, 238 n. 13; historical modes of, 166; immanent sources of, 63; instrumental acts of, 51; interlocking of, 151–52; of meaning, 50; organization of (logical, methodical, transcendental), 193, 196; partial terms of, 51; potential acts of, 50–51; potential and principal acts of, 239 n. 17; principal acts and terms of, 50, 51; of 'real,' 233 n. 53; reconstruction of (*see* reconstruction); reduction of, to knowledge, 49–50; sources of, 51; statement of (*see* Interpretation, statement of); structure of, 49–53 (and cognitional theory, 50); theory of, 49, 161; transformation of, and new viewpoints, 53; types of, 123; universe of (*see* Universe of meanings)

Meaning, control of: and hermeneutical method, 59; and metaphysics, 46, 50, 53; and self-appropriation, 195; and transcendental method, 152, 195; and universal viewpoint, 76; and upper blade, 59

Meaning, stages of, 65, 123–24; and basic context, 124; examples of supplementary expression, 166, 212; and explanatory differentiations, 68–69, 168; historical differentiations of notion of being, 69; models for understanding of cultures, 167, 214; and statement of interpretation, 124, 161, 173; result in modes of expression, 239 n. 29. See also Meaning, historical modes of; Modes of thought

Mentalities: differences in, 167; Hebrew, Greek, etc., 103, 107–108, 110, 123, 130, 168, 173

Metaphysical equivalence, 238 n. 9

Metaphysics: anticipation of structure of universe of being, 72–73; critical, and integration, 47; and ethics, 128; expansion of, 80; explicitly tertiary in *Method*, 191; a foundational task, 236 n. 125; generalized semantics, 53; and *Gesamt- und Grundwissenschaft*, 127–28; grasp of universal order, 96; highest viewpoint, 72; as horizon, 203, 213; priority of, 10, 214 (led to faculty psychology, 191); shift from, 109, 121, 124, 146; starting from concrete subject, 198–99; supreme science on objective viewpoint, 126; and transcendental method, 128; and universe of meanings, 74; unrestricted view, 73, 74; and wisdom, 47–48, 207

Metaphysics, dialectical, 44–48; explicit metaphysics, part of, 48, 71; a philosophy of philosophies, 48; and universal viewpoint, 74, 96

Metaphysics, explicit: and ascent to universal viewpoint, 96; contemporary form of wisdom, 77; and control of meaning, 50, 70; definition of, 40; and development of meaning, 53; dialectic a part of, 45, 71; a generalized semantics, 50; genesis of, 59, 70; heuristic integration, 45; highest viewpoint, most comprehensive integration, 47, 48, 71, 73; historical progress towards, 59; integration of universe of meanings, 45, 48, 73–74;

336 Index

and metaphysical wisdom, 74, 77, 96, 132; single unified view, 44, 45; transition to, 44, 48, 59; and universal viewpoint, 71–74, 76, 77, 211. *See also* Generalized empirical method

Metaphysics, explicitly dialectical, 47, 48, 71, 73, 74

Method: and appropriation of interiority, 213–14; automatically theological, 134; and conversion, 193; dialogical, 213, 215; and differentiations of consciousness, 197; and dynamic view of sciences, 194; and emergent probability, 196; of ethics, 86–87; existential character of, 137, 138; as foundational, 136–39; and foundations, 153, 157; framework for creative collaboration, 196; as general dynamics, 192–95; as HCF, 153; and heuristic structure, 33–34; as horizon, 155–58, 213, 189–92 (replaces metaphysics as horizon, 203); horizon analysis, 129; illumination of, by faith, 102; indirect (Rahner), 287 n. 44; key to integration, 116; makes explicit the goal operative in knowing, 256 n. 29; mediation of theory and common sense by interiority, 197; mere superstition without understanding, 29; and order, natural and supernatural, 193; philosophic, 43; and philosophy, disadvantages of the term, 194; post-Hegelian, 194; problem of, 105; and return to concrete, 214; scissors movement in, 184; and technique for overcoming aberration, 106; transcendental (*see* Transcendental method); and universal viewpoint, 196, 212, 213 (*see also* Transcendental method and universal viewpoint); no watertight solution, 271 n. 63; and wisdom (contemporary form of, 105;

inherits role of Thomist, 203; sapiential function, 135; sapiential part of theology, 203–204). *See also* General method (1959); General method (1962); Generalized empirical method; Transcendental method

Method, theological: a priori and a posteriori, 204; and canon of relevance, 167; coincides with foundational part of theology, 136; and dialectic of values, 153; openness of, 166, 179, 212; problem of, 136, 147; subject-object polarity in, 96; theological component of, 209–10; and totalitarian ambitions, 165; and transformation of cognitional structure by faith, 139; and universal viewpoint, 197–200; and wisdom, 203–205

Methodical horizon, 128–31, 210; new context for theology, 154; subject-object polarity, 190; and total and basic horizon, 129; and transcendental horizons, 129, 153; and transcendental method, 146; and universal viewpoint, 130, 132, 211, 265 n. 32. *See also* Total and basic horizon

Methodological viewpoint: and metaphysics, 126; not static, 115; shift to, 118, 124, 160, 172, 197

Methodology, of present study, 10–12

Method of metaphysics, 40–44; dialectical, 43; a genetic wisdom, 43; subject-object polarity in, 95; takes over epistemological functions of wisdom, 43

Methods: comparative, organistic, genetic, dialectical, 119, 130, 131; structural unification of genetic and dialectical, 45; transcendental and particular, 266 n. 45

Models, 69; derived from data of consciousness, 167; and supplementary

expression, 166, 168; for understanding of cultures, 214
Modes of thought, 106–107, 110
Moreau, J., 257 n. 64
Moving viewpoint, 71, 139, 195
Munus nobilissimum, 101, 135, 139
Mystery, 46, 69
Myth, 46, 69

Naturwissenschaften, 193
Newman, J.H., 12, 213
Nihil amatum nisi cognitum, 144
Niṣkāma karma, 215
Nominalism, 214
Notion of being: a priori, 32; and being, 62; differentiation of, 48; explanatory differentiations of, 168; fundamental heuristic notion, 35, 36; inchoate wisdom, 35, 36, 74; and intellectual light, 35; and pure desire to know, 34; rudimentary view of the whole, 35, 96; and universal viewpoint, 207
Notion of being, protean, 38, 75; and basic context, 122; and dialectical metaphysics, 62; differentiation of, 62; explanatory differentiations, 68; and universal viewpoint, 61
Notion of universal viewpoint. *See* Universal viewpoint, notion of

Objectification of subjectivity, 182
Objectivity: cognitional question, 233 n. 54; fruit of authentic subjectivity, 164, 213; phenomenological, Bultmann's perspectivism, 122; theory of (and hermeneutical method, 53, 54; and history, 173; and idealist account of history, 171)
Objects to operations, shift from, 136
Ontology, first *quoad se*, 27
Operational: habit, 109; potency, 109 (and universal viewpoint, 110); specializations (breakthrough to, 139; related to levels of consciousness, 140)
Operators: a priori, 32; develop positions, reverse counterpositions, 182; questions, 64
Orientation(s): habitual, 40, 241 n. 65; patterns of experience, 241 n. 64; problem of, 56
Other things being equal, 169, 173. *See also Caeteris paribus*
Outer words: refer to inner words, 49. *See also* Expression

Panikkar, R., 186
Parmenides, 70
Pascal, B., 144
Past, challenge of, in scholarship, 164
Perspectivism, 122, 171
Philosophia perennis, 92
Philosophies, new, and problem of method in theology, 136
Philosophy: of action, 143; concerned with concrete realities, 198; disadvantages of the term, 193, 194; modern type of, faces a critical problem, 137; and self-appropriation, emphasis on, 198; and theology, distinction not separation, 198; total, four parts, 127; total and basic science, 190; in traditional sense, and hierarchy of sciences, 193; turn to concrete, return to theology, 134, 138, 146
Philosophy of philosophies: a priori for history of philosophy, 112; and chapter 14 of *Insight*, 39; and dialectical analysis, 37; and dialectical metaphysics, 48; and dialectical theorem, 39; and universal viewpoint, 109; upper blade for philosophy and theology, 109
Piaget, J., 108, 111, 114–15, 117, 124, 125, 131, 195

338 Index

Pincer movement: echoes of, in *Verbum*, 19; and heuristic structure, 33; interpretation a result of, 18; marks all knowing, 3, 28; military metaphor, 226 n. 10; original, 35; and pure form of speculative development, 208; subject-object polarity in, 95; and wisdom, 76. *See also* Scissors action

Plato, 70, 257 n. 64, 258 n. 66, 284 n. 99; and dialectic as philosophical dialogue, 187; and group-use of dialectic, 110

Pluralism of theologies, way of controlling, 196

Polymorphism, 39, 78; in earlier chapters of *Insight*, 45; and wisdom in cognitional terms, 42

Positions, development of, 70

Positions and counterpositions, 70; anticipated to dialectic, 181; in ethics, 86; and foundations, 180; and grasp and communication of insights, 52; identification of, 75–76; and objectification of horizon, 182; and theology, 92

Positive research, integral part of theology, 135

Positive theologies, specialized, 267 n. 15

Positivism: problem of, 17, 19, 29

Posterior Analytics, 154

Potency and formal object, 125, 131, 146

Praxis, strong and weak sense, 288 n. 66

Pre-understanding, 11, 119, 162, 213. See also *Vorverständnis*

Principle of the Empty Head, 119

Priora quoad nos, 91

Priora quoad se, 91, 214

Problem of evil, divine solution to, 83; and positions, 81–82

Problematik, 259 n. 3

Processio intelligibilis, 239 n. 13

Progress: in knowledge, 28; liberal notion of, 110

Projection, subjective, 56, 59

Providence, 215

Prudence, 116, 117, 146

Psychological introspection. *See* introspection

Psychology, Thomist, 19

Pure desire to know, 36, 48, 84, 86. *See also* Intellectual light

Pure form of speculative development, 17–19; an a priori scheme, 18, 19; demonstrable conclusion, not hypothesis, 18; diachronic upper blade, 27, 208; generalized tool of interpretation, 30; not mentioned in *Verbum*, 19; and universal viewpoint, 30; and wisdom, 27

Pure reason: dethronement of, 143; does not exist, 198. *See also* Speculative intellect, overcoming of

Pythagoras, 70

Questions: and heuristic structures, 33, 35; no further relevant, 163; operators, 64

Rahner, K., 126, 196, 266 n. 8, 285 n. 1, 287 n. 44

Reconstruction: of context of author, 163; of meaning from immanent sources, 55, 62, 63; universal viewpoint key to, 96

Reexpressions, 83, 91

Regina scientiarum, theology as, 95

Relativism, problem of, 3, 104, 169–70, 171; and descriptive viewpoint, 56; handled by dialectic, 169, 172

Relativity of interpretations to audiences, 3, 57, 58, 75, 120

Religious experience, 142

Index   339

Reproducieren, 277 n. 33
Research, 159–60, 172
Research, interpretation, history: not auxiliary disciplines, 198; and problem of standpoints, 212; and transcendental method, 173
Resolutio in principia, 21
Responsibility: repeated mention of, 137; and theological method, 139–40
Revelation, communication of, 91, 92
Ricoeur, P., 213, 284 n. 95
Romanticism, 121, 123, 263 n. 82, 277 n. 33
Rudimentary view of the whole, 35, 74, 206

Sache, die, 11, 119, 162
Sala, G.B., 190, 231 n. 22, 261 n. 48, 285 n. 3
Satire, and universal viewpoint, 84
Scholarship: advantages of, 164; and interpretation, 162; and new anthropology, 152
Science(s): architectonic, wisdom as ontology, 21; Aristotelian notion of, 111, 116 (and traditional theology, 152); community as carrier of, 187; conflicting notions of, 104, 146 (root problem in theology, 105); demonstrative and empirical notion, 152; explicitly conscious operational habit, 109; general (total and basic horizon, 190; translation of *Gesamt- und Grundwissenschaft*, 190); Greek notion of, 116; modern notion of, fits better with Catholic fact, 116; natural, necessitarian ideal, 196; natural and human, 118, 193; not value-free, 153, 177; notion of, 117 (and problem of method in theology, 136); of sciences, wisdom as ontology, 21
Scientific: interpretation (*see* Interpretation, scientific); investigation, a priori and a posteriori movements in, 108
Scissors action: between categories and data, 168; in history, 122; in human knowledge, 3, 58; and method, 184; between method and data, 191; of method of physics, 191; and notion of being, 35; and pincer movement, 33; in theological method, 204, 205; between transcendental method and data, 168; and universal viewpoint as goal, 201; and wisdom, 76. *See also* Pincer movement
Seignobos, C., 170, 279 n. 79
Selbstvollzug, Christian church as, 7
Self-appropriation, 75, 88; and classification of philosophies, 104; and control over meaning, 59, 195; and derivation of categories, 7, 156; and dialectic, 178, 181, 182, 187; and epistemological wisdom, 41; and foundations, 181, 183; and intellectual light, 41; and introspection, 41, 64; and method of metaphysics, 41, 43; and projection into the past, 104; and stages of culture, 104; starting point of philosophy, 138; subject and object, interaction of, 95; upper blade for history, 104. *See also* Introspection
Self-correcting process of learning: and enlargement of horizon, 118; and understanding the text, 11, 162
Self-criticism, 177–78
Self-knowledge: and critical thought, 23; and development of meaning, 53; and dialectic, 41, 75; empirical, scientific and normative, 26; and epistemology in Aquinas, 22; higher control of meaning, 59; historical progress towards, 59; and interpretation, 59; introspection and wisdom,

21; and method of metaphysics, 41; scientific, 24
Self-mediation: mutual, within a tradition, 138; with respect to a tradition, 138
Self-scrutiny, 59
Self-transcendence, and discernment of ambivalence, 178
Self-understanding, 11; in dialectic, 177–78
Semantics, generalized, 50, 53
Shields, M., 259 n. 9
Simple interpretation. *See* Interpretation, simple
Snell, B., 166, 167, 278 nn. 54, 55
Specialized positive theologies, 267 n. 15
Specifically theological principle, shifted to point of transition, 140, 147, 180, 187
Speculative intellect, overcoming of, 143, 193. *See also* Pure reason
Stages: in cultural development, 197; of human thought, 110; of meaning (*see* Meaning, stages of)
Standpoints, problem of: cannot be handled by history, 171; handled by dialectic, 177; partial elimination of, in history, 170
Standpunkt, 169, 172
Starting point: of philosophy and theology, 138, 139, 146; of theology, 140, 141, 147, 172
Statement of interpretation. *See* Interpretation, statement of
Statics to dynamics, shift from, 194
Subject: concrete, 114, 146, 183; focus on, 114
Subject-object polarity, 95–96; and generalized empirical method, 95, 190–91, 205; of horizon, 125, 132
Sublation, 145, 266 n. 8. See also *Aufhebung*

Supplementary mode of expression. *See* Expression, supplementary mode of
Swartzentruber, P., 74, 243 n. 93, 248 n. 197
Systematic mode of thought, emergence of, 110

Tekippe, T.J., 4–7, 62, 74, 223–34 nn. 11–16, 224 nn. 18–25, 248 n. 196, 250 n. 46
Theological foundations. *See* Foundations, theological
Theologically transformed universal viewpoint: as base, 91, 201; and basic context, 121; and classical fundamental theology, 208–209; deductive transition to, 146, 199; fate of, 146; includes special categories, 201; includes truths, 90; and magisterium, 91; and methodical horizon, 130; not a high and distant goal in *Insight*, 8; and theologians, 91
Theological method. *See* Method, theological
Theological principle, introduction of specific. *See* Specifically theological principle, shifted to point of transition
Theological viewpoint (Tekippe), 5
Theologizing in India, 214
Theology: a priori and a posteriori, 184; as *Aufhebung der Philosophie*, 126; categories for study of prescientific stages of, 107; classical notion of, 108, 145, 212; classicist assumptions of, 152; collaborative enterprise, 185; and conversion, 198; deductive, starting point in truths, 134, 141; dogmatic-speculative, 92; emphasis on tradition, 198; and human sciences, 94–95, 113–14; of *Insight*, ignored religious experience, 197; introduction

to, *Insight* a contribution to, 88; parts of, 135–36 (*see also* Functional specialties; Operational specializations); largely empirical, 141–42, 147, 159 (and foundations, 141, 201; starting point in data, 141, 201, 210); and positive studies, 101–103, 104, 113; primarily systematic, 108; problem of, 105, 113 (and positive theology, 105); proper independence of, 160; properly methodical notion, 197; sapiential or methodical part of, 95, 135; as science, 113; two modes of, 140; universal relevance of, 195; and universal viewpoint, double movement towards, 201

Theology, dogmatic: differentiation of, 140; and *munus nobilissimum*, 131, 135, 139; and problem of method in theology, 136; and speculative theology, 91; stabilization of name, 134–35

Theology, historical, 103, 107; and doctrinal identity, 91, 92, 94, 101; requires an upper blade, 108; and universal viewpoint, 92–94

Theology, positive: differentiation of, 140; dogmatic, concerned with transpositions over contexts, 134–35; and dogmatic, distinction between, 134–35; and horizon, 151; *in oratione obliqua*, 139; and problem of method in theology, 136, 147; and speculative, integration of, 105; stabilization of name, 134–35

Theology, speculative: and positive, relations between, 101, 105, 108; relevance of, 113; seeks universal formulations, 91, 92; and transmission of revelation, 91; and transpositions, 102

Theorem: dialectical (*see* Dialectical theorem); Gödel's, 88; new organization of data, 233 n. 43

Thomas Aquinas, St, 19, 237 n. 135, 245 n. 140, 259 n. 6, 278 n. 54, 288 n. 58; and Augustine's vision of eternal truth, 22; and critical program, 21, 23; and development of positions, 70; epistemology, 22, 24; and judgment, 213; knew and practiced introspection, 20, 23, 47; knowing by intentionality, 22; and meaning organized by logic, 193; mounting up to his mind, 30; option for knowing by what we are, 22; reduction of meaning to knowledge, 49; and self-knowledge, 21, 23; use of Aristotle for theology, 94, 167; and wisdom, 12, 42, 43 (epistemological, 21; genetic, 205; transposition of, in *Insight*, 208)

Thomistic epistemological reflection, 24, 26, 42, 47

Total and basic horizon, 125–28, 210; and basic context, 132; generalized empirical method, 190; and metaphysics, 126, 131, 211; objective pole of, 127; total and basic method, 190

Total and basic science: philosophy, 190; total and basic method, 190

Tradition: appropriation of and handing on, 205; and interpretation, 120; and understanding a text, 162

Transcendence, pseudo-problem of, 38

Transcendental: deduction, validity of, 235 n. 105; doctrine of methods, 126; foundations of methods, logics, ethics, 193, 195, 196; and historical, interaction between, 204–205; horizon (*see* Horizon, transcendental); in Kantian sense, 117; in scholastic, in Lonerganian sense, 116–17; and subject-object polarity, 190; three meanings of (scholastic, Kantian, Husserlian), 191

Transcendental method, 125, 130, 225

n. 50; appropriation of operations on four levels, 192, 195; and authenticity, deliberate quest of, 153; base of dialectic, 172, 175, 177; and basic context, 177; and cognitional theory, epistemology, and metaphysics, 189–90, 211; and control over emergent probability, 195; critical, 131; and dynamic viewpoint, 195; and existential level, 192–95; extension to theology, 199–200; first description as, 116; and foundations, circular relationship, 183–84, 211; foundations of all methods, 152, 195; and functional specialties, 158; functions of, 155; as horizon, 155–58; later descriptions of, 190; meaning of, 189; metaphysics tertiary, psychological categories primary, 201–202, 211; and methodical horizon, 132, 189–92, 211; and method of metaphysics, 127; and new context for theology, 154; new control over meaning, 152, 195; and new horizon, 158; and new theology, 158; openness of, 188; philosophy of philosophies, 157; remedy for unauthenticity, 157; rock, 155; and subject-object polarity, 190–91, 205; and theological integration, 156; three basic questions, not four, 192–93; and transcultural categories, 156; understanding of, not a prerequisite, 166–67; as upper blade, 191

Transcendental method and universal viewpoint, 157; t.m. and ascent to u.v., 195–97; t.m. less metaphysical, more concrete than u.v., 192, 202, 211; t.m. more flexible than u.v., 192; t.m. takes over functions of u.v. while including it, 211. *See also* Universal viewpoint and transcendental method

Transcultural: base, of theology, 184; categories for theology, 156; language, image as, 104; principle of transition over cultures, 104

Transition(s): basic problem in method, 105; in Christian theology, 110; from commonsense to symbolic mode of thought, 107; over contexts, Romantic neglect of, 121; over cultures, 104; identifying points of, 12; from indirect to direct discourse, 147, 199–200. *See also* Transposition(s)

Transposition(s): over contexts, 130; between types of knowing, 102. *See also* Transition(s)

Truth: appropriation of, 54; attainment of, linked to entire human person, 68; and control over meaning, 46; criterion of (*see* Criterion of truth; Criterion of truth, remote); definition of, 54; and expression, 54: and hermeneutical method, 53–54

Tübingen school, 120

Two vectors of human development, 198, 205; and scissors-action of theological method, 205

Unauthenticity, radical or derived, 129

Understanding: act of, and inner word, 238–39 n. 13; habitual, and interpretation, 28–30, 50; the text, 28–30, 162, 173; and universal viewpoint, 60

Universal viewpoint: 3, 60–74, 80; an actual viewpoint, 6; a priori, 3, 31–33 (and Kantian a.p., 31–32, 60–61); ascent to, 68–70 (is finality of being, 70; historical, 9, 70, 96, 106; personal, 70; and transcendental method, 195–97); and basic context, 121, 124, 132, 210–11; centrality of, 10; common vision of a common goal, 72, 73–74; and conceptual identity in difference,

93; and conversion, 9, 120; and development, ontological analysis of, 88; and dialectic, 75–76, 161, 200–203 (remains part of upper blade of d., 203, 211); and dialectical method, 87, 96; directions for moving towards, 6, 182; and emergent probability, 76; expansion and transformation of, 7, 78–81, 208; explanatory unification from, 92; and faculty psychology, 88, 195, 208; functional persistence of, 145; functioning of, 66–68; a general hypothesis, 246 n. 151; generalized, and theological viewpoint, 5; generalized tool of interpretation, 30, 64, 76; and God, 80; habit of, 9; and Hegelian dialectic, 60; and hermeneutics, 119; an intellectual habit, 86; of an intelligent and reasonable being, 73–74; and introspection, 30, 76, 96; and level of doing, 84, 87–88, 96, 192, 208; and levels and sequences of expression, 64, 66, 75; limitations in, 84–88, 96, 111–12, 209; and meaning, 19, 96 (new control over, 76; and principal acts of, 63); a metaphysical construct, 88, 96, 112, 201, 208; and metaphysics, 71–74, 76, 77, 211; and method, 196, 212, 213 (*see also* Transcendental method and universal viewpoint); and methodical horizon, 132, 146; and notion of being, 61, 207 (protean, 61–62, 76; structure of protean, 66); and notion of universal viewpoint (*see* Universal viewpoint, notion of); operational habit, 109–10; operative component, 207; post-*Insight* occurrences of the term, 4, 112, 128, 145, 200, 210; potential, 8; progress towards, 76; and pure form of speculative development, 30, 64, 76, 96; rooted in tradition and contemporary developments, 213; and satire, 84; self-appropriation, replaced by, 64; and self-knowledge, 63, 64; synchronic and diachronic, 30, 76; and theological method, 197–200; totality of viewpoints (grasp of virtual, 19; ordered, 4, 64; potential, 4, 75); and total and basic horizon, 132, 146; and transmission of divine solution, 83; and universe of meanings, 74; unrestricted, 73; and upper blade, 65, 208; and virtual grasp, 61; and wisdom, 9, 206 (*see also* Wisdom, and universal viewpoint)

Universal viewpoint, notion of, 62, 63, 75, 207; definition of, 60; a heuristic structure, 60–63; and metaphysics, 73; and protean notion of being, 76; proximate achievement, 201; and transcendental method, 187. *See also* Universal viewpoint

Universal viewpoint, theological transformation of, 80–84; in *Method*, 198, 199–200; patterned on classical fundamental theology, 90; a personal act, 89

Universal viewpoint, theologically transformed. *See* Theologically transformed universal viewpoint

Universal viewpoint and comprehensive viewpoint, 175, 176, 187, 200, 207; both potential, 5; coincide in extension, 211; discrepancy between, 6; Hefling on, 7–8; Lonergan's self-interpretation, 5–7; Tekippe on, 4–7

Universal viewpoint as goal, 73–74; of dialectical analysis, 93; high and distant, 8, 62, 70, 201, 207; two senses of, 200–201

Universal viewpoint as heuristic structure, 3, 31–36, 62, 201; for meaning, 4, 63–66, 72; in *Method*, 192, 202; part

of derived general categories, 201–202, 211
Universal viewpoint and transcendental method, 9, 157, 189–97, 192, 195; functions of u.v. taken over by t.m., 201; u.v. remains part of t.m., 211. *See also* Transcendental method and universal viewpoint
Universal willingness, and universal viewpoint, 85–86
Universe of meaning(s), 73; emergent probability in, 9; and explicit metaphysics, 45, 48; integration of, 48; structure of, and universal viewpoint, 72
Universes of discourse, 213
Upper blade, 208; basic context, 121, 122; at beginning of a science, 28; dialectic and foundations, 164; for fields resistant to conceptualization, 110; genetico-dialectical, 111; and heuristic structures, 33–34; higher control over meaning, 59; for history, 103, 108, 210; in human knowledge, 3, 58; multiplicity of, in philosophy and theology, 109; necessity of (in interpretation, 3; in historical theology, 108); original, a spontaneous notion of being, 35; positive research weak on, 102; and revealed truths, 209; and scientific interpretation, 59; and self-appropriation, 75, 204; stages of meaning as, 110, 168; synchronic and diachronic, 27; in theology, 102, 204; of transcendental method, general categories, 184; universal viewpoint as, 3
Upper context: and basic context, 121; and level of doing, 87–88

Value(s): control over, 172, 177; notion of, 143, 147, 210

Vécu to *thématique*, transition, 199–200, 204
Verstehen, 163
Vertin, M., 184, 194, 195, 285 n. 23, 290 n. 89
Via analytica, 91
Via inventionis, 92
Via synthetica, 91–92
Viewpoint(s): acquisition of, 55; approaching texts from, 17; classicist, 160; descriptive, 56, 58, 59; dialectical sequences of, and transcendental horizons, 128; dynamic, 194, 195; explanatory, 56, 58, 59; genetic and dialectical development of, 59, 167; genetic sequences of, and relative horizons, 128; highest and most comprehensive, 47; historicist, 154; humanist, 84, 88, 89, 95; methodological, 115, 126 (shift to, 118, 124, 160, 172); moving, 71, 139, 195; new, and communication, 53; objective, 126; ordered totality of, 4, 64, 74, 96; philosophical, and scholarship, 102; shift from cognitional, to existential, 109; shift from, to horizon, 125–26; static and dynamic, 194; terminal, 83; theological, 5; unrestricted, 126; of wise man, 203
Vorverständnis, 119, 162. *See also* Pre-understanding

Walgrave, J., 272 n. 75, 289 n. 86
Weltanschauung, 169, 172
Wendung zur Idee, 118, 263 n. 82
Whitson, R.E., 186
Wirkungsgeschichte, 165, 262 n. 67, 276 n. 28
Wisdom: architectonic science, 21, 212; Aristotle's first philosophy, 42; cognitional, 42 (and dialectical, 43; and theological, 204); and common

sense, 42; communitarian, 203; and dialectic, 106; dialectical oscillation in, 27, 28, 30; divine, 25; dual role, epistemological and metaphysical, 21, 27–28, 74, 95, 132, 212; explicit references to, in *Insight*, 42; and first principles, 21; and foundation(s), 9, 43 (for theology, 105); and generalized empirical method (*see* Generalized empirical method, and wisdom); genetic, 27, 36, 43, 205, 208; gift of Holy Spirit, 42; growth in, 25, 36, 85; and heuristic structures, 76, 77, 206–207; as individual habit, 106; infinite, 27; infused, 144; and integration, 116; and introspection, 27; and judgment, 21, 106; and knowing the real, 25; Lonergan's sources, 12; and metaphysics, 43, 47–48, 207; methodical, 203; as ontology, 21; original pincer movement, 76; paradox of, 206; and prudence, integration of, 116, 117, 146; and pure form of speculative development, 27; replaced by generalized method and dialectical metaphysics, 96; selects basic terms, 43, 237 n. 8; and self-knowledge, 26–27; speculative virtue, but also practical, 251 n. 62; and theological method, 203–205; third type of, 42, 43; total and basic horizon, 128; unity of, 27; universal context, 40; and universal viewpoint, 9, 74, 85, 206 (key to interpretation of, 95, 203); unrestricted viewpoint, 126; upper blade, 28 (original, 28, 208)

Wisdom, epistemological, 208; and generalized empirical method, 40, 77; and introspection, 20–21, 26, 28; and method of metaphysics, 43; and self-appropriation, 41; and self-knowledge, 27

Wisdom, inchoate, 206; and intellectual light, 25, 27, 76; and notion of being, 35, 36, 48, 74; original pincer movement, 35; universal anticipation, 27–28

Wisdom, metaphysical, 208; and dialectical metaphysics, 47; and explicit metaphysics, 77; and shift to methodical w., 203

Wittgenstein, L., 291 n. 18

World(s): and general method, 115; of interiority, 116

www.ingramcontent.com/pod-product-compliance
Lightning Source LLC
Chambersburg PA
CBHW030301080526
44584CB00012B/401